MW01031063

The Mayor

Also by Brian Hicks

Sea of Darkness

City of Ruin

Toward the Setting Sun

When the Dancing Stopped

Ghost Ship

Raising the Hunley (with Schuyler Kropf)

Into the Wind (with Tony Bartelme)

to V.C & Kitty
What a special
and priceless gift
to be reunited
with you
Your old
and devoted
friend
Jim

The Mayor

Joe Riley and the Rise of Charleston

BRIAN HICKS

Foreword by Pat Conroy

Published by
Evening Post Books
Charleston, South Carolina

First edition

Editors: Rick Nelson, Mitch Pugh and Bob Kinney
Designer: Gill Guerry

First printing 2015
Printed in the United States of America

A CIP catalog record for this book has been applied for from the Library of Congress.

ISBN: 978-1-929647-25-5

This book is dedicated
to the memory of

Cynthia Hurd
Susie Jackson
Ethel Lance
DePayne Middleton Doctor
Clementa Pinckney
Tywanza Sanders
Daniel Simmons
Sharonda Coleman-Singleton
Myra Thompson

and for my mother,
Judy Lynn Hicks

Contents

FOREWORD

By Pat Conroy

Charleston is a city in love with dreaming backwards. It is the only American city ever to start a war against its own nation. In its convoluted history, it has offered itself up as grand opera, morality play, drama of travail, marketplace of stories, and theater of the absurd. It is built on a peninsula, yet has always been insular, braided with a passion for secrecy and a preference for mystery. Charleston has never gone in for braggadocio or chest-thumping, yet feels superior to any place that you and I might hail from. Even Europeans go silent with liturgical awe when they wander through the narrow streets South of Broad, with its splendid houses turned away from the streets and its profusion of intimate, well-composed gardens sheltered against the intrusion of the stranger's eye. At its finest, the city looks as though it were imagined by a committee of Anglicans appointed by a tasteful deity. Yet by firing on a ship carrying the American flag, it doomed itself to becoming a footnote in the grand parade of great cities.

One hundred and fourteen years later, Joseph P. Riley was elected mayor of Charleston, and it was then that the city answered the call to its own vision of greatness. With his election, the city began its transformation and because of this singular visionary man, it has taken its position again as one of the most magical places on Earth. It is a story most fitting and moving. Joe Riley is a native son of Charleston, as much a part of the landscape as a perfect, deep-water harbor or the great salt marsh itself. His 40-year career as mayor of Charleston has already become legendary.

This extraordinary book will tell you why. Brian Hicks has experienced a long and prize-winning career as a journalist for The Charleston Post and Courier, the traditional newspaper of record in the South Carolina Lowcountry. He has written one of the best political biographies I've ever read. It reads with the smoothness and power of a novel, and several times while reading this book I was reminded of my first encounter with Robert Penn Warren's *All the King's Men*. It has the edginess and raw bite that politics always brings to a narrative. Over and over again, as Mr. Hicks relates the highs and lows of Joe Riley's career, you discover that the citizens of Charleston are opinionated, irascible, articulate and lion-hearted in their defense of their city. Some of these townsmen descend directly from the fire-breathing folk who started the Civil War and would happily do it again. Joe Riley himself is a direct descendant of a Confederate soldier. But Mr. Hicks has assembled a vast and brawling cast of characters almost Shakespearean in their variety.

As a Southern writer, I've watched the rise and luminous arc of Joe's career since he was a cadet at The Citadel to his imminent retirement as Charleston's mayor 40 years later. The association has been as up close and personal as any novelist could imagine. I arrived on The Citadel campus in 1963 when Joe was a greatly respected senior in F Troop. Though I found the plebe system challenging almost beyond my capacity to endure, I came to admire some of the seniors and strongly wanted to emulate their leadership skills. Since Joe was in a different battalion, I heard stories of him through the eyes and ears of my classmates and the four seniors I served as a knob who lived next door. The Citadel is a dark matrix of discipline, and a crucible of authentic efficiency in the molding of its cadets. Since its founding in 1842, The Citadel has served as a fountainhead for leaders in the world of politics, business and all the branches of the armed forces. By the length of his service and accomplishment, Joe Riley has a strong claim on being the most distinguished graduate in The Citadel's long history.

In 1970, I first met Joe in his Broad Street office where he agreed to be the lawyer who would read my first book, *The Boo*. I had written the memoir of a charismatic assistant commandant at The Citadel by the name of Thomas Nugent Courvoisie, who struck both fear and devoted awe in the hearts of a generation of Citadel men. He had a voice that sounded like an artillery shell fired by the battery he'd commanded at the Battle of the Bulge. His last name proved unpronounceable to the Corps of Cadets and his nickname, The Boo, became legendary in the barracks. My book did great, but not irreparable, damage to the English language and Joe Riley had read the entire manuscript when The Boo and I walked into his office. I had complained to The Boo that we needed a more experienced lawyer, but The Boo silenced me and said, "Joe Riley has as much integrity as anybody I ever met who came through The Citadel. If I ever went into battle, I'd want a guy just like Joe Riley fighting beside me. You'd be the last guy I'd ever choose, Conroy."

That day, Joe proved to be a superb lawyer; he told me that I had left The Boo and myself open to hundreds of lawsuits because I had used the real names of that sorrowful nest of loser-scoundrels The Boo had encountered over the years when they'd broken one of the many byzantine laws of Citadel culture. Joe sent me home with the assignment of changing every single name in the book. That night, because The Boo still intimidated me, I made up over two hundred names and handed Joe the corrected proofs the next morning at breakfast. In my over-litigated life, no lawyer ever made me work harder. Five years later, Joe Riley would be elected the mayor of Charleston and would serve with rare distinction for the next 40 years.

I've watched his career closely and in awe. This book will explain both my long attention and my awe.

There is no city on Earth quite like Charleston. From the time I first came there in 1961, it's held me in its enchanter's power, the wordless articulation of its singularity, its withheld and magical beauty. Wandering through its streets can be dreamlike and otherworldly, its alleyways and shortcuts both fragrant and mysterious, yet as haunted as time turned in on itself. It is a city that cries out for artists and poets and souls aflame in wildness, yet it has produced very few of those. The city itself grants its own mirage of art and it is often enough to live beneath its canopies of trees and the harmony of its bells and secret gardens. In Charleston, you can have the illusion that you are living in a work of art every day of your life.

But until the arrival of Joe Riley, Charleston was a sleep-walking, underachieving city with its eyes still fastened on a past where its citizens began the most calamitous war in American history. The story of Joe Riley is the story of the renaissance of a city restored to greatness by the dauntless vision of a single man. The Charleston of 2015 looks and feels nothing like the city that turned its keys over to Joe Riley in 1975. He has turned it into one of the great cities of the world, a city with five-star hotels, a world-class arts festival, a lineup of restaurants that draws tourists from Paris, a first-rate university, a state-of-the-art aquarium, a new museum and library, and the Joseph P. Riley Jr. baseball stadium. He has released a city ensconced in the amber of its own history and set it free to attain its name as one of the great destinations of the discerning traveler.

But, for me, Joe Riley will always deserve acclaim for his non-negotiable belief that the South has harmed all of its black citizens by its legacy of Reconstruction and its shameful Jim Crow laws. Though it is not widely known, the civil rights movement had an indelible effect on many Southern white boys and girls who watched in horror as the fire hoses and police dogs were turned against peaceful demonstrators in Alabama. The police charge at the Selma bridge sickened many of us. The assassination of Martin Luther King Jr. altered many of our lives for all time, and many young men and women set out after that moment to change that part of our heritage that had grown malignant to us. In Georgia, one of them was Jimmy Carter; in Arkansas, Bill Clinton. In South Carolina, Ernest Hollings won a Senate seat. Dick Riley, John West and Jim Hodges served as governors. Joe Riley set out to change the way African-American citizens of Charleston were treated by city government, and had been for over 100 years.

There was nothing shy or reluctant about Joe's embrace of civil rights. In his first year as mayor, I heard a Charleston matron with an unpronounceable name refer to him as "Nigger Joe." But that seemed harsh even by Charleston standards, and it got softened to "Little Black Joe" and finally LBJ. Black Charleston repaid Joe Riley by offering him their overwhelming support for 40 years. When he hired the irrepressible Reuben Greenberg as Charleston's first black police chief in 1982, I think the city was more shocked that the new chief was an observant Orthodox Jew. A cynical Republican confided to me that Joe only made the hire to lock up the Jewish vote on the peninsula. I disagreed, because I knew Joe had the Jewish vote sewed up since his first election. When Joe Riley retires, I believe Charleston will remember him as the greatest civil rights champion of his era – white or black.

Early in my writing career, I became friends with Joe and Charlotte Riley and they would let me stay in their Charleston house to write while they moved out to the family beach house on the Isle of Palms. I wrote the first three chapters of my novel *The Great Santini* at their dining room table, and then wrote the first chapter of *The Lords of Discipline* there a few years later. On various occasions, I've contributed money to his campaigns and even traveled with him to do fundraisers in various cities in the year he ran for governor of South Carolina. When I was living in San Francisco in the early '90s, I received a letter from Joe asking me to join a board that would oversee the construction of the city's first aquarium. For the next 10 years, I was part of that coma-inducing nightmare as the bureaucracy of building codes and architectural plans moved forward at the pace of a wounded escargot. Though the meetings were agonizing with the discussion of minutiae, I noticed that Joe Riley never missed one of them, even though he sometimes attended 10 other appointments before he reached our roundtable discussion. I marveled at his attention span, the ardor of his vision, the absorbent power of his brain to deal with either crises or small adjustments, and the quiet resolution of his leadership. He had the patience of a novelist and I first went with him to see a vacant lot poisoned by chemicals and then remembered him on the opening night of the South Carolina Aquarium watching as he eyed a moray eel coming out of a cave of false coral. For me, it had been like building a pyramid. For Joe Riley, it was just another day at the office.

When Joe organized a march from Charleston to Columbia to protest the fact that the Confederate flag still flew over the Statehouse, he called and asked me to join the march. I drove up with my wife Cassandra King and met up with the novelist Anne Rivers Siddons and her husband, Heyward. We joined a larger, boisterous crowd and Joe delivered one of those speeches for which he's become famous. I heard him deliver a speech on the Custom House steps after Hurricane Hugo had swept through the city with catastrophic results. Charleston looked like a city bombed out during an enemy air raid and the citizens were still in a state of collective shock. Joe's words took hold of that crowd, offered them soft expressions of comfort, spoke of resilience, toughness, and issued a vow and a promise that Charleston would come back stronger than ever. Joe Riley was as good as his word. He was always as good as his word.

In Marion Square, before he would lead his march to Columbia to remove the Confederate flag, Joe delivered one of his eloquent stem-winders, telling of the shameful history of slavery and the treatment of black people after the Emancipation Proclamation. The flag served as a symbol of a war fought for the right to own slaves and still flew atop our Statehouse as a brutal reminder that "old times there are not forgotten." The flag was like a fishhook stuck in the eye of every black man, woman or child that had to pass beneath it. To bring the flag down would be a sign that South Carolina was moving beyond its past, was finally growing up, and would deliver a message to the state's black people that the most egregious symbols of the racist past would be retired to the walls of museums. Because the flying of the Confederate flag hurt the feelings of every black person who saw it, it was time for the flag's honorable retirement. The Legislature agreed to remove the flag from the top of the Statehouse and move it to the Confederate memorial on the grounds of the Capitol. Joe Riley's march from Charleston received national attention.

In the summer of 2015, Mayor Joseph Riley's 40-year effort to improve race relations delivered an unexpected dividend when Charleston suffered one of the worst tragedies in its history. In the middle of a June heatwave, a young South Carolina white man joined a group of parishioners at Emanuel African Methodist Episcopal Church. Led by the Rev. Clementa Pinckney, who was also a state senator, there was a small gathering of people who got together weekly for Bible study. This complete stranger was invited to join the discussion and treated with a sense of great fellowship. He stayed and listened for an hour before he pulled a pistol and murdered nine people for committing the unforgiveable crime of having been born black.

The murders of these God-fearing men and women touched the heart of Charleston with a power that seemed mystical and spirit-born. White people and black people, young and old, gathered outside Mother Emanuel to pray and grieve. There was the constant embracing of strangers and shedding of tears that came from the eyes of both aristocrats and dockworkers. Joe Riley was covered by the national media, and when he spoke America understood how lucky the city of Charleston had been for 40 years. In his own sorrow Joe was magnificent, and he led the city in its rites of sorrow. His eloquence was tear-stained, soft and transformative. His city had suffered a wound to its soul and Joe had earned the right to help us all heal. I believe it will always remain his finest hour.

By reading Brian Hicks' book, I learned how a city works, and of the quiet heroism required of the public servants who make it work. I couldn't put the book down because I couldn't take my eyes off the renaissance man embodied by Joe Riley. Even after reading this book, there is something that is indefinable, enclosed and even private about Joe. He has turned the city of his birth into one of the most wondrous cities on Earth. Mr. Hicks brings his career to astonishing life. He writes with grace and when he comes to the massacre at Mother Emanuel, Brian Hicks raises his game and his writing gains power, even a sense of grandeur. Joe Riley has been lucky once more and has found the right biographer to explain his life to the world.

I was lucky to meet Joe Riley as a young man and even luckier to love him still, 50 years later.

PROLOGUE

April 3, 2000:
Marching out of Dixie

Joe Riley feared he could not go on.

He was stranded in a cheap motel 50 miles out of Charleston, his feet so blistered that he couldn't walk on the coarse carpet in his room. The march had been far more arduous than he'd anticipated, and that surprised him. All those years of running – of keeping himself in shape, of full-dress parades at The Citadel – had not prepared him for this. In little more than 24 hours he had walked himself bloody, and he still had three days – and nearly 70 miles – to go. But at the moment, that seemed impossible.

Joseph Patrick Riley Jr. rarely failed, and had never quit anything in his life. Now he realized there might be no other choice. It was too late to call this off. Ten miles away, hundreds of people that he'd led out of Marion Square on Sunday were trudging up Highway 176 toward Holly Hill – the second stop on their journey to Columbia. This "Get in Step With South Carolina" march was perhaps the most ambitious gambit in his 25 years as Charleston's mayor. It had two purposes: to show the nation that not everyone in South Carolina wanted the Confederate battle flag atop the Statehouse dome, and to pressure the state Legislature into taking it down.

For years, Riley had badgered lawmakers to do just that. He did not like the message the flag sent, the negative publicity it brought to South Carolina, the stereotypes it conjured. He wanted the rest of the world to know that not everyone in his home state blindly worshipped relics of the Lost Cause. It was bad for business and bad for race relations – the two dominant issues of his entire political career. But over the years he had made little progress. The General Assembly had never seriously considered moving the flag, not even when the National Association for the Advancement of Colored People declared a boycott on the entire state. Riley had made it his mission to change all that.

When he first had the idea for a march, the mayor shared it with some of his friends, bluntly asking them if he'd lost his mind. The very notion was out of character for Riley. He was not the typical South Carolina politician; he did not garner publicity for outrageous comments like Fritz Hollings, had never been a divisive figure like Strom Thurmond, Ben Tillman or John C. Calhoun. He was simply a moderate Democrat in a state becoming more conservative every day. Despite that, Riley had been successful in politics. In the past quarter-century he had rebuilt Charleston twice and worked to heal the scars that lingered more than a hundred years following the Civil War. He accomplished all this through the considerable force of his unwavering will.

Publicity stunts had never really been part of the Riley playbook. Other politicians considered him a Boy Scout – which he had been – a man perpetually positive, sometimes naively so, even though he could be a bare-knuckled Irish political brawler behind the scenes. But his critics claimed this march was exactly that, a stunt meant to embarrass the state. He could not disagree. And as the media attention proved, it was working. More than 600 people had turned out on a Sunday afternoon for the first leg of the journey. The showing bolstered his faith, confirmed his belief that the people of South Carolina were more moderate, more inclusive, than the totality of their elected officials suggested. Even the critics were forced to concede that he had a point. Somehow Riley had managed to draw a crowd that was two-thirds white, proving the flag was not only an issue in the African-American community.

The march had taken on a life of its own, helped by some of the state's most noted celebrities – author Pat Conroy, singer Darius Rucker, football coach Lou Holtz. Already the Washington Post and New York Times had written about the mayor's quest, and international papers followed suit. Good Morning America wanted Riley to appear live on national TV. No journalist could resist the irony of it all: the mayor of the city that started the Civil War leading a march against the Confederacy's most enduring symbol.

"Get in Step" had troubles in the beginning, but Riley's staff kept much of it from him. Conroy – perhaps South Carolina's most famous citizen, and certainly one of its best-known liberals – had been down with the flu. But the author did not want to miss the march and disappoint his fellow Citadel alum. Conroy saw Riley as a character in one of his novels: a progressive man in a conservative state, in love with his beautiful, yet flawed, home while also appalled by some of the things its past represented. Riley had a Lowcountry heart much like Conroy's.

So Conroy had been there as the people marched out of Marion Square carrying the blue, palmetto-laden state flag up Meeting Street. It was an ambitious statement to make, Riley knew, but still he had been surprised by the bitter backlash. Already, roadside signs urged South Carolina residents to "Keep the Flag, Dump Riley." There had been threats, nasty anonymous emails, including one that warned, "If you march your niggers through Calhoun County, I'll put you in my gun sights."

The intimidation could not stop Riley, but it forced him to take precautions. He wore a bulletproof vest, and police officers in plain clothes and flak jackets surrounded him as he marched. In some ways, he knew, this only added to the story's value. His mission had struck a nerve, and the fact that these threats had not dissuaded him or his followers only enhanced the importance of their statement.

The marchers showed no signs of fear, singing as they went – "We Shall Overcome," "Highway to Heaven" and "Father, Lend Me Your Walking Shoes." In some ways, it felt like a modern-day civil rights march, and that idea appealed to Riley. In his office, he had a framed photograph of Martin Luther King Jr. taken during the March on Washington – the event that first stirred his political conscience. There was one difference in this protest, however, and his friend and former Statehouse colleague Alex Sanders noted it early on Sunday.

"This time," Sanders said, "the police are on our side."

The need for that protection was clear by early Monday. For most of the day, the marchers endured the taunts of people set up at intersections along the route, many of them waving Confederate flags and hurling insults. Silence, Riley had said, was the best way to respond to such hatefulness. Most followed the mayor's lead. They ignored the crowds singing "Dixie" beside the road, and the man in the pickup truck who buzzed the march with "A Country Boy Can Survive" blaring from his stereo. The marchers just kept going. David Rawle, an advertising executive who had been with Riley since his first campaign in 1975, soon realized it was the same half-dozen people at every crossroads.

At one intersection, the crowd turned more aggressive. One man yelled, "Come and take it down, you just try," prompting highway patrolmen and agents with the State Law Enforcement Division to detain and search him. Rawle didn't believe the mayor was in danger, but there was no way to predict what these people might do. A mob mentality was brewing. Riley had attacked their heritage, or so one man claimed. But the mayor told reporters, "That is not his heritage; that is his hate."

Within a day, the march took its physical toll on Riley. He could handle the hecklers and ignore the Lowcountry sun baking him in the heavy Kevlar vest, but his feet could not take any more punishment. His 57 years soon caught up to him, and he developed a blood blister on one foot. A doctor traveling with the march burst it and Riley kept going. But by midafternoon Monday – somewhere in the pine tree-lined rural landscape of Berkeley County – Riley had been forced to leave the procession. A police officer drove him to a motel on the outskirts of Harleyville.

Riley knew it shouldn't matter if he walked every mile of the route. The purpose was to show the country that South Carolinians wanted the Confederate flag off the Statehouse dome, and he was only one of those. But the mayor also realized he was the focal point – the leader, the man reporters flocked to interview. He was the catalyst for all this, the self-appointed spokesman for progressive South Carolina. This march was his statement. What would it look like if he could not go on? That was a bit of symbolism Riley did not want broadcast to the world.

Riley had faced many difficult trials over the years. He was an unlikely candidate for mayor in 1975 – a quiet, 32-year-old lawyer with a baby face and an aversion to campaign hyperbole. His advisors worried that voters might consider him too young to be mayoral material. Twenty-five years in front of the cameras had changed that; his time in public office had aged him considerably. But through it all, the mayor still clung to the politics of a much younger man.

Riley had been that way for his entire political career. He'd fought for civil rights, for racial equality, since he was 26 years old. He was the first white man in South Carolina to propose a state holiday for Martin Luther King Jr., an idea that 1970s South Carolina was not ready to embrace. In those days, that was not the modus operandi of a man whose great-grandfather had been a Confederate soldier. It was not the way a graduate of The Citadel conducted himself. Like Conroy, Riley wore The Ring – the symbol of a true Citadel man – but he was determined to prove that did not make him a Confederate flag-waving cracker fighting to keep the 20th century at bay.

He soon learned that some Charleston residents wanted to do exactly that. During his first years in office, Riley brought in an international arts festival and promoted plans to build a massive hotel-shopping complex in the heart of the city's central business district. These were monumental changes for sleepy Charleston, and many of the city's oldest residents did not cotton to change. In fact, they considered it heresy.

Charleston was still a proper Southern town steeped in tradition when Riley was elected, a place where a person's worth and identity were measured by their ancestors. And those people did not want to see any alterations, big or small, to their city. Riley believed Charleston should embrace its historical past, but also needed a vibrant core to survive and grow. These were wildly unorthodox ideas in the 1970s, but Riley could not be steered off course. And over time he had been proven right.

In the years before Riley was ensconced at City Hall, Charleston was dying a slow, agonizing death – and growing more racially divided every day. It had never seen the troubles Alabama or Mississippi suffered, but then South Carolina was slow to join the civil rights movement. As a young state representative in 1969, Riley had witnessed the National Guard occupy his town during a strike of African-American hospital workers. He had watched the 1971 mayoral election with growing alarm as nearly every black voter cast a ballot for one candidate while whites overwhelmingly voted for another. Riley knew that was not the message Charleston needed to send.

Thanks to his efforts to foster racial progress at the Statehouse, Riley won the mayor's office with a broad swath of support from old families South of Broad and black voters who lived largely north of Calhoun Street. It had been front-page news when he received the endorsement of a black lawmaker, the local newspapers shocked that the Rev. Robert Woods would support a white man when a black candidate was in the race. Riley would go on to build bridges in his city, literally and figuratively. At first the old guard fought, but eventually he won over most of them. Through it all he maintained the support of the black community. Somehow he managed to become an ally to both old Charleston and the new. And he won re-election, time and again.

Fourteen years into Riley's tenure, just as Charleston was beginning to resemble his vision, disaster struck. A Category 4 hurricane tore through the city, causing more destruction than the Yankees had ever imagined. Riley rode out Hugo at City Hall, watching the winds punish Charleston from a peephole cut into the boards covering the building's front door. At one point, he saw a chunk of metal crash down on Broad Street and lamented, *Someone has lost their roof.* Later he learned it was City Hall's own roof.

Most of Charleston fared far worse than City Hall, and Riley spent years picking up the pieces, tirelessly pursuing federal funds to rebuild his hometown. He publicly fought FEMA, and used his Washington connections to help neighboring counties. Riley became mayor of an entire region. He even appeared on the Oprah Winfrey show. Already influential among other mayors around the country, Riley became a national figure. And he rebuilt his city a second time, with an emphasis on saving its most important artifacts. The preservationists, many of whom had once eyed him warily, now embraced him – as did much of the city. In parts of Charleston, his approval ratings hovered near 85 percent.

By 2000, Riley had become one of – if not the –most influential Charlestonians of the 20th century. Even his critics, and he had many, conceded that he was the father of modern Charleston – a city on its way to becoming one of the most visited tourist centers in the world and a major shipping port. The city was the crown jewel of South Carolina. Riley returned Charleston to a prominence it had not enjoyed for nearly two centuries. He was the architect of the city's true Reconstruction, more than 100 years after the war that nearly destroyed it.

So how, he wondered, could he allow a little thing like blisters to stop him now? It would not matter if 600 people paraded through Columbia and up Gervais Street in three days. If Riley was not leading the "Get in Step" procession, the march would be branded a failure. It might be excuse enough for the Legislature to ignore the entire protest. And Riley did not believe in losing.

For the moment, it was out of his hands. As the march continued up Highway 176 that Monday afternoon, he sat alone in his motel, staring out the window at a vacant RV lot and waiting for his physical therapist.

The news was worse than he'd feared.

Frank Santangelo, Riley's physical therapist, arrived late that afternoon. He made the drive from Mount Pleasant to Harleyville in little more than an hour, surprised to find the mayor of Charleston holed up in such dingy environs. But Santangelo was more shocked by Riley's condition. Frankly, he was a mess. Both his feet had been split open by huge blisters – the kind of trench foot usually found on soldiers after long marches, the sort of wounds that benched professional athletes. If the wounds became septic, Riley would have much more to worry about than a political statement.

Santangelo couldn't explain why the march had taken such a toll on Riley, but he knew if the mayor tried to walk another 70 miles he would end up in a hospital. But there was no way to simply tell him to go home. He didn't dare. Santangelo had known Riley a long time – long enough to know it wouldn't do any good. Riley was too stubborn, and this march was too important to him.

So Santangelo patched up Riley the best he could. He gave the mayor a complicated set of instructions: He would have to cover his feet in "second skin" – a lotion much like Vaseline – and then wrap them in gauze, changing the dressing every time he stopped for a break. To reduce pressure, he should change shoes at least once a day. Santangelo cut the toes out of Riley's running shoes to reduce the pressure, and told him to lie down and elevate his feet – prop them on a tree – at every break. It would allow the blood to flow out of them. This, Santangelo said, was the only way he could continue. And still he might not make it.

As soon as Santangelo left, Riley called a police officer to drive him back to the march. The cruiser sped down Highway 176, past the corner stores and old churches, until the mayor finally saw his people trudging along with their signs and the state flag. The scene made him proud. A few miles south of Holly Hill, Riley got out of the patrolman's car and took his place at the front of the procession.

For more than an hour, Riley walked along the highway, shouting words of encouragement to his followers and returning calls from reporters on his cell phone. Within an hour, the group arrived in front of the old, yellow-brick Holly Hill town hall – the end of the road for the night. Riley thanked everyone and asked them to be back in front of town hall at 7 a.m. Then he climbed into a police car for the trip back to the motel. Walking for just an hour had been painful, but he hoped to feel better after 12 hours of rest. And if he didn't, he would likely continue anyway.

For Riley, this was the beginning of the final leg of a political journey that began in the 1960s. In some ways, it felt as if no time had passed at all. The last time South Carolina made national news for a controversial civil rights protest, Riley was just a young man trying to find his political voice.

But even then, Joe Riley did not believe in failure.

PART I

The Land of Opportunity

April 30, 1969

The troops had rolled into Charleston a few days earlier.

There were more than 500 National Guardsmen patrolling the streets in green fatigues and combat helmets, carrying rifles with bayonets, their armored vehicles parked on Calhoun Street alongside Ford Fairlanes and Volkswagen Beetles. The governor had deployed them as back-up for an overworked police department in a city once again under siege. Charleston had not seen such a military presence in more than 100 years, the last time the city commanded the nation's attention. Set against a backdrop of sun and palmetto trees, the troops – and their armored personnel carriers – were familiar echoes of another lost cause being fought at that very moment on the other side of the world.

The Guardsmen were primarily a precaution. The protesters had proven mostly passive, walking the streets in paper union hats, a few carrying simple handmade signs. The politicians just assumed trouble would result from the ongoing hospital strike, now in its sixth week. State officials were nervous, mainly because the vast majority of these protesters were black – agitators, they called them. Despite those fears, Charleston had suffered little more than some mindless vandalism: a few fires, a rock thrown through the window of Edwards 5-and-10.

Earlier in the week, demonstrators had blocked the entrance to the Francis Marion Hotel at the corner of King and Calhoun in the heart of downtown. Twenty-five teenagers were arrested, most of them promptly returned to their parents. Police Chief John Conroy had neither the inclination nor the room to hold protesters for long. But that would soon change. The old county jail on the banks of the Cooper River was being cleaned up to make room for the eventual, and expected, overflow of inmates. Another precaution.

The temporary blockade of the Francis Marion came at the end of a march that had crossed the historic district, through the Four Corners of Law, bringing the civil rights movement to the doorstep of City Hall and within earshot of the rich neighborhoods South of Broad, as well as the tiny law office of state Rep. Joseph P. Riley Jr. Six weeks of these protests had cut into the business of downtown merchants. Save for the occasional march, the streets were largely deserted. Most people had decided to stay away from Charleston until the trouble passed.

Things would get worse before they improved.

On this day, Coretta Scott King was in town to lead yet another march, an event that attracted the network news and The New York Times. King's appearance was a show of solidarity and support for more than 500 workers – most of them poor, nearly all of them black – from the Medical College and the county hospital. These "non-professional" workers were being paid 30 cents below the federal minimum wage, and they had had enough. They were fighting for fairness, for equal treatment, for dignity. This did not go over well with hospital administrators or the local power structure. The dozen or so workers who organized the union, and the ensuing strike, were promptly fired.

Since then, the hospital district had become one large protest rally, the police working overtime to handle the daily picketing. Martin Luther King Jr.'s Southern Christian Leadership Conference arrived with reinforcements, and the slain civil rights leader's successor, Ralph David Abernathy, was quickly arrested. When Coretta Scott King arrived on April 29, Abernathy was still in the Charleston County Jail. He refused to post bail.

Abernathy had been arrested for violating one of the ludicrous rules imposed on the protesters. A judge decided there could be no more than 10 people on the picket line at any time, and all of them had to remain within a spot on the sidewalk only 20 yards wide. No other protesters could be within 500 yards of the hospitals. Mary Moultrie, one of the movement's organizers, had been jailed for 11 days simply for ignoring this edict. Her arrest sparked a new protest outside the jail. Finally, the judge just let her go. Moultrie was not even fined.

Moultrie was free in time to greet Mrs. King, who arrived the night before the march to motivate a crowd of 3,000 at Emanuel AME Church – the oldest African

Methodist Episcopal Church in the South and home to some of the nation's earliest civil rights pioneers. King compared the hospital workers' plight to the labor dispute among garbage workers in Memphis – the strike her husband had been trying to resolve when he was killed a year earlier.

Standing in the pulpit at Mother Emanuel, King said the Charleston hospital strike had become a national test of purpose like Selma, Ala., and vowed, "I am in this historic struggle no matter what the consequences, no matter what sacrifices may be necessary."

Those were strong words coming barely a year after her husband's death. And it did little to calm the nerves of Charleston officials, especially Chief Conroy, who did not want to see his city torn apart by violence – or become infamous for the death of another member of the King family. Conroy, a fair man and moderate on issues of civil rights, worried about what his police force – which, like most Southern police departments of the day, employed a fair share of bigots – might do if anyone got the least bit out of line.

Charleston of 1969 was an anachronism. Its 300th anniversary was just a year away, but it seemed all the clocks had stopped a century earlier. Once among the country's largest and most sophisticated cities, it was now merely a small, quiet seaside town most noteworthy for a large collection of antebellum homes protected by the nation's first serious preservation movement. Although the city's near-religious affinity for preservation was ahead of its time, some suspected this had more to do with a yearning for the way things once were than an appreciation for architecture.

Charleston had been the cultural center of the South in its heyday, a busy seaport, the summer home of wealthy planters. Once, it had been *important*. By the 1960s, however, many of those fine homes were in disrepair and the central business district was filled with aging, decrepit buildings and failing businesses. The folly of Reconstruction had done little for Charleston. The city was just another Civil War casualty.

The city's lower peninsula still looked much as it did during the War Between the States, except that now many of the oversized homes had been subdivided into apartments. Few of Charleston's residents needed 5,000-square-foot homes, or had the means to maintain them. Above Broad Street, the city was a mix of historic storefronts and a few modern chain stores. The greatest – perhaps only – signs of growth at the time were the new buildings going up around the Medical College. But the hospital could do little to remedy the city's overall declining health.

Charleston's economy never really recovered from the war, but the peninsula had remained busy until a decade earlier, when many residents began to move to the suburbs west of the Ashley River. A naval base on the Cooper River north of the city had kept the town alive. Charleston of the 20th century avoided a completely moribund economy only because of the same federal government it had once fought for independence. Most residents refused to acknowledge this irony and, in fact, perpetuated it. In the historic neighborhoods South of Broad, society's forebears carried on beneath the Spanish moss as if their time had not passed.

It was nothing short of miraculous that Charleston had avoided the controversies of civil rights for so long. The city was literally built on slave labor. Charleston had been the port of entry for most enslaved Africans until the practice was outlawed in the early 19th century. Charleston's role in the slave trade was, more than anything, a matter of convenience. At the height of the "peculiar institution" there were 4 million slaves in the United States, and a full 10 percent of them lived in South Carolina. These enslaved men and women produced the rice, cotton and indigo that made their owners rich. At one point, African-Americans made up more than half the state's population, and 36 percent of Charleston's.

Despite the city's role in the slave trade and its prominence in the Civil War – the first secession vote was cast at St. Andrew's Hall, the first shots were fired on Fort Sumter – Charleston had never struggled with the civil rights movement. While Birmingham and Montgomery were torn apart by violence, Charleston sat idle through the fight for equal rights with little more than a few lunch counter sit-ins. There had always been an uneasy détente among black and white Charlestonians, as if matters of race were meant to be avoided. Such unpleasantness had no place in a polite town of Southern manners. And so the town limped along.

The hospital strike threatened to change all of that. When Moultrie and her colleagues demanded equal treatment and equal pay, it forced the community to face lingering inequities. It was not clear which made the city's old guard more uncomfortable – confronting issues of race or labor unions, which had never been welcome in South Carolina. In some ways, the hospital strike felt like the death of old Charleston. Now the city was on a path to becoming just another divided Southern town.

Mrs. King set out from Morris Brown AME Church just before noon, wearing a finely pressed dress, fashionable sunglasses and a paper union hat. She held her head impossibly high, her posture almost regal as she passed sidewalks crowded 10 people deep. For most of the march, King walked arm-in-arm with Moultrie and Rosetta Simmons, a county hospital worker who was Moultrie's counterpart. Nearly 2,000 people followed behind, the entire group circled by Conroy's officers and dozens of newspaper photographers. It was a spectacle unlike anything Charleston had seen.

King issued a statement to the press just before the march began that said Charleston, "like Selma and Memphis, has become a national test of purpose with tremendously important implications for decent-minded Americans everywhere." The hospital workers and hundreds of others walked through the streets for more than an hour, the marchers singing "We Shall Not Be Moved" as they paraded past Ashley Hall, a private school for girls – white girls. The contrast was deftly noted by The Times.

The march brought Charleston to the attention of the White House and President Richard Nixon ordered South Carolina to end this embarrassment quickly. The state did not particularly welcome instruction from Washington, but on this occasion South Carolina officials found themselves in rare accord with the federal government. As King marched for the cameras, lawmakers 100 miles away in Columbia were plotting their response to the hospital strike.

They were determined to make sure Coretta Scott King was wasting her time.

For years, South Carolina Gov. Robert McNair had been praised for his pragmatic attitude toward civil rights. Unlike many Southern governors, McNair guided his state through the troubled waters of the 1960s with a delicate touch – most famously calming protesting students on the campus of its most famous historically black institution, South Carolina State College. Perhaps he benefited by comparison to other politicians, but McNair was considered such a moderate that he'd been on the vice presidential shortlist for the 1968 Democratic ticket.

But South Carolina's national silence was broken in February 1968, when local college students in Orangeburg – a small town halfway between Charleston and Columbia, and the home of S.C. State – picketed a local bowling alley that refused to allow them inside. On the third night of the protest, highway patrolmen opened fire on the picketers, killing three black men and wounding 28. McNair called the Orangeburg Massacre one of the saddest days in the state's history, but blamed the incident on "black power" advocates, which was hardly a sympathetic position on civil rights. After that, it did not matter that McNair's delegation to the 1968 nominating convention included the state chapter president of the NAACP. His national political aspirations were over.

Since then, it seemed South Carolina had been making up for lost time. In Denmark, students at the predominantly African-American Voorhees College took over the campus at gunpoint, demanding more black-studies programs and black faculty members. It was a dangerous situation, and McNair sent in the National Guard. The hospital strike arose at about the same time, and by then the governor had had enough. He had troops spread out across the state, and his sympathies had become nearly as strained as the National Guard.

The day before King's march, McNair called legislative leaders into his conference room on the first floor of the Statehouse. He said the state would not negotiate with striking hospital workers, that South Carolina had never recognized unions – and that was not about to change. When lawmakers left the room nearly an hour and a half later, they had their orders. One legislator told reporters the governor was standing firm. Another said, more ominously, that "There's one thing that's never been tried before – force."

The South Carolina Statehouse was not a particularly hospitable environment for equal rights. In 1969, the 170-member General Assembly was composed of 169 white men and one white woman. Atop the Statehouse dome, the Confederate Naval Jack flew below the South Carolina and U.S. flags. The flag had been hoisted nearly a decade earlier, allegedly to honor the centennial of the Civil War. Some people considered the banner a subtle protest of the civil rights movement, something many Southern states had done in the wake of the monumental Supreme Court decision *Brown v. Board of Education*. Georgia had even redesigned its state flag to incorporate the Confederate battle flag image. South Carolina's own Confederate flag remained in place four years after the war's centennial ended. In the South, old times were not forgotten.

About the time King began her march, legislators convened to debate a resolution hastily drafted after their meeting with McNair. The resolution said: "That there being no Constitutional or statutory authority permitting the state, its subdivisions, agencies or institutions to bargain collectively with their employees, the public policy in this regard as announced by his excellency, the governor of South Carolina, be and the same is hereby affirmed." It was little more than a position paper, a signal that the Legislature would not intervene on behalf of hospital workers.

Some Charleston lawmakers complained that they hadn't seen the resolution until it was presented for a vote. Sen. Robert Scarborough said Charleston County lawmakers would support the measure, but claimed that did not indicate a lack of concern for their home county. In truth, they simply would not cross legislative leadership, or McNair. In 1969, such rebellion was not condoned at the South Carolina Statehouse. The Democrats who controlled the state were a tightly regimented organization and the few Republicans who held seats did not protest – not on this particular issue. Condemning a striking union was as close as South Carolina came to bipartisanship.

In the House of Representatives, one freshman lawmaker sat listening to the debate with growing alarm. A long parade of speakers had taken the floor, and their tone was increasingly dismissive, derogatory and aggressive. Nearly all of these men were Democrats, but they did not sound like their national counterparts. Their words echoed the sentiments of their ancestors, the ones who started the secession movement in 1860. State Rep. Joe Riley Jr. felt the debate was, at the very least, embarrassingly disrespectful to black people. At worst, he realized, the state was once again coming down on the wrong side of history.

Riley was just three months into his first term of public office, and he hardly cut an imposing figure. Although he carried himself with an air of maturity beyond his 26 years, he was slight, reserved and quiet. His cherubic face looked so young that colleagues still occasionally mistook him for a legislative page. Sometimes they even asked him to fetch Cokes. He was not a man who commanded much authority, at least not at that moment.

In this, his first session as a member of the General Assembly, Riley's most significant contribution had been a bill to expand absentee voting – just as other states had done recently. The Charleston News and Courier's editorial board derisively called his legislation a case of "monkey see, monkey do," and Riley took it personally. He couldn't understand why anyone would oppose voting rights; he considered it the very foundation of democracy. Although he bristled at the criticism – as he would for years – Riley would not be stopped by it.

Riley already had a growing stable of allies and friends at the Statehouse. State Rep. Thomas Bryant of Orangeburg had noticed Riley's poise and maturity during an organizational session in December, when he was assigned a seat in the back left corner of the House directly behind the Charleston delegation. In his first few months, Bryant noticed Charleston lawmakers were constantly fighting some injustice or another, always in an uproar. But Riley sat quietly, doing his work and going about his business methodically. While most House members went to lunch with lobbyists, Riley often stayed at his desk. Bryant thought he would be a good person to know and emulate, and the two became fast friends.

Before this day, Riley had taken the podium to address the House only once – a short speech in support of a statewide kindergarten program. That had been one of his campaign platforms and he was passionate about it. His remarks had made little impression on his colleagues, most of whom did not support the plan. But they would not ignore his second speech so easily. As Coretta Scott King marched through the streets of his hometown, Riley decided it was time. He asked Speaker Sol Blatt if he could address the body.

Riley knew enough to realize he couldn't persuade the House to reverse its vote – he was no starry-eyed idealist. But he felt the need to say something largely because there were no African-Americans in the Legislature, no one to defend workers who were only fighting for equal treatment. He would speak on behalf of the hospital workers – they were his constituents, after all. Riley didn't intend to come off as a zealot; he just wanted to appeal to his colleagues' sense of decency, of fairness. He simply believed the House was being unjust.

In his brief remarks, Riley reminded House members that the hospital workers were protesting peacefully, just as the Rev. Martin Luther King Jr. had always suggested. The strike had been mostly orderly – the vandalism was regrettable but to some extent had been sensationalized by the media. The hospital workers were only standing up for their rights as human beings. He talked about the civil rights efforts of Henry Aaron, star outfielder of the Atlanta Braves. If nothing else, Riley – a baseball fanatic – assumed everyone shared his respect for Hammerin' Hank.

In truth, Riley had little information about what was happening back home. The Charleston legislative delegation had been briefed on the situation, but he had no inside knowledge of the negotiations. He only knew that nothing had been accomplished in six weeks, and that it was wrong to uniformly dismiss the very real concerns of people who wanted nothing more than fairness. The Legislature's resolution drew a line in the sand that only ensured the strike would continue, and increased the chance that someone might be hurt.

"The situation is serious and so important that nothing should have gone through this House today without serious consideration and study," Riley said. "It should be emphasized, however, that the resolution that was passed today says simply the state can't negotiate without specific legislation being passed to permit it."

And that is exactly what Riley wanted.

Riley had no desire to stir the pot, and thought he'd struck a moderate tone. A student of political history, he knew a rabid stance caused people to become even more intransigent. And race was a sensitive subject, not just in South Carolina of 1969, but all of America. So he tried to be subdued. Still, his remarks raised eyebrows even among those closest to him. He sounded exactly like a child of the '60s, a liberal idealist from New York or California – places many folks in South Carolina did not particularly care for. These remarks were the first public acknowledgment of Riley's deepest beliefs, his true political agenda.

State Rep. Alex Sanders watched Riley with both admiration and amusement. He was in his second term as a House member, a tenure long enough to know exactly what Speaker Blatt and the leadership would think of this tongue-lashing from a mere freshman. They might not ostracize Riley or relegate him to meaningless committee assignments – not yet – but they would keep an eye on him now. He could be trouble.

Sanders had struck up a solid friendship with Riley despite their very different personalities. Not yet 30, Sanders nevertheless had an old soul and already had cultivated a reputation at the Statehouse of a hilarious raconteur. Sanders may have talked like a typical good ol' boy South Carolina politician, but that belied a philosophical spirit in tune with Riley's progressive political convictions. Sanders was no old school, yellow-dog Democrat; he was a liberal. He and Riley quickly became allies.

Still, Sanders couldn't understand why Riley always seemed so damned serious. He wasn't impolite, and had a wit so dry it was easy to miss – a trait Sanders greatly appreciated. But Riley seemed far more intense than most people his age, even among lawmakers. When he was working, Riley was all business. The long hours, and his aversion to socializing with lobbyists, led some people to misunderstand the young lawyer. Sanders admired his gumption and his work ethic, but realized legislative leadership didn't know what the hell to make of this preachy, baby-faced kid from Charleston. Riley did not go along with the program, and that did not bode well for his political future.

Riley never considered the repercussions of his speech, but it wouldn't have stopped him if he had. Although he'd been in office only a few months, Riley did not concern himself with treading lightly as most freshmen did; he felt comfortable at the Statehouse. He had been around politicians all his life – his father was a recognized civic leader in Charleston, a major player in the county's Democratic Party and a vocal ally of Congressman Mendel Rivers. Politicians had been in and out of the Riley home every week when he was growing up.

By the time he was elected to the General Assembly, Riley had spent years observing legislative bodies in action. He had interned in Rivers' Washington office one summer during college and, in his first two years of law school, worked for then-Lt. Gov. McNair and his successor, John West. Riley understood politics and already knew all of the state's most influential leaders. He considered many of them friends. They did not intimidate him.

Although Riley was on good terms with many of the state's pro-segregation politicians, he did not share their views. In some ways, Riley's politics were inspired by the times. He came of age during the country's greatest period of change, and it had made an impression on him. He still remembered a hot summer day in 1963 just before his senior year of college. It was the moment everything started to fall into place, when he began to make sense of contradictions that had bothered him his whole life.

Riley had spent that day at his family's summer home on the Isle of Palms. It was a busy, tense time. His oldest sister, Susanne, was in labor at the hospital – soon to deliver the family's first grandchild. With his parents preoccupied, Riley was forced to entertain himself and eventually turned on the television. Most stations were broadcasting grainy black-and-white pictures from the mall in downtown Washington, where the Rev. Martin Luther King Jr. stood on the steps of the Lincoln Memorial and related his dream to 250,000 people. Riley was inspired.

He remembered that speech as he evoked King's name in his remarks to the House of Representatives. The civil rights leader had been dead a year and his widow was at that moment marching through the streets of Riley's hometown. In some ways it was as if the world had not changed. Despite the Civil Rights Act, and all of King's work, the same people were still fighting the same battles. But now, six years after that day he watched King on TV, Riley believed he was finally in a position to join the cause.

Coretta Scott King's march broke up shortly after passing the main campus of the Medical College's west wing on Ashley Avenue. As she circled back to the parking lot where the march began, about 150 demonstrators broke off and formed a picket line in front of the hospital. It was a clear violation of the court order, a show of defiance. When Chief Conroy reminded them of the rules and asked them to move along, they refused.

"Do you want to go to jail?" the police chief asked.

"Yes, yes, yes," the people chanted.

But Conroy did nothing, and no one would question his judgment. A few days earlier, the local Rotary Club had given the chief a standing ovation for keeping the city safe during the strike. Conroy took this job seriously and, if he had any sympathy for the demonstrators, he did not let it show. But he told them they could stay for a while; his men would be back later to arrest them. At the moment, Conroy had far more pressing concerns. He desperately wanted to make sure Coretta Scott King got out of Charleston unharmed – both for her sake, and the city's. The protesters could wait.

The next day, Gov. McNair declared a state of emergency for Charleston and imposed a curfew from 9 p.m. to 6 a.m. He feared the city was in for a long siege. Some predicted the next step would be martial law, especially after The News and Courier reported that the curfew had failed to stop the violence: "Fires, gunfire, false alarms and gang attacks flared sporadically after the 9 p.m. curfew began in Charleston."

Protesters threw rocks at police officers and soldiers patrolling the streets. A storage shed on Queen Street was set afire when someone tossed a Molotov cocktail into it. Two National Guardsmen claimed they had seen "two Negro youths" running from the building just before the fire was detected. Later that night, two unoccupied Highway Patrol cruisers parked on President Street were riddled with bullets. The strike was becoming less peaceful every day.

Save for a few troublemakers, the city was a ghost town on the first night of the curfew. The News and Courier noted that when the bells of St. Michael's chimed 9 o'clock, Charleston was already asleep. The restaurants and movie houses were quiet, and the go-go dancers – as the paper euphemistically called them – were temporarily out of work. The city was living under armed occupation. Checkpoints were set up on the bridges leading to the peninsula from West Ashley and Mount Pleasant. Guardsmen searched cars and checked identifications, allowing only doctors or other approved night-shift workers entrance to the city.

Tensions grew more strained when a local lawmaker, state Sen. Rembert C. Dennis, suggested that the Legislature pass a resolution praising the governor and the Medical College for their stand against these protests. Herbert Fielding, a local funeral home director and chairman of a black civil rights organization called the Political Action Committee, pointed out the senator was a trustee at the Medical College – perhaps not the most unbiased judge of the situation.

Fielding said politicians like Dennis had casually dismissed the concerns of hundreds of citizens, turned Charleston into an "armed camp" and refused to even discuss a solution. He called on local leaders to "start immediate discussions between state officials and the workers now on strike." Fielding demanded the troops leave Charleston.

"We are all citizens of this community, vitally interested in the social, economic and political development of our people, most certainly the several hundred workers now in conflict with the Medical College Hospital," Fielding said. "We recognize and respect you as our political leaders, but remind you that such leadership demands faithful, forceful, dynamic and imaginative action in times of crisis. We would only further petition you to understand that law and order without justice is neither realistic nor lasting."

Fielding was basically restating the same case his friend Riley had made on the floor of the House days earlier. And just about as many people listened.

Finally, the city offered a gesture of good faith. Charleston Mayor Palmer Gaillard appointed a committee of citizens to sit down with hospital officials and striking workers in hopes of defusing the hostility. Gaillard said he wanted to find some common-sense middle ground. Both sides agreed to try, and for weeks the newspaper was filled with promising headlines predicting a break in the strike. But that didn't happen, and soon the threats from the hospitals resumed. Medical College President Dr. William McCord said that "if the union keeps up the pressure … the hospital will have to close."

The Legislature remained in session until June, but Riley saw the effects of the hospital strike every day. His wife, Charlotte, was pregnant and due any time, so he drove home from Columbia at night to ensure he would not miss the birth of their first child. Every evening, he saw the picketing workers, the checkpoints and the deserted streets of the peninsula. It saddened him to see the city going through such turmoil, and frustrated him that the General Assembly had taken such a hard stand.

One weekend night in May, Riley was forced to break that curfew and rush into the heart of the hospital district. Charlotte had gone into labor, and he dutifully helped her to the car and set out on the quiet streets. The trip was mercifully quick, at least until they were stopped at a checkpoint. It wasn't hard for the guards to figure out what was going on. Charlotte was clearly very pregnant, and a distressed Riley – not relying on anyone's powers of observation – told the soldiers, "My wife is going to have a baby any minute." The troops waved them through, and Joe Riley III was born safely, just blocks away from Charleston's ongoing strife.

For weeks, it seemed Charleston was in a time loop. There would be a march, people were arrested, and when they were released the cycle began anew. Ralph David Abernathy was released from the Charleston County Jail on Friday, May 2 – the same day his "letter" was published in The News and Courier. In it, he assured the city that the Southern Christian Leadership Conference only wanted equal rights for all people, that they were not Communists. "We want and will have no part of a godless, atheist, totalitarian form of Communism. But neither will we have a dictatorial, repressive so-called Democracy."

The following Monday, Abernathy was back in Charleston to lead yet another march. He returned several times until he was finally jailed again on June 20 for organizing a nighttime protest. This time, Abernathy vowed to not post bail until the strike was settled. Protesters responded by throwing bricks at police officers, and the governor quickly reinstated the curfew that had been lifted three weeks earlier. This time, the mayor had requested it, because conditions in Charleston seemed to get worse each day.

As the summer began, 17 U.S. senators asked the White House to send in mediators, and they arrived just in time to witness Abernathy's second arrest and the violence it precipitated. The AFL-CIO came to the union's aid and threatened to shut down the Port of Charleston unless the strike was settled. Finally, the pressure was too great to ignore any longer. Local civil rights activists, including Bill Saunders of Johns Island, were able to broker a deal with officials from the two hospitals.

The strike ended on June 27, 100 days after it began. McCord said the employees who had been fired would be rehired, and the rest could come back to work. All of them would be paid at least $1.60 an hour – the federal minimum wage – and a grievance process would be established to handle any future trouble. The hospital even set up a credit union for the workers, something they didn't have before the strike. One of the final sticking points was the reinstatement of Mary Moultrie, the woman who started it all. Moultrie learned she had her job back while watching TV in a hotel room in New York City, where she had been sent on a speaking tour to raise money for her striking colleagues.

The county hospital settled with its workers a month later, rehiring everyone but Rosetta Simmons. Hospital officials said they had hired another LPN in her absence and had no job for her. Five months passed before the hospital offered her another position. That was effectively the end of the episode, but medical workers knew all too well that some wounds took a long time to heal.

The strike had cost taxpayers more than $22,000 in extra police protection over the three months, and many residents would not soon forget it. But Mayor Gaillard praised the two sides for finally settling their differences. "The entire matter has caused considerable concern and hardship on all Charlestonians, and I hope that the community will now get back to normal and get on to the business of promoting our community."

Riley praised McCord, Chief Conroy, Gaillard and Saunders for their work, but he soon noticed a change in Charleston. Victory in the hospital strike had convinced African-Americans that they did not have to bow to the city's power structure. They had found their voice and soon became more involved in local politics. That fall, black garbage workers would stage their own strike, and that did not bode well for Palmer Gaillard. Although the mayor got some of the credit for resolving the strike, a few of the statements he made during the crisis offended many people in the black community.

Their resentment would linger into the city's next mayoral election.

The Rileys of Charleston

He had always known politics was in his future.

Before Joe Riley ran for a seat in the state Legislature, before Fritz Hollings suggested he seek public office, even before he was president of the senior class at Bishop England High School, he was drawn to that world. History and the government and retail politics had intrigued him from a young age. He was fascinated by it all – not because it seemed unattainable, but because he'd been around it his whole life.

Joseph Patrick Riley Jr. was born to public service. It was learned behavior in his family, part of his DNA, passed down from one generation to the next. For nearly a century before his birth, Riley's family – men and women alike – had been involved in every facet of Charleston's municipal, charitable, fraternal and religious communities. It came as naturally as breathing. It was simply what they did.

Patrick and Ann Collins Riley arrived in Charleston around 1850, at the end of a massive influx of Irish immigrants that began nearly 30 years earlier. The Rileys came from Ballymena in County Antrim, perhaps hoping to escape the harsh economic realities of 19th century Ireland. When they landed at the docks that lined the peninsula's eastern shore, they found a new home much larger than the town they had left in the northern Irish countryside.

To the Rileys, Charleston must have seemed like a bustling seaport – a big American city full of opportunity and prosperity. But actually it was a town on the wane, its best days decades behind it. The nearly 1,000 Irish immigrants who arrived with the Rileys during the 1850s accounted for much of the city's modest growth in the 1860 census. In the years before the Civil War, whites were only about 57 percent of the city's 40,000 residents – and the Irish were a small subset of that statistic. Slaves made up nearly one-third of the population; free blacks – who carried papers to prove their status – accounted for most of the rest.

In Charleston, everyone had their place. Free blacks fell into a social-order chasm somewhere between whites and slaves, and the Rileys soon found they were only a notch or so higher in that pecking order. People of color were not the only ones discriminated against in 19th century Charleston. Catholics like the Rileys were not readily accepted into the Holy City's culture. It was a town dominated by French Huguenots and Episcopalians, as it had been for almost two centuries.

The Irish were not shy, however, and took the country's land-of-the-free slogan at its word. About the time the Rileys landed, the Irish were building the Cathedral of St. John and St. Finbar on Broad Street, a grand temple that would dominate the skyline for a brief time. It would take decades before the Irish Catholic community was accepted into Charleston society, but that did not stop them from integrating themselves into the city.

Patrick Riley had trained as a weaver in Ireland, but found more attractive opportunities in his adopted hometown. He took work as a general laborer, and soon found a permanent job in the gas business. Charleston was just beginning to line its streets with gaslights, and there was plenty of work harvesting natural gas, coal and oil. He and Ann started a family, which eventually grew to include two daughters and four sons. One of those boys, Andrew J. Riley – the grandfather of Joe Riley Jr. – was born in the city on April 4, 1854, making him one of the family's first Charleston natives. Ultimately that would be the most important fact on his resume, at least by the measure of other Charlestonians.

When the Civil War began, Patrick Riley volunteered to fight for the Confederacy, as many Irish immigrants did. But his skills in the manufacturing and delivery of gas were deemed more important to the South, so he stayed home. His son, Andrew, was far too young to join the war effort. Instead, he came of age during Reconstruction, a depressing period in the city's history. Opportunities were not abundant, but he soon found a calling. Andrew took work as a pipefitter apprenticed to a local plumber. When his mentor died, Andrew Riley inherited the business. By the turn of the century, when the city was cleaning up from the devastating earthquake of 1886, Riley was installing Charleston's first water and sewer lines.

Andrew J. Riley kept his plumbing business open on King Street well into the 20th century. By then, he had also taken an interest in local politics. Between 1888 and 1915 he served Ward 9 on City Council, working alongside a half-dozen mayors – including the administration of one of his closest allies, Mayor John P. Grace. Riley eventually became president of the board of trustees at Jenkins Orphanage, a home for black children. And in 1896, he joined the city board of firemasters. All this made Andrew Riley a very busy – and visible – man.

Riley was an influential fundraiser for the Sisters of Our Lady of Mercy in their efforts to build St. Francis Hospital. He was a delegate to the Irish Race Convention in 1919, and the next year became chairman of a committee that planned the visit of President Eamon da Valera of the Irish Republic to Charleston. It was the first time a foreign sovereign had visited the city, but it would not be the last.

Andrew Riley married the former Mary Emily Oliver, a woman who took just as much interest in Charleston's welfare. She was treasurer of the local Red Cross chapter, sat on the board of the city's orphan asylum and was the first president – and a founder – of the Charleston Diocesan Council of Catholic Women. Andrew and Mary were a busy couple with a large family – six boys and three girls. Joseph Patrick Riley, their eighth child, was not born until Andrew was already 58 years old.

Many Irish Charlestonians were drawn to public service because it helped them more quickly become an accepted part of the community. But for the Rileys, there may have been more to it. Perhaps they were inspired by Mary's father, Henry Oliver, a local building contractor and native of Charleston, a man the papers hailed as "thoroughly devoted to her welfare and best interests." Oliver had been born in Charleston in 1839, the son of an Englishman who landed in New York 15 years earlier, traveling as an indentured servant to pay for his passage to the New World. It was a common tale in the 19th century.

Andrew Riley's father-in-law was something of a local hero. The Evening Post called Henry Oliver "one of the best and most gallant soldiers which Charleston furnished to the Confederacy." As an infantryman, Oliver had fought in the battles of Chickamauga, Spotsylvania, Petersburg, Cold Harbor and Gettysburg – and somehow lived to tell about it. Oliver was a survivor. He was in the middle of another skirmish along the James River in April 1865 when Gen. Robert E. Lee laid down his sword at Appomattox Courthouse, effectively ending the War Between the States.

Oliver walked home from Richmond and started a successful contracting business, a calling for which he had abundant talent. He built the Cogswell Building and Printer's Row on East Bay Street, the Wilson-Sottile House on College Street, the YMCA-Women's Exchange on King Street, as well as Francis Silas Rodgers' home – later known as the Wentworth Mansion. He served as general contractor on an 1883 renovation of City Hall and, according to family lore, succeeded the original contractor and finished construction of the new Cathedral of St. John the Baptist – replacing the Cathedral of St. John and St. Finbar, which was destroyed in the fire of 1861.

Oliver made significant contributions to Charleston's architecture, but his true passions were public service and organizing reunions of his fellow Confederate veterans. When he died in 1910, The Evening Post reported that "Mr. Oliver never held public office, but he was always willing to contribute his services in a modest way to the promotion of the public good."

Andrew Riley died just 14 years after his father-in-law. By then, he had retired from all his civic duties except the firemasters board. Still, his death was a shock to the community "as it was not generally known that he was desperately ill." The flags at City Hall and every fire station in the city were lowered to half-staff to mark his passing. Fire Chief Louis Behrens noted that, "We had been friends for at least half a century and I keenly feel his death." When he died, Andrew Riley left Mary to raise their children in the family home on Calhoun Street, not far from the College of Charleston. His son, Joseph, was only 12.

Later, Joe Riley Sr. would credit his mother for his lifelong interest in public service. Although she was a widow with nine children, Mary Oliver Riley still spent part of nearly every day doing some sort of community work. She devoted 30 years to the Red Cross alone, and taught her son to give a few hours of every day to something "worthwhile." It was the least he could do for his city.

Between his studies at Catholic elementary school and, later, Bishop England High School, Riley worked for his mother. The family owned some property around town and he was charged with collecting the rent. He did not realize it at the time, but he had found a vocation. After high school, Riley left Charleston to attend the University of South Carolina in Columbia. But the Depression was in full swing and his family needed money, so he returned home and took work as an elevator operator in a cigar factory. Later, Riley joined the Civilian Conservation Corps, a job that took him no farther than Round O in neighboring Colleton County. He stayed for a year before returning home.

Charleston was a desolate city in those days. It had never recovered from the war and, more than a half-century later, the area's largest industry was the Navy base north of the peninsula. The city was turning into a military town, and a seedy one at that. North of Broad Street, many streets – especially those lined with bars and strip clubs – were considered inappropriate for proper people to visit. The City Council tried to regulate this foot traffic, declaring public parks off limits to sailors and, of course, black residents. After all, segregation was the law of the land.

One day, Riley heard the speaker at a civic group suggest that Charleston's young men should leave town to find work because "there are no jobs, no opportunities here." Charleston, the man said, was dying a slow and agonizing death – the Yankees' last revenge. This hopeless assessment made Riley determined to stay and start his own business. In 1937, when he was just 25, he opened the Joseph P. Riley Real Estate and Insurance Company.

Even though he was busy building his company into a local empire, Riley followed in his parents' footsteps, serving on the advisory boards of Jenkins Orphanage and the Red Cross. He joined the Hibernian Society, like all good Irish did, and worked for the Boy Scouts and Catholic Charities. He was intimately involved in the expansion of St. Francis Hospital, as his father before him. Between all that, Riley found time to get married. One of his competitors provided him with a bride.

Riley knew John Edwin Schachte from their mutual business – both sold real estate and insurance, and both had their offices on Broad Street. Schachte had worked for his father's firm, Henry Schachte & Sons, all his adult life. The Schachte family hailed from Germany, and had been involved in banking, construction, real estate and insurance around Charleston for the better part of a century. John Edwin Schachte had married Susie Knobeloch of Charleston in 1912, and the couple had two children – a son named for his father, and a daughter named Helen.

Helen Louise Schachte was a quiet, reserved woman who in many ways was ahead of her time. She had attended the College of Charleston – finishing second in her class – and Jefferson Medical College. She worked as a medical technologist, but in another era Helen would have undoubtedly become a physician. She was bright and, like Riley, became involved in several charities. After a long courtship, Helen and Joe Riley were married on Nov. 11, 1939.

Helen Riley took up even more local causes after she quit her job to raise a family. The Rileys' first child, Susanne – named for Helen's mother – was born in the spring of 1941. She was followed 21 months later by Joe and Helen's only son, who was named after his father.

Joseph Patrick Riley Jr. was born on Jan. 19, 1943, an unseasonably warm winter day in Charleston. The 70-degree weather, which would not survive the week, was the only local news of note. The city was consumed mostly with reports of the war in Europe and the inauguration that day of Gov. Olin Johnston. Johnston, a man with a slow and deliberate South Carolina drawl, had been re-elected to the governor's office after serving a previous term in the mid-1930s. On the day Joe was born, Johnston promised to bring Prohibition back to South Carolina – and fight the growing national calls for desegregation.

It was a particularly busy time for the Riley family. A week earlier Joe Riley Sr. had bought the building at 13 Broad St., which eventually would become the home of his real estate and insurance company. Joe Sr. was also heavily involved in the war effort, acting as treasurer of the Charleston Service Men's center and a member of the civilian defense council. He also took regular shifts watching the coast for German submarines from lookout posts on the Isle of Palms.

Riley was enamored of the island, had been for years. He had tried to buy the Isle of Palms outright, but couldn't get the bank loan and eventually lost out to a developer named J.C. Long. As consolation, Riley built a summer home for his family there at 3rd and Carolina and bought several acres of property on the island – in turn selling oceanfront lots for $875. The Riley family had owned a summer home on Sullivan's Island when Joe Sr. was a child, and his mother kept it long after Andrew Riley passed away. Joe Sr. grew up acclimated to the island life. He not only loved fishing and boating, but realized the barrier islands were an emerging real estate market. Or they would be, one day.

Except for summers, when they stayed at their beach house, the Rileys lived in an apartment house on Rutledge Avenue just two doors up from Julian Mitchell Elementary School. With Helen, Susanne and Joe secure in the apartment in late 1943, Joe Sr. left port on the Army Hospital Ship *Shamrock*. He'd tried to join the service when the United States entered World War II, but his eyesight – not his age – prompted the military to pass on him. So Riley signed up as crew on the 602-patient ship when it sailed from Charleston. The *Shamrock* spent months supporting Gen. George Patton's operations, rescuing soldiers in Europe and North Africa. While her husband was away, Helen fussed over baby Joe, refusing to cut his hair until his father returned.

During the year Joe Sr. was gone, Helen moved the family to a house on Grove Street, north of Hampton Park. But that was too far away from downtown, and her family, so by the end of 1945 the Rileys relocated to a duplex at 63 Gibbes St., south of Broad Street. They lived on the first floor and rented out the upstairs. There, Helen had two more children – daughters Mary and Jane.

The family would not grow any larger – Jane was the last – but the Rileys had no shortage of relatives in Charleston. Mary Oliver Riley died in 1945, when Joe was just 2, leaving him with no memory of his paternal grandmother. However, his father's sisters had never married and aunts Emily and Habby (Margaret) lived nearby – as did "aunt" Dorothy, Joe's second cousin. Dorothy had grown up with Helen in the Schachte house after her mother and father died at a young age. All of these women doted on the Riley children; Emily was Joe's godmother. Helen's parents, Ed and Susie Schachte – Ned and Nana, as the kids called them – also lived close by on Beaufain Street. The Rileys often took their Sunday dinner there.

One of Joe's earliest memories was Ned Schachte sitting in his chair next to a stand-up radio cabinet. He would climb into his grandfather's lap and together they listened to whatever Major League Baseball game the local station was broadcasting that day. It became their shared passion. While Joe was still in elementary school, his grandfather took him to College Park stadium to see his first baseball game. It was opening night for the Charleston Rebels – one in a series of minor league teams that would call the city home – and Joe was immediately enamored. His grandfather taught him the game in the grandstand bleachers behind the first base line, recording the plays on a notepad. Soon, Joe could keep his own scorecard.

His favorite team as a boy was the Brooklyn Dodgers, in part because he was fascinated by the exploits of Jackie Robinson, the first black man to play Major League Baseball. But in truth he simply had a love of the game. Helen, unmistakably her father's daughter, did her best to encourage Joe's interest. When school forced him to miss a World Series game – which in the 1950s were played during the day – Helen would watch on television and keep score so she could give her son the play-by-play as soon as he got home. Joe sat at rapt attention, memorizing every detail.

In the 1950s, Charleston was a very poor town. Even the aristocratic families South of Broad had little money then, but the Joseph P. Riley Real Estate and Insurance Company became more successful each year. The Rileys were quickly ensconced firmly in the upper-middle class. Joe Sr. took great pride in his family, and every fall hired a professional photographer to take the picture that would grace their Christmas cards. One year the photo was set around the family dinner table, another year around the tree. Eventually, they would take most of their portraits on the front porch of their home.

Riley did not spoil his children, but he provided for them well. He once bought them a pony, quite the extravagance in downtown Charleston. The children often took the pony for rides in the nearby horse lot and, before moving to Murray Boulevard, kept it in the impossibly small back yard on Gibbes Street. The animal found these accommodations somewhat lacking, and one day escaped. Helen placed a frantic phone call to her husband's office. The horse, she reported, had gotten out.

"I know," Riley calmly told her. "I just saw it running down Broad Street."

In those days, Charleston streets were not too busy for the occasional random horse to pose a problem.

Those streets became the Riley children's playground; they rarely needed to venture much beyond their neighborhood South of Broad. Susanne took music lessons from a woman who lived a few blocks away, and proved to be something of a prodigy. Helen Riley hoped that her son had the same music gene and sent Joe for lessons, too. He hated it.

Joe had no interest in playing music; he wanted to be outside with his friends. Once he returned from his lesson without any sheet music to practice on the family piano. When his mother asked him about this, he claimed the wind had blown his homework out of the basket on his bike and down a storm drain before he could catch it. Neither his piano teacher nor his mother believed the story, but for the rest of his life Joe swore that is exactly what happened. Besides, he would later say, the sheet music was for "The Happy Cowboy" – and who wanted to play that anyway?

Soon after that, Joe was allowed to discontinue his lessons. Still, he sat through his sisters' recitals without complaint, most likely content to know he did not have to join them onstage.

Joe attended Catholic grammar school on Broad Street, as his father had, and every day he rode his bike to school – a trip of about a half-mile if he took the right route. The streets of the lower Charleston peninsula were his back yard, and by the time he was old enough to venture out on his own, Joe knew every alley intimately. More than 60 years later, he could still point out the storm drain that ate "The Happy Cowboy."

His teachers would remember him as a good student – very good, close to excellent – but were mostly struck by his budding leadership skills. Joe was quick to organize games on the playground and call attention to any infraction or unfairness. In the classroom, he was the student who told the others to be quiet when the teacher was out of the room. Joe did this in part because of his fondness for the school's principal, who was also his eighth-grade teacher – Sister Mary William.

Joe thought Sister Mary William was kind and attentive – and attractive – and treated the children with respect. He wanted to make her proud. Sister Mary William believed young Joe was simply trying to be a good citizen, a trait she attributed to his parents. Riley's mother was often in the school helping out, and the nuns considered her a kind, gentle woman. His father spent little time on campus, but always showed up for PTA meetings.

Joe was a well-behaved child. He may have teased his sisters, but never harassed them. Susanne often complained that she spent all her time studying, yet her brother never seemed to exert himself. He needled her about this, claiming he didn't need to study – he could do just fine without it. But Joe did study; he just did it quickly. And he spent a lot of time reading, poring through a series of children's book biographies of Thomas Jefferson and Robert E. Lee. Behind baseball, history was one of his greatest interests.

Joe's best friend was Pat Brennan, who lived nearby on Tradd Street. The pair had a routine they followed every day. When school let out at 1:50 they went home, and Joe had dinner with his family. Susanne, who attended Ashley Hall, got out at the same time. Afterward, Joe and Pat would get on their bikes and go exploring. They played baseball, football – whatever was in season – and nearly every day stopped at the local service station to drop 13 cents on a Pepsi and a pack of Lance crackers. On the days he wasn't roaming the streets with Pat, Joe walked his sisters to Burbage's Grocery on Tradd, where they could use sticks to spear their own pickles.

It was an idyllic childhood, he would later say. Joe and Pat hung out with a large contingent of friends from the neighborhood and their school. The gang nearly reflected the spectrum of Charleston's socio-economic structure in the 1950s, although they had few black acquaintances. Even in adolescence, Joe and Pat realized there were unnatural barriers in their hometown.

When Joe was about 12, the family bought a large home on Murray Boulevard overlooking the Ashley River and Charleston Harbor. By then it wasn't just the children who brought home their friends. Joe Sr. often had guests over, many of them famous South Carolinians. The girls remembered Gov. Jimmy Byrnes coming for dinner once; Fritz Hollings, a rising political star, lived just down the street. Congressman Mendel Rivers visited Murray Boulevard frequently. He was one of Joe Sr.'s closest friends – Riley even served as treasurer on his campaigns. At the time, Rivers was easily the most influential politician in the city.

The Riley children were always welcome at these power-structure gatherings, and Joe Sr. often called on Susanne to entertain their guests on the piano. Big Joe, as people began to call him, was not particularly strict but taught his children proper manners – and expected them to be on display at all times. He once put up a sign in the kitchen that read, "Be pleasant until 10 a.m. and the rest of the day will take care of itself," a message that Susanne assumed referred to her penchant for waking up grumpy. But the children rarely disappointed their father. They grew accustomed to a house filled with people, and never failed to impress guests. They also learned a great deal from these visitors. Nearly everyone they saw – including their parents – was somehow involved in the community. Joe grew up believing that was just what everyone did.

None of those distinguished guests, however, talked about the increasingly contentious nature of South Carolina politics – not in front of the children anyway. All of that was still a decade away.

A Lowcountry Heart

When school let out in May, Joe and Helen Riley moved the family to their Isle of Palms beach house for the summer, often staying until classes resumed after Labor Day. Big Joe eventually sold the first beach house and built a second one at Carolina and 8th Avenue. There, Helen took her children to the beach twice a day. The kids swam and fished and played in the sand, the Lowcountry sun tanning them a deep brown. The Riley children learned a healthy respect for the unique South Carolina environment from their parents.

Joe quickly fell in love with the coast, and spent countless hours exploring the beach and the marshes behind the island. It was a world apart from downtown Charleston, with its own customs and traditions. When Big Joe got home in the evening, he always jumped into the ocean – in part a baptism to wash away the day, but also because their house had no air conditioning. Afterward, he often took Joe fishing, either in the Intracoastal Waterway or offshore.

Pat Brennan spent at least one week each summer on the island with Joe, and it was a time for shrimping, crabbing and messing around in whatever boat Big Joe owned at the moment. Brennan considered Joe the brother he never had, and the Rileys his second parents. Helen Riley made the best butter beans he would ever put in his mouth, a dish he would always remember. The Rileys encouraged a full house. Big Joe was happiest when he was surrounded by people. Susanne often brought home boarding students from Ashley Hall to stay for the weekend; Mary and Jane, like Joe, went to the Catholic school, and had their own friends over. Helen never knew how many people she might be feeding on any given night, but she never complained.

Joe and Pat ultimately joined the Boy Scouts, which afforded them even more time to stay outdoors. The summer before they started high school, they went to Camp Ho Non Wah, a 145-acre spread on Wadmalaw Island overlooking Bohicket Creek – a completely different experience than the Isle of Palms. One day, the two were at the camp swimming pool when they saw a boy coming toward them. This young man was clearly a teenager and, they believed, much older. Joe and Pat were still on the edge of puberty, but this boy had hair on his chest and his face. They were intimidated.

The young man introduced himself as Bill Robinson, and simply asked, "Are you guys going to Bishop England? Are you going to play football?"

Joe and Pat followed Robinson's lead and tried out for the football team. Pat became a defensive end. Joe – who enjoyed football, but didn't exactly have the size for it – tried out as a back and an end before he was finally assigned to the offensive line with Robinson. At the time Joe weighed about 135 pounds (although the program listed him at an optimistic 170), and guard was the only position he could reasonably play – tackles and centers were generally much larger. Joe took a beating on the practice field, but he handled it without complaint. He even endured the track team, which the football coach required of all his players.

Joe played football throughout high school. He got into some games as a junior, and by his senior year had secured the job of second-string left guard. Then, five games into the season – just before Bishop England's rivalry game with Charleston High – the starter got hurt. Suddenly Joe was a first-string guard, a position he would hold the rest of the season. In that game, he played well enough to earn a mention in the newspaper article chronicling BE's 12-6 victory.

Perhaps his best showing, however, came during his greatest challenge. Bishop England was playing St. Andrew's High, which at the time had an all-state defensive tackle. For the entire game, Joe faced off against the tackle – who was not only better than him, but every player on the BE team. Joe took a beating, but he got his licks in and held his own. He was fast, and knew that even big guys fell when you hit them at the ankles.

At Bishop England, Joe proved to be a serious student and his interest in politics began to take shape. He was drawn to a book written by a Massachusetts senator named Jack Kennedy, who had commanded the torpedo boat PT-109 in the Pacific during World War II. Riley was inspired and, as a junior, was one of two students selected to attend the American Legion's Boys State, a government education program that allowed students to set up mock cities and run them. The next year, he was president of the senior class; Robinson was treasurer.

High school afforded Joe his first taste of independence, and he had a typically active social life. His first date was a double date with Pat Brennan, but mostly Joe and Robinson left the Friday night football games together and ended up at the high school's sock hops. They were witness to the birth of rock and roll on AM radios and spent their evenings on the familiar streets of the Charleston peninsula. This was life in a small town.

They never got in serious trouble, never ran afoul of the law. Robinson later said he didn't even taste a beer until his senior year. Brennan recalled that whenever the kids hatched a plan to pull some prank or make mischief, Joe was most often the one who said, "Guys, we don't need to do that." Brennan later said that Joe led by example. "Even when you knew somebody was suggesting something that wasn't a good idea, you didn't want to be the one to say it. But Joe would."

Joe later said that sports kept him and his friends out of mischief, but they claim he kept them in line. Even though he worried about looking like a nerd or a square, Robinson thought Joe was preternaturally concerned with right and wrong. He had an unerring moral compass – sometimes he was almost too good to be believed. That did not mean Joe was above stumbling into occasional trouble.

Once Joe was teaching his cousin, Jack Riley, how to drive the family's Jeep at the Isle of Palms house. Jack judged a turn wrong and took out the house's front steps – leaving him and Joe scrambling to repair the staircase before Big Joe got home. They rebuilt the steps, but Joe confessed to his father anyway. The new stairs, he later conceded, were perhaps not structurally sound.

It was on the family's 1958 vacation that Joe once even made his mother mad. The family piled into their station wagon for a long trip up the East Coast – Mary and Jane forced to sit in the third seat, which faced backward. Later, they lamented that their seats allowed them to see only where they'd been. The Rileys visited Williamsburg, Va., Mount Vernon, Washington, D.C., and New York before dropping Susanne off in Connecticut to visit friends from Ashley Hall. The enduring memory from the trip, however – the one the entire family would talk about for years to come – was the night they stayed in a rural Virginia hotel.

Helen Riley carried a bottle of Scotch for her and Big Joe's nightly drink. It was a reward, her daughters said, for sitting in the car with them all day. Helen kept the bottle wrapped discreetly in a towel, but that night one of the girls asked Joe for a towel. He grabbed the first one he saw, the one that held the Scotch. Later, he explained that when someone asks for a towel, you don't just hand it to them – you are required to pop them with it. When he playfully snapped the towel at his sisters, the bottle went flying and smashed onto the inn's tile floor. Since it was a dry county, the Rileys were left with no nightcap that evening. Although it was an accident, his parents were not very pleased with 15-year-old Joe.

That was about as much trouble as Joe ever found himself in – if no one counted his rebellions when it came time to see the doctor. Joe hated the sight of blood and abhorred needles, a trait that he blamed on a shot he got in his heel as a baby. One of the most famous family stories involved the children's trip to the doctor for their annual booster shots. Joe was 6 or 7 at the time, but already a headstrong young man. When his turn came, Joe bolted out the door – the doctor chasing the little escapee up Rutledge Avenue. They eventually caught him on the sidewalk, where he was attempting to hide in a parked Chrysler.

Joe was both a typical and model young man, mature beyond his years and fiercely devoted to his family. Joe was as protective of his mother as he was his younger sisters. Jane in particular benefited from his watchful eye, and later said the only time her brother ever spoke harshly to her came when she made the mistake of griping about an order from their mother in his presence. Even as a teenager, he could not tolerate disrespect – especially not any directed toward his mother.

After graduating from Bishop England in 1960, Joe enrolled at The Citadel. College was not an automatic decision – at the time, fewer than half his graduating class would move on to higher education. His father had attended the University of South Carolina, but didn't push his son to follow that path. Joe was drawn to the strictly regimented military education, and had an uncle who'd attended the school. The fact that Brennan and Robinson were going to The Citadel also may have played a role in his choice, but not completely.

Joe wanted to join the military, but hearing problems that had afflicted him since childhood made him ineligible. The family blamed his hearing loss on a bout of scarlet fever he suffered as a child, and recruiters considered it a permanent disability. Big Joe's most powerful friends – Rivers and Hollings, who was governor at that time – tried to intervene, but it was no use. Even Gen. Mark Clark, then president of The Citadel, couldn't help. Riley's only taste of military life would come in college.

Joe later said it was the school's emphasis on devotion to honor and duty that most attracted him – at The Citadel, everyone went in as equals. He majored in political science but took a wide variety of classes, sampling nearly every discipline. One day Robinson, his roommate for most of their time in college, asked why he bothered with all those courses on cultural and classical arts, things that had little place in Charleston of the 1960s.

"One day I might need it," he said.

If Joe suffered hazing beyond what cadets normally inflicted on underclassmen, he never said. He took whatever was thrown at him stoically and, like most members of the Corps of Cadets, this gave him pride in the school – and himself for getting through the plebe system. Riley stayed busy in college, selling advertising for the school's yearbook, joining the literary society, the rod and gun club and the Catholic choir. He was a member of the yacht club for three years, eventually becoming commodore. But The Citadel had access to the river only through a small cut at the Charleston Yacht Club, and then only at high tide. The cadets mostly spent their time polishing the college's boats.

On weekends, Joe Riley took his best friends to Murray Boulevard for a little time away from Padgett-Thomas Barracks. Helen fed the boys and Big Joe gave them all keys to the house, told them they were welcome any time. Joe's friends considered his father one of the most powerful men in Charleston. Although not any sort of public official, it seemed he was involved in everything. Big Joe recently had been appointed head of the state tourism commission by his neighbor – and Citadel alumnus – Gov. Fritz Hollings. Riley's friends would remember him as a kind man, albeit one with a short fuse and near-famous Irish temper. But he would do anything for his son's friends, even find them jobs. Murray Boulevard was exactly the sort of environment Citadel cadets needed.

During Riley's plebe year, Charleston began celebrating the centennial of the Civil War – and those festivities extended to the military college's campus. The school was proud of its role in the conflict. In January 1861, cadets on Morris Island had fired the first shots at the *Star of the West*, a ship out of New York secretly bringing supplies and reinforcement to the federal troops at Fort Sumter. The ship was unable to land at Sumter because of Citadel men. The school considered that attack on the *Star of the West* the actual first shot of the war.

Those old times were not forgotten at The Citadel. The cadets waved Confederate flags at football games and the band played "Dixie" with gusto. Riley's own company – Foxtrot – routinely displayed battle flags in their class photos for the *Sphinx*. Joe thought little of it at the time. Civil War history was unavoidable in Charleston, and he could relate given the extensive exploits of his great-grandfather, Henry Oliver. To Joe, the flag was merely an expression of Southern patriotism. At 18, he did not detect any racial overtones or realize that anyone would be offended by the banner. The Citadel was several years away from integration.

Only later did Riley learn the flag's other meaning, the manner in which it had been hijacked by hate groups. His political conscience was formed in part by his classes at The Citadel, where he learned about Jim Crow laws, Pitchfork Ben Tillman and the state's ugly tradition of mistreating black citizens. A child of the South, Riley knew all about Charleston's love of the past – but he was quickly learning that not everything about that past was good. By the summer of his senior year, when he watched Martin Luther King Jr.'s "I Have a Dream" speech, Riley knew enough to understand its importance.

Joe later said, without overstating the case, that King's speech changed his life.

His senior year at The Citadel began in 1963. That year a skinny basketball player from Beaufort walked through Lesesne Gate to begin his knob year, and the military college would never be the same. Donald Patrick Conroy was a military brat, the son of a domineering and abusive Marine colonel from Chicago. The Citadel could not inflict any punishment on Conroy that was worse than his childhood, and he grew to have a love-hate relationship with his college.

Within a few years of graduating, Conroy would turn The Citadel on its ear with his first book, *The Boo* – an ode to the assistant commandant of cadets, Lt. Col. Thomas Nugent Courvoisie. With that book and *The Lords of Discipline*, a novel written nearly a decade later, Conroy immortalized the world of South Carolina's military college in the 1960s. It was not always a pretty picture, but both works were unflagging in their affection for The Boo.

Conroy's work was a reflection of Joe's time at The Citadel; it was no revelation to him. He knew The Boo – who called cadets "lambs" or "bums," depending on his opinion of them at any given moment – could be the stern disciplinarian one minute and a generous father-figure the next. Riley thought he had a particularly gruff personality and avoided him as much as possible, which wasn't often. At some point, everyone drew the ire of The Boo. His favorite sport was catching bums in the act of sneaking on or off campus. Of course, one night he caught Cadet Riley.

Joe had a weekend pass to sell advertising for the *Sphinx*, and he and Robinson used it as an excuse to visit a classmate. Brennan had already departed the college for medical school, which was allowed at the time. Cadets Riley and Robinson did not realize, however, that on this particular weekend the passes expired on Saturday night – usually it was Sunday. When they got back that Sunday evening, The Boo caught the pair with his usual, and obvious, pride.

The Boo rubbed it in their face how he'd outsmarted them, and showed them just how subjective his punishment could be. Robinson, whose father had attended The Citadel with Courvoisie, got off with a warning. Joe was busted down a rank and forced to walk tours. That meant marching back and forth on the second battalion quadrangle with a shouldered rifle. The cadets called it a monumental waste of time, the military college equivalent of writing on the blackboard or standing in the corner.

Although his parents were disappointed, they said little. Joe and Helen Riley realized their son was not up to anything too bad, he'd simply not paid attention to the pass. By cadet standards, it was a fairly minor infraction. Joe was much harder on himself – but did not complain. He just marched. And marched. Finally, The Boo took pity and ordered him to stop.

"OK, Bubba, you've walked enough," Courvoisie said.

Joe kept marching, and told The Boo he would finish his tours. Either out of pride or an innate stubbornness, he would pay his debt.

That incident did nothing to tarnish Joe's Citadel career. Late in his junior year he was selected as a member of the Summerall Guards, a precision-drill platoon that had once marched in President Dwight Eisenhower's inauguration. The Guards went through intense training to learn a special drill performed to a silent count. Membership in the Summerall Guards was considered one of the school's highest honors, given to only 61 students each year. By military measures, Joe was in the top of his class.

By the time he graduated in 1964, Cadet Riley was assistant leader of Foxtrot Company's Second Platoon, while Robinson held the same position for the Third Platoon. They were still roommates in the Padgett-Thomas Barracks, but their paths soon would diverge. Robinson went into accounting and Joe decided that, if he could not get into the Army, he would go to law school. After graduation, after getting The Ring that marked him forever as a Citadel man, he took a long trip to Europe, meandering from one country to the next. When the locals discovered he was American, they often asked Joe about the assassination, just months earlier, of the young president who had been one of his boyhood heroes.

Joe's decision to attend law school did not pass without incident in the Riley home. His father expected Joe to join him in the real estate and insurance business, and did not like the idea of his only son taking off to become a lawyer. He had built the Riley Real Estate and Insurance Company into a formidable Charleston business, and hoped that one day his son would take over. But Joe had other ideas. His sisters listened to the tense discussion, the long argument that ended with Helen stepping in to support her son's decision. Eventually, Big Joe gave in, too. He quickly realized it was pointless to argue. When Joe Riley Jr. made up his mind, few people could change it.

Other than a summer when he worked as an intern for Congressman Mendel Rivers in Washington, Joe had never lived away from Charleston. And like his father, Joe's three-year stay in Columbia at the University of South Carolina School of Law would mark the last time he resided anywhere other than his hometown. That first year, Joe moved into a house on Greene Street with several other law students, which eventually included fellow Citadel alumnus Mike Duffy. Another Citadel graduate, Capers Barr, was already in his second year of law school. They had known each other only slightly in college, but soon became close friends.

It was during his first year in law school that Joe began his political apprenticeship, working as a page for Lt. Gov. Bob McNair and, later, John West. He learned how the Legislature worked, which was fascinating to a young law student. He watched politicians write the laws he would one day use in his practice. Watching the process could have soured him on politics, as it did many people, but the optimistic young law student was only inspired. This was exactly what he wanted to do.

He did not realize it at the time, but Joe was making connections that would serve him his entire life. A new generation of South Carolina leaders was coming of age in the mid-1960s. Duffy would one day become a federal judge. Jean Toal, who Joe had known since he was 9, was destined to become chief justice of the South Carolina Supreme Court. And Barr would be his lifelong friend – and campaign manager. At the time, Joe's interest in politics was quickly on the rise. At one point he organized a campaign to entice his family neighbor, former Gov. Fritz Hollings, to run for the U.S. Senate.

In the spring of his first year at law school, Joe returned to The Citadel to watch a friend graduate. He saw old pals and teachers, walked the parade grounds and remembered those experiences unique to those who wear the ring. At one point, he saw some girls he knew in front of Bond Hall and went over to talk with them. There was an attractive young woman in the group he didn't recognize, but he was drawn to her immediately. Her name was Charlotte DeLoach, and she was from Camden. She had just moved to Charleston.

Joe later said "she was not only attractive, she was a wonderful person. And one of the first things I learned was that she had a good sense of humor, that she could easily laugh."

Charlotte's father had been in the Army, and the family moved often before settling in Camden. After discarding plans to join the ballet, she moved to Vienna to get a degree in German at the Institute of European Studies. Later, Joe would discover that Charlotte was in the background of a photograph he took in Austria during his

European trip a year earlier.

After returning to the States, Charlotte moved to Charleston in hopes of finding work as a German translator for a shipping line. When that didn't work out, she took a job with a mortgage company instead of relocating to the North (where such positions were readily available). She and her three roommates lived in a house converted to apartments on Rutledge Avenue. One of them knew Joe, and introduced them at The Citadel that day. A week later, Joe called and asked her out.

"I remember we double-dated, but I can't remember where we ate dinner," Charlotte recalled years later. "It was definitely not a fancy place."

Joe saw Charlotte often in the following months. He was home for the summer, staying at his parents' house on Murray Boulevard. When he returned to Columbia to start the fall semester, Charlotte often drove up on weekends to see him. Of course, the bachelor pad where he lived was not a suitable environment for a young woman, so Charlotte stayed with Barr and his wife, Ellie, who lived across the street from campus. Within a year, there was little question in anyone's mind that the couple were made for each other.

Joe and Charlotte were married in August 1966, just before he started his final year in law school.

The newlyweds lived in married student housing that first year, a large, nondescript building that Joe later speculated must have been built as public housing. But the apartment was like a palace to the young couple – there was an extra bedroom where Joe could study, and he even bought a washing machine. For Christmas, he sprang for the dryer. When he wasn't in class, Joe clerked for a Columbia law firm and Charlotte took work in another attorney's office. She planned to work for Joe when he opened his own practice in Charleston and, she said, "I wanted to learn the ropes."

After graduation, Joe and Charlotte moved back to Charleston and bought a townhouse on Logan Street, less than a mile from his family home. He took the second floor in his father's building at 13 Broad St. – the building Big Joe bought the month Joe Jr. was born – and converted it into his law office. The room had once served as Mendel Rivers' district office, and the congressman's sign was still on the door. The space wasn't perfect – there was no running water upstairs – but the rent was right. Suddenly, Joe was a Broad Street lawyer, the top of the social order in old

Charleston. He was barely 25 years old – the same age his father had been when he started his own business.

About a year after he opened his practice, Joe sat in his office on a Saturday afternoon and wrote a letter addressed to Vietnam. Capers Barr had gone into the Army after law school and was nearing the end of a two-year tour of duty in Southeast Asia. Much of the letter was news from the homefront – "We have seen Ellie and little Capers, not as much as we'd like, however." Joe wrote that he and Charlotte had drinks with Barr's parents a week earlier and laughed about the picture of Barr standing by his Army Jeep with a sticker for Riley's legislative campaign on it.

"I wanted to show it to the newspapers but I was afraid your commanding officers (like "Westie") might not appreciate it," he wrote.

But the true purpose of the letter was to invite Barr to join him as partner in his small law firm. "I feel ridiculous even mentioning this, knowing that you will get many fine offers," Joe wrote.

Barr was so touched by the letter he kept it for decades. He later said that, despite the other offers, Joe's proposition was a "no-brainer." So in January 1969, Barr joined what came to be called the Riley and Barr law firm. It was a small operation to be sure, just Barr and Joe and Charlotte (who was pregnant with the couple's first child and would soon quit to take care of the baby).

The world had changed a lot since Barr had gone to Vietnam, and he would see far less of his partner than he imagined for those first few months. Joe had not only passed the bar and opened his own law firm, he'd won election to the state House of Representatives by campaigning as a champion of early childhood education. In his first try at elected office, Joe won more votes than all but the delegation's most entrenched politicians.

So less than two weeks after the Riley and Barr law firm went into business, Joe Riley began his political career.

A Change is Gonna Come

On March 1, 1970, Charleston funeral home director Herbert Ulysses Fielding announced his candidacy for the state House of Representatives. The news did not come as a surprise; he had campaigned for the position just two years earlier. In fact, Fielding first ran for the office in 1952 – when it was hard enough for a black man to vote, much less win an election. Fielding had never held public office, but he'd been involved in politics his entire life.

His father opened the Fielding Home for Funerals on Logan Street in 1912, and it had become a Charleston institution. This was in large part due to Herbert's grandmother, Felicia Fielding Goodwin – who, the family joked, was actually the funeral home's founder because she put up the money. Goodwin made a good living as a seamstress, sewing dresses for wealthy women who lived South of Broad. In her spare time, she distributed clothes to the poor on James and Johns islands. She was the rare person who traveled in every social circle. In her own way, Goodwin was a civil rights pioneer.

Born in 1923, Herbert Fielding came of age as the nation was struggling with issues of civil rights, and his grandmama taught him the importance of that cause. She had been instrumental in founding the city's YWCA, an organization that helped women with domestic issues and promoted racial justice, and served as its first president. The Charleston YWCA promoted a progressive social agenda and made national headlines in the 1950s when it gave a platform to several civil rights activists, including Waties Waring.

U.S. District Judge Julius Waties Waring could trace his family's Charleston roots to 1683. The son of a Confederate soldier and slave owner, he grew up in the wake of Reconstruction, raised by a nanny who herself was a former slave. For most of his life, Waring followed the expected path of a Charleston scion: He became a lawyer, dabbled in local politics and married a girl of equal social standing. In a town with more than 50 societies and exclusive clubs, he was a member of most of them. For much of his life, he seemed completely insulated from the outside world. But by the 1940s he realized that all was not right in that world, or his.

Waring divorced his first wife, even though such a thing was not legal in South Carolina, and married a redheaded woman from the North. That was reason enough for social snubbing in Charleston, but soon the judge began to dabble in civil rights. He ordered pay equalized between white and black teachers, defended a black World War II veteran who had been attacked by a white police officer, and ruled that black people had a right to vote in the Democratic primary. He even hired black court officers. Some people did not approve – the judge received threats, bricks were thrown through his windows and crosses were burned in his yard.

Waring was defiant, called his attackers "savages" and declared it "time for South Carolina to re-join the Union." It was practically a declaration of war in a state where, only a few years earlier, Gov. Olin Johnston had told civil rights advocates that white people had run state government for generations and he intended to keep it that way. "You cannot mix the races and have no trouble," Johnston said. "God didn't see fit to mix them and I am tired of people agitating social equality of races in our state."

The state's U.S. senators eventually tried to have Waring impeached. His own nephew – editor of the Charleston News and Courier, which at the time supported segregation – attacked him in print. The judge was ousted from every organization in town, including the Episcopal Church. He became a national figure in President Harry Truman's crusade for civil rights, sparked a resurgence of the Ku Klux Klan and prompted a political movement headed by Gov. Strom Thurmond, who abandoned the Democratic Party to run for president as a "Dixiecrat" – a party whose only platform was segregation.

By then, Waring's only remaining friends were black Charlestonians. Herbert Fielding became a frequent guest at the judge's Meeting Street home, and Waring became his hero. Here was a white man – a powerful jurist, no less – espousing the same political positions as his grandmama. It gave him hope, and perhaps inspired him to first run for the state House of Representatives in 1952. Fielding later said he knew he wouldn't win; he only wanted to increase black participation in local elections.

Through Waring, Fielding soon met NAACP attorney Thurgood Marshall – and he was inspired even more. Marshall had come to Charleston to file a lawsuit on behalf of Clarendon County citizens whose schools were not maintained nearly as well as neighboring white schools. But Waring told the future Supreme Court justice he was thinking too small, fueling a racist system by arguing for the "equal" in separate but equal. The NAACP recast its lawsuit, and Waring gave the group detailed instructions to file the complaint in a way that ensured it would be heard by a panel of judges. Waring knew the NAACP would lose, but he also knew any case heard by a panel of three federal judges was automatically appealed to the United States Supreme Court.

Waring had orchestrated a plot that forced the highest court in the land to make a ruling on segregation. When the case was finally heard, as an amalgamation of five cases titled *Brown v. Board of Education*, the court largely used Waring's own dissent in Marshall's *Briggs v. Elliott* to strike down segregation in America. The judge did not get any credit, however – the court feared the South would never accept a ruling with Waring's name attached.

All of that happened in the same neighborhood where Joe Riley grew up – Waring's house was only a half-mile from the Riley residence. He knew nothing of these dramatic events as a child, however. Race was not an issue addressed in his house, or many others in Charleston. But even as a boy, Riley found himself sensitive to issues of fairness and equity. It was something he picked up at Catholic school – and from his family.

For his entire life, Riley would remember a rare evening when his family went to eat at one of Charleston's finest restaurants – one of only three in the city at the time. The waiter, a black man in a starched white cotton jacket, at one point asked young Joe a question. He listened and politely replied, "Yes, sir." When the waiter was gone, his parents gently reminded him that black people were not addressed as "sir." He wondered why – a question that would nag at him for more than a decade before he realized that "all men are created equal" was more of a platitude than the actual law of the land.

Fielding, a full two decades older than Riley, understood better than most what was happening on the Charleston peninsula. He realized that the nice man who lived on Meeting Street – who had invited the Fielding family into his home – had manipulated the judicial system to outlaw segregation in the United States. A white man from Charleston society had changed the country. It motivated him to take a more active involvement in the fight for civil rights.

Eventually, Fielding formed an organization called the Charleston Political Action Committee to give a voice to progressive ideas and civil rights. He made bail for arrested protesters and found them legal representation. He defended striking garbage workers and publicly rebuked Mayor Palmer Gaillard for failing to bargain. Fielding spoke up for hospital workers during the Medical College strike. The man had no fear – he partly blamed the problems of African-Americans on complacency in the black community, and urged them to get involved. But Fielding warned that if blacks continued to be dismissed as agitators by white people it would lead to unfortunate militant ideologies. He preached against the escalating politics of "white fear and black rage," elements that could create roadblocks to civil rights.

But Fielding also bristled at the idea that any black man who supported a white politician was an "Uncle Tom." He was not simply interested in statistics; he was more interested in a candidate's agenda. For that reason, in 1968, Fielding supported Congressman Mendel Rivers in the Democratic primary over an African-American lawyer named George A. Payton. During the race, Rivers and his campaign treasurer, Joe Riley Sr., asked Fielding to work alongside Riley's son.

Later, neither Riley nor Fielding could remember the circumstances of their first meeting, but they immediately knew they shared a political vision. They became friends during the Rivers campaign, Riley stopping by the funeral home to put campaign signs into Fielding's car. Working for a white candidate, and against a black opponent, was tricky for Fielding. He was on the 1968 ballot for state representative, and failing to support another black politician could be troublesome on several levels. People chose funeral homes based on friendships, and the Fielding family could not afford to offend potential customers. But then, Fielding had no fear.

In June of 1968, Rivers easily recaptured his party's nomination for the 1st District congressional seat, and Riley – in his first run for elected office – finished in the middle of the pack on a primary slate of 11 countywide Democratic candidates for the state House. Riley had campaigned on a platform of more competitive pay for teachers and better technical education, protection for Charleston Harbor and a new bridge to James Island. He said nothing about civil rights, but it was already on his mind. Both Rivers and Riley would go on to easy wins in November.

Fielding lost his 1968 bid for the Statehouse, but he would not give up. In the succeeding two years, Fielding had made it the business of his Political Action Committee to get black representatives elected to the Legislature. The General Assembly needed more diversity if anything was going to change. Riley was reminded of that when he admonished the House for its treatment of the Medical College's striking workers.

So when filing for the 1970 state races opened, Fielding resigned as chairman of the Political Action Committee to run a third time. His platform was simple – he wanted to stop the soaring crime rate in the city, conceding that there was a need for "real justice" as well as law and order. He spoke of closing the generation gap, trying to inspire young people to tackle problems that had lingered in the state for generations. He made little or no mention of his service in the Army during World War II, although it might have helped. He felt there were more pressing issues at stake.

In April of 1670, a ship called the *Carolina* sailed into the vast bay that one day would be known as Charleston Harbor. The *Carolina* had left England the year before carrying settlers to the New World, accompanied by two other ships that would not survive the journey. Seven years earlier, King Charles II had given the Province of Carolina to eight of his friends, and these men – the Lords Proprietors – had planned for this moment ever since.

The *Carolina* slipped past a peninsula littered with oyster shells and sailed several miles upriver before finding a spot on the south bank with hundreds of acres of high ground. This was their destination. It was called Albemarle Point, a location scouted by the explorers sent in advance of the settlers. The land had been recommended to the explorers by a local Indian tribe, the Kiawahs. This would become their new home, the beginning of the grand city envisioned by the Lords Proprietors.

The settlers built a fort, not as an insult to their Native Americans friends, but as protection against the Spaniards. Here these Englishmen learned about all the wonders of their subtropical new home, which included hungry insects so small they could not be seen and the fragrant odors of a strange black muck that they would come to call pluff mud. Within two years, the fort gave way to a planned city – the first in the Carolinas – and the residents named it Charles Town in honor of their generous benefactor. Within two years, the population would exceed 200.

Three hundred years after that historic landing, more than 7,000 people sat bundled up in the bleachers of The Citadel's football stadium on a cool spring night for the opening performance of "Three Centuries of Charleston." The pageant featured dancing girls, Confederate soldiers and hundreds of Boy Scouts and Girl Scouts, all singing "Happy Birthday" to Charleston. The show included 14 scenes, from that landing at Albemarle Point to a ball attended by George Washington during his 1791 visit to the city. At one point, the entire cast – some barely 7 years old, others approaching retirement – danced the Virginia Reel. Later, they unsurprisingly did "The Charleston."

The Tricentennial was officially underway.

Everyone, it seemed, got in on the act. Mayor Palmer Gaillard, who celebrated his 50th birthday on Charleston's 300th, was spotted around town wearing knickers and a powdered wig. A parade on the official birthday – April 4 – wound through the streets of the former Oyster Point, where the settlers moved after 10 years at Albemarle Point. The biggest treat of the parade may have been a full-scale model of the Best Friend of Charleston, an 1830 steam locomotive that was the first built in the United States. The Best Friend provided regular passenger service to the people of Charleston for six months, moving at heady speeds of up to 25 miles per hour. Then it set another American record, becoming the first locomotive in the United States to have its boiler explode.

The weather was perfect for a parade. On this sunny day, men in tricorn hats marched through the streets with Scouts and marching bands. The crowds along the route were 20 deep. Police Chief John Conroy said there were at least 150,000 people watching the parade. Joe Riley Sr., the parade chairman, estimated at least 380,000 people watched. And that did not include the television audience, which he optimistically suggested might top 4 million.

That evening, Gov. Bob McNair attended a Tricentennial banquet along with U.S. Sen. Fritz Hollings, Lt. Gov. John West and Mayor Gaillard. The Municipal Auditorium was draped in Spanish moss for the occasion, and the "Lords Proprietors" made an appearance with their wives. The most rousing ovation was reserved for the 10th Earl of Shaftsbury, Lord Ashley Cooper – the Proprietor whose name adorned the city's two rivers.

In his remarks, Gov. McNair heralded the opening of a new state park at Albemarle Point, site of the city's original settlement. The state had purchased the land for nearly $5 million and planned a natural park that would tell the story of the state's founding. McNair said he hoped Charles Towne Landing would become as famous among schoolchildren as Plymouth Rock or Jamestown. But bad weather and construction delays muted the grand opening of Charles Towne Landing.

When the Tricentennial began, workers were still finishing the administration building and pavilion. The animal forest had not been completed and the movie theater would not be ready for several weeks. The problem was with some of the contractors, and the state attorney general threatened to bring suit against all the companies involved in building Charles Towne Landing. But those delays – and the inevitable political bickering that resulted – could do little to dampen the city's spirit.

The Tricentennial was a festive celebration. There would be parades and galas for weeks. The trouble with the hospital strike the year before had been largely forgotten. Charleston was doing what it did best – celebrating its history.

Two weeks after the Tricentennial opening, state Rep. Joe Riley presented a commemorative plaque from the celebration to House Speaker Sol Blatt. Riley led the Charleston County delegation in the ceremony, thanking Blatt for his "many kindnesses" to the Holy City. The speaker was gracious, complimented the delegation members for their abilities and wished them good luck in their re-election campaigns. Finally, Blatt thanked Riley for the plaque and noted he had a "warm spot in my heart for the people of Charleston."

Riley was not sure he could reciprocate the sentiment. Although he thought Blatt a kind man, he had come to believe the speaker far too conservative. Riley and his progressive colleagues felt Blatt was holding the state back. Everything they attempted – raising teacher pay, ethics reform – went ignored. For their efforts, Riley, Alex Sanders and a few other young lawmakers had been dubbed the Young Turks. The name stuck, but it had different meanings depending on whether the newspapers or legislative leadership used it. Times were changing everywhere, it seemed, but within the walls of the Statehouse.

The 170 members of the Legislature were predominantly small businessmen, lawyers and farmers – people with the means to largely ignore their businesses for five months of the year. For the most part, Riley believed these men (and one woman) wanted to do good work for South Carolina. But the definition of "good" varied greatly among the body. Many of these people held ideas far different from Riley on race, education, ethics – and just about everything else.

Riley had most recently run afoul of his colleagues by lobbying to shorten the legislative session. He did not like spending so much of the year at the Statehouse, away from Charlotte and Joe, who was approaching his first birthday. Clearly, lawmakers extended the process far longer than needed – Georgia accomplished the same amount of work in two months. Riley stayed in Columbia as little as possible, driving up on Tuesdays and back on Thursday afternoons so he was away from home only two nights a week. He even skipped traditional legislative picnics and political events on the weekends. But he never missed the Thursday morning session to go home early. He always stayed long enough to do his job.

Most lawmakers believed the length of the session was just fine; some even told Riley the General Assembly was like "going to a convention every week." There were receptions held in their honor regularly, and lobbyists bought most of their meals just for the chance to discuss pending legislation. In those days, some savvy lobbyists kept open tabs at restaurants and bars near the Statehouse so lawmakers could charge anything they wanted. To many legislators, especially those from little towns, Columbia was a big city – a place they could go out every night for a steak and a drink. There was no way anyone could persuade them to spend less time there.

Riley kept his distance from lobbyists, but he did not consider them evil; they served their purpose. So many bills floated around the Statehouse that it was impossible for a part-time legislator to keep up. Lobbyists were more than happy to explain the legislation and make their pitch for it. The trick was to hear from both sides. Riley would talk to them in the Statehouse lobby, but he and most of the Young Turks avoided hitting the bars and restaurants with these hired guns.

Usually, Riley and Tom Bryant, Tom Smith and a few others took their meals at the Market Restaurant, where Sanders held court daily – spinning one tall tale after another. Every week, Riley had at least one new story to tell Charlotte when he got home. Sanders used his friends to hone his act, an ever-evolving commentary on the state of South Carolina and the world. At the same time, the Young Turks were becoming a well-known clique among lawmakers. But their seemingly standoffish nature did little to endear them to some of their colleagues.

The Young Turks lost more fights than they won. The Riley-Sanders Amendment – or the Sanders-Riley Amendment, depending on which of them described it – called for an increase in the state income tax to fund teacher raises. Through sheer tenacity, Riley and Sanders gathered enough support for the bill, but the opposition rallied and killed it. Sen. Dick Riley, a sympathetic man destined to be governor and U.S. Education Secretary, tried to move the measure through the Senate, but couldn't. Like so many battles waged by the Young Turks, raising teacher salaries was a losing proposition.

The South Carolina General Assembly was simply not progressive enough for Joe Riley. Although Democrats held the vast majority of the seats, most were far more conservative than their national counterparts. Riley believed the Legislature needed more women, more black members – people inclined to think more liberally than farmers and small-business owners. He would make it his mission to bring diversity to the Statehouse. But Riley had learned that very little got accomplished without the blessing of leadership, and Speaker Sol Blatt – the man he had just presented with a Tricentennial plaque – was one of the most conservative. If there was going to be any real change, Blatt had to step down. But Blatt had been speaker for 30 years, and he wouldn't go willingly.

Within a year, the Young Turks would begin their most ambitious campaign.

The General Assembly adjourned in June, just in time for the state primaries. In 1970, the Democratic primary was in essence the election because the Republicans often failed to field a single candidate. Even when they did, they usually stood no chance in the November general election. This made the primary particularly important for Herbert Fielding. He had to get his supporters to the polls.

Luckily, he was not the only African-American on the ticket. Lonnie Hamilton III, a band director at Bonds-Wilson High School, was seeking a seat on Charleston County Council. And two others joined Fielding on the slate for state House: Jim Clyburn, a former teacher at C.A. Brown High School and executive director of the state Commission for Farm Workers, and George Payton, the attorney who ran for Congress against Mendel Rivers two years earlier. This suggested a heavy turnout in the black community. Fielding would need it.

At the time, all 11 of the county's House members were elected at-large, which meant everyone in the county got 11 votes on the slate. It forced candidates to campaign throughout Charleston County, which ran nearly one-third the length of South Carolina's coast – and had the effect of diluting the minority vote. The turnout in the city would have to be above normal for Fielding, or any African-American candidate, to have a chance.

The June 9 election suggested that Charleston was more progressive than most of the state. Riley was renominated with the third-most votes on a slate of 22 candidates, only 700 behind the leader. Fielding ended up 2,000 votes behind Riley, good enough to finish fifth and ensure him a spot on the November ballot. Clyburn finished 1,800 votes behind Fielding, taking the eighth spot on the ticket. Riley's two hand-picked candidates were both headed to the general election, and he wanted to find a way to help them win.

Herbert Fielding led the victory celebration that evening at Brooks Restaurant, which sat across Morris Street from the Brooks Motel. These two black-owned businesses had seen more than their share of civil rights history; the Rev. Martin Luther King Jr. stayed in the motel once. Fielding told the crowd the true winners were "a whole ethnic group of people who for once in their lives have realized something." He said it was now up to blacks and whites to work together, the same message he had been preaching for two decades.

Charleston's Tricentennial celebration was still going weeks after the primaries.

Although most of the parades, balls and plays had been scheduled for the first half of April, perhaps the most momentous event was still to come. The Municipal Auditorium was staging a local production of the Gershwin opera *Porgy and Bess*. In 35 years, it had never been performed in the city where it was set, and where it was written. Local customs had prohibited it.

The opera was based on Charleston native DuBose Heyward's 1925 novel *Porgy*, the story of a crippled street beggar living on the fictional Catfish Row in Charleston. Heyward, the descendant of a signer of the Declaration of Independence, was for a short time the city's most famous author – he won national praise for writing about black characters without condescension (although he did resort to some stereotypes). Still, the story of Porgy was so rich, including characters who spoke in the Gullah dialect, that composer George Gershwin was immediately enchanted.

Gershwin came to Charleston in the summer of 1934 and rented an oceanfront cottage near Heyward's Folly Beach cabin. There, he composed much of the music that would make up his most famous opera. Heyward even contributed some of the lyrics. *Porgy and Bess* premiered on Broadway in the fall of 1935 with an entirely black cast. That was risqué even in New York at the time, and completely out of the question for Charleston. As a result, Heyward never saw his own play in the city of its origin. By 1970, *Porgy and Bess* had been staged in 29 countries, but nowhere near the inspiration for Catfish Row.

Local producers were developing their own production even before the Tricentennial began. Using Charleston residents, all of whom were African-American, the play began rehearsals the previous November. By the time it premiered on June 25, word of mouth had reached such a crescendo that the first show at the Municipal Auditorium – a black-tie event – sold out quickly, as would many of the subsequent performances during its two-week run. Even Heyward's daughter, Jenifer, attended the opening night gala.

For days, The News and Courier carried stories about *Porgy and Bess* on its front pages, and local merchants advertised "Porgy specials" to cash in on the publicity. But no one – not the newspaper, Heyward's daughter, nor anyone else – addressed the lingering question of why it had taken so long for the most famous opera of Charleston to be performed locally. No one wanted to admit that, until 1970, the city would not permit a troupe of black performers to take a public stage.

The audiences for *Porgy and Bess* were largely integrated, but all was not well in Charleston a year after the hospital strike. It was apparent in letters sent to The News and Courier, in which some people complained that television coverage of the Tricentennial parade focused too much on "two particular bands" while other outstanding military bands and dignitaries like Strom Thurmond – who "does a lot for the South" – were passed over. "I don't think Charleston or South Carolina owes any favors or apologies to any group," one woman wrote.

After 14 performances, more than 25,000 locals had seen *Porgy and Bess* – a number The News and Courier said proved that "Porgy did what the skeptics said was impossible." Gov. McNair said the production should go on tour throughout the state, but Frank Gilbreth, who wrote The News and Courier's metro column under the pen name Ashley Cooper, disagreed. "Let the people come to us! The whole reason that 'Porgy and Bess' is a huge hit, at this late date, is that it's being played where it was written, by the descendants of the people it was written about."

The Municipal Auditorium, where *Porgy and Bess* premiered, had been open only two years and would soon be renamed the Gaillard, after the mayor. By the time it was rechristened, however, Gaillard would be out of office. And that had much to do with race relations in Charleston – which could not be smoothed over with a simple opera.

With the legislative session and the primary behind him, Riley turned his attention to his family and his law practice. At the time, there were about 200 lawyers in the county, and nearly every one of them had their offices on Broad Street. Locals called this assemblage of power brokers "The Broad Street Ring" with a mix of awe and disdain. The Riley and Barr firm was a small fish in this pond. They were in the right place, but Riley did not look particularly powerful – especially the day the newspaper published a photograph of him riding his bike to work with the headline "Life of Riley." The young state lawmaker said biking was simply good exercise, and meant one less car on the road – a theme he would return to in the coming years.

Riley and Barr was a general-practice law firm in every sense of the word. They took on any work they could. As Barr later recalled, "It was a time when the older lawyers wouldn't let the young ones starve – they would throw them business." The pair got more than their share of wills, and the occasional accident. Of course, proximity to Riley Real Estate helped enormously. In those early years, residential real estate closings were the firm's bread and butter.

Business sometimes came in from Riley's and Barr's own connections. One day a Citadel professor asked them to file suit against The News and Courier. The professor was upset by a story that suggested local landlords did not maintain their properties and often mistreated tenants. This hit too close to home, as the professor himself was a landlord. But neither Barr nor Riley was enamored of the idea of suing the local paper, and eventually sought their own legal counsel.

Gedney Howe was the paragon of the local bar, a prominent player in local politics and a mentor to young Charleston attorneys. Riley and Barr took the professor's case to Howe for advice, and his answer was unequivocal: "There are two people you are not going to win an argument against: Your wife and the newspaper. You will never get the last word, especially with people who buy ink by the barrel." They didn't take the case.

The Citadel would provide the firm some work, however. Riley got a call one day that gave his heart a momentary jolt. The voice on the line reminded him of walking tours in a wool uniform under the unforgiving Lowcountry sun. It was Lt. Col. Thomas N. Courvoisie, "The Boo." Riley had heard what happened to The Boo – everyone had. In 1968, Courvoisie was removed as assistant commandant of cadets and assigned to the supply room, where he spent his time handing out toilet paper. The reason for the demotion was unclear. The school said something about Corps morale, but some alumni believed The Boo had simply become too popular. Courvoisie was indignant, but he didn't complain – much.

Courvoisie explained that a former cadet had written a book about him, and he wanted Riley and Barr to "lawyer it" – make sure there wasn't anything libelous or otherwise troublesome in the text. The author was a Citadel graduate – a chronic bum, to hear The Boo tell it – who had written the memoir at the colonel's Mount Pleasant house. But they could not find a publisher, so Courvoisie put up the money himself; that's why he worried about liability. And that was how Riley first met Pat Conroy.

Riley had been a senior during Conroy's knob year, so they didn't really know each other in college. But they quickly hit it off, no doubt due to their shared experiences and political views. At the time, Conroy was teaching black students in a one-room schoolhouse on Daufuskie Island, a remote spit of land in Beaufort County accessible only by boat. Riley admired Conroy's chosen profession. Conroy later recalled The Boo telling him some real good Citadel lawyers were going to look over the book, men with great experience. When Conroy asked how long they'd been in practice, The Boo said, "About a week."

"Well," Conroy said, "at least they have experience."

Ultimately, Riley agreed to vet the book and suggested changing only some names and one anecdote about a less-than-admirable incident on the campus. He said the embarrassing story could prove troublesome, given emerging laws on the right to privacy. But The Boo suspected – erroneously – that Riley wanted the episode excised because it was about him.

"Bubba, I always knew it was you," The Boo said.

The fall campaign should have been easy, but the Republican Party was showing signs of life and attacking the entrenched Democratic leadership at the Statehouse. Riley spent much of October 1970 countering claims that Democrats were cutting teachers and education funding, leaving fellow Democratic House candidate Arnold Goodstein to pick up his mantra on raising teacher pay. Fielding spoke to groups about the need for better medical care in rural, outlying communities of Charleston County. The entire fall was a long slog from one campaign event to the next.

To help their candidates reach more people in the sprawling county, the party set up the Democratic Action Team. The plan was simple: Each candidate put his campaign contributions into a fund, and the team ran television ads for all of them, singling out one candidate in each spot it aired – basically something along the lines of "Support Joe Riley and the Democratic Action Team."

Riley had won his seat in 1968 with more votes than all but a few veteran members of the county delegation. Now, with a record of reform – and a good family name – he figured he was a lock for re-election on merit alone. Some people assumed he would get the most votes of any House candidate in the 1970 election, which would make him chairman of the county's legislative delegation. It was an honorary position, and Riley could not have cared less about it.

That fall, Riley asked the man running the campaign for the Democratic Action Team to pull all his television ads. He didn't think he needed the boost, but Fielding and Clyburn did – so Riley told the team to divide his money between the two. Electing black members to the General Assembly was far more important to Riley than seeing himself on television – or becoming chairman of the delegation. He did this without fanfare, without telling Barr or even Charlotte. She found out only when one of the candidates thanked him at a rally. "That was a nice thing to do," she told him.

Later, Clyburn would speak warmly of Riley's generosity, and credit that simple gesture for sparking a long political career. Fielding was touched by his friend's gesture. He understood politics well enough to know that Riley was taking a real chance, no matter how safe he thought his prospects for re-election. Fielding knew a few votes one way or the other could end a career.

But Riley was right; he had nothing to worry about. On Nov. 3, the weather was pleasant enough to lure nearly two-thirds of registered voters to the polls. While Lt. Gov. John West swept 46 counties to win the governor's office, the Democratic Action Team celebrated a night of happy returns at the Francis Marion Hotel. The Republicans, gathered in another meeting room at the hotel, glumly watched the returns roll in. Riley garnered the fourth-most votes in the House races behind three other incumbents, and Goodstein easily made the cut. But the biggest news of the night was Fielding.

"We are now well assured all segments of Charleston County are represented," party chairman Dr. Gordan B. Stine told the raucous ballroom crowd. "Finally, South Carolina is not one of two states in the nation without black representation in the state Legislature. We are proud that we were able in Charleston County to help break this barrier."

Herbert Fielding became the first African-American member of the Legislature since the years immediately following Reconstruction. He would join two other new representatives from Richland County as the first black Democrats ever in the South Carolina General Assembly. It was a historic night, one that Riley could not have imagined just a year earlier.

Jim Clyburn was also celebrating that night – unofficial returns showed him finishing in 11th place, which would award him the final seat in Charleston County's House delegation. By the next morning, however, he had been edged out by two Republicans. Local GOP Chairman John Bourne was nearly 200 votes ahead of Clyburn, but the seat eventually went to former state Rep. Sidi Limehouse, who bested Bourne by 700 votes.

Clyburn may have been the victim of dirty tricks by disgruntled Democrats. Some people had gone around the county handing out sample tickets that listed the slate of candidates, but omitted his name – along with Fielding's and County Council candidate Lonnie Hamilton III's. Clyburn conceded the trick hurt, as did rumors that he was "militant" – a thinly disguised code that suggested he cared only about black issues.

Clyburn joked that he'd been called "militant" by whites and "Uncle Tom" by blacks in the same day, yet he would not contest the results. In the end, he said, "I didn't get enough votes."

Clyburn's gracious attitude did not go unnoticed. Governor-elect John West was impressed with the young man's maturity and humility – and the fact that he did not make any trouble for the party. By early December, rumors around South Carolina claimed Clyburn was up for a job in the West administration. Clyburn initially denied it but before the holidays he took leave from the Commission for Farm Workers to serve as assistant to the governor for Human Resources. Eventually, he became the first African-American to serve in a governor's Cabinet since Reconstruction – an opportunity Clyburn said he got only because of Joe Riley.

Riley spent the holidays with his family, savoring the time before he had to return to Columbia in January. He was now a veteran lawmaker about to begin his second term. He was both a rising star and a rabble-rouser, but now he had reinforcements.

He would need them, because Joe Riley had a lot of plans for South Carolina.

The End of an Era

Joe Riley returned to the Statehouse in January 1971 with education on his mind. He needed his delegation's approval for the local school district to raise taxes, wanted to secure additional funding for the College of Charleston and renew efforts to increase teacher pay across South Carolina. He also wanted to expand the statewide kindergarten program that had been gutted when he first proposed it two years earlier.

There really was only one thing standing in his way: House Speaker Solomon Blatt. As the session convened, Blatt was beginning his 16th term as speaker – a reign that dated back to 1937, minus a few years in the late 1940s and early '50s. He was a bald, bespectacled man, the son of a Russian Jew. He'd fought in World War I. Riley did not dislike Blatt, he just thought the man literally came from a different time – and that time had passed. But no one had the guts to tell Blatt.

He was the leader of the "Barnwell Ring," a group of powerful politicians who hailed from that rural county on the state's southwestern border. For years, these men had held undue sway over the entire state. Blatt – along with House Ways and Means Chairman Winchester Smith and Senate President Pro Tem Edgar A. Brown – had controlled just about everything that passed through the Statehouse since the 1930s. If they didn't like an idea, it was ignored, buried in committee, even publicly ridiculed. They had amassed so much political capital by the 1940s that Strom Thurmond ran for governor on a platform of breaking up the ring. In fact, Thurmond had coined the term "Barnwell Ring" – and it stuck. Blatt, Smith and Brown were too conservative even by Strom Thurmond's standards.

Blatt had been perhaps South Carolina's strongest opponent of desegregation, introducing 28 pieces of legislation to stop the integration of public schools. He had vowed to keep the University of South Carolina "for white students only" and, when his efforts were declared unconstitutional by the courts, Blatt tried to pass a bill exempting Barnwell County from integrating. The speaker was not above playing favorites, and he didn't much care what anyone thought about it.

When the session began, Blatt made an announcement that crushed Riley's entire agenda. The speaker said he would personally block any attempt to raise teacher pay. He claimed South Carolina teacher salaries were increasing at a faster clip than the national average, conveniently failing to mention this was because their pay was so low to begin with. Blatt was defiant, claiming that, "I refuse to participate in any program that will give teachers a salary increase while other departments suffer."

Despite Blatt's line in the sand, Riley would not give up, even if he realized the chance of success was slim. At least he had additional allies now. When the House made its seating assignments for the new General Assembly, Riley had Fielding assigned the desk next to his. He wanted to keep his friend close, show him the ropes. Soon, they were spending time together outside the Statehouse. At one point, Riley realized that Fielding was the first black man he'd ever had dinner with.

Fielding and Arnold Goodstein quickly joined the ranks of the Young Turks, which did not make a great first impression on leadership. Nearly every idea the group proposed was shot down or buried in subcommittee, including Fielding's plan – co-sponsored by Riley – to waive probate court administration fees on estates of less than $2,500. Since Democrats controlled the Legislature, Fielding assumed the team would stick together, that there was no need for bipartisanship. But that was just naivety. Goodstein soon realized that in any other state, Blatt and most of his allies would have been Republicans – and conservative ones.

Fielding was one of three black members of the House of Representatives that year. Along with Jim Felder and I.S. Leevy Johnson, he was among the first African-American lawmakers since 1902. This was not a cause for much, if any, celebration among most of the General Assembly. Fielding found Columbia state Rep. Isadore Lourie, a leader of the Young Turks, to be one of the few welcoming members. Lourie spoke proudly of their election – something he relished not only because they represented racial progress, but because he assumed they would be allies.

Others legislators were not so kind. Fielding later said he was not disparaged, simply ignored. Some members of the old guard would not even acknowledge his presence – and these were fellow Democrats. He also took no solace from his treatment by leadership. Any time Fielding stood to ask a question, he got the same exasperated recognition from Blatt. "What do you want now, Mr. Fielding?"

Fielding and Goodstein mostly followed Riley's lead. They accepted a bill legalizing mini-bottles in restaurants because Riley said it was the only liquor legislation that could get past the staunchly stick-in-the-mud Upstate delegation. Of course, he didn't say that publicly. Goodstein quickly discovered that Riley was a master of diplomacy, although he was only 28. "Even people who disagreed with him respected him." Goodstein recalled later. "He knew how to disagree without being disagreeable."

Riley was fast becoming a leader of the Young Turks, but he often didn't have many followers. Few people would cross leadership to support the Turks' progressive legislation. Social and economic justice didn't exactly fit into the priorities of good 'ol boys in the South Carolina General Assembly, and even freshmen learned it was unwise to cross Blatt. Riley's friends said it would have been understandable if he'd gotten frustrated during that session, but he was too optimistic to let one setback after another depress him.

Riley may have been diplomatic most of the time, but he was not above playing hardball to get his way. The regular legislative session ran from noon on Tuesday until adjournment sometime in the early afternoon on Thursday. One Thursday, he couldn't get the votes to pass a resolution and noticed dozens of House members were gone. He quickly discovered that many members headed home on Wednesday nights – still collecting their Thursday per diems, of course. It made him mad. Riley had argued for a shorter session because he didn't like being away from his family, but he would not skip out early. And he didn't believe anyone else should either – especially while accepting an expense account from the taxpayers.

The next week, the Young Turks requested a roll call on Thursday morning, and the members who were actually in the chamber went ballistic. They called it a stunt, correctly claiming it would give their opponents an issue to criticize them on during the next election. Traditionally, it was not something sitting members did to one another. One Upstate lawmaker even told Riley to go back to kindergarten

– because "that's where you had to take roll."

But Riley would not back down, and eventually penned an op-ed piece on the practice that some newspapers around the state published. In it, he argued that legislative pay should be increased to $4,000 per year but members should not get their $25 per diem unless they show up to work. A roll call every morning would keep everyone honest. It was principle, Riley argued. The voters had elected these people to do a job; they had a responsibility to attend. This stand made Riley wildly popular back home, but it did little to further his career at the Statehouse.

The Young Turks were learning that many of their causes – ethics reform, open meetings, freedom of information – were more popular with the public and the press than with their colleagues. So they started talking to reporters. As the coverage increased, opposition to the Young Turks' reform efforts slowly melted away. They eked out a few victories but still could not get their most progressive reforms through the chamber – not with Blatt at the helm. And that included Riley's idea to shorten the session and put a deadline on the introduction of statewide bills. Many veteran lawmakers resented this relative newcomer trying to tell them how to do their jobs.

Riley did not back down. Instead, he took the fight directly to the Statehouse leadership.

The news that Sol Blatt would face opposition in the next speaker's race surfaced in June. The Associated Press reported rumors that Speaker Pro Tem Rex Carter of Greenville was planning to challenge the leader of the Barnwell Ring in January. Blatt said all the right things – that he was fond of Carter, that he was "shocked." And then he talked about all his work for the state recruiting industry, improving education and keeping taxes low.

It sounded as if, for the first time in years, Blatt was actually campaigning.

The idea to oust Blatt had been brewing for months. Some speculated that House members were upset when the speaker invited Republican Vice President Spiro Agnew to address the chamber that spring. A few openly suggested Blatt was repaying the administration for appointing his son to a federal judgeship. The rumors were so rampant that Gov. John C. West had to issue a statement denying any involvement in efforts to get rid of the veteran speaker. Not even the governor had the stomach to challenge Blatt.

Blatt was not nearly as shocked as he claimed – nothing happened in the House without his knowledge. By the time the story was published, the speaker had been trying to do damage control for weeks. He knew the Young Turks were behind Carter's candidacy, and tried to apply pressure to them in not-so-subtle ways. In the final weeks of the session, Blatt had called state Rep. Tom Bryant into his office, just to test his allegiance.

Bryant understood the Legislature's power structure well. His father had been a member of the House – had served with Blatt – and later was elected Orangeburg's state senator. Bryant even attended sessions with his father as a boy. He was under no illusions about why he had been summoned, and did not particularly relish the idea of confronting the speaker alone. But Bryant was solidly progressive and, like Riley, convinced Blatt must go.

The speaker was friendly and accommodating; Sol Blatt was no fool. But he quickly got to the point. He'd heard there were rumblings that some people were supporting Carter for speaker, and it disturbed him. Bryant said yes, some members believed it was time he stepped aside. "You're crazy," Blatt said, "I'll die in this office." After continuing his tirade for a few minutes, he finally asked Bryant if he could count on his support. Bryant apologetically told the speaker he, too, was voting for Carter.

"After all I did for your daddy?" Blatt said.

It was going to be a long summer.

Riley did not hide his role in the effort to remove Blatt – he went on the offensive. He spent the summer campaigning for Rex Carter, even turning to unlikely allies: Republicans. In August, Riley told the Metropolitan Exchange Club in Charleston that the people of South Carolina "are tired of the barons of power controlling the affairs of state." He said no one would stand for one man to be governor for 30 years, and the House speaker should be no different – particularly when he stands opposed to progress.

Throughout the summer of 1971, Riley attacked Blatt's record. Usually courteous to a fault, Riley could slice up a politician with sarcasm and pointed condemnation when he wanted. He derided the speaker for undermining the state's kindergarten program – and ridiculed Blatt's regular boast that he was "proud of South Carolina."

"Pride shouldn't stand in the way of fact or progress," Riley argued. "I hope the Republican Party will get some interest in the reform movement running through a large segment of the Democratic Party and give us a hand."

The rebellion against Blatt dominated the news for much of the summer, even though most polls suggested that the speaker was in no danger of losing his job. Riley continued to criticize Blatt, but could not even persuade all the Young Turks to vote for Carter. Goodstein flatly refused. "If you shoot at the king, you sure as hell better get him," he told Riley.

Goodstein didn't think Carter stood a chance, but he also felt obligated to Blatt. The speaker had appointed him to the powerful House Judiciary Committee as a freshman, while he was still in law school. Such gestures had a way of genuinely fostering loyalty. Riley didn't push; he understood. As a freshman, Riley's request for House Judiciary had been ignored.

By September, the Associated Press reported that Blatt had 42 solid votes to Carter's 29. One other candidate, Rep. Harold Breazeale of Pickens County, had 3 votes. A full 50 members of the House were wisely staying out of the fight. Political reporters speculated that Blatt held the upper hand, but his influence might be on the wane. The 1970 reapportionment was moving several rural House seats – where Blatt was strongest – into urban areas. Even Charleston was getting an additional seat. That improved the chances of electing more progressive members.

But Riley knew better; he was at odds with most of his own delegation. Clyde Dangerfield publicly defended Blatt, arguing, "When you have a good man who has done a good job, you don't kick him out." Even state Rep. Thomas Knight of Berkeley County spoke derisively of Riley's efforts. He basically called the Young Turks a bunch of petulant children.

"If I were going to kindergarten, I would vote for Joe Riley of Charleston or Rex Carter of Greenville," Knight said. "But since I am not going to kindergarten, and I don't need somebody to hold my hand up to go to the bathroom, I will vote for Sol Blatt."

Riley kept up the campaign into the fall until a deal finally emerged. In early November, Carter bowed out of the speaker's race. Charleston lawmaker Tommy

Hartnett cried foul, claiming Carter "made a deal that would feather his own nest but hurt his supporters." At the same time, Blatt announced he would step down in mid-1973 and throw his support behind Carter for speaker. Both publicly claimed there was no deal, but it seemed a lot of thought went into the dual announcements: Newspapers reported that Carter had agreed to keep Blatt's committee assignments in place for a year and name Blatt speaker emeritus.

Riley was disappointed, but realized the campaign had forced the speaker's retirement. He told The News and Courier that Carter "has taken an approach which is very unselfish. I am very pleased that victory is in sight." And he criticized Hartnett – a childhood friend – for riding the fence in the speaker's race. Their relationship would grow more strained when Hartnett later switched parties.

The Young Turks could claim partial victory, having nudged the Legislature into the 20th century. Carter would be a much more progressive speaker and actually allow votes on all those things Blatt opposed – raising the gas tax and the state income tax, as well as increasing pay for teachers. But Carter would not take over until 1974. By then it would be too late for Riley.

Mayor J. Palmer Gaillard announced his plans to seek an unprecedented fourth term in early 1971. Only one man had held the job as long as Gaillard – William McG. Morrison, the man he had defeated in 1959 – and another term would ensure him a spot in the history books as Charleston's longest-serving chief executive. Gaillard's record in office was solid, and his background was impressive – a Navy pilot in World War II, small business owner, two terms as a city alderman. He should have been a lock for re-election. But first he had to get past an opponent in the June primary, local attorney William Ackerman.

Most of his supporters considered Gaillard very much a bread-and-butter mayor, but in some ways he was visionary. He had gone to court for the right to annex across rivers, and soon expanded the city's size for the first time in more than a century. His forays into West Ashley and James Island would double the size of Charleston. On his watch, the city had built the new Municipal Auditorium and cleaned up a few of the seedier areas of town. He had hired a popular police chief, John Conroy, when there had been tremendous local pressure to hire from within the department.

Gaillard had proven a fair man on civil rights issues, which made him progressive by South Carolina standards. When he took office, the mayor inherited an NAACP lawsuit against the city that demanded the new municipal golf course be opened to people of all races. Gaillard did not even contest the suit. The city's attorney told him the law was on the NAACP's side, and that was all it took. The golf course became the first integrated public facility in South Carolina.

Despite all this, Gaillard had troubles in the Democratic Party and the black community. He had angered Democrats by endorsing Richard Nixon for president in 1968, and some African-Americans did not feel the mayor had done enough to help workers during the hospital strike. It made his efforts seem even weaker when, several months later, he got into a dispute with picketing sanitation workers. The issue was minority hiring – many people in the community felt city government did not employ enough black residents. But then, Gaillard didn't hire much of anyone. He was notoriously frugal – the mayor didn't even have an administrative assistant.

The depth of the community's discontent was not entirely apparent until June 8, the night of the Democratic primary. When the polls closed, Gaillard had a decent lead, although the vote was closer than he would have liked. Ackerman's campaign had challenged the legitimacy of more than 500 ballots cast by people who had voted in the Feb. 20 Republican congressional primary – a special election necessitated by the death of Congressman Mendel Rivers in December. When the ballot boxes from predominantly black wards came in, Gaillard's margin narrowed considerably. The News and Courier went to press without calling a winner. The next day, it appeared the mayor's margin of victory was only 91 votes.

A recount, and the argument over the validity of Republican ballots, fell to the city's Democratic Party Executive Committee. Local attorney Thomas Tisdale, who the mayor had appointed to a municipal judgeship the year before, slogged through ballots for four days before declaring Gaillard the winner. Ackerman petitioned the state Board of Canvassers for a new hearing, still fighting to have the GOP votes nullified.

It was late July before Gaillard secured the nomination. The Board of Canvassers pointed out that, for all his protests, two of Ackerman's own alderman candidates had also voted in the Republican congressional primary. But the attorney would not give up, and Gaillard suspected he was now conspiring with the Republican candidate for mayor, former state lawmaker Arthur Ravenel Jr. Within weeks, Ackerman appeared as an alderman candidate on Ravenel's ticket.

In the fall campaign Gaillard went uncharacteristically negative. He accused Ackerman of trying to destroy the Democratic Party by siding with Ravenel, who had served in the Legislature as a Democrat before joining the Republican Party in the early 1960s. Gaillard said "a renegade Republican and a renegade Democrat have joined hands to have their own party." Eventually, the Democrats sent in their heavyweights – Gov. John West and U.S. Sen. Fritz Hollings – to stump for the mayor. The party took out a huge ad in local newspapers, featuring the photographs of all the public officials who had endorsed Gaillard. The page included everyone from Hollings to state Rep. Joseph P. Riley Jr.

In December, Gaillard suffered another close race. At one point his lead was only 193 votes, which was a veritable insult considering his opponent was a Republican. For a time, it looked like the mayor was destined for more hearings and recounts. But when all the challenged ballots had been settled, Gaillard won his fourth term – by a mere 704 votes.

Many community leaders considered the election an unmitigated disaster. If Gaillard had not annexed so much of West Ashley and James Island, he almost certainly would have lost. But worst of all, the mayor had been re-elected with almost no support in the black community. At a time when civil rights were a foregone conclusion, it was not a good message to send.

Riley was deeply troubled by the election. He liked Gaillard, believed he was a fair man who supported civil rights. It was unfortunate the race had been distilled down to black versus white, but he feared it would only get worse. He wanted to do something to help. A few weeks after the election, Riley wrote the mayor a letter. It was a thoughtful note, not critical in the least; Riley took his time and was proud of the final product. He thought he was doing Gaillard a favor.

Riley told the mayor the election had created a real opportunity for him to reach out to the black community. He suggested Gaillard attend events in black neighborhoods to build bridges. The city needed a mayor to heal those problems the election had proved still existed. The letter reflected Riley's own sense of social justice. But when Gaillard showed it to his staff, one of them said, "That sounds like a candidate for mayor in four years."

Riley believed he was just offering sound advice to a friend; there were no political overtones intended. In truth, he hadn't given the mayor's office a second's thought – Riley had never even attended a City Council meeting. He believed his political destiny was in Columbia, where he could concentrate on issues that affected all of South Carolina – education, poverty, integration. Riley thought he was in the right job, and if he wasn't, he would run for higher office. Municipal politics had never occurred to him. At that moment, he had his eye on another job.

In September 1972, Riley was well on his way to re-election for a third term in the House when he made a bold announcement: He would seek the chairmanship of the powerful House Judiciary Committee. The longtime chairman, Rep. Fay Bell, had been defeated in his June primary, so the seat was open – a rare occurrence in South Carolina. The heir apparent was Rep. Robert Kneece of Columbia, vice chairman of the committee. Riley was a longshot; he had been on the committee for only two years. But he was ambitious and thought it would help the Young Turks advance their goals. As Judiciary chairman, Riley would have a much larger role in setting the legislative agenda.

His friends thought Riley was crazy to make a play for such a coveted position. Although Riley argued that there would be at least 10 new members on the 27-member committee – and they choose their own chairman – he had to know Sol Blatt was still pulling the strings. And the odds that the speaker had forgotten Riley's open campaigning for Rex Carter were slim to none. Tom Bryant feared his friend was setting himself up for failure.

Riley was re-elected to the House easily, and by December claimed he was within one vote of winning the Judiciary chairmanship. Blatt had even moved one of Kneece's supporters off the committee. But the speaker apparently knew more than Riley. When the vote was taken, Riley lost. Later, he would concede that Blatt likely blocked any chance he might have had. So long as Sol Blatt was speaker, which was only through the 1973 session, Joe Riley would get nothing of importance. But by then, Riley was no longer interested in waiting out the speaker.

Had he been elected Judiciary chairman, Riley later said he might have remained in the state Legislature a little longer. He would have been in a position to effect more change in the state and perhaps set himself up for a bigger campaign one day. But since he didn't win the chairmanship, he decided this third term would be his last.

There were other issues that factored into the decision, but the predominant reason was family. Charlotte wanted her husband at home. For five years, Riley had been gone almost half the week for half the year – a long time to spend away from his young family and his law practice. Although he routinely ignored weekend legislative retreats and events, and turned down most invitations while he was home, it was still a tremendous drain on his time.

And there was this: Charlotte was expecting their second child, all the more reason he felt he needed to be home. Riley conceded his wife was right and agreed he had fulfilled his public-service duties. He would find other ways to serve, just as his father always had. But he would keep this decision to himself for more than a year. He knew that a lame-duck politician had very little influence, and he still had much he wanted to do.

In 1973, Riley tackled a variety of issues that were overwhelmingly unpopular with his colleagues. He fought to increase the state gasoline tax by a penny – from 8 cents on the gallon to 9 cents – because inflation had prevented the highway department from keeping up with road repairs. He fought a bill that would allow coroners to carry guns – a silly proposition since, as he noted, they weren't law enforcement officers. And he began a movement that would force lawmakers to disclose the names of their campaign contributors and any conflicts of interests they may have on votes they took.

He continued his crusade against his colleagues' wallets when he tried to outlaw legislators from serving as attorney for any group regulated by state boards. In the 1970s, utility companies routinely hired lawyer-legislators to represent their interests before the state's Public Service Commission. The panel set rates for all the electric, water, gas and phone companies in South Carolina – and held hearings every time one of these businesses wanted to raise its rates, which was often. The companies argued that hiring legislators was good business because these men, more than anyone, understood the process and could look out for their interests.

That was just the way things were done, Riley realized. It was the system, and it had been that way going back to the days when the PSC's main job was overseeing railroads. Even though he had no evidence that anyone was abusing the system, Riley knew it looked bad. After all, Public Service commissioners had a hard time turning down the request of any company represented by a state lawmaker. The Legislature appointed the members of the Public Service Commission.

Riley introduced legislation that would prohibit sitting lawmakers from appearing before the Public Service Commission. At first his proposal barred lawmakers from appearing before all regulatory boards, but his colleagues suggested he start small. Of course, the idea met with serious opposition – such a law would take money out of the pockets of several members, who were paid handsome fees for their legal work. It only made matters worse that Riley and his co-sponsors were these Young Turks who shied away from parties and lobbyists. Other lawmakers were suspicious, but there was little they could do when stories about the practice made the papers.

Still, the proposal would linger in committee for more than a year.

Most of Riley's legislation suffered the same fate, but he hoped to get a fair hearing after Rex Carter took over as speaker in late 1973. Riley spent the summer attending to his law business, but was often distracted by legislative work. He sat on delegation committees that argued over the consolidation of all Charleston County governments, as well as a separate plan to redesign Charleston City Council into a body with fewer alderman – and single-member districts. Riley was appointed chairman of that committee, a role he called the greatest honor bestowed upon him since he was chosen to erase the blackboard in grammar school.

For his last session of the General Assembly, Riley focused on civil rights – the issue that mattered most to him. Along with Fielding, Goodstein, Sanders and Bryant, Riley had a new ally: the Rev. Robert Woods had been elected in 1972 as the second black state representative from Charleston County. Woods, an active member of the Southern Christian Leadership Conference, gladly went along with all of Riley's plans. Woods recognized a kindred spirit when he saw one.

As the 1974 session opened, Woods and Riley introduced legislation to designate Jan. 15 as Martin Luther King Jr. Day in South Carolina – an idea Goodstein predicted would go over like "a lead balloon." Similar efforts were underway across the South. The Georgia Legislature had approved a plan to hang King's portrait in the Statehouse, but Lt. Gov. Lester Maddox had blocked efforts to designate a state holiday in honor of the slain civil rights leader. It wouldn't be much easier to get the support of South Carolina officials.

Woods took the House floor that January to praise King as "a great teacher who led us through a long and dark period." The freshman lawmaker – one of only three black members of the House that year – said King's dreams, and the lessons he taught, would not soon be forgotten. "Together, as blacks, whites, chicanos, Indians and others, we shall overcome. This is the dream that cost Martin his life; that is the dream he lived."

It was a rousing speech, although nothing less would have been expected of a preacher. But as Goodstein predicted, the measure was wildly unpopular. Riley and Woods managed to get the bill called up for debate on the House floor, where it was promptly attacked by a Spartanburg Republican as "an outrage and an insult." State Rep. Richard Hines, a 25-year-old businessman, argued that King taught people to make their own decisions about which laws they should obey. He called King's teachings the antithesis of non-violence. He suggested instead a holiday to honor law enforcement officers killed in the line of duty.

Hines refused to debate Riley, who went on to claim the bill would not declare Jan. 15 an official state holiday; it was simply a day for South Carolinians to recognize King in any way they wanted. In the past 25 years, he said, no other country had made as much progress on racial issues without a violent revolution – and King was largely responsible for that. Riley said that in the black community, "no other leader is more revered than King."

The House continued to fight over the King legislation for nearly a month. State Rep. Roger Kirk argued that it was a bad precedent. "We could set aside 365 days to honor famous South Carolinians," Kirk said, naming several white people he would rather honor. In the end, it was another ally of Riley – newly elected Rep. Mendel Rivers Jr. – who chastised white lawmakers who had always "feared King for his ability to motivate blacks to seek equality." In the end, the bill passed 64-25. The victory was short-lived; the Senate refused to approve it.

Riley spent the remainder of the session tidying up unfinished business. He renewed efforts to outlaw milk price-fixing – an issue he had championed during his first term – and expand laws for absentee voting. His greatest victory was ethics reform. Using the press to bring attention to the issue, the House voted 95-1 to make lawmakers' campaign disclosures public. The only new legislation Riley floated was a proposed waiting period on handgun purchases, but he was too far ahead of his time. The bill was ignored.

As the session drew to a close, Riley announced he would not seek re-election. He said the same things many politicians did, that he wanted to spend more time with his family. The difference was, Riley meant it. His son, Bratton, was still in diapers and Riley told reporters he wanted to be home to see more of his boys' "formative years." His friends understood, but those who did not know Riley assumed there were other reasons.

Some reporters speculated that changes in election laws played into Riley's decision. Candidates for the state House would no longer run as a countywide slate – the U.S. Supreme Court had ordered South Carolina to establish single-member districts to better represent the ideal of one-man, one-vote. And Riley had been drawn into a district with two other sitting lawmakers. Riley dismissed the speculation, noting that both the lawmakers drawn into his district had already promised to not seek re-election. The seat was his for the taking; he just didn't want it anymore.

Riley's announcement was a shock to the state power structure, and several people asked him to reconsider. A week after Riley said he would retire, Speaker Carter announced that a study committee would look into shortening the legislative session. Carter said the time demands of a five-month session had cost the state the service of a lot of good men. Riley was the example he used.

Eventually, Riley was summoned to the governor's office, where John West – his former boss and a friend of the family – also tried to change his mind. West told Riley that he was a future state leader, that it was not a good time for South Carolina to lose progressive voices. But Riley politely disagreed. He was finished.

When Joe Riley walked out of the Statehouse in June 1974, he thought his political career was over. He spent the summer supporting Pug Ravenel's gubernatorial campaign, then returned to Columbia for a special session in the fall. But he was simply fulfilling his commitments. Riley had always wanted to be involved in politics, and felt he had made a difference in the fight for more education funding. There were many things still wrong with South Carolina, he knew, but he'd done his part. Charlotte wanted him home, and he knew it was a reasonable request.

He had served six years in the state House of Representatives, and now it was time to tend to his law business and his growing family. So Riley left Columbia without regret, convinced his name would never appear on another ballot.

He would continue to believe that for nearly six months.

The Campaign

On Jan. 24, 1975, Charleston Mayor J. Palmer Gaillard announced that he would not seek a fifth term of office. He didn't make a big deal out of it; Gaillard simply summoned reporters to City Hall on that Friday morning and read a short statement. In a town unaccustomed to change, this was monumental news. By the end of 1975, the city would have a new chief executive for the first time since the late 1950s.

And Charlestonians rarely approved of anything new.

Gaillard had been mayor for 15 years already and on City Council for eight years before that. Many people couldn't remember a time when Gaillard was not a prominent name in local politics. But most insiders were less than surprised. Even the local newspapers, which carried the story on their front pages, did not treat it as a bombshell – there were no screaming banner headlines. Gaillard's decision to retire from public office was, at least in the eyes of the political intelligentsia, a foregone conclusion.

After the 1971 election – a campaign Gaillard won so narrowly it prompted recounts and election commission hearings – many believed the mayor was simply done. He had to realize another campaign would be a bloody battle, one he might not survive. Since the last election, the political landscape had changed considerably. Voters recently had approved a restructuring of City Council, and that added a new dynamic to municipal elections. Instead of 16 aldermen elected at-large, the council now would be composed of 12 members elected in single-member districts. That almost certainly ensured the council would include significant black representation for the first time in the modern era. And that spelled a heavy turnout in black precincts, where Gaillard – despite his moderate record on civil rights issues – had been soundly thumped in 1971.

If any such political calculus figured into his decision, Gaillard said nothing of it during his announcement.

"For the past 15 years, I have been honored to have served as mayor of this city and I shall always be grateful to the citizens for having elected me to this high office on four consecutive occasions. This rare privilege is something that I shall never forget and to all Charlestonians, I express my sincere and heartfelt thanks," Gaillard said.

The mayor said that, "Should Almighty God spare my life until the end of this term, it will mean that for 16 years the citizens have known only one mayor." Between that time and his eight years on council, he had served a quarter-century – and Gaillard said that was a long time for one person to be involved in city government. The mayor said he wanted to make the announcement early enough so "all qualified individuals" interested in the job would have time to make a decision and mount a campaign.

The reporters gently grilled Gaillard, asking if he could be "drafted" to run for another term – a point on which he was slightly cagey. The mayor acknowledged "public service is in my blood," noted he was still young at 54, and didn't consider himself finished with politics. But ultimately, he said, "The time has arrived for a new name to occupy this important position; someone, hopefully, young with new ideas and a fresh approach to our problems but, above all, an individual with undisputed integrity."

It was a very specific description, enough that some people believed Gaillard already had a candidate in mind. This seemed to jibe with speculation circulating among the city's political establishment. Once insiders knew Gaillard was unlikely to run again, they began to talk about finding someone who could bridge the city's growing racial gap – a candidate who would appeal to black and white voters, and work with what would most likely be the most diverse City Council in Charleston's 300-year history.

When reporters asked if Gaillard was talking about former state Rep. Joseph P. Riley Jr., the mayor said his description shouldn't be interpreted as an endorsement of anyone. However, he said, "Of all the people mentioned so far, I would be comfortable with Mr. Riley."

The mayor's announcement may not have garnered World War II-size headlines in the local newspapers, but it was more significant than anyone understood at the time. Even Gaillard did not realize that he had just changed the course of Charleston's history.

Joe Riley had been a private citizen for only a few weeks when Gaillard announced his retirement. His term as a state representative officially ended when the new General Assembly convened, but Riley had been home for months tending to his law business. Throughout the fall, as Gaillard's plans became more apparent, people began to approach Riley about running for mayor. Some even dropped hints in the newspapers.

Capers Barr could not believe the courtship process. He knew when politicians said they had been "asked to run" it was most often a bunch of bull – they wanted to run but were trying to appear modest. That was not the case with Riley. Barr saw people parading into the law office at 13 Broad St. every week, most of them urging Riley to consider moving down the street to City Hall.

Riley had never given much thought to local politics. "I'd never imagined or aspired to be mayor," he would later say. His interests to that point had been focused on state issues – managing growth, delivering services, improving education. He always believed he was best suited to be a legislator, perhaps one day governor. Municipal politics never occurred to him. Riley had never even attended a City Council meeting, an amazing fact given his family's long involvement in civic life.

Riley had adjusted to his homecoming with ease. He and Barr were slowly building their business, finding new clients while still taking as many residential real estate closings as they could from Big Joe. Riley was finally living on a normal schedule. Following family tradition, he had taken Charlotte and the boys to the Isle of Palms for the end of the summer, where they had just built their own summer home.

A few years earlier, Riley had bought an oceanfront lot on the Isle of Palms for $7,500 – 10 times what his father paid 30 years earlier. Still, the value of barrier island land was appreciating so rapidly Riley devised a plan to build his family a beach house that wouldn't cost him anything beyond his initial investment. He took out a mortgage on the lot and used the cash to build a modest home. They rented the house to monthly tenants during the winter for exactly what it cost to make a mortgage payment.

In the summer, he could get the same amount for a weekly rental. So by midsummer, their annual costs had been covered, and the family spent a month or six weeks living on the island. It became a sanctuary, a getaway, a continuation of a family tradition from his childhood. And, just like his father, when Riley got home in the evenings the first thing he did was jump into the ocean with his sons. Then he would retreat to the porch, where he sat with Charlotte overlooking the vast Atlantic.

During one of those summer stays at the beach, Riley lent the Gibbes Street house to Pat Conroy. The Citadel alum, who Riley got to know while vetting *The Boo*, was writing a novel and needed a quiet place to work. After college, Conroy had taken a job teaching poor black children on isolated Daufuskie Island just south of Hilton Head. But he had ambitions to be more than a babysitter in a shack of a schoolhouse, and lobbied Beaufort County school officials for additional resources. He wanted to do far more for these children than school officials thought necessary, and they bristled at the pressure. The school district eventually fired him, and he wrote a book about the experience, *The Water is Wide*. The nonfiction account was well-received and ultimately turned into a movie. With two works of nonfiction behind him, Conroy was ready to try his hand at fiction. He told Riley he wanted to write a novel inspired by his abusive father, a man Conroy and his siblings called "The Great Santini."

By the late fall of 1974, there was a consensus building. One day, local attorney and former municipal judge Tom Tisdale stopped by 13 Broad. He told Riley he had been approached to run for mayor, but declined. "I just want you to know that I'm going to support you," Tisdale said, offering his services on the inevitable campaign. Riley thanked him for the offer, but said nothing to indicate he was committed to running.

Riley could not escape the talk. He rarely ventured out that he didn't meet someone who said, "You've got to run for mayor" or at the very least ask, "When are you going to run for mayor?" Riley was flattered, of course. His father had talked about the job before, although Riley knew his mother would have never allowed it. Big

Joe liked to be involved in community decisions, but from behind the scenes. His temperament was not suited for public office – he was far too candid, too easy to rile. And although Riley was undoubtedly his father's son, his temperament was far more reserved, like his mother's – even though, in later years, he occasionally displayed a short fuse. Still, he was clearly the true politician in the family.

It seemed the Charleston power structure already had its man, whether Riley liked it or not. One day, he ran into the mayor on the street. Gaillard told him confidentially that he'd decided to not run again and would make the announcement soon. He suggested Riley should consider taking his place. Riley thanked the mayor for the advance notice, but would not commit. He could not avoid the question much longer, however. And, in truth, he had to admit the idea held some appeal.

Riley's former colleagues in the legislative delegation were actively trying to recruit a candidate. They polled black leaders around the city, asking for a consensus candidate. Who was someone both white and black voters could support? State Reps. Herbert Fielding and Robert Woods did not have to give it much thought. Riley had fought for a Martin Luther King Jr. Day, had helped create the state Human Affairs Commission, tried to expand voter rights. He was a liberal who'd supported John Kennedy and civil rights. Eventually, they sent Fielding to recruit Riley.

Coming from his old friend, Riley took the request seriously. He knew the city had a lot of issues to address: a diminishing downtown, an unsteady economy, concerns over racial progress and inclusiveness. Gaillard had been roundly criticized for not hiring enough blacks to work in city government, and Riley knew that hurt him in the 1971 election. Those were all issues that interested Riley greatly, and he later said he felt a growing sense of responsibility as winter fell.

He was still thinking about it as the holiday approached, when local leaders applied still more pressure. On Dec. 12, 1974, about 400 people attended a "nonpartisan" reception for Riley at Hibernian Hall. None of the speakers mentioned the mayor's race, although County Councilman John Seignious wore a homemade "Riley for mayor" sticker on his lapel. The official reason for the event was to honor Riley for his legislative accomplishments – something not often done for three-term lawmakers. Lt. Gov.-elect Brantley Harvey gave Riley a scrapbook filled with testimonials and kind letters from his legislative colleagues, as well as Gov. John

West and Gov.-elect James B. Edwards.

Many of the Young Turks turned out to toast Riley, one of whom even performed a musical number for his outgoing colleague. But it was the incoming lieutenant governor who sang Riley's praises the loudest. Harvey said Riley had lived up to his great promise during his time at the Statehouse, that he was "a young man of keen intellect, moral courage and dedicated service. He is totally fair and honest."

Riley was modest in his brief remarks, and said he had the good fortune to serve in a time "ripe for reform." He talked about the continuing need for social justice and said he was glad to have the opportunity to "try to bring people of all races together." To some, it sounded very much like a campaign speech. Within a week, News and Courier columnist Barbara Williams wrote that although the event may have started innocently enough, it had turned into a mayoral rally for Riley.

One of the event's sponsors was Rep. Robert Woods, who was also considering a mayoral bid. Other organizers pointed to his participation as proof that there were no nefarious purposes behind the appreciation dinner. But that did not stop Robert Ford, a community activist and expected City Council candidate, from showing up to distribute a press release about plans to elect Charleston's first black mayor.

A week later, Riley talked to Clyde Johnson, an African-American columnist at The Evening Post who'd been speculating on the mayor's race for months. Johnson had written that Riley already had the backing of several influential sectors of the community, and predicted he would eventually run. In their conversation, Riley admitted he had been approached by several people and conceded that he was considering the idea. During the course of the phone call, Riley lamented the state of housing on the peninsula, the prevalence of crime and the growing concerns over the health of the central business district.

Riley spoke of social and racial understanding, about tapping citizens to get involved. "All communities have this talent, but we have more than our share," he told the columnist. Johnson came away impressed with Riley – and convinced he was about to announce his candidacy. "I believe that Riley has a discerning eye on the community and what ails it," Johnson wrote. "I, too, believe that being a public servant affords one an opportunity not found in many other endeavors. To be a success, public officials must really enjoy their work. I sense that Riley loved serving in the General Assembly and I predict he will run for mayor in 1975."

By the time Johnson published that opinion, it was Christmas Eve 1974. And he was right – Riley had just about made up his mind. But first he needed to talk it over with his family.

Big Joe was thrilled with the idea. He always talked of running solely for the purpose of changing the form of government to a city administrator-run system. Many of the people he admired most were politicians, and he was proud of his son's work in the Legislature. Helen Riley was not nearly as enthusiastic; she likely knew such a campaign would be far different than running on a slate of candidates for the Statehouse. A mayoral candidate stood alone on the ballot. It was more personal and would leave her son open to attack – something she preferred to avoid. Ultimately, Riley's parents supported his candidacy, as did his friend and law partner, Capers Barr. All he needed was his wife's blessing.

Riley would not run without her consent.

Charlotte Riley had just reclaimed her husband from politics, and could not have been thrilled by the idea of a full-time job in public office. But she knew he had a strong desire to serve, and understood that. At least as mayor, he would work less than a mile from the house. He would be home every night, close by in case of emergency. As political jobs went, mayor certainly beat state legislator.

She was not apolitical – Charlotte was, in fact, one of her husband's closest advisors. Her main concern was privacy, and she worried about what such a high-profile job would mean for her and her sons. She had no desire to be in the spotlight, did not like the idea of being Charleston's first lady. Riley promised she would never have to do anything that she didn't want to do, and that he could keep his political and personal lives separate. Besides, Riley said, if he won he would serve only one term.

Joe Riley kicked off his mayoral campaign in February 1975. The general election was not until December, but there was a primary to consider and, with an open seat, any number of people might decide to run. The best course of action was to start early and strong, and possibly scare off the competition. Riley wanted to get out and talk to voters, and his campaign staff wanted to reassure people he was up to the job, since he looked much younger than his 32 years – which some people might consider a tender age for a chief executive.

His staff had a point, which became abundantly clear in March. Riley was out greeting voters in the Mazyck-Wraggborough neighborhood, reporters in tow. Some of the people Riley talked to mentioned that they remembered him as a "runny nose" boy hanging around his father's office. One woman even said, "Oh, you're a little fellow. We were expecting to see a much bigger man."

At 5'9" Riley was not a particularly short man, but he was slight of build – and seemed more so because he had started running with Barr to keep in shape. Between the jogging and the mixed-doubles tennis matches he and Charlotte played with Capers and Ellie Barr on the weekends, the candidate was as thin as he'd been as a cadet. Riley didn't give much thought to the issue of his age. In those days, 32 was considered much older than it would be just a generation later. Riley had grown up around men who returned from World War II in their early 20s but had as much maturity as any 40-year-old.

Riley spent as much time campaigning in black neighborhoods as white. He found that many African-Americans felt alienated from city government, and that presented many problems. The candidate talked to black voters about the need for better affordable housing, more police protection and greater employment opportunities. He promised to hire more black workers in city government. Through his political friends and meet-the-candidate events at Morris Brown AME Church, Riley had the support of most power brokers in the black community. But he wanted to connect with regular citizens. He refused to take their support for granted.

Some black candidates for City Council had already endorsed George Fuller for mayor. At the same time, Fuller – a black deputy coroner for the county – had secured the support of soul singer James Brown. This helped little in terms of electoral math, but it brought him a brush with fame, and publicity. Riley's campaign staff feared Fuller might cut into their margins in the community, at least enough to hurt. But the Rev. Robert Woods, the state representative, endorsed Riley in May. Woods put out a statement that left no doubt who he believed had "best addressed himself to the needs and priorities of this city."

"I hope the black community will support a man not based on his race or color, but on his credentials," Woods said. "Joe Riley Jr. is the candidate who has the best interest of the people of our city at heart. I know he is committed to unifying our community and recognizes the need for the black and white communities of our city to join together and work for the common good of all."

Woods gave the Riley campaign a huge boost – it made the front page of The News and Courier – but Fuller tried to downplay its importance. He said the state representative's statement was merely a response to his endorsement from James Brown. Fuller even suggested that Woods had promised to support him for mayor just a few months earlier. His endorsement, Fuller said, would have no effect on the election.

"I think it's going to mean that he has one more vote," Fuller said.

The two candidates sparred throughout the spring, sometimes with dueling press conferences. Fuller staked out a much more conservative position than Riley, and criticized his crime initiatives. He said Riley's idea for a citizen's police review board was "unnecessary bureaucracy." Riley mostly ignored Fuller, and proposed opening police storefronts on King Street and the East Side, home of many of the peninsula's poorest, and most crime-ridden, neighborhoods.

Riley set up a network of volunteers that would eventually grow to 250 people. Although his campaign headquarters was in an old motel on Lockwood Drive, he met with his West Ashley coordinators in a diner there every week. He wanted to be in every corner of the city. He told voters that West Ashley had been ignored by the city, Charleston needed better parks and a greater focus on revitalizing downtown. Peninsular merchants had seen their profits drop considerably as people moved out of downtown. Riley tried to address everyone's problems.

In April, President Gerald Ford named Palmer Gaillard deputy assistant Secretary of the Navy for Reserve Affairs, following a nomination from Sen. Strom Thurmond. The appointment was not a stretch – Gaillard was a Navy vet who enlisted two days after the attack on Pearl Harbor. He spent four years as a pilot in the Navy before returning home to Charleston following the war. No one could say the appointment was simply a soft landing pad for the mayor. But this meant Gaillard would not finish his term.

The timing of his departure ensured there would be another mayor before voters went to the polls – City Council would appoint one of their own to finish Gaillard's term. But this would not give any candidate an advantage; none of the aldermen had filed to run for mayor. On Aug. 19, they unanimously elected Alderman Arthur B. Schirmer, who had been on council 14 years. He became the first Charleston mayor to live west of the Ashley, and may have been selected because he had no plans to continue in the office – or even as a member of council.

Schirmer made it clear he would only serve out Gaillard's term and then return to his landscaping and paving business. But while he was in office, Mayor Schirmer acted as much more than a caretaker. He cut a deal to share city pools with the school district and tried to annex the entire James Island Public Service District – a position candidate Riley said he would support if the residents approved.

The mayoral field continued to grow as the year dragged on. Lamar Brabham announced he would challenge Riley in the Democratic primary. He was only 22, a former assistant manager at Piggly Wiggly who listed "rat control" as one of his campaign platforms. Still, his entry in the race forced the Riley camp to spend money that could have been saved for the general election. By August, only the Republicans had failed to field a candidate. But rumors around town suggested the GOP had an ace in the hole.

After years of insignificance, South Carolina Republicans had gained a lot of confidence in recent years. Arthur Ravenel had come close to beating Gaillard in the 1971 mayoral election and the party had just taken the governor's office for the first time in a century. State Sen. James B. Edwards, an oral surgeon from Mount Pleasant, had been a party activist for years before winning the governor's race on just his third campaign for elected office. Despite Edwards' appearance at the Riley appreciation dinner in December, the party assumed the governor would endorse their mayoral candidate – especially since she was another longtime Republican activist.

Nancy Dinwiddie Hawk had been a force of nature in Charleston for two decades. She and her husband, John, brought their family to the city in 1951 when he took a job with the Medical College. Nancy Hawk moved her nine children into a huge house at the foot of Meeting Street and soon became just as involved in the community as the Rileys. She was on the board of First (Scots) Presbyterian Church, founded what became Mason Preparatory School in her basement and took an active role in the arts. She was also a Republican long before it was in vogue in South Carolina.

By 1975, Hawk was perhaps best known as founder and chairman of the Save Charleston Fund. The preservationist group had led a campaign to stop the city from demolishing several old warehouses on East Bay Street, a cause that the Historic Charleston Foundation very publicly supported. Hawk fought to keep high-rise buildings out of Charleston, a popular position among downtown residents. As a result, Hawk had quite a following among her neighbors – Riley's neighbors – South of Broad. Riley knew Hawk was popular and later said, even with the Democratic Party behind him, "I was not overconfident."

Riley trounced Brabham in the Democratic primary on Sept. 30 – taking 85 percent of the vote – but still had to face three candidates in the general election. Besides Fuller and Hawk, former judge and Gaillard advisor Kenneth Rentiers was running as an independent. Riley was the odds-on favorite from the start, but with so many people in the race, anything could happen. But there would not be a runoff. According to the rules of the municipal election, a candidate needed only a plurality to win – not a majority. Riley only had to get one more vote than his next closest competitor.

Riley's team grew considerably as the campaign went along. Besides Capers Barr, Riley had the support of attorneys such as Robert Rosen, Thomas Tisdale and Bill Regan, businessman Dick Davenport and future advertising executive David Rawle, who he met while working on Pug Ravenel's gubernatorial campaign. Riley also had many prominent black community leaders in his corner, not only Woods and Fielding, but Marjorie Amos – the first woman, and one of the first African-Americans, to win a seat on Charleston County Council. Nearly every faction in the city was supporting Riley.

The one man who might have helped Riley's campaign the most did not get involved. In later years, local folklore suggested that Big Joe was so powerful he simply rallied the city's power brokers to unite behind his son. But Riley did not give his father an official role in the campaign, nor did he consult with him. Riley wanted to win on his own. He would later concede, however, that his father had a lot of influence in the community and almost certainly was an independent advocate.

A campaign for mayor was far different than running for a House seat. For one thing, Riley learned he had to pay more attention to fundraising. He hated asking for money, and did so grudgingly, but proved proficient at it. Over the course of the race, Riley collected $66,000 – more than twice as much as Hawk. A good amount of that money was spent on television advertising.

Rawle hired Albert and David Maysles, acquaintances of his, to film a series of campaign commercials for Riley. The Boston-born brothers were legendary film-makers, the men who made *Gimme Shelter* – a documentary about the final leg of the Rolling Stones' 1969 tour which ended in disaster at Altamont, California. It was a wealth of talent for local TV. If nothing else, the campaign was assured of slick television advertising.

The Maysleses worked from Rawle scripts that highlighted Riley's three biggest campaign themes: crime, traffic and the need for better public parks. Rawle, who handled strategy and polling as well as advertising, broke down the commercial schedule to neatly fit each of those issues. One of the first spots focused on the city's growing problem with congestion, which went along with Riley's proposal to build a new bridge to James Island. Rawle rented a room at a hotel that locals simply called the "round Holiday Inn," and set up his crew on a balcony overlooking the twin bridges connecting the peninsula with West Ashley.

Crew members took their positions just after the 3 p.m. check-in while Riley and Rawle sat in the room talking and glancing at the TV – assuming the crew was getting the footage they needed. But at 6:15, one of the brothers stuck his head into the room and asked, "When does the traffic start?" Riley and Rawle were panicked until they checked the bridges for themselves and saw what, in Charleston, passed for gridlock. For the Maysleses, who were accustomed to New York City traffic, it seemed like they were wasting their film.

Rawle soon learned that Riley was a sometimes troublesome candidate. He could be stubborn, made almost every decision himself and would not do anything if it didn't seem just right. One evening they planned to film a parks-themed commercial at a local playground. The script called for Riley to stand in front of the camera and say, "This is one of Charleston's parks. The equipment is falling apart, there is no lighting and it's empty."

It should have been simple. But at one playground the crew found a couple of guys playing basketball on a net-less hoop. Rawle asked the pair to step aside for a moment so they could film, but Riley refused to say his lines. "I can't do this here," he said. "The script says it's empty, but there are guys playing ball. I'm not comfortable with this."

The next park was even more desolate and run-down. The scant plot of land had a single swing set, complete with one rickety swing. Riley was supposed to blame Charleston's soaring crime rate on the lack of recreational facilities for its children, but again, there was a problem. Riley saw a homeless man dozing in the bushes. He refused to stick to the script.

"I can't say no one comes here – he's here," Riley said, pointing to the sleeping man.

The commercial was rewritten.

Riley campaigned six days a week through the fall, eventually attending at least 50 breakfast meetings, more than a dozen "coffees" and two-dozen luncheons. He knocked on doors every day except Sunday, when he stayed home with his family. There was a debate for all four candidates at the Jewish Community Center, but mostly the campaign devolved into a war of words between Riley and Nancy Hawk – the two sides swapping barbs in The News and Courier and The Evening Post. By December, Riley had held 38 press conferences.

Riley suggested the city leverage money from the South Carolina Arts Commission to bring in more festivals; he called for a development board that would lure new businesses – and new jobs – to the city; he proposed a police community-relations program to help lower the crime rate; and promised to build additional downtown housing, especially along King Street, to replenish the peninsula's flagging population. But Riley said Charleston's greatest need was a mayor who could unite the city.

In one stump speech after another, Riley promised that City Hall's doors would be open to everyone, that his administration would hire more minorities. He preached inclusiveness every day, warning that Charleston could not solve its problems with crime, economic development, housing or transportation unless "all segments of the community come together."

"We shouldn't have to live on the East Side to be concerned about better housing. We shouldn't have to live west of the Ashley to be concerned about traffic. We shouldn't have to live South of Broad to be concerned about preserving our architectural heritage. We shouldn't have to be a merchant to be concerned about King Street revitalization," he said.

Nancy Hawk ran on a platform of fiscal conservatism that was in direct opposition to most of Riley's positions. She criticized Charleston city government for owning public housing outside of its borders and complained that the city got ridiculously low rents "to the benefit of special interests." She opposed a downtown campus for Trident Technical College, arguing the city instead needed more taxpaying businesses on its rolls. She derided the idea of a citizens police review board, suggesting that instead anyone with complaints could take them to their councilman. Hawk had the less-government mantra down to a science.

As the campaign rhetoric grew sharper, Hawk's campaign manager called Tom Tisdale and suggested their candidates agree to a set of rules for the election. Tisdale thought about it briefly, but ultimately declined. He couldn't see how agreeing with Hawk on anything helped his candidate. Soon, Hawk was calling Riley's campaign staffers a "bunch of gutter rats." The Democrats laughed it off, and soon began using the term to refer to each other.

And then they really made Hawk mad.

When Riley released a list of his campaign donors and expenses, Hawk labeled it "smear tactics." She claimed that while Riley had "painted himself and his campaign as ethical, open and above reproach," her donors had been harassed by his supporters. Riley said it was only "an attempt to belatedly excuse her failure to disclose her personal financial interests and the names of her contributors and the amounts they are putting into her campaign." He said the last thing Charleston needed was a negative campaign. But that was what the city got.

Although the city's movers and shakers were largely in Riley's corner, Hawk's support was not unsubstantial. She had raised $26,000 and drew support from a half-dozen Republican City Council candidates and even President Ford's sister-in-law. Eventually the Republican Party brought in Gov. Edwards, who praised Hawk's "leadership, dedication and courage." But Hawk's support would not decide the race – Riley's would. The News and Courier speculated whether, in a general election, Riley could maintain sufficient levels of support in the black community with Fuller in the race.

Barbara Williams, the city's top political journalist, reported in The News and Courier that out of the six black City Council candidates on the ballot, two unquestionably supported Riley. But another candidate, Robert Ford – who had come to town for Martin Luther King Jr.'s Southern Christian Leadership Conference during the 1969 hospital strike – said he was more inclined to support a black mayor rather than someone who had simply won the Democratic nomination. Since Woods chose not to run, Ford hinted that he would support Fuller. "My obligation," Ford said, "is to the black community."

Although he sometimes took the criticism personally – his critics claimed he was thin-skinned – Riley understood the politics at play. But no one was prepared for the nastiness of the campaign's final weeks. Riley's younger sister Mary could not even watch the news with all the talk of gutter rats and the like. Her brother was being dragged through the mud daily. The opponents in his legislative campaigns had never been so vicious, so personal. But this time Riley was not one of a dozen candidates for 11 House seats – he was fighting for the top job in the city. And it was apparent the stakes were much higher.

In the end, the election wasn't even close. On Dec. 9, nearly 15,000 Charleston residents voted in the municipal elections and Riley won 7,485 votes – 11 more than his three opponents combined. Nancy Hawk finished with an impressive 4,855 votes. She took most of the West Ashley precincts, but not by nearly enough votes to overcome Riley's strength on the peninsula. And Hawk could not blame municipal election rules for her defeat. Riley not only had a plurality of votes, he won slightly more than 50 percent. Even if election laws required it, he would have avoided a runoff. In the end, Fuller was not a factor. Riley won 75 percent of the black vote.

That night, Riley's friends and family gathered at the Gaillard Auditorium, which City Council had renamed in honor of the former mayor two months earlier, to celebrate his victory. Before the mayor-elect arrived, however, he went home to see his sons. He then drove over to 27 Tradd St. to surprise his two surviving aunts, Emily and Habby. The women who doted on him as a boy weren't expecting to see him, but Riley felt the need to visit all of his family this night – and he knew his parents and Charlotte would be at the Gaillard.

When Riley finally appeared at the auditorium, he had no monumental speech to deliver. He honestly had no idea whether he would win, and had chosen to spend his final hours campaigning instead of writing remarks. So he simply walked into the party, climbed onto a chair in the middle of the room and shouted, "Did we do it or did we do it?"

That night he thanked his supporters and credited them with the victory. He said that together they had taken "the high road to unity, togetherness and positiveness, rather than the low road of divisiveness, factionalism and polarization." He pledged to do the "kind of things you want done" to make Charleston a progressive city. No one in the Gaillard Auditorium that evening realized they had just changed the course of the city's history – not even Riley. At that moment, it had not yet sunk in.

Joseph Patrick Riley Jr. had just been elected mayor of Charleston. He was 32. And he would take office in six days.

PART II

"Lift Every Voice and Sing"

Two Worlds

Charleston City Hall sits on the northeast corner of the intersection at Broad and Meeting streets. The four-story building, most notable for its European-inspired architecture and sweeping twin staircases leading up to its front porch, was built between 1801 and 1804 as a branch office of the First Bank of the United States. When Congress revoked the bank's charter in 1811, the property – which had been the site of a meat market in the 18th century – reverted to city ownership. The building sat empty for seven years before local officials decided to convert it into their grand, almost-new City Hall in 1818.

Aside from housing the second-oldest continuously operating council chambers in the country – New York City's opened six years earlier – City Hall makes up one-quarter of what locals call the "Four Corners of Law." The Meeting and Broad intersection is also the site of the county courthouse, the federal courthouse and the post office, as well as St. Michael's Episcopal Church. In one stop, Charleston residents have access to local, state, federal and ecclesiastical law, which, they joke, is everything you need in life – and death.

When Joe Riley walked into City Hall on Dec. 10, 1975, he knew the building as well as any local, which is to say not very. He passed it every day, but rarely had occasion to go inside. He never attended City Council meetings and seldom had reason to visit the mayor. Now, he was five days away from having a set of keys handed to him. The following Monday, he would become the 38th man in the city's history to call the historic old building his own personal office.

That morning Riley was meeting with outgoing Mayor Arthur B. Schirmer and his department heads for a crash course in city government operations. It was craziness, he thought, installing a new mayor less than a week after the vote – but the compressed election schedule left little choice. Already, election planning was one of many things on his list of things to fix in Charleston. For the moment, he would just have to make the best of it.

Mayor Gaillard didn't have a large staff and Schirmer had certainly not added to it in four months, so Riley had limited resources at his disposal. He told the newspaper he wanted to "familiarize myself with administrative details as much as possible in the short period of time left." Schirmer was gracious, the staff courteous, and they did all they could to help him get a handle on the job. After all, he was the new boss.

Although he must have been somewhat overwhelmed, Riley later said he never had a moment where he wondered, "What have I gotten myself into?" Taking over the day-to-day operations of a city was a monumental challenge in itself, and Riley did not want to be a simple caretaker – he planned to remake Charleston from the ground up. But he also had to make sure there was a continuity of basic services; that was the bread and butter of City Hall. For that reason, Riley decided to keep most of the staff from the Gaillard/Schirmer administration, including Police Chief John Conroy. There really wasn't much choice, at least not at first. The people he worked with well would remain for years, the rest would be replaced over time.

Riley needed as much institutional memory as he could get. He would be working with a City Council of 12 members, 11 of them as new to the job as he was. Riley was no novice at the workings of government, but this was the executive branch – far different from his experience as a legislator. He expected a sharp learning curve, and could not have been comforted by a News and Courier editorial, published two days after his election, that suggested no one envied him the job. "The situation is unprecedented in Charleston's modern times," the editors wrote. "It presents challenges to the new mayor in terms of diplomacy and leadership which are equally unprecedented."

Riley understood the symbolism of this new era – it had been one of his campaign themes. He had promised a more open, inclusive government, and that would start with the inauguration. All previous ceremonies for installing the mayor and council members had been conducted in City Council chambers, a room that held barely 100 people. Riley moved the 1975 inauguration onto City Hall's front porch. The city would set up rows of seats stretching into Broad Street, allowing more people access to the event. For the first time since Reconstruction, half the members of council would be black – and Riley wanted as many people as possible to see that. He delayed the start time until 3 p.m. so that even schoolchildren could attend.

On Monday, Dec. 15, the weather was unseasonably warm and, luckily, free of rain. Campaign staffers had reserved the nearby Hibernian Hall for the inauguration in case of bad weather, but that wouldn't be a problem. It was a perfect day to be outside – a perk of Charleston winters. Riley showed up at City Hall early, eager to start but still trying to shake off a nasty cold that had eaten up half his orientation week. At least the downtime had given him ample opportunity to write his speech.

The ceremony began with an invocation from the Bishop D. Ward Nichols of the Seventh Episcopal District, AME Church. Then Big Joe held the Bible as his son took the oath of office, which was administered by the Rev. Robert Woods – the state lawmaker whose endorsement had helped Riley win three out of four black votes in the election. By choosing Woods to give the oath, Riley wanted to illustrate he was serious about civil rights. And in case anyone missed the gesture, almost his entire inaugural address focused on the unification of Charleston. In the opening minute, he even referenced the Declaration of Independence's "all men are created equal" passage.

"The new City Council represents small and distinct districts – single-member districts – and not the electorate at large. Some among us fear this change. We should not fear it – we should welcome it. Free and full debate, a hearing of all varieties of political opinion, is the healthiest method of government. We have nothing to fear from honest disagreement about how people should govern themselves," Riley said.

The mayor's speech echoed his campaign themes, promising swift action on crime, inviting the people of James Island to join the city and vowing to develop affordable neighborhoods in the city. "The easy way would be to take narrow and selfish positions and never compromise, to leave the problems of housing to the East Side, to leave the problems of transportation to West Ashley, to leave preservation to downtown, and to leave the redevelopment of the central business district to the merchants." But Riley argued things that "affect one segment directly, indirectly affect us all."

Riley invoked Martin Luther King Jr.'s quote about the South's "tragic effort to live in a monologue rather than a dialogue" and his daughter's more recent remark, which fit Charleston so well, "We may have come over in different ships, but we are all in the same boat today." For that reason, Riley said the city's boards and commissions "must reasonably reflect our population." He promised more black citizens and women in positions of authority – something the mayor said was more important than even growth to Charleston's survival.

"The monuments to this administration's accomplishments may not be visible in marble or brick; rather in fewer of our children falling prey to a life of crime, and more, many more in constructive jobs and professions; increased business in our shopping district, and a lively and exciting atmosphere on King Street; a citizenry that has trust and confidence in government," Riley said. "We shall seek unwritten memorials, graven not so much on stone as in the hearts of people."

Woods led the crowd in raucous applause – one of six times Riley was interrupted in his 17-minute speech. And if there was any doubt the mayor was serious about this commitment to racial harmony, the program included a performance of "Lift Every Voice and Sing," a turn-of-the-century hymn often heard in the AME Church. Some people referred to the song as the "Black National Anthem." Riley even had the lyrics printed in the inauguration program.

After the ceremony, the new mayor and City Council mingled with the crowd during a reception in Washington Park while the band from Burke – the peninsula's predominantly black high school – played late into the afternoon. This was an entirely different scene, and an entirely different city government, than Charleston had ever known. The new, 12-member council was comprised of six black members and six white. Three of the council members were women, and two were Republicans. Some were older, and some were very young – Riley was still a month away from his 33rd birthday. For many people, it was an exciting time. But some older natives felt only trepidation. This was change, and that was not often welcome in Charleston.

Long after the crowd dissipated, and the businesses on Broad Street closed for the night, the mayor returned to City Hall. Using his new set of keys, Riley – with his lawyer buddies Bill Regan, Thomas Tisdale and Robert Rosen in tow – decided to check out the mayor's office without the distraction of staff or audience.

The mayor's office encompasses the back half of City Hall's second floor, with smaller offices on either side of it. It is a room wider than it is deep, with windows looking north and into Washington Park. There are two doors that open into the main hall, but they were permanently locked and no longer used. In all, it is a warm, comfortable and elegant room.

For hours, the men sat in the office drinking beer and smoking cigars, laughing and telling stories. It had taken nearly a year, but they had arrived. And now there was finally a moment to relax. But Riley was rarely content to sit idle, and at some point decided to redecorate. At the time, the mayor's office was dominated by a large conference table where City Council held its Ways and Means Committee meetings. It was pushed up against the mayor's desk, forming a great "T" in the room. The table had to go.

There were no open-meeting laws in the 1970s, so council could sit at the table and hash out any deals it wanted without the public – or the press – in attendance. Riley would eventually stop that practice, and didn't even want the table in his office. Together, the mayor and his friends scooted the table up against one wall, moved the flags and finally put the desk exactly where Riley wanted it. Satisfied with their work, they turned out the lights and headed for home.

The next morning, when Riley arrived for his first official day on the job, he found the mayor's office had been restored to its former arrangement – conference table in the middle of the room, abutting his desk. City Hall staffers had arrived earlier and panicked when they realized someone rearranged the office. It would take months for Riley to convince long-term employees that things were different now.

During the campaign, Riley's pollsters found that in parts of Charleston the fear of crime was worse than in New York, Cleveland, Detroit or any other big city. The polling suggested a panic that went far beyond even Charleston's less than stellar crime rate. This was a problem, Riley knew, because the fear of crime could be just as polarizing – if not more so – than actual crime itself. After all, crime affected only a certain number of people. Fear could afflict anyone. And in Charleston, it was epidemic.

The mayor's first priority was increased police protection in the most crime-ridden areas of the city – the East Side and the Neck Area of the peninsula. Before the end of December, he announced plans to begin "team policing" throughout the city. The police department would set up substations, which he called "storefronts," in some neighborhoods by February. The idea was for police officers and the people they protect to become better acquainted, and the best way to do that was have the same officers on the same streets every day. The department would start with one substation on King Street and another at Meeting Street Manor, a public housing development.

Riley secured the money for his substations from the federal government. A mid-Census count claimed Charleston had lost nearly 12 percent of its population between April 1973 and 1974, and that cost the city $250,000 in federal revenue sharing. Mayor Schirmer had been arguing with Washington officials over the discrepancy – the city claimed it had added population – but had little luck. Riley took over the fight and soon recovered $166,000 of the lost money. That gave him the idea to hire more police with federal grants. Within months, he added 12 officers to the force. He would pay their salary, in part, with state and federal programs aimed at stopping drug-related crime and rehabilitating abusers.

It was a savvy idea, but amending the budget would prove troublesome. The former administration and City Council had set the 1976 budget before leaving office, and when the new council wanted to make adjustments, it led to the first fight of the new era. Some white council members wanted to eliminate a program designed to "educate and rehabilitate wayward black girls," a euphemistic description if there ever was one. The money stayed in the budget when Riley sided with the six black members of council. It was a box score that would become common in those first years.

Soon it became apparent that Riley's talk of equality and inclusion were more than kind words. He set up a committee to plan a black-history trail in Charleston complete with markers, plaques and brochures. This ran afoul of a similar panel established by Mayor Schirmer, but Riley believed that group was doing little more than spending money with few tangible results. Members of the Schirmer committee complained that Riley was confusing the issue. "Well, you've got a new mayor now," Riley told the group publicly. "I need a committee that can do more than ask for $50,000."

Riley wanted the community to see an immediate change in the city, not hear more talk about nebulous plans for some unspecified future date. Less than a month into his term, he declared Jan. 12 the beginning of the Rev. Martin Luther King Jr. week – a tribute to "a man of peace who led the historic battle against segregation and racism armed only with his belief in the equality and dignity of men." Riley and his council also voted to hang a portrait of the slain civil rights leader in City Hall. The mayor believed the portrait was a symbolic message that all were welcome in City Hall.

But some people did not see it that way.

During his first months in office, Riley set up a number of boards and committees to study everything from annexation to city parks. The newspaper hailed Charleston's new era of citizen input, but others complained that Riley had gone overboard. Some of that criticism seemed to be thinly disguised disdain for all the new faces on these panels. A few even complained publicly about the King portrait in City Hall. One South of Broad resident wrote a letter to The News and Courier claiming, "The only justification for that would be to pay off political debts." Basically, the writer was accusing the mayor of pandering to black voters.

Riley expected some grousing from white residents; he had lived in the city all his life and understood old Charleston racial attitudes very well. But he was more surprised when a few black citizens publicly criticized him, too. Eugene Jenkins, the leader of an East Side grass-roots organization, said the mayor had promised him $20,000 for community development but refused to hand over the money. Riley had met Jenkins while touring the East Side in March 1976 and was initially impressed. At a meeting of the city's Commission on Redevelopment and Preservation a month later, however, Jenkins said he couldn't pay for his new programs to create jobs and improve recreation on behalf of the organization People United to Live and Let-Live. In front of a small audience, Jenkins screamed at the mayor.

"You have deceived me, you have deceived the people in the community who look to me for information," he said.

Riley's staff claimed they helped Jenkins apply for the funds, but the commission had decided against giving all its money to one organization without a clear plan for how it would be spent – a subtle critique of Jenkins' plans. Jenkins could hardly make a legitimate case that he'd been wronged. Two weeks before his outburst, the city had hired him as the first East Side community developer. But since he now suggested the mayor and City Hall had deceived him, Riley said he assumed Jenkins would resign.

"Sir, I am still doing the work in my community," Jenkins said.

"Well, we'll talk about that tomorrow," Riley said.

The mayor spent much of his first year courting James Island residents. In the 1960s, Mayor Gaillard had won a court case that allowed the city to annex across rivers, and he used that victory to claim much of West Ashley. Riley considered this one of Gaillard's greatest accomplishments, a move that saved Charleston from a rapidly diminishing population and tax base. He knew that a city had to grow to survive and, as the Census mid-decade count had found, Charleston was not growing very much. In 1976, the city had a population of only about 57,000.

The city was trying to annex property in the Neck Area of the peninsula before the newly formed city of North Charleston could take it, but that had become an uphill battle. In July, Riley went into full campaign mode, meeting Neck Area residents at Geer Drug Co. to explain how joining Charleston would save them money – and help the city grow. There was certainly an industrial tax base to tap, but the area had only about 11,000 residents. It would be a nice boost to the city's population, but other areas held far more promise.

The logical progression of what Gaillard started, Riley knew, was to move the city onto James Island. He'd wanted to do that since his days in the Legislature. By 1976 the island had about 32,000 residents, enough to boost Charleston's population to almost 90,000. That kind of growth would leverage more federal money for the city, and Riley believed services were more effectively delivered by one large government. For years, he had been a strong supporter of metro government. But there weren't enough people who felt the same to make any referendum feasible.

The biggest obstacle to annexing James Island was its public service district. Although the island was largely rural, many of its residents lived within the boundaries of a PSD that provided them some level of municipal services – mainly fire protection and garbage pick-up. In essence, the public service district was a small city government, and that meant politics muddied the water. Many James Islanders saw no benefit to joining the city, or paying city property taxes, when they already had fire protection and trash pick-up.

Riley tried to argue the PSD was a duplication of services, that the city could do a better job. He pointed out the public service district's taxes had gone up 142 percent in the past six years, while the city's rate had climbed by 33 percent. Riley hosted public meetings through the spring and summer, but ran into strong resistance. Eventually, he appointed a committee to study the annexation of only those James Island neighborhoods not in the public service district.

The mayor did not realize it at the time, but he was starting a fight that would last for decades.

In August 1976, several members of the city's Spoleto Festival committee walked into Riley's office to deliver bad news: they had just returned from a disappointing trip to Italy and recommended Charleston scrap its plans to become the American site of the international arts festival. Spoleto, they feared, would be a disaster and drive the city to financial ruin. Better to avoid the trouble, these committee members said, and bow out before it was too late.

It was not what the mayor wanted to hear. The Spoleto Festival was scheduled to open in nine months.

Spoleto had been in the works secretly for nearly two years. The idea was for Charleston to host a 10-day arts festival that would become the U.S. counterpart to Spoleto, Italy's Festival of Two Worlds. This was the brainchild of Italian-born composer Gian Carlo Menotti, a two-time Pulitzer Prize-winning composer who wrote his first opera when he was 11. He won both Pulitzers in the 1950s, for *The Consul* and then *The Saint of Bleecker Street*, but was perhaps best known for his Christmas opera, *Amahl and the Night Visitors*.

In 1958, Menotti chose Spoleto for the site of his festival because it was an inexpensive, small town with appropriate venues to host operas and concerts. The "two worlds" part of it was the co-mingling of European and American arts. He wanted Italian audiences to see American performers, which he believed would give those artists a truly sophisticated audience – a not-so-subtle dig at U.S. arts patrons. When the festival became a success, he wanted to start a companion festival in America. Soon, the National Endowment for the Arts got involved.

The NEA staff advised Menotti to find a Southern city for his festival. They feared an American Spoleto would become lost in the noise of the busy Northeast corridor, and believed Menotti could make more of an impact in the South. Menotti looked at Winston-Salem and Savannah before finally approaching Charleston on the advice of a friend. The city set up a committee to study it, and stacked the panel with influential locals, including College of Charleston President Ted Stern and banking executive Hugh Lane. Riley had been asked to join the board before he was elected mayor.

The public announcement of the Spoleto Festival came in March 1976. The committee had originally wanted to start the festival that year, but there was no way to plan it around the myriad Bicentennial events already scheduled in the city. Instead, Spoleto Festival USA would open on May 25, 1977. The program would feature two opera companies, 17 chamber music concerts and 14 ballets. In all, the festival would include 65 performances. Menotti released a statement promising to enrich the city's very life. "Art is not something for after lunch … it's something to live with … it's part of life itself."

Riley believed the festival would change Charleston forever. It would expose local residents to more culture than they had seen in centuries and draw thousands of visitors to the city, which was just beginning to see the economic benefits of tourism. In June 1976, Charleston had hosted classical pianist Charles Wadsworth at the Dock Street Theatre as a dry run for the festival, and the event was an outstanding success. The Holy City, it appeared, was ready for the high arts. But the festival's own committee was suggesting the show close before the first curtain was raised.

The Festival of Two Worlds was a financial mess, according to these local committee members, and they feared Menotti's plan was to make Charleston liable for the Italians' debt. They also thought the composer was disagreeable, hard to work with. They argued that Spoleto looked like more trouble than it was worth – even if it attracted visitors, where would they stay? The city might have to bring in cruise ships to accommodate guests. A better plan, the committee argued, would be for the city to start its own arts festival without Menotti.

Riley thought it would be a disaster to back out of the agreement, and tried to stall. But a few weeks later, in September, the Spoleto Festival Committee met on a Sunday in a Queen Street bank's boardroom. The mayor knew what would happen before he sat down. As soon as the meeting was called to order, Hugh Lane made the motion to cancel Spoleto. Riley was in a panic. One of the festival's greatest boosters, Ted Stern, was out of town, and the mayor had no idea how the other board members felt. But fresh from the Legislature, Riley resorted to the only trick he could manage: parliamentary procedure. "I move to table that motion."

"This is a once-in-forever chance," he said. He went on to make an impassioned plea for the festival, as best he could off the cuff.

Riley feared he had just made himself look foolish, but surprisingly his motion carried by one vote. Spoleto still had a majority of the committee's support, albeit barely. The losing side did not put up much of an argument; Lane and several others decided it would be best if they stepped down. With their departure, the remaining members looked at the mayor and said, "Now you're chairman of the board."

Riley suddenly had the weight of Two Worlds on his shoulders. That afternoon he walked into his house and was forced to tell Charlotte, "You're looking at the chairman of the board of Spoleto." He knew what she'd think of him taking on additional duties, but he would soon hand the reins to Stern, who he felt was more qualified for the job. Later, the mayor said that meeting – that vote of confidence – was the true beginning of Spoleto in Charleston.

The rift on the Spoleto board leaked within days. Nella Barkley, the festival's general manager, denied rumors that Spoleto had been cancelled, but did little to dissuade them when she said there were "problems" she could not talk about. "I will be very relieved to discuss things openly when I can." A few days later, Lane showed no such reservations. He claimed the box office receipts for Spoleto would be used to defray the costs of other festivals – not finance Charleston's.

"All donations raised nationally would go into a common pool," Lane said. "These changes from the original plan, in my judgment, made the funding of the Charleston festival ... infeasible and meant, as I interpreted it, that we could be raising money and selling tickets, the proceeds of which would not necessarily be used for the

American festival. I felt that if I continued my efforts to bring a Spoleto Festival to Charleston that it would at least be an endorsement of fiscal and management policies to which I cannot subscribe."

Riley was suddenly in a tight spot. He didn't want to damage the festival, but agreed with Lane's contention that money raised in Charleston must stay in the city. The mayor said he would iron out these differences with Menotti soon, and promised a positive outcome. Barkley was not so supportive and tacitly endorsed Lane's analysis. "I am not fundamentally in disagreement." By the week's end, Barkley had resigned as Spoleto's general manager.

Menotti was performing in Portland, Oregon when Riley tracked him down – after first checking with someone about the proper pronunciation of the composer's name. To avoid any social faux pas, Riley finally decided to just call him "maestro." The mayor invited him to Charleston for discussions, but Menotti had heard about the local controversy, the board resignations, and at first refused.

"I do not want to come to a place where I'm not wanted," Menotti said.

Riley assured him that Charleston most certainly wanted the Spoleto Festival, and finally Menotti agreed to meet. With some cajoling, the composer promised Spoleto USA would not be used to subsidize the Festival of Two Worlds or anything else. Later, David Rawle, who was involved with Spoleto for years, said Riley did nothing less than save the festival. He would have to do so often in the years to come. Menotti was crisis-oriented, prone to melodrama and he constantly pushed the mayor. But Riley knew what he could give and what he couldn't, and deftly conducted the maestro. He realized anyone who wrote his first opera at the age of 11 had to be high-maintenance, and took that into account.

Menotti's visit put the funding crisis to rest, but the festival's problems were far from over. Spoleto still had not been planned, and now didn't have a general manager. And the show was less than eight months away.

In October, James Island residents who wanted to be annexed into Charleston met with Riley at City Hall. The city had a merger referendum scheduled for Nov. 23 that would ask voters in the Neck Area, West Ashley's St. Andrew's Public Service District and James Island to join the city – and these residents wanted to run the campaign.

On James Island alone, Charleston stood to gain 32,000 residents, $388,000 in property taxes, as well as $273,000 in taxes on beer, wine and liquor and, more importantly, about $550,000 in federal revenue sharing. The mayor said in turn the city would spend more than $850,000 in fire and police protection on the island, and $250,000 on parks and leisure services. It would cost the city $83,000 more than it would gain in taxes, but it was growth – and that's what mattered to Riley. He gave the James Islanders his blessing to campaign on behalf of the referendum.

It was an ugly fall. James Island merger opponents put out a fact sheet that made false claims about city water rates and warned that islanders, if annexed, would be forced to pay personal property taxes on boats (which they already did). There was a nasty racial undercurrent in the fact sheet. It proclaimed James Island was safe while Charleston residents were afflicted by crime, implying crime would spread to the island. But the point that sent Riley into a rage was an assertion that the parks he promised to build on the island would attract "undesirables."

Riley went on television to refute the misinformation, but it did little good. The opposition had passion, momentum and a slick propaganda campaign working in its favor. The pro-annexation camp was simply outfoxed. On Nov. 23, the merger lost by a 2-to-1 ratio. All 11 James Island precincts voted overwhelmingly against joining the city. The city had spent $30,000 to find out that James Island, the St. Andrew's Public Service District and much of the Neck Area wanted no part of Charleston. The mayor had never suffered such a defeat.

"I really believe that they would have benefited greatly from improved services," Riley said. "The real loss in the long run will be theirs and not ours."

The Evening Post blamed the loss on an anemic campaign by merger supporters, an aggressive opposition and the typical fear of political change. But the paper's editorial board disagreed with the mayor on one point: The editors said the loss would hurt both the city and the areas that had refused to join it. This was the beginning of a decades-long struggle. James Island had won the first round, but it would not be the last they heard from Riley.

In December, Riley declared his first year as mayor a success. He told The News and Courier that a crackdown on delinquent taxes had brought in enough money to give city employees a raise. The city had a new focus on improving parks, and his program to rehabilitate East Side housing was well underway. But most importantly, Riley said, the new form of government was more open and representative of Charleston.

"Certainly if I had a hand-picked slate, then I would have reason to expect them to do what I want to. With single-member district council members, I have reason only to expect support because what I'm doing is right," the mayor said.

The mayor always maintained a public show of optimism and, in truth, it was a mostly accurate reflection of his attitude and personality. But he had his share of growing pains too. The merger referendum defeat ate at him, and he was working too many hours. One day a man stopped Riley in Washington Park and complained that he had sent a letter to City Hall but the mayor hadn't responded. After a few minutes of griping, Riley argued back – something he rarely did. He later called the man to apologize, but his staff said he was stretching himself too thin. "You need to delegate more," one staffer told him.

Riley had little time to slow down or delegate, however; he was putting together his first city budget and it included a radical plan to put even more cops on the streets. His $14.7 million budget called for a 15 percent tax increase, nearly all of which would be used to hire 19 additional officers and buy the equipment they needed. Riley knew any tax increase would be unpopular, but figured he was still in his honeymoon phase and could get away with it. Besides, no one could deny that the police department needed reinforcements.

The budget proved more unpopular with the fire department than taxpayers. The 1977 spending plan included 5 percent raises for all firefighters – and 10 percent for police officers. Firefighters called it an insult, a slap in the face, and claimed they deserved just as much as the cops. Riley argued that firefighter salaries were in line with the regional average, but the police in Charleston were paid far less than in other cities. He said the city had to offer better police pay to keep good officers and attract new ones, and City Council went along with him.

The firefighters did not give up so easily. Off-duty firefighters began to picket outside the homes of City Council members, and on Christmas morning stood in front of the mayor's Gibbes Street home. Riley could hear them through the window as the boys opened their presents, and when the family left for church they had to run the gauntlet of mad firefighters – some of whom carried signs that said "Longest Hours, Most Dangerous Duty, Lowest Pay. Why?"

The mayor was not offended by the demonstration; he actually found it mildly amusing. But he would not back down, even after the firefighters remained outside his house into the New Year.

Riley finally met with the firefighters on Jan. 4, 1977. They had moved their protest to the steps of City Hall, and there was no way to avoid them. But the mayor simply repeated what he said in the council meeting – Charleston firefighters are paid fairly, but police officers are underpaid. The firefighters again requested a mediator; once more Riley refused. Within days the city was preparing for a firefighters strike. The prospects concerned many people, given Charleston's unfortunate history with fire.

The protests continued for a month until City Council asked the Board of Firemasters to step in. The board promised a salary and benefit study comparing the Charleston Fire Department with ones in Columbia, Greenville and Spartanburg. But that did little to ease the tension. Eventually, firefighters went to state officials for help and asked voters to demand a "pay parity" ordinance that would tie Fire Department wages to police salaries.

The threat of a firefighter strike loomed throughout the spring, and those fears increased in April when Fire Chief Wilmot Guthke canned the president of the local firefighters union. Raymond Avant had made disparaging comments about the chief during an interview with a local TV station, and, after he was fired, claimed it was retaliation for insulting the chief and threatening a work slowdown. Guthke said Avant had violated several department regulations, one of which was providing a false address. Avant sued the city, and the lawsuit dragged on for two years before the courts ruled against him.

By then, the idea of firefighters being paid the same as police was long dead.

On May 25, 1977, Spoleto Festival USA held its opening ceremonies on the Cistern Yard at the College of Charleston – and the world took notice. Time, Newsweek, The

New York Times and the television networks parachuted in for coverage, giving the city more attention than it had seen since the 1969 hospital strike. But this news was overwhelmingly positive. Newsweek even called Riley "Charleston's Cagney-like mayor," describing him as a new Southern politician in the mold of President Jimmy Carter. The first night Tchaikovsky's opera *The Queen of Spades* was performed at the Gaillard, soon to be followed by Menotti's own *The Consul.*

For 12 days, Menotti, dance troupes and orchestras took over Charleston. By the time they were done, festival officials declared Spoleto a success – which meant it might come close to breaking even. It didn't. Local businesses were disappointed mostly by the lack of tourism generated by Spoleto. More than 80 percent of the tickets had been bought by Charleston residents despite an extensive regional marketing campaign. The festival had blocked off rooms in Savannah and Myrtle Beach to handle the overflow, but local hotel managers said they were no busier than any Memorial Day week. David Rawle told disheartened merchants the festival would pay off sooner than later, if for no other reason than all the publicity Charleston garnered by hosting Spoleto.

"We're in a perfect position for next year," Rawle said.

Ticket sales for Spoleto had exceeded expectations by more than $100,000, enough for the newspapers to declare the event a success. The News and Courier and The Evening Post credited Riley – along with Rawle, Ted Stern and Pug Ravenel – for saving Spoleto after Hugh Lane and Nella Barkley bailed out. Stern had taken over the local festival committee at Riley's request, and basically ran Spoleto out of the College of Charleston. The mayor had spent his time repairing relations with the local arts community, which initially eyed Spoleto warily. In April, Riley had gone so far as to declare "Symphony Week in Charleston."

After Spoleto ended, Riley and Charlotte flew to the Festival of Two Worlds in Spoleto. Italian officials had invited the mayor in order to cement their new bond. Alicia Paolozzi – a part-time Charleston resident who had put the city on Menotti's radar – paid for the trip and hosted the Rileys at her home. The mayor said the foreign press had been calling already, so the trip would benefit Charleston. No one could argue that Spoleto had earned the city a lot of favorable international attention. And the mayor finally got to see the festival his committee had criticized a year earlier.

Riley returned from Italy to find himself under attack from the one group he least suspected: The National Association for the Advancement of Colored People. The Rev. Omega Newman had criticized the city's hiring practices, claiming black applicants were passed over in favor of whites. His real complaint was the mayor's decision to fire a black city employee named Kent Byas. In June 1977, Byas was charged with six counts of obtaining property under false pretenses. He worked in a department that helped local residents find new housing when they were displaced to make way for city projects. If families met the criteria, they were given $200 in moving expenses. The police said Byas was taking a portion of that $200 from every resident he helped. Riley fired him immediately.

Newman said the mayor had convicted the man without a trial and denied him due process over claims that he had stolen just $535. Riley said any city employee facing criminal charges would be suspended, but when those charges were related to the person's job, "firing is the only alternative." He offered Byas the option of taking his grievance to the city's personnel committee, but believed he'd done the right thing – no matter what Newman said.

The criticism stung Riley. For his entire political career, he had made a point of inclusiveness and was actively recruiting African-Americans to work in city government. But now he was taking heat from both sides. He was criticized for Martin Luther King Jr. week and had been attacked for allowing a portrait of Denmark Vesey to be displayed at Gaillard Auditorium. Vesey was a free black man convicted of plotting a slave revolt in Charleston during the 1820s. Locals claimed Vesey planned to slaughter the city's white residents as part of his uprising, although the evidence used by the court to convict and hang Vesey had been conveniently lost. The controversy over Vesey would not die anytime soon, even though Riley argued that Vesey was simply a man trying to overthrow the evil institution of slavery.

The mayor was so focused on the concerns of the black community that some locals started calling him "LBJ," short for Little Black Joe. Herbert Fielding even called Riley one day and warned, "You need to stop doing so much for black people. You are hurting yourself in the white community. This will damage you politically."

Fielding was right – Riley had angered some whites. But the mayor was not overly concerned. More than anything, he was touched to hear concern in his friend's voice, as well as the acknowledgment that he was trying to do the right thing, that he was making a difference in the black community. "Herbert, it's OK," he said. "I have to do this. It is important that I'm responsive to African-American neighborhoods."

Soon after Newman's tirade, The News and Courier defended Riley in an editorial that sported the unfortunate headline "Mayor Riley and Black People." The editors credited the mayor for his restrained attitude, his defense of civil rights, and lamented that "what he gets for all that is a panning from black critics." The paper defended Riley's firing of Byas and warned that "If it were not for Mr. Riley and his sense of fair play, spokesmen for disgruntled black citizens would have a hard time getting their complaints heard beyond their own small circle. They just don't have much of a following. To make their attack this week, they took advantage of the mayor's personal desire to turn council meetings into a forum for community complaints."

City Councilman Robert Ford, who had campaigned against Riley in 1975, argued that the mayor's hiring practices were fair game and not all that laudable. Ford also rose to the defense of Byas, claiming the man had been railroaded – that a white person accused of embezzlement would have been given a chance to resign and get a job somewhere else. But that was unlikely (and would be proven untrue years later). The courts took one look at the evidence Riley used to make his decision and, within months, sentenced Byas to three years in prison.

Race relations in Charleston suffered a much more serious threat by summer's end. On Friday, Aug. 26, a dozen local high school teams converged on The Citadel's Johnson Hagood Stadium for the annual Sertoma Charities Football Classic. The event, in only its seventh year, had already become a local tradition. Area football teams faced off for short games in advance of the season, with the proceeds from ticket sales going to help Lowcountry charities. The Sertoma Club had raised more than $100,000 since starting the event.

That night, more than 10,000 students and parents were in the stands cheering on their teams, even though the scrimmages had proven mostly uneventful. North Charleston and C.A. Brown opened the jamboree, but neither was able to score. Garrett managed just 8 points against Lincoln. The most impressive team of the night by far was Stall High, which put up 24 points on Hanahan – nearly equaling the 27 points scored by the 11 other schools combined. It was a night of defense on the field. The offense was elsewhere.

Late in the evening, a group of kids – some of them apparently not even in their teens – rushed the stadium ladies room. Then they ran into the parking lot, throwing rocks and assaulting people on the way to their cars. Two teenage girls were thrown to the ground, beaten and then molested by more than 40 boys. Before it was over, 18 people had been sent to the emergency room. It was simple luck that no one was killed.

The finger-pointing began the next day. Some people who had been at the stadium criticized the police for standing by and watching the attacks without subduing the first suspect. A few people claimed the officers had said they weren't allowed to make arrests. This was soon interpreted as a nefarious racial policy by Riley, since most of the kids in the mob were black.

By Monday, people were demanding to know what the mayor was going to do about the violence. Riley could feel the eyes of the entire city on him. It was time to act on the promises he made on inauguration day, and he knew everyone would be watching closely.

But most of Charleston's problems could not be solved overnight, a lesson Riley was destined to learn the hard way.

A Golden Haze

On Aug. 31, 1977, nearly 250 people gathered in the James Island High School gym to launch their own investigation of the violence at the Sertoma Charities Football Classic. They wanted a citizens' committee to investigate the incident because they didn't trust Charleston police. The city, they believed, was the problem. As they sat in the stifling gymnasium, the crowd grew angry. Their criticism of the city, its police department and the mayor became more racially tinged every minute.

One man told the crowd he had to do the police's job for them, grabbing a "black boy" who was causing trouble at the game and putting him in a headlock. When the man said he hit the child, the people cheered and applauded. But when a white teacher from Burke High, which sat next to Johnson Hagood Stadium, noted that a black teen was injured in the attacks, the crowd broke into jeers and catcalls.

"We don't want your kind," one woman screamed.

Hollywood could not have scripted a more stereotypical Southern, lynch-mob response. But not everyone took such hateful tones. A West Ashley man tried to calm the audience, explaining how three black police officers had surrounded him, his wife and their 12-year-old daughter to protect them from the violence. And Ed Varner, the James Island chiropractor chosen to lead the citizens' investigation, urged the crowd to be fair. "If you hate a person, hate his personality, not because of the color of his skin."

But it seemed the entire debate was about skin color. The mayor had said there was no evidence the incident was racial, that the victims were black and white, but some people thought otherwise. Reports indicated all the suspects were black, which gave the crowd all the ammunition they needed to perpetuate stereotypes.

Riley supporters did not think it coincidental that the most vocal criticism came from James Island. They didn't want to be annexed by the city but were happy to sit across the river and condemn it.

Chief Conroy tried to appease the critics, conceding it wasn't always fair to equally blame blacks and whites. But he said the evidence suggested the trouble started with an attack on a black youth named Edward Taylor. According to Taylor, he was attacked in the stadium bathroom by five white kids, one of whom hit him in the eye with brass knuckles. The story seemed to fit the facts, as Taylor was the first person treated by paramedics on the scene. City Councilman Robert Ford said he saw a group of black teenagers chasing whites outside the stadium, and assumed the fleeing kids were the ones who had assaulted Taylor. Soon black ministers announced their own study, fueling the perception that this was a black-versus-white incident.

The idea that white kids might have started the melee did not sit well in some quarters. Critics said Conroy's explanation only proved the city pandered to black residents. But the chief said his officers were more focused on getting people safely out of the parking lot than chasing the teens. He pointed out there were 10,000 people in the parking lot, and three-dozen cops couldn't be expected to control that many people. The best course of action was to help victims, he said. But that was not what anyone wanted to hear.

The Sertoma Club Board of Directors quickly announced they would return to Johnson Hagood Stadium for the next football classic, and Riley was relieved by the board's political courage and level-headedness. It reinforced his message that the incident was an aberration. He even attended a high school game between C.A. Brown and Garrett to show there was no danger. Then he went on TV to outline his plans for increased police protection. Shortly after he received the police report on the incident, Riley went home and spent four hours outlining a speech he would deliver live the next evening. The mayor promised stricter crowd control at games, including assigned seating. Arrests, he promised, would be much more common for any disturbance.

"Those who commit assaults or are guilty of disorderly conduct will not be given a warning, will not be ejected from a game, they will be arrested and taken to jail," Riley said. "The potential for more violence caused by an incident like this must indeed make it a more serious offense. I want the message to ring loud and clear – one who assaults the person of another in the city of Charleston must be prepared to lose his freedom."

Riley understood this was a test of his ability to lead. Everyone wanted to see what he would do, and the mayor felt the pressure from the citizens' groups and the media. He also knew some people already eyed him suspiciously. He was Little Black Joe, after all, and his critics assumed he would cover up – or minimize – black crime because he had been elected on the strength of African-American voters. But that conspiracy theory did not take into account one bit of contradictory evidence: Crime had been the other cornerstone of his campaign. His position on policing was hardly liberal. Riley knew that, more than anything else, he had to keep the city safe and reassure people the police were doing all they could.

News and Courier columnist Barbara Williams called the Sertoma violence the mayor's "trial by fire," and noted he handled the crisis in a forthright manner that surprised many people. He came off tough and strong. "Some note that if Riley had been considered anything less than a racial moderate, the reaction would have been far different. But he could give the speech he gave without major repercussion because of his reputation of moderation in the black community."

After Riley announced his plans, the issue slowly died down. In the following weeks, the tension eased and there were no protests – although the police struggled to arrest anyone related to the mob violence at Sertoma. But there would be other chances, more violence to shock Charleston before things got any better.

The Sertoma incident was one of the few stories that could distract Charleston from another growing controversy. In July, Riley had announced plans for the city to work with a private developer to build a giant hotel and convention center on the site of the old Belk property at King and Market streets. The department store had moved to a shopping center in West Ashley, selling its property in the middle of downtown for just under $1 million. The building had been demolished and planning for a facility on the site was underway. The mayor said the city would add a parking garage to support the convention center.

It should not have been a surprise to anyone. The mayor had mentioned the facility months earlier while talking with reporters about the downtown parking shortage. And in 1976, a hotel-convention center for the central business district was one of the primary recommendations in a revitalization study conducted by the consulting firm Barton-Aschman Associates of Washington. The consultants said a 350-room hotel wouldn't compete with the Francis Marion Hotel a few blocks to the north, and would likely prove to be the economic game-changer Charleston desperately needed.

In most cities, the redevelopment of an indisputable eyesore would have been lauded as a vision of urban renewal. But this wasn't most cities. In Charleston, some people believed any change was a cardinal sin.

About a month after detailed plans for the complex were unveiled, the Preservation Society of Charleston asked the city for a "serious reconsideration." The society opposed plans to demolish parts of other buildings in the central city. They suggested limiting the size of the hotel-convention center to the Belk property – or simply building a parking garage for another department store and other shops. The next week, downtown residents formed the Charlestowne Neighborhood Association and elected Nancy Hawk as its president. Hawk, who had challenged Riley in the 1975 election, did not care for his hotel-convention center plan – and she wasn't the type to suffer in silence. Her appointment as neighborhood association president solidified Hawk's role as Riley critic-in-chief.

At first, the mayor tried to mollify the opposition. He argued that the center would revitalize downtown, bring in nearly 1,000 jobs and fill the city's coffers with new tax revenue. "If we don't rebuild the tax base, people won't be able to afford to live in the historic area. If we kill this opportunity … it would be the worst kind of crime for us and those who follow us." But Riley soon found he could not reason with his critics. He had started a fight with the single most powerful force in the city of Charleston – history.

At the beginning of the 20th century, Charleston was an insular society dominated by the elite South of Broad residents. They prided themselves on following the traditions of their ancestors, lived and socialized only among themselves – and controlled the city's politics. What happened above Broad Street seemed to concern them very little, even as the town sank into deeper economic depression and crime. Although few of these people ventured far from the shopping district on King Street, they did not want anyone else to touch their city. They held a powerful nostalgia for everything that was Charleston, and the one thing they hated above all else was change.

In 1920, the Society for the Preservation of Old Dwellings was formed at an afternoon tea in the front parlor of 20 South Battery. The society was born in response to the feared demolition of the 1802 Joseph Manigault House, one of the thousands of wonderful old homes and buildings spread across the Charleston peninsula. Despite massive fires, hurricanes and earthquakes – and a handful of military invasions – old Charleston still looked much as it did in the early 19th century. Some blocks dated back to the 18th century. Susan Pringle Frost, a suffrage activist and one of the first female Realtors in Charleston, said she looked at the city's architecture "partly through a golden haze of memory and association." Many residents felt the same, so Frost had little trouble organizing the society.

Frost claimed her group did not fear development or growth – they just wanted it to occur elsewhere in the city. She said that "members of our society are not opposed to progress, that we would like to see industries, smoke stacks, and everything that would advance Charleston commercially, come once more to Charleston; but we want them properly located, and not at the expense of the beauty and charm of Charleston's distinctiveness, which annually brings so many visitors to its doors."

In 1931, the society persuaded City Council to enact zoning ordinances to protect historic structures – the first laws of their kind in the country. For once Charleston was considered a national model, and the society's work sparked similar movements in other cities. The laws were somewhat strict. The city designated 138 acres of the peninsula as the "Olde and Historic District," an area that would eventually grow to protect and regulate nearly 5,000 historic buildings. And the city established a Board of Architectural Review to police the alteration, renovation or demolition of any building in that district. In 1957 the society renamed itself the Preservation Society of Charleston, and its membership rolls grew larger each year. In Charleston, nothing was held in higher regard than its historic façade.

"Let us keep to the things that have stood the test of centuries," Frost once said.

The mission of the Preservation Society proved immensely popular. Even though it went against the local conservative mindset, many residents welcomed a quasi-governmental body charged with nothing less than telling people what they could do with their own property. Their devotion to the past was so ingrained they considered it a solemn duty to stop the "desecration" of Charleston's historic landscape. That attitude would only spread.

In 1947, the Historic Charleston Foundation was established to save aging peninsular houses and promote their preservation through annual house tours – similar to the open houses the Preservation Society sponsored. The foundation used this money for various local projects: it saved the Bennett Rice Mill, helped the Charleston Museum pay off the mortgage on the Heyward-Washington House, bought the Nathaniel Russell House to showcase the finest examples of early 19th century neoclassical architecture and funded the rehabilitation of the Old Exchange Building's pediment. Two decades later, Nancy Hawk co-founded another preservation group, the Save Charleston Fund, and fought to protect old warehouses on East Bay Street and thwart the construction of downtown high-rises. Her fight was so popular it propelled her into the 1975 mayor's race. And now her devotion to preservation would draw Hawk into another campaign against Riley.

For some residents, opposition to the hotel-convention complex, initially called Charleston Center, had little to do with preservation. The city proposed demolishing the back end of some Meeting Street buildings, but would save their façades and as much of the buildings as possible. Although some preservationists considered the idea heresy, they believed the greater threat was tourism. In the past year, the number of tourists flocking to Charleston had grown by 20 percent, due in part to the Spoleto Festival, the Miss USA Pageant broadcast from the stage of the Gaillard Auditorium and an aggressive advertising campaign. Slowly, the city was earning a reputation as a pleasant, year-round vacation destination. When it was too cold to go to the beach, visitors could tour any number of historic homes and gardens. It was becoming a regular industry for the city.

Many peninsular residents detested the tourists, the congestion, the horse carriages that clopped by their homes all day. These visitors littered in their yards, one man told the newspaper, while the horses polluted the streets and residents tripped over fishing gear on The Battery. Some older residents said they didn't want to live in that atmosphere, and threatened to move to the wilds of West Ashley. Far too many mornings they had seen people on historic district streets climb out of their cars, where apparently they had slept all night.

Tourism business owners said the naysayers were looking for quick and easy solutions that didn't exist. But Riley tried to appease his neighbors. He ordered sanitation workers to clean up the streets more diligently and asked City Council to consider a number of ordinances to regulate downtown tours. The mayor even suggested that carriage horses wear diapers. None of these solutions came easily. Many city officials were wary of tourists and new laws to regulate them. City Councilman Rutledge Young, whose district covered half the historic district, said Charleston had to walk a delicate tightrope.

"The Southern tradition is that we ought to welcome these people. They spend a lot of money and create a lot of jobs," Young said. But if things get out of control, tourism will "kill the goose that laid the golden egg."

That was an argument that would not subside anytime soon. In fact, it was a debate destined to become an indelible catchphrase in modern Charleston's history.

Before he even suggested Charleston Center, Riley knew it would be difficult to build such a massive project in the heart of the old city. For more than a decade, development had been moving away from downtowns and into the wide-open suburbs. That was killing a lot of American cities, as Riley learned from his work with the National League of Cities and the U.S. Conference of Mayors. He knew it was essential to jump-start the downtown economy, and believed this complex would do it. The hotel and its convention center would be a catalyst, an economic generator. But he had lived in Charleston long enough to know it would be controversial. "There was always a group ready to say we're going to tear the place up," he later recalled.

When the mayor didn't immediately give in to their demands, downtown residents and preservationists launched a full-scale campaign. The head of the Preservation Society threatened to cancel the group's fall tour of homes if the city continued on its reckless course. A defiant mayor called his bluff, suggesting he do just that. Hotel opponents soon flooded City Hall to protest during council meetings, so mad their venom permeated the old room. One night, a South of Broad lady walked up to Riley and did the harshest thing she could imagine: She stuck her tongue out at him. He did his best not to laugh.

Another night, the tension got so bad Riley was forced to call a recess. When the people in the audience got up to stretch their legs, the mayor remained at his desk on the podium. He soon heard a commotion, looked up and saw one particularly stocky – and angry – man charging him with fists clenched. The man was about to swing when Councilman Danny Richardson, a former stevedore and good friend of the mayor, grabbed him in a bear hug. Riley was shaken. If the man had landed a blindsided punch, he could have been seriously hurt. That is how mad change made Charlestonians.

By late November Riley was running his own campaign, lobbying local business leaders to support the hotel-convention center complex. When The News and Courier lauded Hawk's new neighborhood association for protecting itself and the city, the mayor responded with what would become a Riley trademark: a multi-page letter dissecting his critics and methodically outlining his point of view. The newspaper printed the full text of Riley's letter, which took up parts of three pages. The mayor argued that the city had taken strong steps to regulate tourism and detailed his plan to create additional green space downtown and clear up traffic with more mass transit. He did not mention Charleston Center, but chastised his neighbors for failing to show up when he first asked for citizen input.

But by then, that was no longer a problem for the mayor.

The Historic Charleston Foundation eventually joined the critics and called for a study of the proposed complex. The group feared a hotel with 400 rooms may be "more than this area can support." They were disappointed that the proposed height of the building was 99 feet in places, and suggested the center would spawn too much congestion. They even wanted a smaller parking garage – 500 spaces instead of 750. The foundation, like the Preservation Society, opposed the demolition of any King Street buildings – no matter if their façades were saved. Riley listened to all these demands, but he would not back down.

Eventually, all these complaints would be repeated – in court.

After two years in office, Riley believed Charleston was on the right track but the city hadn't grown as much as he wanted. He spent the spring of 1978 fighting the James Island Public Service District's bid to expand sewer service, knowing that it could stifle his annexation efforts. He also found himself constantly at odds with North Charleston Mayor John Bourne over control of the Neck Area of the peninsula. The area was mostly a collection of poor neighborhoods, but they were surrounded by the industrial heart of the region. That was a tax base worth the trouble, and Riley believed even the neighborhoods would be far more valuable one day. But Bourne was just as determined, in part because North Charleston desperately wanted to surpass Charleston in population.

Riley did not shy away from the fight. He knew people had questions about him, and was sensitive to the idea that people considered him mild-mannered, a lightweight. People who said that didn't know him. Riley could be a brawler and, between his tussles with Bourne and the preservationists, it was beginning to show. His friends told The News and Courier that Riley's critics could no longer call him "The Boy Mayor."

His true mettle should have been apparent from the city's attempts to beef up law enforcement. Riley had added 23 officers to the force, and his team-policing concept had stopped the city's rising crime rate for the first time in years. Charleston police now solved 21 percent of crimes in the city – not a particularly great statistic, but better than the abysmal 9 percent it had been before officers were assigned to specific neighborhoods. The city was safer, but crime would continue to plague Charleston.

A few days before Riley outlined the police department's improvements in his 1978 State of the City address, former city alderman Peter Lempesis was shot to death in front of his Columbus Street dry-cleaning store. The coroner ruled the death a homicide, probably the result of a robbery gone bad. Lempesis was carrying $37 in his wallet, but the gunmen didn't have time to take it before they shot him and ran. Police arrested two teenagers for the crime in July, but a jury eventually acquitted the alleged triggerman. The other teen, who had turned state's evidence on his partner, later went to jail for 24 years on another charge after robbing and raping a local woman.

Shortly after the Lempesis murder trial, a Charleston police officer was shot and killed with his own gun while trying to stop shoplifters in the historic district. Riley visited the officer's family in the hospital and urged the community to get involved. He asked ministers to preach against crime and the Legislature to change criminal justice laws. The mayor wanted to make it tougher for criminals to make bail, and he wanted longer sentences. Just weeks after Riley lobbied the Legislature to support his crime measures, a mistrial was declared in the case of a man accused of killing a beer store owner. The key witness had been gunned down with a shotgun.

Riley went on a crusade, publicly criticizing the courts anytime a suspect was granted a low bail. In response, the governor named him the chairman of a statewide criminal justice task force. Although his critics claimed he was too liberal, Riley never wavered in his support for law enforcement – sometimes to the point that it threatened to hurt him politically. In April 1978, the Fraternal Order of Police called for an investigation of Chief John Conroy, who they accused of being inside The Copa, an exotic dance club, that allegedly was serving beer after hours. Riley said Conroy had every right to be out in the bars, that it was his way to "keep his finger on the pulse of the community."

Many people believed the complaint against Conroy was politically motivated. The man who made the complaint didn't live in Charleston, and asked reporters if the city would "cover this one up like Sertoma?" Riley stood by his chief, and eventually the complaint went away.

In March 1978, Riley shocked some downtown residents when he declined an invitation to the Hibernian Society's St. Patrick's Day Banquet. The annual event was a grand tradition, and it was unfathomable that an Irish mayor – who, along with his father, was a member of the club – would bow out. When The News and Courier called to ask why, Riley initially demurred. But finally he called out the Hibernians, starting a controversy that would plague the group for years. The mayor said he wouldn't attend the banquet because the society once again had not invited Lonnie Hamilton III, the first black chairman of Charleston County Council.

The year before, Riley had privately complained about the Hibernians' decision to snub Hamilton. He said the group always invited ranking public officials, especially the chairman of County Council. The Hibernians ignored his protests, and since he was already on the program and scheduled to make the annual toast, Riley kept the commitment. But he would not do that again. When the mayor took his concerns public, Hibernian Society President Carl Pulkinen called the club a "benevolent and social organization. Our by-laws prohibit the discussion of politics and religion. If Mr. Riley wishes to engage in politics, he must go elsewhere."

Pulkinen claimed the Hibernians sometimes invited public officials to their events, and sometimes didn't – there was no such thing as an automatic invitation. But some people believed the Hibernians had asked former Mayor Palmer Gaillard to give the response to their "toast to the city" instead of Riley because of his criticism. City Attorney Bill Regan soon joined the fight, telling the paper he would not go to the event either, "because I am sick to my heart of racism in this community." Regan said most members of the Hibernian Society weren't to blame, just the leadership.

Hamilton told the paper he appreciated the gesture of anyone who favored a color-blind community, and claimed the Hibernians had rules that prohibited blacks or women from becoming members. The Hibernians denied that, arguing that membership was available to anyone who was proposed by a member and had two sponsors. There was no discrimination – the Hibernians said any member could bring a guest of any color they chose.

Riley hadn't wanted to stir up controversy – he was a Hibernian, after all – but believed as mayor he had to make a leadership stand. New Orleans Mayor Moon Landrieu told Riley he had once informed the city's largest Mardi Gras krewe he wouldn't attend its annual ball if no black people were invited. Riley had never forgotten that story. That, he thought, is part of a mayor's job. So he would not shy away from the issue.

The next year, Riley would try his best to drag the Hibernians into the 20th century. He agreed to appear at the St. Patrick's Day banquet and bought two tickets, listing retired insurance executive Arthur J. Clement Jr. as his guest. He made no effort to disguise Clement's name – he listed it in full. When the tickets arrived in the mail, Riley was relieved; he hoped it meant the Hibernians were serious about members bringing anyone they chose. But when word reached society officials that Riley's guest was a prominent black activist, the mayor heard rumors that he'd ruffled feathers. The Hibernians would not admit this, however. President Marion

Stone told the newspapers that he "hadn't seen the guest list."

Clement told reporters he didn't consider his attendance "earth-shaking. If anything happens that makes me feel uncomfortable, I'll be surprised." And nothing did happen. When Riley and his guest walked through the door, a North Charleston doctor immediately walked up to Clement, shook his hand and told him they were glad to have him. Riley thought it was a wonderful gesture, and felt he'd done his job.

A month after Riley publicly snubbed the Hibernians, he found himself on the other end of racial controversy. City Councilman Robert Ford urged African-Americans to boycott Spoleto because the "black community is completely cut off" from the festival. Ford said only one black person sat on Spoleto's 24-member board, and there were none on its five-member staff. Riley argued that the Spoleto advisory committee included two dozen black members, and numerous black artists performed at the annual event. "Robert, you like to politicize everything," Riley said. "And an arts festival is not a political event."

Spoleto certainly didn't need bad publicity. The second festival was due to start in a month, and ticket sales were not nearly as strong as they should have been. Riley knew it would take time for the festival to catch on but had hoped to have all the city's hotel rooms booked, especially since there were so few. Unless something changed, it appeared the festival would lose money again – and it had already cost the city business. The Miss USA Pageant announced it likely would not return to Charleston for a third year, claiming – among other things – that it was too hard booking the Gaillard around Spoleto.

The city was betting heavily on Spoleto and Riley knew it had to be a success, sooner rather than later.

In August, Riley left City Hall by 6 p.m. most evenings and drove across the Silas Pearman Bridge. From atop the towering span he had a breathtaking view of his city, its expansive harbor as well as the barrier islands and Lowcountry saltmarsh spreading out beyond it. In the distance, the tiny manmade island of Fort Sumter glowed in the falling sunlight and, beyond that, the vast Atlantic shimmered in brilliant hues of blue and green. Riley never tired of the sight.

Once he reached Mount Pleasant, Riley turned onto Coleman Boulevard, following it to the Ben Sawyer Bridge and Sullivan's Island. He crossed Sullivan's until he reached the Isle of Palms and his summer home. It was a much longer commute than he had most of the year, when the short hop from Broad Street to Gibbes took only a couple of minutes. But the extra time in the car was worth it to uphold family tradition.

By 1978, Riley's sons had grown accustomed to this schedule and always joined him on his nightly baptism in the cool waters of the Atlantic. Joe and Bratton found it amusing when their father walked out of the breakers, his arms held high as if in triumph. Then he would retreat to the porch with Charlotte and have one of the two beers he might drink in a night.

This adherence to family tradition was in part learned behavior, but it was also a conscious decision to spend every moment he could with his family. City Hall had largely changed Riley's life. As a legislator, he was only one cog in a giant machine; as an administrator, his job was not only crucial – it was never done. Most of his routines pre-1975 had ceased to exist, so he decided to devote his hours away from the job to family.

Riley and Charlotte wanted to make the most of their children's early years. They knew once the boys were old enough to drive, their time with them would be scarce. So the mayor largely eschewed hobbies – he didn't play poker with the guys and wouldn't take up golf until his sons were old enough to play with him. When his friends asked him to go hunting, he politely declined unless Joe and Bratton were also invited.

Most of the year, Riley spent his weekends at Little League games, fishing with the boys, working in the yard with Charlotte – the flowers he planted every May along the beach house's front walk were a great source of pride for the mayor. They watched television as a family, the boys complaining that their notoriously frugal father wouldn't pay for cable. They often pointed out all the City Council members had it – a bit of trivia they knew from accompanying the mayor when he delivered handmade fruit baskets to his colleagues at Christmas. Finally, Big Joe sprang for his grandchildren to have more than three channels. Then, they could at least watch baseball with their dad.

Still, Riley's mayoral duties sometimes interfered with that family time. On the second and fourth Tuesdays of the month, when he presided over council meetings, he missed dinner with Charlotte and the boys. If he had to attend an evening reception, he showed up early, was first through the receiving line – and the first to slip out. He never drank at these events, not because he worried about appearances, but because it took up time. His top priority was making it back home in time for dinner at 6:30.

Riley sometimes found time for his friends during the day, and he used these breaks to bounce ideas off them or just unwind. He and his lawyer buddies – Robert Rosen, Tom Tisdale, and Capers Barr – often met at the King Charles Inn. It was a throwback meeting, reminiscent of a time when the city's attorneys ran everything in Charleston. Of course, all that had changed for Riley. He didn't think it was right to practice law while serving as mayor, so he left the firm in the hands of Barr and his cousin. But getting together with the guys was a way to feel normal and remember the old days. Rosen recognized the nostalgia better than anyone. He often arrived at the inn first, christening their table with a sign that read "The Broad Street Ring Meets Here."

Riley had much less time to spare once plans for Charleston Center began to take shape. In April 1978, the city won a $4.15-million Urban Development Action Grant to buy property surrounding the old Belk land, relocate some area businesses and widen Market Street. It was a major coup for the project. Hundreds of cities from around the country had requested a total of nearly $800 million, and the feds only had about $150 million to award. Charleston got every penny it requested, which helped because the cost of the project had risen to $48 million. Riley called the grant a sign that the city's program was "effective, well-designed and well thought-out" and said federal officials recognized Charleston was on the right path to "conservation and revitalization."

The preservationists and neighborhood associations did not agree with that assessment and filed a lawsuit. They questioned the city's ability to issue bonds for a project that would ultimately benefit a private developer. The Monday following the grant announcement, Riley was forced to defend the plan in a 9th Circuit courtroom. He said the area around the site was a blight on the community and the city was trying to revitalize the central business district.

Some of the buildings that needed to be partially demolished housed The Copa and the Corinthian Room – two places that featured semi-nude dancing girls – as well as the Lion's Head Inn, a hangout for Charleston's largely underground gay community. The city had started buying some buildings, and for a few months actually owned one of the strip clubs. This prompted Bill Regan to joke, more than once, that he needed to go down and check on their investment.

The city won the first round in court, but the Preservation Society appealed that summer. Riley had tried to appease them by giving preservationists a seat on the citizens committee he set up to review plans for the hotel-convention center. But when they shot down nearly every aspect of the project – it was too large, too tall and bad for the city – the mayor was livid. He said the committee's job was to evaluate the design, not determine whether the project was a good idea.

"That's not their function," Riley said. "This isn't multiple choice."

The preservationists suspected the committee was just for show, claimed Riley ignored eight of their 10 proposals – and they had little interest in "fiddling with the cosmetics." Henry Cauthen, executive director of the Preservation Society, said it was clear no one cared about the committee's opinion. Soon, the preservationists and neighborhood groups stirred up local merchants – who began to complain that the city was offering too little for their property. The mayor's signature redevelopment project was in serious trouble.

Riley spent the summer of 1978 fighting what he called "misinformation" being spread by several groups, particularly Hawk's Save Historic Charleston Fund. He noted that designers had already reduced the hotel's height by three stories, and argued the center would blend into surrounding property and prop up a commercial district that was quickly dying. The business owners who complained about competition would actually benefit from increased traffic, he said, and Charleston Center – along with the city's tourism management plan – would revitalize and save the peninsula. The preservationists disputed every point and criticized the plan so much that the newspaper even tired of reporting it. The fight would have to be settled in court.

On Aug. 31, 1978, the state Supreme Court gave the preservationists their victory. The justices ruled unanimously that the city could not go into business with a developer – or transfer powers of eminent domain to private business. "The critical issue in this case is whether the city of Charleston can condemn land and lease it to a private corporation for the construction of a parking facility and convention center containing rental commercial space. We believe it cannot." The court said the city couldn't evict existing businesses and offer their space to other private companies. The justices didn't see where the center provided enough public use to warrant the city using its powers of eminent domain.

The Preservation Society said the ruling protected historic buildings in Charleston more than they ever had been – and gave them a victory far beyond what they had sought. And that worried them. The mayor claimed the project would add millions of dollars to the city tax base and create 1,000 jobs – and the preservationists and downtown neighborhood associations had killed every bit of it. They quickly realized a court victory was not necessarily good public relations when News and Courier columnist Frank Gilbreth sarcastically praised the group for saving a dilapidated block of downtown Charleston from "ruin" by Mayor Riley and private developers.

Soon after they were ridiculed in print, Cauthen tried to moderate the group's message, claiming they had only wanted to reduce the size of the project. "The Preservation Society never objected to the development of … empty property. Our main position in opposition was the demolition of as many historic buildings as was involved … but we really think that vacant land should be developed for the tax base of the city."

It was too little, too late. By then, many people believed the Preservation Society was anti-growth and content to let Charleston die – the group had saved buildings just so they could sit empty and crumble. But the damage had been done and, public relations disaster or not, Riley conceded that the court ruling was a huge setback. He vowed to push on, but didn't sound overly confident.

Within days of the ruling, Riley was back at work. The state Supreme Court had provided the city a detailed roadmap of the proper way to use eminent domain. The mayor would study the justices' words closely and find a way to restructure the deal.

One way or another, Riley was determined to build Charleston Center.

A Walk in the Park

In January 1979, a Pennsylvania charity gave the city $600,000 to buy 14 acres of waterfront property on Charleston's lower peninsula. Appraisers valued the land at a little more than $1 million, and the Parklands Foundation's anonymous benefactors suggested the city use the gift to leverage enough federal money to purchase the lot outright. Riley said this gift would allow Charleston to build a "park of almost national significance" on the harbor.

And that was exactly the plan.

The mayor had coveted the Concord Street land for years. This rough collection of parking lots and marshland overlooked the Cooper River, the harbor and the abandoned island fort of Castle Pinckney. It was very nearly the last available waterfront property on the peninsula, and Riley knew it could rival even The Battery for the city's best view.

The problem was the owner had no intention of selling. William Murray, a developer, financier and Atlanta architect, intended to build a massive $75 million retail and residential complex on the property. It was Murray's announcement a few years earlier, in fact, that first drew Riley's attention to the acreage. Since then, the mayor had become determined to stop the development and to get the land.

Riley's idea had been percolating for nearly three years. Barely a month after he took office, a City Council committee reviewed an ordinance for waterfront conservation zoning drafted by the planning commission. The proposed law banned buildings on peninsular marshland and certain highlands along the banks of the Ashley and Cooper rivers. The council eventually punted on the idea – a holdover from the Gaillard administration – but the debate had been enough to draw out Murray, who showed up at City Hall to protest.

Riley thought Murray's idea was ghastly; it ran contrary to his vision for downtown Charleston. Well on his way to an apprenticeship in urban design, Riley believed that blocking public access to the water would hurt the city. The idea behind Charleston Center was to jump-start the central business district and bring in tourists. He thought those visitors – and locals – should be able to enjoy some of the most breathtaking views on the Eastern Seaboard without hotels or condominiums blocking their access. Privately, he even dreamed of opening up the State Ports Authority's waterfront property on the lower peninsula. He'd told his friend Thomas Tisdale that the port's Union Pier property just north of Murray's land one day might be the most valuable urban rehabilitation project in the United States.

Riley knew he had little chance of getting the port property, but he thought the city could acquire Murray's land. After taking a public relations hit for trying to use eminent domain on the Charleston Center property, he first tried to bargain with the developer. But when the mayor quietly made overtures, Murray claimed his land was worth about $12 million – but the value didn't matter because he wouldn't sell.

In October 1977, Riley had persuaded City Council to hire an appraiser, the first step toward buying, or taking, Murray's property. The mayor said as Charleston grew, there would be a much greater need for open spaces and public parks. And that meant more to him than the additional taxes Murray's planned "Market Square" development might bring in. But some people argued the city had more than enough open space already. Besides The Battery – the city's most famous overlook – Charleston had several significant waterfront holdings.

Decades earlier, a Midwestern philanthropist had given the city Brittlebank Park on the Ashley River; another couple donated Cypress Gardens, a pristine patch of land that included the only known cypress forest gardens in the world. It was a grand park, but in Moncks Corner – more than 25 miles away from downtown Charleston. And in the late 1960s, Charles and Elizabeth Woodward landscaped and rehabilitated North Adger's Wharf, the ruins of a finger pier on the Cooper River just south of Murray's property.

All that was not enough for Riley – he wanted the last open vista on the Cooper River. When Murray balked, the mayor went on the attack. He criticized the development, said it "defies my wildest imagination" to cram so many buildings on such a small piece of land. Out of the 13.4 acres, city planners estimated only 2 acres of it was high ground. Murray conceded he might have to fill some wetlands, but promised to plant shrubs to make up for the lost marsh grass.

Riley considered condemning the land, taking it with the city's powers of eminent domain – public relations be damned. But he thought better of it, and the idea for a waterfront park sat dormant until the Parklands Foundation came along.

The foundation was basically Charles and Elizabeth Woodward, the couple who had turned Adger's Wharf into a park more than a decade earlier. Riley had explained the dilemma and they agreed to help. They saw the park as an extension of what they had done at Adger's, which abutted the Murray property. So the couple set up Parklands to donate the money, an attempt to keep their names out of it.

The secrecy immediately put reporters on alert, and they smelled scandal. They suspected Riley was trying to take the land for developers who were his friends. Already, some downtown residents had started a rumor that the mayor's interest in Charleston Center had much to do with the fact that his father was in the real estate business. This mysterious donation seemed to support that conspiracy.

Riley fought with editors at the newspapers and managed to keep the worst allegations out of print – which wasn't too difficult since the reporters had no facts to back up the theory. The mayor wanted to protect the Woodwards from negative publicity, and knew that a whiff of scandal would make it nearly impossible to do that. It would not be the last time the mayor had to deal with such allegations.

In early March 1979, Riley asked the South Carolina Department of Parks, Recreation and Tourism to match the Parklands Foundation's $600,000 gift with federal pass-through money. He said $1.2 million would be enough to pay fair market value for the property. Murray said it did not matter – he would not sell, and told the newspapers that Riley's attempts to bully him made him look like a dictator.

This, the mayor realized, was not going to be any easier than Charleston Center.

Riley had spent the fall of 1978 trying to revive Charleston Center following the catastrophic state Supreme Court ruling. In September, he hinted that the convention center might be downgraded to a conference center in response to complaints about its size. He traveled to Washington to brief the President's Advisory Council on Historic Preservation on the project, and to "help correct misinformation spread about the project by the Save Historic Charleston Fund." But the negative publicity grew faster than he could combat it.

People who owned buildings near the site accused Riley of trying to intimidate them into selling. They claimed he regularly sent fire and building inspectors to harass them. Robert Kaiser, who owned five Meeting Street properties in the path of Charleston Center, accused the mayor of dirty tricks. One of his buildings, which housed the infamous Copa, had burned down over the summer and he claimed the city was attempting to prove it was beyond saving. The mayor conceded inspectors were checking downtown buildings, but denied it was harassment.

"There are no orders going out ordering people to fix up their property while this case is in the courts," he said.

Most of the center's opponents focused their ire on Riley instead of the city or council members. He had put himself in that position by becoming Charleston Center's biggest cheerleader and publicly fighting preservationists. The mayor had no qualms about feuding with anyone he believed was wrong – he would even take on the newspapers if he felt his redevelopment goals were criticized too harshly. But the newspapers were largely supportive of Charleston Center, and Riley. It became apparent that not everyone felt the same on Dec. 19, 1978, when a woman called a local television station to issue a death threat for the mayor.

"I'm not going to tell you who I am, but Mayor Riley will be killed tonight," the woman said.

An engineer at WCSC, the city's oldest television station, said the woman sounded "very serious," but before he could ask any questions, she hung up.

At that moment, Riley was presiding over a council meeting open to the public. The police sent extra officers to City Hall while others tried in vain to track down the source of the call. Within a week, Police Chief John Conroy ordered higher security at City Hall – the call was not the first threat. Police officers in plainclothes had been strolling the building's halls for two weeks, "checking for patterns of movement," the chief said. He conceded the security could be better. One City Hall employee said it wouldn't be hard to take better precautions. "It's always easy to improve on nothing."

Riley said little about the threats. Preservationists weren't exactly the violent type, and he considered the calls nothing more than scare tactics. Besides, the mayor had little time to worry about nebulous problems – there were enough real crises. In December the Spoleto Festival's new general manager had quit, claiming she could not work with Menotti. Weeks later, Ted Gould – the developer of Charleston Center – was sued over a similar project in Virginia. And some City Council members were lobbying for a 33 percent raise. Despite all these annoyances, Riley said in his State of the City address that Charleston's greatest era was just beginning.

The next week, Riley got a call at his home on Sunday evening that he felt certain was a prank call – probably from Bill Regan. Because the voice on the other end of the line said, "Is this Joe Riley? This is Jimmy Carter."

Riley knew the president, had ridden in the motorcade when Carter visited Charleston a couple of years earlier. He could not imagine why the president would be calling him, especially at home on a Sunday evening, and suspected he wasn't. But he decided to play along because he knew it was Regan. He could dish it out as well as he could take it.

"Hello Jimmy," he said. "How have you been?"

Riley kept it casual – dropping "Jimmy" into the conversation as much as possible to let Regan know he was in on the joke. But as the call continued, Riley had the slow and horrifying realization that he actually was talking to Carter. He immediately changed his tone, and changed "Jimmy" to "Mr. President." Carter, who called to talk about federal grants for the city, didn't seem to notice.

Riley didn't have much time to dwell on his faux pas, as the preservationists were on the attack, dragging the mayor into one battle after another. In February, a public meeting to discuss the project's environmental impact statement turned into a circus. Nancy Hawk and Henry Cauthen asked if their consultants could speak, and the mayor let them go first. When the consultants finished, the center's opponents heckled anyone who spoke in favor of it. They objected to every positive statement, mocked citizens who claimed the plan would revitalize the city.

Riley told Hawk and Cauthen they didn't understand the word "compromise." The city had already lowered the hotel's height by 37 feet and reduced the size of the parking garage and conference center. But Hawk called the hearing an illegal mockery of the process and walked out. Riley later called a news conference to demand an apology from Hawk and the Preservation Society for their "outrageous behavior." He said their opposition made him more determined than ever to build Charleston Center.

On March 8, more than 1,500 people attended an "appreciation reception" for Riley at the Gaillard Auditorium. The event was hosted by former College of Charleston President Ted Stern and County Councilwoman Marjorie Amos, who read a telegram praising the mayor from the president. Carter was apparently unfazed by their earlier phone conversation.

The reception was widely viewed as a prelude to Riley's re-election campaign. News and Courier columnist Barbara Williams had reported weeks earlier that a Washington pollster was surveying residents on the mayor's behalf. Although many of the questions were about civic issues – opinions on Charleston Center, an assessment of Police Chief John Conroy's job performance, the effectiveness of city services – some focused on possible mayoral candidates.

There was no shortage of potential hopefuls, and the rumors ranged from the plausible to the outlandish. Many expected Nancy Hawk to seek a re-match, and others believed City Councilman Robert Ford would run. A few suspected Riley friend state Rep. Robert Woods would launch his own campaign. There was even some speculation that two former mayors, Palmer Gaillard and Arthur Schirmer, were interested in the job. The poll asked about every one of them. But the mayor did not make an announcement during the reception. He did, however, concede the last three-and-a-half years had been the most exciting of his life.

For Riley, there was not much debate. He had too many projects in the works to walk away. Charleston Center was in jeopardy, the waterfront park still far too tentative. The mayor realized all these things might fall by the wayside under a new administration that did not share his goals or enthusiasm. The only reservation he had was his promise to Charlotte that he would serve just one term.

Riley had proven adept at separating his political and home lives, and working a mile from the house was much better for the family than spending half of every week in Columbia. Still, City Hall took up a considerable amount of time – but, he could argue, not much more than any other job. So he finally broke the news to Charlotte that he wanted to run again. His friends later joked that Riley told her it would be only one more term.

On Monday, April 2, Riley – surrounded by 100 friends – made it official. "We've made substantial progress on a broad and substantial agenda and I'd like another four years to complete the work we've started," he said. Riley vowed to continue the battle against crime and his quest to revitalize downtown. He would build Charleston Center and, if that hurt his chances for re-election, so be it. But it wouldn't. Within two weeks of Riley's announcement, every hopeful had quietly removed their name from contention. Even Republican Party officials said they would likely skip the mayoral race and focus on picking up a few City Council seats. By summer, Riley was all but assured of a second term.

Without an opponent in the mayoral election, Riley was free to spend the summer promoting the redesigned Charleston Center. He took his message directly to the newspapers, carrying architectural renderings and a slide show to illustrate just how much the hotel and convention center had been whittled down to placate the opposition. The time for compromise was over, Riley said. "The hotel can't be made any smaller. What we've got is this or nothing."

Within days, both The Evening Post and The News and Courier published largely positive editorials urging the city to stop fighting and "get on with it." The News and Courier noted nothing will ever satisfy the opponents, but the mayor had made a good-faith effort. And for the first time in a year, that seemed like a realistic option. On May 3, 1979, the state Supreme Court unanimously ruled in favor of the city's new plan for Charleston Center.

The justices said the city had an inarguable right to condemn property for the public good, so long as it was actually used for public space. The city had basically reconfigured its original plan based in part on advice from the court's previous ruling. It would build only a 532-space parking garage and manage it. No private property taken by eminent domain would be turned over to the developer. The preservationists argued that a parking garage served minimal public good, but would help developers tremendously. The court, however, had the final say. Bill Regan joked to the newspapers that, "I bet Riley's down there digging right now."

City Council approved a memorandum of agreement with the developers within a month.

And the preservationists would strike back before the ink was dry.

The mayor's efforts to redevelop downtown Charleston attracted the notice of the National League of Cities, the Smithsonian Institution and the U.S. Conference of Mayors. At a time when suburban sprawl was nearing its peak, Riley was rebuilding his inner-city's core business district – and doing it with great care. Projects that did not fit into his vision were dismissed out of hand, no matter how lucrative they might be. In June, the Academy of Contemporary Problems and the German Marshall Fund of the United States invited Riley to discuss urban development on a two-week tour across Europe. Riley said the trip would give him ideas, and it was a chance to take a vacation with his wife. The academy paid his way; the mayor paid for Charlotte to go with him. He wanted her to share the experience, and she watched as he studied European public spaces and found several ideas he would carry back to Charleston.

In his absence, City Council annexed 2,800 acres of West Ashley, a move that enlarged Charleston's total acreage by more than 20 percent. The city took in the immense Shadowmoss subdivision, large swaths of the Pierpont neighborhood, as well as land owned by Clemson University and the U.S. Department of Agriculture. The annexations did little to increase the city's population – most of the land was undeveloped at the time, although that would change – but it effectively killed any expansion of the St. Andrew's Public Service District.

Soon, Riley also had the land for his waterfront park. Murray had decided to deal, but told the mayor he wanted more than the city's appraisal of the land – $30,000 or $40,000 more at least. Riley was close, and wanted the park so badly he considered agreeing to the counter-offer. Finally, Bill Regan had to talk him down, tell him it was a bad idea to get caught up in Murray's numbers game.

"Joe, you are young, and if you pay more than appraised value for this land, you will get in political trouble," he said.

Regan was a smart attorney, and Riley trusted his instincts. He turned down the counter-offer. But the city had to find another way to let Murray believe he'd gotten the better deal. In the end, even the mayor conceded the plan was "complicated and quite unusual." Murray wouldn't take the city's offer in cash for the Concord Street property, but said he would trade it for 80 acres in Mount Pleasant that fronted Highway 17. The city took $1,275,000 – including $600,000 from the Parklands Foundation and $637,000 in matching funds from the federal Heritage, Conservation and Recreation Service – and bought the Mount Pleasant property. The owners claimed their land was worth much more, but donated the rest to the city as a charity tax write-off. Then the city traded its new land for Murray's.

The newspapers questioned the deal, speculated that friends of Riley had somehow made a tidy profit, but could find nothing illegal or unethical – or anyone who had gotten the better of anyone else. Riley ignored the criticism; he only cared that he finally had his waterfront park. After the papers were signed, there was a reception at the Colony House where Murray told the mayor, "You remind me of Winston Churchill."

"Bill, that's a lot nicer than when you called me Hitler," Riley said.

For the moment, everything was going Riley's way. Aside from a brush with Tropical Storm David that forced him to apply for federal clean-up funds, the mayor had a few good months. In October, proponents far outnumbered opponents at a public hearing on plans for Charleston Center. And two days before Riley won re-election in November, The News and Courier offered him an early victory present: an editorial supporting his hotel-convention center. The paper conceded that the plan wasn't perfect, but noted the developers had made one concession after another while the opposition piddled with technicalities. "We don't think that Charleston can do better at this point. It could do worse." Mainly, everyone was finished with the fight. Even the sardonic Ashley Cooper had tired of the grousing. Frank Gilbreth admitted he was just as bored with the Preservation Society's crusade as everyone else.

The opponents should have taken it as a sign: Riley was re-elected without opposition, he had the support of the city's two daily newspapers and the preservationists could no longer muster a majority at public hearings. But instead of slinking away, they turned up the rhetoric. In January 1980, PBS' MacNeil-Lehrer Report aired a testy debate between Riley and Nancy Hawk in which she called Charleston Center completely incompatible with the wishes of preservationists and downtown residents. "It is something very inappropriate – like putting a carnival next to a terminal nursing home." But that, Riley said, was exactly what he was trying to prevent: allowing downtown Charleston to become little more than a home for old folks.

The next lawsuit landed a month later. The National Federation for Preservation Law filed a request in federal court to stop the project from accepting any federal money – a tactic concocted with the Preservation Society and the Charlestowne and Harleston Village neighborhood associations. It was a more lethal strategy than contesting eminent domain. The preservationists already had delayed Charleston Center by years. Every month that passed, the costs went up – forcing the city to rely more heavily on federal dollars. The project simply couldn't be done without assistance from Washington.

A week after the lawsuit was filed Riley announced that the city's Tourism Management Study Committee would be put on hold. Preservation Society President Norman Olsen Jr. said Riley was "punishing downtown residents" for participating in the lawsuit against Charleston Center. The mayor denied it was retaliation, even when The News and Courier accused him of playing a little too much hardball. Riley said his legal staff could not work on tourism guidelines because all their time was being consumed defending the city against frivolous lawsuits.

The mayor didn't care how it looked, or what Olsen, Hawk or any of the other litigants said. He had public opinion on his side. And he quickly drew first blood in the new fight: the city successfully petitioned to have the new case heard in local U.S. District Court. And the National Federation for Preservation Law couldn't find a single Charleston attorney who would take the case.

For once, the federal courts moved more quickly than the state's. In late April, a U.S. District judge ruled the city could accept $7.1 million in federal grants to build the hotel and conference center. It was a key victory, and nearly took the fight out of the city's opponents. Only Nancy Hawk remained indefatigable. She papered the city with 2,000 handbills that claimed Charleston soon would be overrun with conventioneers and new hotels would rise on Concord Street – a not-so-subtle dig at Riley's planned waterfront park. But most of her colleagues were about ready to concede defeat.

The winter of 1980 had passed quickly. Civil rights pioneer Septima Clark held the Bible at Riley's second inauguration, and he began his second term the same way he did his first: working in the black community. The mayor planned to rehabilitate more East Side housing and persuaded City Council to pass a resolution promising that at least half the workers hired to renovate Hampton Park would live in neighborhoods surrounding the park – and at least half the workers would be African-American. Before the end of January, the city would annex 1,800 acres of James Island, inching closer to black neighborhoods where the local PSD did not offer services.

That same month Riley proposed a $100,000 renovation of old College Park, the baseball stadium where he'd watched games since he was a kid. The city had just landed a new minor league franchise to replace the departing Pittsburgh Pirates farm team. The Kansas City Royals filled the void, moving a Class A team to Charleston. It wasn't the AA team or the franchise Riley really wanted – he was still a Dodgers fan – but it was a start.

Riley was doing his best to instill an abiding love of the game in his sons. They watched baseball on TV, and went to see the new minor league team play regularly. At least once a year Riley took Joe and Bratton to Atlanta, often meeting his old legislative buddy, Tom Bryant, and his sons at the ballpark. The Bryants always got to Fulton County Stadium in time for batting practice, while the Rileys rarely rolled in much before first pitch. The mayor would not allow the boys to miss too much school time, baseball or not.

That spring, Riley was in Atlanta to lure more major retailers to Charleston and lobby Sears and Roebuck officials, who planned to close their downtown store and take an anchor position at the new mall under construction in West Ashley. Riley moved quickly on this information. By summer, the city would annex 253 acres between Sam Rittenberg Boulevard and the Stono River – land that included the new Citadel Mall. The St. Andrew's Public Service District accused Riley of "blackmail," but the mayor said it was just part of the city's aggressive annexation campaign.

In truth, the annexation had been a strategic move. Riley knew if the public service district got the tax windfall from a new shopping mall it would be in a better position to fight future annexations in West Ashley. Now the city had the PSD boxed in. The News and Courier defended the city's move and predicted "The PSD is on its way out. The city is in. For a long time it has nibbled at the fringes of the PSD. Now it is eating its way to the heart."

With his victories in federal court and West Ashley behind him, Riley could relax a bit. That summer, Police Chief John Conroy invited the mayor and the rest of the Broad Street Ring – Robert Rosen, Tom Tisdale, Capers Barr and Bill Regan – to sail down to Florida. Conroy was an accomplished mariner and planned to see the world from the deck of his boat once he retired. Riley almost declined the invitation, not wanting to leave the family behind, but Charlotte convinced him that a boys' trip would do him good. She said he had to go – if for no other reason than to get away from the preservationists.

The gang took their time sailing south. They rode the Intracoastal Waterway all the way to St. Augustine – a nice few days of fishing and drinking beer. Conroy lived up to his reputation as a good captain and Riley enjoyed the trip. He knew the waters from Charleston Harbor up to Bull's Bay as well as any local, but the Intracoastal in southern South Carolina, Georgia and Florida was a new experience. For most of the journey, the waterway was so narrow he could almost touch the marsh grass on either side of the boat.

Tisdale had not been able to make the trip down, but flew to St. Augustine for the return voyage. Conroy had decided to forego the leisurely pace of the Intracoastal and try a little blue water sailing. Not too far offshore they could hit the Gulf Stream and make it back to Charleston in no time. But soon after they sailed out of sight of land, Tisdale spotted a mass of black clouds on the horizon. He nervously asked Conroy, "Can we get around that?"

"No," the captain said.

Within minutes, the sailboat was pinned on its side under 50-knot winds. Conroy had every reef in the mainsail, but still the boat was screaming along at an unbelievable clip. For more than two hours, Conroy and his crew – including Riley, former captain of The Citadel's sailing team – manned the rigging, working furiously to keep the boat from capsizing. Tisdale thought they would not make it, that this would be how he died. Later, Riley admitted the same thing. But eventually the storm passed; the boat had held together. Even in the days before GPS, Conroy still knew exactly where they were. They were on course and, thanks to the storm, made it back to Charleston in little more than a day.

Riley returned to find another storm brewing in Charleston. In his absence, Fritz Hollings had taken up the fight for Charleston Center. Preservationists feared their appeal in the federal case would not go well, so they attempted to win in the court of public opinion. They suggested the senator had used his influence to funnel money to the mayor's project – he was, after all, a friend of the Riley family. Hollings, who had been in politics nearly as long as Riley had been alive, proved too much for the South of Broad crowd. Hollings said hell yes, he'd been working to get money for Charleston – he was a U.S. senator from South Carolina. What else was he supposed to do? He said his work on the project was no secret, and there was nothing illegal or unethical about it. Riley had to admire the senator's crusty candor.

A month later, the 4th Circuit Court of Appeals denied the preservation groups' request for an injunction to stop the city's plans. A final ruling in the case would come later, but the forecast from the court did not look good for the preservationists. Within two months, the Harleston Village Neighborhood Association dropped out of the lawsuit. The judges had already decided that the National Federation for Preservation Law had no standing and kicked it off the case, leaving only the Preservation Society and the Charlestowne Neighborhood Association to continue the fight – and pay the legal bills. And it would not get any cheaper since there was only one more possible stop: the United States Supreme Court.

City attorney Bill Regan could barely contain his glee, wondering publicly if a few obstructionists would really ask the people who had issued groundbreaking decisions on Miranda Rights and *Brown v. Board of Education* to hear such a case.

While the preservationists debated their next move, Riley gave them something new to fret over. That fall the city moved forward with plans to build a new visitors center at Meeting and John streets, site of the 19th century railroad depot. It was a perfect spot – close to the interstate and across the street from the new home of the Charleston Museum, which had opened in April. The city hoped the center would corral and guide tourists into downtown and perhaps even cut down on traffic, which locals said seemed to get worse every year. Riley joked that such grousing was nothing new – his aunts had complained that King Street was just too crowded when he was a kid.

Riley expected no trouble with the visitors center. It sat a few blocks north of Calhoun Street, an area not exactly considered the heart of the historic district in 1980. So he was surprised when, in November, he got a letter from the Preservation Society asking to be included in the center's design. Norman Olsen Jr., the society president, told the mayor his group would "welcome the opportunity to be constructively involved in the early decision-making and design stages for such a center."

Riley couldn't believe the nerve of it, and fired off a vicious response – the result of years of frustration with the preservationists. Olsen was so shocked and offended that he immediately took the letter to Frank Gilbreth at The News and Courier. He assumed the newspaper would lambaste Riley's horrible manners and demand an apology. He was right about only one thing – Gilbreth was delighted by the letter. He thought it was a scream, and published the whole thing. Olsen would not get his apology; instead he had to endure people cheering for the mayor, who had taken an aggressive stand against years of bullying.

> *Dear Norm:*
>
> *I am in receipt of your letter concerning the Preservation Society's desire to be involved in the early decision-making and design stages for the Visitor Reception Center. Please know that I have no intention whatsoever of involving you or the Preservation Society in this project at all. And I find it incredible that you would even ask. You have caused the City to waste $150,000 in legal fees and thousands of hours of City employees' time, not to mention the hundreds of thousands of dollars the taxpayers will pay in inflated prices for property purchases and construction costs.*
>
> *With the Charleston Center, I tried to work with the Preservation Society and to give you the opportunity to, as you suggest, be involved in the early decision-making and design stages and otherwise, and have found that you and your organization, as currently led, are most unreliable and completely impossible to work with. I think it is most unfortunate for our City, because I would like nothing*

better than to work with the Preservation Society. While we are being sued by you and your organization, however, it would be impossible to communicate with you in any way at all. You have slandered me and our City; your organization has misrepresented our actions and intentions, and your organization has irrevocably destroyed any chance of a good relationship with the City Administration.

I tried my best to work with the Preservation Society, to listen to your concerns and, in fact, a number of changes were made as a result of comments and suggestions by the Preservation Society. What did the City receive in return but a costly and wasteful lawsuit? The Preservation Society elected to choose a course of litigation rather than cooperation, and you are now stuck with the choice you made. For the City and for the Preservation Society, this is most regrettable indeed.

Most sincerely yours,
Joseph P. Riley, Jr.
Mayor, City of Charleston

A month later, the Preservation Society gave its tentative support to the design of the new visitors center. Apparently, the group realized it had lost, and if it wanted to have any influence in the city, it had to find a way to make amends with Riley. In December, when the Board of Architectural Review approved the demolition of six buildings to make way for Charleston Center, no one said a word.

On Dec. 23, 1980, the 4th Circuit Court of Appeals gave Riley his expected victory. It confirmed the city's right to build Charleston Center in part using federal money and tossed out the case for good. The Preservation Society conceded it probably wouldn't be worthwhile to take such a case to the United States Supreme Court.

Riley told the preservationists it was over, to drop the fight. He suggested they come together and resume the Tourism Management Committee's work – something he could do if he didn't have to waste any more staff time on lawsuits. Nancy Hawk called it blackmail, but by then there were few people still listening. The fight had gone out of them; Riley had won.

But three years had passed and Charleston Center was still little more than a drawing on a piece of paper.

The Chief

The Washington Light Infantry is one of the nation's oldest militia units, formed in 1807 when a second war with the British seemed inevitable. Like most old things in Charleston, the militia never really went away – it just limped along, one of the city's countless traditions. Well into the 20th century, the infantry maintained a healthy, patriotic membership, many of the men retired from various branches of the service.

In 1907, on the group's centennial anniversary, the Washington Light Infantry bought a rambling building at 240 King St., which sat on a part of the street locals called "the bend" because it literally is where the road takes a sharp turn. The building was too large for the group so it rented out the first floor to a dry goods store while maintaining the infantry's headquarters upstairs. More than 70 years later, the Washington Light Infantry found itself parked firmly in the way of progress.

The group's home base was best known to locals as the Penney's building. The department store chain had rented the ground level in 1935, shortly after the dry goods store went out of business, and stayed until 1975. When its lease expired, Penney's moved to the North Area – becoming yet another suburban expatriate. By 1981, the Washington Light Infantry was renting out the first floor to a variety of tenants, including the city's most famous gay bar, the Garden and Gun Club. The Washington Light Infantry did not discriminate, it merely collected rent.

And now the city wanted the Infantry out.

For three years, Charleston Center developer Ted Gould and various city officials had tried to persuade the infantry to move. The group's leader – Carl Beckmann, a retired National Guard brigadier general – listened patiently to their pleas, but had yet to budge. He was not against the idea of a hotel and conference center, in fact he supported it. But he would not move out simply for Gould; he wanted to talk to the city. He knew Charleston City Council could not invoke eminent domain and force the group to sell, not for a private development. Beckmann wasn't a hard guy – he just hadn't heard an offer he liked. So he was standing firm, for the sake of the militia.

Riley knew the infantry had to move, but did not want to bully the men or even offend them – he considered the Washington Light Infantry one of the most prestigious groups of its kind in the country. Perhaps it was the politician in him, but Riley wanted to make the group happy. The city looked for a suitable replacement headquarters for months, and finally offered to relocate the infantry to the corner of Meeting and George streets, the site of an old Masonic Lodge.

The 1870 building had been built by the federal government, used by the USO during World War II and eventually acquired by a Masonic Lodge in 1947. When the Masons sold the building in 1979, it set off another court battle with preservationists. The Historic Charleston Foundation opposed plans to put a bar and restaurant in the building. A judge sided with the developers, but then the state refused to issue a beer and wine permit – there was always more than one way to skin a cat in South Carolina. In 1980, the building suffered a mysterious fire and had sat empty ever since. Despite the fire damage, the building was still sturdy and sound. Riley thought it was the perfect place for the Washington Light Infantry.

The militia members were not sold on the idea, and their reluctance sparked stories in The News and Courier that speculated the Washington Light Infantry could turn out to be the hold-up that would kill Charleston Center. The problem was one of geography. Even though the Masonic Lodge was only four blocks from their current headquarters, members of the infantry believed the building was too far north on the peninsula – and in a seedy area of town. When he listened to this argument, Riley had an idea.

The Washington Light Infantry's King Street building was notable mostly for its wrought-iron gate. Riley asked architects if they could draw up renovation plans for the Masonic Lodge and add an ornate fence of wrought iron and concrete around the property. In early 1981, he invited Beckmann and other officers to City Hall to see the plans. When the drawings were unveiled, the room went quiet. The building looked good with its classic federal lines, but it was the gate that made a statement. It was strong and elegant, more so than the wrought iron on King Street.

Beckmann and his men played it cool. They promised to consider the proposal, but had to talk to their members. Before they left, Beckmann asked if they could take the drawing with them – and Riley knew he had them. That rendering would show up in the newspaper months later, when the city announced it had come to terms with the Washington Light Infantry. The mayor crossed one more obstacle off his Charleston Center list.

Riley spent the first months of 1981 mending fences as well as building them. In February he invited Preservation Society President Norman Olsen Jr. to City Hall so they could put aside their long-simmering differences. The society had dropped its lawsuit against Charleston Center in January, but also canceled its fall tour of homes. The members were concerned about its impact on tourism, which Olsen said was a very delicate balance. The meeting seemed to go well, with Olsen asking about plans for the waterfront park and the visitors center.

Finally, Olsen suggested the mayor meet with his group to clear up misconceptions about his intentions for these new attractions, and the city. It was ironic, the level of distrust. The mayor was quickly gaining a national reputation both for his devotion to smart urban design and historic preservation, but some local preservationists still thought of him as a meddling interloper – convinced that he, or any change, might destroy the city's heritage.

On March 14, 1981, Riley and his wife joined a U.S. Conference of Mayors delegation on a trip to Taiwan. The Taiwanese government paid their way, eager to show off its successes in housing and economic development, and to repay the mayors for their hospitality a year earlier. It was Riley's first trip to Asia, and he learned Taiwan was economically successful because of its focused efforts – things that didn't fit were not pursued, or accepted – in a way that mirrored Riley's philosophy. It was a world both completely foreign and strikingly similar to home.

Taiwan is an island about 100 miles off the Chinese mainland, smaller than South Carolina but with a population of 181 million – or 177 million more people than the Palmetto State in 1981. More than half the island is covered in mountains that are largely uninhabited; the rest provided a harsh lesson in the realities of urban density. There were challenges to having so many people living in small areas, horrendous traffic chief among them. From his hotel balcony, the night smog made it impossible to see the water or much of the island.

In Taipei, two rivers wind through the city, eventually spilling into the Taiwan Strait. Riley later joked that, unlike Charlestonians, the Taiwanese did not claim the Tamsui and Kelung rivers came together to form the Pacific Ocean. The city reminded him of turn-of-the-century Chicago, a boomtown on the hustle, and he found interesting elements of urban design throughout the city. Many buildings had colonnaded sidewalks similar to what was planned for Charleston Center. And like his own Lowcountry home, the modern city mingled with nature at every turn – it was common to see rice fields alongside sidewalks next to high-rise buildings. Everything just fit together. In Kaohsiung, Riley jogged in a linear park that ran along the banks of a river, near the city's huge port, and he took it as proof that his waterfront park was important. Even in a city dependent on the maritime industry, citizens needed access to the waterfront.

The Taiwanese were eager to show off their innovations, their factories – and their food. Riley was served fresh pineapple every day, and he tried Mongolian barbecue, Peking duck, squid balls, even shark fin soup. When he learned how much the locals took pride in their culinary arts, he was relieved that one of the gifts he carried was a copy of *Charleston Receipts*, his city's famous local cookbook.

Taiwan officials enjoyed their alcohol as much as any native Charlestonian, and far more than the largely temperate mayor. In Tainan, Mayor Su Nan-cheng – who Riley described as a mixture of Richard Daley, LBJ and Huey Long – was eager to share his stockpile of cognac and vermouth. There were local customs, however, which Riley learned when he asked for a glass of vermouth. This was not allowed: the men could drink only the cognac, the women got the vermouth. The Tainan mayor was intent on showing his guests a good time, and suggested everyone get drunk and take the afternoon off. The official translator refused to offer this invitation, but an aide let the mayors know what was in store for them.

The mayors were told you could not simply sip your drink. When you wanted to imbibe, you had to make a toast. It didn't matter what the toast celebrated, there simply had to be one. The proper custom was to *gam bay*, which Riley interpreted as the old tradition of "down the hatch" in one gulp. Mayor Su obviously liked his drink, and kept making toasts, which quickly left the Americans a little light-headed. It appeared the Tainan mayor would get his wish for the afternoon.

Nan-cheng continued to toast the mayors – most of them very moderate drinkers – to the point that they had to retaliate. "Rather than all of us drinking a toast each time the mayor raised his glass, we teamed up on him. Each one of us would get up and make a toast to the mayor. He would, of course, be obliged to *gam bay* his own down the hatch. The problem for the mayor was there were nine of us and only one of him. So for each *gam bay* we had collectively, he had nine."

Mayor Su Nan-cheng did not make it to the official dinner that night.

Riley had the chance to observe Taiwan from a variety of perspectives. He was granted an audience with Premier Sun Yun-Suan, who spoke of his country's struggle for housing and the need for more mass transit. Riley found the premier to be a generous host, but he was most impressed with Taiwan's citizens. Out jogging at 5:30 one morning, he noticed the street was teeming with people. Even in a New York-size city, he thought this was unusual.

Across the city, the breakfast business was bustling but Riley also noticed a lot of people buying and carrying badminton rackets. He followed along as the sidewalk gave way to a trail going up the side of a small mountain. At its end, he found a small temple with about 1,000 people outside of it dressed in tennis gear, exercising to the cadence of one voice shouting out orders. The area had been set aside by the premier for Early-Risers, people who wanted to get up and exercise. One woman even offered the mayor her racket.

Riley was amazed at how different the attitudes toward visitors were in Taiwan, and it upset him to think that few Charleston residents were so kind to tourists. When the Conference of Mayors delegation had landed, they were greeted by bands that played the *Battle Hymn of the Republic* and *The Star-Spangled Banner*, a ceremony so lavish it made him feel like the president. That, he found, was just how the people were in Taiwan.

When he returned to Charleston – after a brief side trip to Tokyo – Riley told The News and Courier that Taiwan "taught me a few things about Southern hospitality."

Charleston had gotten no more hospitable in the mayor's absence. In a News and Courier article meant to be the obituary of the Charleston Center debate, the fight sounded anything but over. Henry Cauthen was back to claiming the city was going to "kill the goose that lays the golden eggs," and Elizabeth Hamilton – daughter of famous local watercolor artist Elizabeth O'Neill Verner – told the newspaper she was outraged over the "rape of Charleston." Some preservationists even claimed the more reasonable Historic Charleston Foundation was merely a front for the mayor. By the end of the month, the Preservation Society would start a letter-writing campaign, trying to get officials in Washington to cancel $7.1 million in federal funds for the project. With a new administration in the White House, one that was preaching fiscal restraint, the preservationists hoped to kill the hotel by cutting off its funding.

It frustrated Riley to be characterized as a proponent of unchecked development when he actually shared many of the preservationists' concerns. The mayor had asked City Council for a zoning ordinance to limit the number of hotels on the peninsula, and fought plans to build a cheap motel across the street from the Gaillard Auditorium. He even asked the Planning Commission to put together a study of how many hotel rooms Charleston reasonably needed – a policy of moderation that Riley's critics conspicuously ignored.

The city would need fewer rooms than anticipated, at least for the moment. In September 1981, The Citadel's Board of Visitors turned down $200,000 from a movie studio that wanted to film an adaptation of Pat Conroy's *The Lords of Discipline* on campus. Conroy's second novel was a thriller set inside the gates of the fictional Carolina Military Institute, a thinly veiled version of El Cid. The plot centered on a secret campus group that used violent measures to rid the corps of unwanted cadets, including its first African-American plebe.

Although many locals considered the novel a love letter to Charleston – *The Lords of Discipline* captures the city's atmosphere as no other book – it was also an unflinching look at life inside a military college. Conroy's depiction of hazing and racism on campus enraged Citadel officials and alumni, and none of them wanted to help publicize this story. The book was banned on campus, just as Conroy's much gentler work, *The Boo*, had been a decade earlier.

The Board of Visitors claimed the filming would be too disruptive for students, but the real reason was the subject matter. Chairman George James said that, "It's not something that is complimentary to the school or to Charleston or to South Carolina, for that matter." Eventually, public pressure forced the board to reconsider its decision – for a minute anyway.

Riley lobbied the Board of Visitors, claiming the movie would have great economic benefit to the city. But he did so delicately, keenly aware of the political sensitivities. Not only had he attended The Citadel at roughly the same time as Conroy, part of the novel had been written in his house. Conroy, who previously used the Gibbes Street house to write part of *The Great Santini*, had returned one summer to recapture the magic while the Rileys were on vacation. It was there he came up with the book's powerful opening line, "I wear the ring." The mayor eventually deferred to the Board of Visitors – but not before noting that the book was just fiction.

"The author has feelings about the beauty of Charleston that will come out very well in the movie," Riley said. "Considered in its totality, the author conveys a very strong appreciation for the concept" of the school.

The Board of Visitors upheld its original decision in late October, forcing the film's production company to shoot at Wellington College in England. Riley persuaded producers to shoot some off-campus scenes in Charleston, however. The Citadel could close Lesesne Gate, but it couldn't stop the movie or Conroy, who wrote a letter to The News and Courier mocking the college's decision to forego easy money.

By then, however, Charleston and its mayor were distracted by another drama.

On Tuesday, Oct. 27, Police Chief John Conroy left the Charleston police station on Lockwood Drive around 4:30 to tape an interview with South Carolina Educational Television. The public broadcasting crew had asked him to talk about guns and the police's use of deadly force – a topic he had spoken on at a recent convention of the South Carolina Law Enforcement Officers' Association. The filming made him late to a class on celestial navigation he was taking in anticipation of his retirement. Conroy planned to sail across the Atlantic in a few years, visiting ports of call in Europe, and wanted to know exactly where he was going. After class, he got notes on what he missed from other students, and asked the instructor for information on upcoming lessons. Charleston Police Lt. T.J. Brandon, who was also taking the course, drove Conroy to his home on Society Street.

"I'll see you in the morning," Conroy said as he got out of the car.

That night, residents in Ansonborough saw Conroy walking his dog around 10:30. The chief often took the dog out for late strolls, and some neighbors considered it part of his job – he was walking the beat, and it made his neighbors feel safe. Of course, the dog also appreciated it. That night, the people who spied Conroy out with his dog were the last to see the police chief alive.

The gunshot woke Conroy's son at 1:30 a.m. Startled, Jay Conroy jumped out of bed and ran downstairs, where he found his father slumped in a living room chair. There was a single gunshot wound to the right side of the chief's head, and Conroy's .38 service revolver was lying on the floor. An ambulance came and took him to Medical University Hospital, where he died at 3:30 a.m. Conroy was 55.

The chief's death was ruled a suicide, but no one could understand what led him to kill himself. His doctors said Conroy had a mild heart arrhythmia, but nothing life-threatening. His job was going well. His secretary, Ann McDaniels, told investigators the chief had been in a fine mood the day before – and she could usually tell when something was bothering him. Some people suspected there had to be more to his death.

Riley was heartbroken. Conroy had not only been his chief, he was his friend and a kindred spirit. The mayor considered him a force for good going all the way back to the hospital strike, when he tried to keep the city and protesters safe during the dark days of the civil rights movement. Under Riley's tenure, Conroy had started to make a dent in the city's crime statistics and recently had been named president of the S.C. Law Enforcement Officers' Association. Conroy was at the pinnacle of his career. His death made no sense.

The chief's sense of fairness had not been forgotten, especially in the black community. Nearly 350 people turned out for a special Wednesday night service at Ebenezer AME Church, where city councilmen remembered Conroy for trying to make the East Side a safer place to live. Robert Ford hailed Conroy as a "great chief and a great man," and Jerome Kinloch memorialized him as "a good warrior who will be missed by the citizens of Charleston."

The mayor thought back to the sailing trip they had taken the year before, how the chief had saved their lives during that violent storm. He was thankful Charlotte had persuaded him to go along. "He was an avid and excellent sailor," the mayor said, describing Conroy's post-retirement plans to reporters. Days later, at Conroy's memorial service, Riley gave the eulogy. "He was a wonderfully broad man in a complex world. He brought us his intelligence, his judgment, his leadership. He gave no superficial platitudes, but rather truth."

Riley appointed Conroy confidante Maj. Charles Sands as acting chief and said the search for a new chief would begin immediately. But he could not let Conroy's death go. Privately, he asked doctors to look at news conference footage of Conroy, to see if they noted any signs of depression. He checked with the FBI, but found nothing to suggest his chief was in trouble. A Berkeley County sheriff had recently been indicted, but federal agents told Riley they had checked out Conroy at the same time and determined him "clean." The mayor finally decided his friend's death must have been a spur-of-the-moment choice, aided by easy accessibility to a handgun.

Riley struggled with his emotions that winter, going through the motions while trying not to think about the loss of Conroy. As resumes for potential new chiefs poured in, he asked his friends and colleagues to sift through them. There was no great hurry – the mayor had confidence in Sands, largely because Conroy had.

Riley turned his attention to the 1982 city budget and his ongoing fight to keep federal money flowing into the city. In December, he traveled to Washington to testify before a House subcommittee planning to decrease loans for cities that had fallen into decay – federal budget cuts would become a constant concern for Riley throughout the administration of President Ronald Reagan. For the moment, however, Charleston's money was safe.

The mayor knew the city needed a source of revenue beyond property taxes to fund all that he wanted to do. He made regular trips to the Statehouse in Columbia, where he lobbied lawmakers to give cities the right to charge local sales taxes and collect hotel-motel taxes on room rentals. He told state officials that without new revenue streams, the burden on property owners – and property tax bills – would become overwhelming. Few lawmakers were interested in attaching their name to anything that would raise taxes, but Riley continued to badger them. It was his standard operating procedure. The mayor believed if he made a logical argument, and repeated it until he was blue in the face, people eventually would listen. It had worked before. But the General Assembly continued to ignore him.

In March 1982, Riley addressed the National Conference of Historic Preservation Officers in Washington. He talked about the city's rehabilitation of Rainbow Row decades earlier, touted Charleston's preservation laws as the first in the nation, and stressed the importance of protecting historical architecture. The only way to keep a city healthy, he said, was to fill in the blank spaces between historic structures with quality development. He said attention to every detail was crucial – and his friends could attest that Riley practiced what he preached. David Rawle would recall Riley inspecting the bricks for Charleston Center and telling one of the leading designers in the country, "This isn't good enough yet."

The mayor remained in Washington to testify before the U.S. Senate Budget Committee on behalf of urban development block grants. The new philosophy in D.C. held that states should have more autonomy and control all grant money directly. But that meant cities would have to wade through an extra layer of bureaucracy to get any funding – if the states didn't simply keep the money. Riley warned the committee that this new federalism would hurt the very cities that made up the country, that block grants were their salvation.

As much as Riley believed that, he had not yet proven it in his own hometown. Trouble continued to plague Charleston Center. When the mayor announced construction would begin in April, it was clear this was, at least in part, wishful thinking.

Nearly 200 people responded to the city's national search for a police chief. Riley had resisted overtures to hire from within the department, and it appeared the choice had paid off. He had his pick of lawmen, which was exactly what he wanted. Crime was still a major problem in much of Charleston, and the mayor felt he needed to hire a big gun, someone with strong credentials. Some of his friends urged him to at least give a black candidate a proper vetting. He was surprised they felt the need to remind him.

Riley was committed to affirmative action. He knew that hiring a black chief would be a monumental signal to the black community, a statement on inclusiveness the city needed to make. Charleston had never had a black police chief and Riley knew there would be several benefits to such a gesture. But he would not simply put a black candidate on his short list to appease anyone; he would seriously consider hiring him. All he had to do was find the right candidate.

Reuben Greenberg, at first glance, was not the guy. His resume stood out from most that poured into City Hall, but Riley was turned off by a photo Greenberg had included. In the picture, Greenberg was standing, staring into the camera, wearing civilian clothes with a rain coat slung over his shoulders. The mayor thought it looked like something out of a fashion shoot for a clothing catalog. Then there was the abundance of education on his resume, which included two master's degrees from the University of California at Berkeley. "He looked like an academic, and I wanted a cop," Riley later recalled. But Greenberg also had serious law enforcement credentials, so the mayor kept his name in play.

Greenberg was a native of Houston, the son of a Russian Jewish immigrant and an African-American mother. Just 39, he had divided most of his adult life between academics and police work, teaching in California and at the University of North Carolina. He had been the undersheriff in Savannah, a police chief in Opa-Locka, Fla., and was currently a deputy director at the Florida Department of Law Enforcement. Greenberg considered his current job too much talking, not enough policing. He'd known and respected John Conroy and, when he learned of the chief's death, decided to apply for the job. But he figured there was no way the city where the Civil War began would hire a black Jew as its police chief.

Riley decided to include Greenberg's name on his short list of six candidates, and asked Bill Regan, Capers Barr and City Councilman Foster Gaillard – son of the former mayor – to make reference calls. Barr ended up on the phone with Janet Reno, then a Florida state attorney based in Miami and a Greenberg friend. Every report they got on him was positive. People said Greenberg was honest and smart, a real cop with a truly genuine personality (a tidbit the mayor would not fully understand until later). Riley still wasn't completely sold. Greenberg sounded too good to be true.

When Riley eventually interviewed Greenberg, the doubts dissipated. This, he knew, was his man. The mayor realized hiring an African-American chief would be a big deal, and help relations between police and residents in the black community. Greenberg commanded respect, and Riley had no doubt he could take it to the criminals – he was anything but soft on crime. His take on the criminal justice system was conservative, typical for a cop, and practically Republican. That was fine with Riley. The mayor may have been exceedingly progressive, but he was also very pro-police and prided himself as tough, and unforgiving, on crime.

Riley planned to introduce Greenberg as the new chief on March 17, 1982. But the day before, Eddie Fennell, a longtime crime reporter at The News and Courier, learned that Greenberg had been hired from Florida law enforcement officials. And he was not in Tallahassee. Fennell called the mayor, who was at Henry's restaurant on the Market with Greenberg and Regan. Riley would not confirm the news, and told Fennell he didn't know where Greenberg was. He didn't like lying to the press, but feared the paper would send a photographer storming into the restaurant. It complicated matters, but Riley was impressed with the journalism – even if it didn't fit his own schedule.

The next morning, The News and Courier carried the story stripped across the top of the front page with a photograph of Greenberg. It was a long morning for Riley. One member of City Council called to say, "We knew you'd hire a black one, I'm just glad you got a good one." Then a prominent citizen called and opened the conversation by asking the mayor, "Are you really hiring a nigger to be police chief?"

At the news conference later that day, Riley said the search for a police chief had been color blind, that Greenberg was simply the best candidate. He lauded the chief's work in cleaning up Opa-Locka and called him a hands-on cop. Riley even mentioned that Greenberg was a compulsive jogger who sometimes arrested people while out for his morning run. The mayor wanted to paint a picture of a very tough chief, something he believed Charleston desperately needed.

Greenberg didn't know about the mayor's early morning phone conversations, but he was braced for the worst. He expected Klansmen to descend on City Hall when he was sworn in, but was surprised by the city's grace, charm and diversity. When he took the job on April 12, after a unanimous vote of City Council, the invocation was given by Rabbi Alan Cohen. Then Greenberg was sworn in by Chief Municipal

Judge Arthur McFarland, who was black. Riley handed him his gun and his badge, and the community held a reception for him that evening on the East Side. It was a warm and elaborate welcome, but it was a gesture from Conroy's widow that meant the most to the new chief.

Greenberg had asked someone at City Hall to help him with temporary housing until he found a permanent place. In less than a day, Alice Conroy offered Greenberg the carriage house behind her home. She normally rented it out during Spoleto, but that was more than a month away and would give the chief time to look. This simple act of kindness changed Greenberg's entire attitude, he later said. He had arrived ready to lead a crusade against racism, but instead was welcomed into the city from a most unexpected corner.

It would not take long for Greenberg to completely shake up Charleston's police department. He demanded all his officers have college degrees – he wanted them educated, not only to ensure better police work, but to make sure his force had a broader sense of the world. Conroy tried to ferret out racism in the department, and had done pretty well, but Greenberg wanted to take professionalism to a new level. Still, the new chief quickly showed the city he was most definitely politically incorrect. While he opened a lot of doors in the black community, some also found him insensitive to suspects – and not above a little racially tinged ranting of his own. Riley soon came to accept that as Greenberg's personality.

"I gave him elbow room because he needed it," the mayor would later say. "I knew he couldn't work in a strait jacket, and knew he would make some outrageous statements."

But he would clean up the streets, and the crime rate in Charleston would fall dramatically. To Riley, that was worth the occasional bad press.

The first pilings for Charleston Center were driven in late May 1982, but only 200 of the 1,000 had been set before the project was delayed yet again. In July, the city halted work when engineers feared the initial pile-driving had shaken the peninsula so badly that some buildings were damaged. Then, Gould had trouble with his construction loans, forcing the city to delay construction of the adjacent parking garage. It seemed Charleston Center was cursed.

The city's new Fort Sumter tour boat facility was not faring any better. Riley was preoccupied for much of the summer fighting the federal government, which initially wanted to locate the pier near the Coast Guard Station on the Ashley River. The mayor convinced National Park Service officials that was too far from the tourist district, and suggested the boats be moored at the old Fleet Landing site near the Market. The feds and the tour boat operator ultimately decided they would build their pier farther up the river, near the Dockside Condominiums. When Riley complained, the Park Service and tour boat owner George Campsen threatened to move the whole operation to Patriots Point in Mount Pleasant.

Despite these headaches, the summer of 1982 was mostly quiet. Riley even had time for a trip to Atlanta with the boys and Tom Bryant where, for the first time in years, it looked like the Braves had a chance to make it to the postseason. It was a nice break from the routine of City Hall. The biggest news there was a committee report that found the mayor was seriously underpaid.

Riley's $35,000 salary was more than most mayors made in South Carolina, but he was the only one who performed more than ceremonial duties. Most cities in the state operated on a weak-mayor, city manager form of government. In Charleston, the mayor was the city manager. And most city managers were paid a lot more. The city was getting a steal – Riley was just as frugal with the city's money as his own. The summer before, council had forced him to buy a new city car. He'd been driving a '75 Plymouth for more than six years, a car he picked up by trading in the Lincoln that Mayor Gaillard had driven. Council members said it was embarrassing to have Charleston's mayor driving around in a jalopy.

The biggest controversy of the year came when the city's tourism management got too overzealous even for locals. In November, the private company that managed the Market for the city ordered Benjamin Campbell – the Peanut Man – to start paying rent or leave. Campbell had been a janitor with the city since the 1940s, spending his days sweeping the Market when it was nothing but a bunch of dusty old vegetable bins. When he retired in 1975, he started selling boiled eggs and peanuts to tourists on the Market and The Battery. He since had been restricted to the Market by the city's new tourism rules.

Campbell certainly wasn't getting rich – he sold about 50 bags of peanuts a day at a profit of 20 cents each. He said $10 a day was enough money, along with his Social Security, to keep him in an East Side apartment. But the Christopher Co. told the Peanut Man he couldn't sell near the Market unless he rented a booth for $7 a day. The newspapers kept the Peanut Man on the front page for a week. It was fine to complain about tourists, but Campbell was a local. The story was only better because Campbell said he sold peanuts so he didn't have to go on welfare.

Riley was livid. He called management company officials and told them to back off, that it made the city look racist. The company immediately complied, and Campbell was grateful. Then he found out the reason the company had asked him for rent; another vendor in the Market had complained about him. The Peanut Man said if he wasn't wanted in the Market, he wouldn't go back.

The mayor eventually visited Campbell at his America Street apartment and asked him to return to the Market. If he was uncomfortable with that, Riley said he could sell his peanuts at City Hall – he already had orders from several staffers. The Peanut Man relayed the entire conversation to the media, and apparently the mayor was pretty blunt: He told Campbell no one should have ever asked him to leave and, if anyone else gave him trouble, City Hall would fix it. Campbell was so overjoyed he told reporters he'd felt like crying.

"The mayor – in my home!" the Peanut Man said. "I'd never met him before."

The mayor declared Jan. 13, 1983, "Francis Marion Day" as the landmark hotel was set to reopen after renovations. The Francis Marion, first opened in 1924, had been a city icon for most of the 20th century – home to one of Charleston's few restaurants when the mayor was a child. The hotel had fallen into disrepair before a local doctor and his brother eventually bought the place, joined the Ramada Inn chain and put in $6 million to overhaul the Francis Marion's public halls and private rooms. Riley called it "an important new beginning for an important business establishment in our community."

It would not be the last time the historic old hotel was resurrected from the dead. Later, Riley would have to save the Francis Marion once again when it went bankrupt and the College of Charleston tried to convert it to dorms. The mayor knew it would look horrible if the city's most historic hotel could not survive, and found other investors to keep it alive.

Charleston's other major hotel project was not faring so well, either. Developer Ted Gould still could not get a loan to build Charleston Center, and hinted that he would sell his shares at cost. When Gould was sued over another development in Miami, attorneys tried to go after his Charleston holdings. Gould was soon off the project. Several banks began sniffing around, but by March 1983 City Council gave Riley approval to apply for another $14.5 million in federal grants to jump-start the project. It took only a few weeks to secure the money. At a news conference announcing the new grant, the mayor wore a T-shirt with a picture of Charleston Center on it with the words "I Believe" in large type.

Just weeks later, in April, Riley confirmed he would seek a third term as mayor. No one had expected any different with so many of his major initiatives still unfinished. Riley would face no opposition in the primary or general election, and most council members weren't challenged either. The entire 1983 campaign became little more than a coronation. That left them free to handle the crisis that consumed much of the year.

In January 1983, a group of Johns Island residents submitted a petition of incorporation to the Secretary of State. These people claimed they wanted to create their own town entirely to avoid annexation into the city of Charleston – even though Riley had said he had little interest in the island. But that changed when the island wanted to form a town so close to the city's border. The mayor knew Charleston could not grow if it was landlocked by a lot of little towns-in-name-only. Before he could respond, however, the Secretary of State rejected the island's petition, claiming any town on Johns Island would sit too close to the existing city of Charleston.

By May, James Island was considering the same idea – and for the same reason. The island had rejected incorporation plans in 1973 and 1975, and now residents suddenly felt the need to defend their homes from annexation. As soon as islanders met to discuss incorporation, the city responded by annexing more than 2,100 acres of James and Johns islands. Riley said he was forced to act when the city was threatened by new towns knocking at its back door. The James Island Citizens Foundation retaliated by immediately petitioning the Secretary of State for an incorporation referendum. Their attorney was Nancy Hawk.

The fight lingered for nearly a year. The Secretary of State would not allow the referendum to go forward, nor would he reject the request. It should have been an easy decision since James Island was even closer to Charleston's border than Johns Island. But James Island had influential friends at the Statehouse. While the Secretary of State's staff looked for a way out of the political landmine, Hawk quite accurately accused them of stalling.

Ultimately, the island would have little luck stopping the city's annexation efforts, either through campaigning or in court. In October, the Westchester neighborhood of James Island overwhelmingly voted in favor of joining the city of Charleston. By the time Riley called checkmate, he had moved on to other campaigns.

In the fall of 1983, the mayor announced a grand plan to link the future waterfront park to the Market, creating a new center city similar to what Baltimore recently had done with its Inner Harbor. Such an area, Riley said, would be the perfect place to build an aquarium.

High-wire Acts

Every summer, Riley took his family to the mountains for a week's retreat near the rocky point where North and South Carolina meet Georgia. It is rugged, heavily wooded, sparsely populated terrain – the place where the movie *Deliverance* was filmed. Riley had discovered the area years earlier on a fishing trip with friends, and promptly fell in love. It would become his sanctuary.

Eventually Riley bought a share of a cabin with a large, shaded porch that sat overlooking the rapids of the Chattooga River's East Fork. Even with his impaired hearing, Riley could always hear the water rushing by, a noise at once chaotic and calming. His sons would later say that mountain cabin was the only place where Riley could truly leave everything behind and relax. There he had no responsibilities, only fishing and Charlotte and his boys. It was a world away from work, and Charleston.

Riley, Joe and Bratton would fish the streams of the Chattooga every morning during their week in the woods. A few years after they bought the cabin, the family met Henry Williamson, a local fly fisherman, and he patiently taught them all the tricks of that majestic art. In some ways it was a far cry from throwing a shrimp net, yet at the same time very similar. Both took much coordination and orchestration. Both were richly therapeutic.

One afternoon during a mountain week in the early 1980s, the Riley family wandered up the road to Highlands, North Carolina. There, they found a small natural history museum that explained and described the unique geography and ecosystems of the region. Riley studied the dioramas and the photos, impressed by how interesting and informative it all was. Even on vacation, he could not help but allow his mind to wander occasionally back to work. Charleston could use a place like this, he thought.

Similar thoughts crossed his mind in June 1982, when the family took what Riley called another of their "Norman Rockwell trips," traveling by car across the country. That summer they drove to Chicago and met up with Charlotte's sister, who lived in nearby Racine, Wisconsin. The trip gave Riley a chance to take his boys to the Windy City's historic baseball parks, but they also found time to visit a number of Chicago's museums before he had to hop on a plane for Minneapolis, site of that year's U.S. Conference of Mayors summer convention. In the Field Museum of Natural History, he was reminded of the tiny exhibit in Highlands. He found it ridiculous that he had to go 800 miles to find an exhibit that explained the ecosystem of a saltmarsh. By the time they toured the Shedd Aquarium, Riley had an idea for a new Charleston museum.

The Shedd was the very model of American aquariums, but by then it had been eclipsed slightly by Baltimore's new National Aquarium. That facility, which had opened late the previous summer, was a cornerstone of the city's Inner Harbor revitalization – an urban renewal project that shared much in common with Charleston's own. The success of Baltimore's Inner Harbor was so great, so immediate, that already other cities were plotting their own aquariums.

That idea would percolate in Riley's mind for more than a year before he brought it up during a public hearing in September 1983. Six months later, in March 1984, the city would join the county Department of Parks, Recreation and Tourism and the Sea Grant Consortium to study whether such a facility was feasible for Charleston. Apparently, the idea was popular – within a few weeks of the study's announcement, the military museum at Patriots Point in Mount Pleasant revealed plans for an aquatic theater featuring dolphin and whale shows. Patriots Point officials said they got the idea from Sea World.

Although that was never a serious proposal, and Charleston officials said Patriots Point's plans did not interfere with their own, it gave Riley pause. For years he had been fighting residents who were convinced he wanted to turn Charleston into Disney World. The Baltimore aquarium was still too new – and the one in Chattanooga years away – for people to truly understand what a modern marine facility could be. If the preservationists thought he wanted to build Marineland on the peninsula, he feared it would make the fight for Charleston Place seem like a mild disagreement.

In the fall of 1984, the aquarium study committee issued a favorable report. If the city put between $6 million and $8 million into such a facility, it could be self-sustaining. Riley suggested locating it on the Cooper River, near the planned Festival Marketplace. But, he stressed, the city was not considering a simple aquarium. Instead, Riley amended his earlier announcement and called the proposed facility a Marine Science Museum. The mayor wanted to distinguish his vision from a Ripley's aquarium or Sea World – or Patriots Point. What he really had in mind was a facility very much like Baltimore's successful new aquarium, which had transformed its city center.

Riley could devote his attention to fanciful things like aquariums because most of his ongoing projects were falling into place. With no opposition in his 1983 re-election bid, he had been able to spend considerable time on other efforts. In February 1984 he helped open a homeless shelter on the East Side, even spending a night as a volunteer. Riley crashed on the shelter's floor in a sleeping bag, not wanting to take up a bed, and the staff told reporters that he got up and swept before leaving the next morning. At the same time, he oversaw a renovation of College Park, the baseball stadium where he spent so much time as a kid.

By March 1984, it appeared all the trouble with Charleston Center was over. Gould had been forced to bow out, and the city brought in Baltimore developers David Cordish and Robert Embry to take over. They in turn hired a New York architect – John Carl Warnecke – and corralled still more investors. The new group went a long way toward calming fears in the city. They immediately lopped four stories off the center and designed the 450 hotel rooms to be much larger than originally planned. The conference facility would be surrounded by restaurants and lounges as well as high-end retail stores. It truly would be a luxury hotel and convention center. Finally, they changed the name. They had decided to call the development Charleston Place.

Even before construction on Charleston Place restarted, it was clear the city was on the cusp of a renaissance. In April 1984, The News and Courier hailed Riley as the "chief architect of a changing city." The front-page story claimed that in his

8½ years as mayor, Charleston had changed more than it had in three centuries. New businesses were moving to King Street, the City Market had become a hub of night life and the Spoleto Festival was quickly becoming a local tradition. Old vacant buildings like the former Sears and the Broad Street Piggly Wiggly would make way for new development, and there were new parking garages and a visitors center on the horizon.

All of that worried some longtime residents, not only those South of Broad but also in Ansonborough, which sat perilously close to the Market. Residents complained about the overcommercialization of downtown, and were upset by a St. Patrick's Day street party that got out of hand. Ansonborough homeowners feared the city was turning into Savannah. They were not appeased by Riley's efforts to strike a balance between tourism and preservation to maintain the special qualities of Charleston. "If you get a Bourbon Street, then you're lost," Riley told The News and Courier.

The mayor did not believe in development simply for development's sake, and any preservationists paying attention could have seen he shared their concerns. Riley blocked plans for a Myrtle Beach developer to build a $30 million, 18-story hotel and condominium complex at the corner of Calhoun and Concord streets, even though the project would have been a windfall for city coffers. But the complex did not fit in with the city's tourism and revitalization goals. Riley would say the same thing to friends who came to him later with a franchise for the popular restaurant/bar chain Hard Rock Café. They wanted to put a Hard Rock on the Market, but the mayor told them that was not Charleston.

And in May 1984, Riley proposed expanding the historic district farther north, giving the Board of Architectural Review control over more of the peninsula's neighborhoods to "prevent irrevocable harm." The revitalization of downtown was moving north, and Riley wanted to control that growth as much as he could.

Riley's growing reputation as an urban planner was not confined to the pages of the local newspapers. The National Association of Housing and Redevelopment Officials appointed him to a task force studying urban design issues, and the U.S. Conference of Mayors elected him to its advisory board. Before the year's end, the conference would send the mayor to Germany to talk about urban challenges in the

United States. Everyone was suddenly listening to the ideas of this young Southern mayor – except in his own hometown.

Riley's makeover of Charleston was becoming so successful, and garnering so much national attention, that locals began to speculate on his political future. Higher office was the next logical step for such an ambitious young man. By summer, there was a rumor around Charleston that the mayor would run for governor in two years. These stories would linger because bits of evidence seemed to pop up everywhere. A reporter from the South Carolina Upstate returned from the Democratic National Convention with a scoop that only confirmed the speculation for many people. A San Francisco cab driver mentioned to the reporter that his last fare had been Charleston Mayor Joe Riley – you know, the guy who's running for governor. The story quickly made it across the country.

Riley denied saying any such thing. He told News and Courier columnist Barbara Williams he had simply discussed the San Francisco mayor's political future with the cab driver. When asked if he had any future ambitions, Riley said he told the cabbie the same thing he had been telling reporters: He was interested in the governor's race, but had made no decision. For reporters, a politician who would admit interest had all but announced his candidacy. A few weeks later, some people showed up at the Municipal Association of South Carolina meeting on Hilton Head Island wearing "Riley for governor" buttons.

Riley was vacationing with his family on the Isle of Palms at the time, so reporters conceded he wasn't handing out the buttons. But that didn't mean his staff or inner circle didn't have a hand in the upstart campaign. Charleston city attorney and Riley friend Bill Regan was seen at the meeting sporting his own button. When asked about it, Regan quipped that he got the button from a Hilton Head cabbie.

Riley did his best to discourage the talk. He said that he was committed to finishing his term as mayor, and cited family responsibilities. In truth, Riley did not want to go through a statewide campaign and face the possibility of moving to Columbia while Joe and Bratton were still in school. But the more he protested, the more people saw Riley gearing up for a campaign. That fall, the mayor endorsed Strom Thurmond for re-election. If the mayor – a dyed-in-the-wool Democrat – was supporting a Republican, most people believed there was only one explanation: He was trying to ingratiate himself with conservative voters across the state.

The speculation was fair. The Thurmond endorsement was a notable course change – in previous campaigns Riley had openly supported the senator's opponents. But the mayor discounted the idea that he was playing politics with the electorate. He said Thurmond was instrumental in securing funds for the waterfront park and Charleston Place, and Riley believed as the city's leader he had a responsibility to promote anyone who assisted it. Thurmond had undoubtedly helped Charleston secure federal money.

In truth, Riley and Thurmond had become unlikely friends – and pretty much for the exact reasons the mayor publicly offered. A decade or more earlier, Riley had skipped an appreciation dinner for Thurmond hosted by Big Joe himself – an absence noted by the local papers. Although Riley claimed there was nothing to that, it was clear Thurmond's politics – and his history of opposition to civil rights – were anathema to his own. The mayor was much closer personally and politically to the state's other senator, Fritz Hollings, a Riley family friend and one of his mentors.

But Thurmond had won over Riley with his unflagging support of Charleston projects and his attitude about their working relationship. Thurmond never held it against Riley when he endorsed his opponents. He simply continued to do his job, which included bringing home the pork so long as it was being doled out. Riley had taken to working out of Thurmond's office when he was in D.C. to raise money for the waterfront park, and the senator flattered him by saying he'd never seen anyone work so hard. Ultimately, Riley had to admit he liked the old man. But his endorsement of Thurmond made his decision to campaign against Congressman Tommy Hartnett that same year even more contentious. After all, Hartnett was a childhood friend.

Hartnett was only a year older than Riley, and they had grown up within blocks of each other. As children they played cowboys and Indians in the same group and, later, baseball and basketball. They sometimes rode to school together, and Hartnett even liked to claim he had dated one of Riley's sisters (even if it was only for a week in the sixth grade). Riley had been a groomsman in Hartnett's wedding and, for a while, it seemed their lives were almost running in parallel. When Riley won a seat in the state House, Hartnett had already been there for two terms. But in

1972, Hartnett said he was no longer comfortable as a Democrat, switched parties and won election to the state Senate as a Republican.

Riley later conceded he and Hartnett grew apart as their political philosophies veered off in drastically different directions. Political reporters blamed Riley for the estrangement, claiming he took Hartnett's snubbing of the Democratic Party personally. And in 1980, Hartnett defeated Riley friend Pug Ravenel to become the 1st District's first Republican congressman since Reconstruction. But Riley did not need petty political reasons to oppose Hartnett. As soon as he was elected to Congress, Hartnett began to interfere with Riley's revitalization efforts.

Although Hartnett publicly refused to criticize Riley – often saying, "He is a decent and honest person. He is a good mayor." – he opposed nearly everything the mayor wanted to do. First, Hartnett fought plans to give federal funds to Charleston Place. Then he tried to cut money for the waterfront park and aquarium projects. Riley realized Hartnett was following President Reagan's political philosophy of slashing government spending – and that began with the very aid that had put Charleston on the path to revitalization. But there was something a little too strident in Hartnett's opposition. Thurmond shared that conservative philosophy but said so long as money was being handed out, South Carolina should get its share. Hartnett, however, was trying to derail funding for projects in his own district. After years of criticizing Reagan administration policies, Riley could not support anyone intent on carrying them out – especially to the detriment of his own hometown.

Hartnett knew better than to expect an endorsement from Riley, but he thought the mayor would sit out the campaign in deference to their long history and friendship. Instead, the mayor took an active – and public – role in the campaign by helping Democrat Ed Pendarvis try to unseat Hartnett. Pendarvis was also a Riley friend; they had gone to The Citadel together. But the mayor admitted Hartnett's stand against federal funding for Charleston Place influenced his decision. Riley believed he needed as many Democrats as possible in Congress to stop the president from cutting Housing and Urban Development grants.

Riley's endorsement set off a year-long blood match with Hartnett. He later said it was just business, and not meant as a slight to his old friend. Obviously, Hartnett didn't hold a grudge forever – 25 years later he gave the mayor a rare Brooklyn

Dodgers World Series jacket. By then, the former congressman said he'd never opposed Charleston Place or the waterfront park – he just didn't think local projects should get federal money when Congress was struggling with a budget deficit. As vicious as it got, Hartnett later dismissed it all as political theater.

"It gave us something to scream about," he said.

In February 1985, the Civil War returned to Charleston, this time in the guise of a film crew shooting an adaptation of John Jakes' *North and South*. In this incarnation, however, the first shots were fired at City Hall. A group of downtown residents protested the inconvenience of having their streets covered in dirt for the filming. This was an altogether different type of tourism, and one that some South of Broad residents said had very questionable value to the city. Riley had met with officers of the Charlestowne Neighborhood Association the previous summer to let them know about the shoot, but some people in the neighborhood claimed they were never informed.

The mayor told residents it was too late to cancel filming, but that did not stop several of them from doing everything possible to make the film crew's job harder. Nancy Hawk put a prominent sign in her window announcing that her house was not to appear in any scenes, and rumor had it she even parked her Mercedes on the curb just to screw up wide-angle shots down Meeting Street.

As the grousing continued, Riley asked residents to please put up with dirt on the streets for a few days. He believed movies and TV shows filmed in the city were free advertising for Charleston. *North and South*, which showed off the Calhoun Mansion and Boone Hall Plantation, became one of the most popular television miniseries of all time – and a great Civil War tourism generator. That only made some locals angrier, especially when Solicitor Charlie Condon introduced Riley at an event as the only man who had the "courage to load up a dump truck full of sand and put a beach in front of Nancy Hawk's house."

The Charlestowne Neighborhood Association endured *North and South* in the spring, but regrouped when the production company returned that summer to shoot a sequel. By then Riley had already decided some guidelines were needed, and City Council agreed. But the neighborhood groups considered it a victory won by exerting pressure. Emboldened, they started working with Congressman Hartnett to block federal money for the waterfront park.

The mayor had predicted the waterfront park would alleviate traffic South of Broad and draw many tourists away from The Battery, which should have been enough to earn the support of downtown neighborhoods. But they either didn't believe him or just targeted the park in retaliation for one defeat after another.

Federal officials told the Charleston newspapers that Hartnett's efforts would have little effect on the city's $9.9 million grant, but the congressman kept at it. Through the summer and fall of 1985, he worked tirelessly to undo everything Thurmond had put in place for the waterfront park. By February 1986, the grant had been cut to $3.7 million. A few days later, HUD outright turned down Charleston's request. Agency officials said the entire program was in danger due to budget cuts by the Reagan administration.

Riley and Hartnett publicly feuded over park funding into the summer of 1986. The mayor accused the congressman of sabotaging Charleston's HUD grant while he was helping other cities secure federal funding. Even Big Joe stepped in, telling reporters that Hartnett and Congressman Carroll Campbell had cut a deal: if Hartnett would help Campbell get elected governor, then Campbell would appoint Hartnett to Thurmond's Senate seat if the old man died in office.

It was a rare instance of the mayor's father publicly stepping into his son's business – not that Riley needed any help. In April 1986, he provided the newspapers with records that showed Hartnett's real estate company was paid $3,800 in federal tax dollars for an appraisal of the waterfront park land. And Hartnett earned $4,600 in federal revenue sharing funds for appraisals related to Charleston Place. Riley provided photocopies of the checks. In essence, the mayor was calling Hartnett a hypocrite.

Hartnett's defense hurt more than it helped. He said his real estate company was hired because it was the best, and he thought the money was city funds. Then the congressman said he was unaware his company had taken federal money and offered to repay it. He asked that Riley write him a check for the same amount out of city coffers. Riley, recognizing the tactical blunder, went in for the kill.

"It sounds like he's asking me to fool around with the city's books," the mayor said.

Within weeks, the federal government announced that the Urban Development Action Grants program would continue, and Riley knew he had won. The city didn't reapply for waterfront park money; the mayor said he had already made his case. Within two months, he and Thurmond – with help from Sen. Hollings – secured $6.3 million from the feds to help build the waterfront park. Riley made the announcement from atop a downtown parking garage, a very visible place to declare victory.

"I regret that Charleston had to fight its own congressman on this project and defend itself against a string of misstatements and demagogic attacks from him," Riley said. "But in the final analysis, the box score will read: the citizens of Charleston, 1; Congressman Hartnett, 0."

Riley's parking garage news conference was the second high-wire act Charleston had seen in a month – the first came during the opening of Spoleto. The festival, in its 10th year, was more popular than ever but still struggled with money problems. Spoleto had paid off a $250,000 debt but predicted another $300,000 shortfall due to state and federal funding cuts to arts programs. A year earlier Riley had been forced to ask local businesses to contribute to the festival's operating budget. That campaign was a success – local businessman Charlie Way contributed $150,000 on the first day. But even such a grand gesture could not save the festival entirely.

Ticket sales for Spoleto 1986 were flagging enough to worry festival organizers, and they needed something to generate some free publicity. On the Tuesday before the opening ceremony, Riley asked his friend David Rawle to help. Since his work on the mayor's first campaign, Rawle had become the leader of the city's largest public relations firm – and had been involved with the festival from the start. It was a tough assignment, but Rawle was pleased to see that, after 11 years in office, the mayor had learned to delegate. Rawle came up with an idea within a day.

The Spoleto bill that year included the Circus Flora, a 75th birthday gift to festival founder Gian Carlo Menotti. The circus featured members of the Flying Wallendas, a legendary family of acrobats who had been performing for more than 60 years. Rawle showed up at the circus' practice and asked Delilah Wallenda if she would do a tightrope walk for the opening ceremony. He wanted her to traverse a single cable stretched from City Hall to the Post Office, 100 feet over the Four Corners of Law. Wallenda thought about it briefly and finally agreed to do it – for $5,000.

City workers spent two days looking for a suitable wire to string between the buildings, and eventually found some cable at the Navy base they believed would work. But the cable had been heavily greased to prevent rusting – not exactly ideal conditions for a high-wire act. The crew spent a day trying to find something to remove grease from the slick cable.

The promise of a free performance by one of the Flying Wallendas won Spoleto national media attention, particularly when it was announced that she would perform without a net over Charleston's most famous intersection. Just eight years earlier, Delilah's grandfather had died trying to walk a tightrope between two wings of a Puerto Rican hotel. Karl, founder of the Flying Wallendas, had fallen to his death when a gust of Caribbean wind blew him off the wire. Now, Delilah would work without a net as well, and if she failed it would be a disaster for the festival. But Rawle had faith – right up to the moment Delilah began to climb the steps of City Hall. She turned to him and said, "I've never done this before."

Wallenda's walk generated exactly the buzz Spoleto needed. The festival received a $100,000 gift to pay performers that day. The mayor reported that the show would go on.

In June, Riley's entire family flew to Puerto Rico for his inauguration as president of the U.S. Conference of Mayors. He had been part of the group's leadership for several years, first as a member of its advisory council and then as its vice president. Technically, he was already president. Earlier that spring, New Orleans Mayor Dutch Morial – the city's first black chief executive – had to resign as conference president when his term in office ended. Riley had been filling in ever since.

The praise for Riley was effusive, particularly from South Carolina officials. Spartanburg Mayor Lewis Miller, who had followed Riley as president of the state's municipal association, said the conference admired the mayor's work in housing and urban development, promotion of the arts and job creation. Even North Charleston Mayor John Bourne had kind words that day. He said Riley would make a great president, and hinted that he could use his new clout to help North Charleston. The compliment that meant the most to Riley, however, came from his father. Big Joe rarely spoke publicly about his son's job performance, but on that day told reporters, "Anything he tackles will be done superbly."

After a family trip to the nearby Virgin Islands, Riley returned to the country as mayor of the mayors. He used this new platform to take his ideas national. That fall he led a group of city executives through the halls of the U.S. Capitol, where they pushed for tougher drug laws to weed out crime in the inner-cities. He lobbied Congress to restore cuts to a revenue sharing program and low-incoming housing aid, and called on state legislatures to make up the difference when Washington failed.

Riley's signature achievement as president of the U.S. Conference of Mayors would not only outlive his term in office, it cemented his reputation as America's mayor. He had spent a decade in the conference befriending mayors around the country, and learned most cities faced challenges similar to Charleston's – they needed economic shots in the arms to survive. And that came from the revitalization of their downtowns, but most mayors did not have the resources to pull off such feats. Riley believed there should be an organization to provide them with support.

He had been kicking the idea around for a year or so. In January 1985, the mayor had written to Jacquelin Robertson, dean of the University of Virginia's School of Architecture, expounding on his idea for an institute where city officials could learn about urban design. "Twenty-five years ago the obituary of the American city was being written. No more. The cities in the United States are not dying but are being rebuilt. The issue is no longer cities dying, but rather what kind of cities are being rebuilt. Will they be of human scale, oriented to the people, or ugly, brutal and cold?"

Riley said mayors were in a unique position to influence the directions of their cities, and "the more sensitive the mayor is to good urban design, the issues of livability, scale, diversity, etc., the more willing and able the mayor will be to help develop higher quality." He asked Robertson if the University of Virginia would like to work with the Conference of Mayors to set up an institute to help train the nation's mayors. Riley used his standing as president of the conference to get the National Endowment for the Arts involved, and it eventually agreed to help fund what came to be called The Mayors' Institute on City Design.

The program that developed from Riley's idea was simple. The institute would hold private training sessions for mayors where a staff of professionals listened to the unique problems of their cities and helped them devise solutions. The sessions proved popular, and other groups eventually got involved. Within a decade, the institute would be hosting at least six sessions each year across the country – one of them always held in Charleston.

The mayors came alone – no staff, no reporters – and talked frankly about their problems, whether it was downtown revitalization, finding new uses for decrepit old buildings or rallying public support for new parks. Riley often attended the sessions, and even traveled to some cities – Roanoake, Va., Minneapolis – to help mayors figure out the best use of the resources they had. For the next 30 years, more than a thousand mayors from around the country would credit Joe Riley with helping their cities return to a beauty and prominence long lost. Outside of Charleston, it would become perhaps Riley's most lasting legacy.

At the same time Riley was busy planning the Mayors' Institute, he realized another signature achievement – the project he had championed since his first term of office. On Sept. 2, 1986, Charleston Place finally opened.

It had taken eight years, a handful of lawsuits, nearly a dozen redesigns, and a last-minute change in developers. But when construction on the hotel and conference center began in 1985, it took less than two years to build the complex that would forever change Charleston. When the grand opening arrived, there was still work to be done, tenants to move in, but the building was finished. The Omni would run the hotel, and Banana Republic was among the shopping center's first stores. The cost had gone far beyond early estimates, peaking at $80 million. The mayor estimated Charleston Place would have a $60 million economic impact on the city every year and create more than 1,000 jobs. He said the opening was one of the most important events in contemporary Charleston history.

On that day, Riley was the first person to sign the hotel's guest book, and The News and Courier called it the "vindication of Charleston Place." King Street was already undergoing a renaissance based solely on the promise of the new center. When the idea was first suggested in 1976, property values in the city's shopping district were lower than they had been in 1948. Now, that real estate was among the most valuable in the city – and the state – and prices would not go down again.

Sen. Fritz Hollings praised the complex a few days later, calling it the result of "competent political leadership." Hollings claimed Riley could have been governor already if he hadn't stuck around to get Charleston Place opened. Although Hollings and Thurmond helped secure the federal grants to build the complex, it was clear that Riley was the linchpin – the one who had believed from the start and tenaciously soldiered on when everyone else gave up. Even the center's detractors were forced to admit Charleston Place had been integrated into the shopping district with little harm to King Street's historic façade. Eventually, the Preservation Society would award the center and Riley with the Carolopolis Award for preservation, the group's highest honor.

Three months later, on Dec. 10, 1986, Riley was scheduled to make an appearance at Charleston Place – something about welcoming a visiting group to town. But when he arrived, the mayor instead found 1,000 supporters – including Hollings and Thurmond – at a surprise party in his honor. When Riley walked into the room, the crowd began to chant "Four more years."

South Carolina's two senators, who had been publicly feuding over President Reagan's role in Iran arms sales, set aside their differences to agree that Riley had been a great mayor for Charleston. Thurmond praised Riley for creating 3,500 jobs, luring more than $2 million in private investments to the center city, and bringing culture back to Charleston. "I have not known a mayor in South Carolina who has shown more zeal, been more dedicated or worked harder for his people than Joe Riley."

Hollings joked that, "I'm glad to find something Strom and I agree on." He said the mayor had forced Washington to listen to the concerns of cities all over the country. Riley, he said, put Charleston on the map – a place it hadn't been in more than a century.

Riley was gracious, and noted that he had a lot of help. Over a period of time, he said, these were accomplishments not of a single leader, "but of a community." The mayor did not commit to running for a fourth term that night, but most people considered it a foregone conclusion. Riley may have realized his first dream for the city, but he had plenty of others.

At that point, no one expected Joe Riley to go anywhere.

Helen Riley with Susanne, 3, and Joe, 14 months, in March 1944. This photo was taken at the house on Grove Street that Helen rented while her husband served aboard a World War II hospital ship. (Provided by the Riley family)

In the early 1950s, Joe Riley Sr. bought this grand home on Murray Boulevard. Each year, the family posed at the house for a photo that would go on their Christmas cards, a tradition that endured until Joe moved out after college. This is one of the earliest in the series, from 1952. Joe, in the front seat with his father, is 9. (Provided by the Riley family)

The Riley children decorate the Christmas tree in another holiday photo commissioned by their father, this one from 1957. Mary is on the ladder, with Jane sitting next to it. Joe is 14. (Provided by the Riley family)

The Riley Christmas photo from 1955 showcased the children's musical talents. Susanne was considered a prodigy on the piano; Joe, 12 at the time, did not play accordion – it was merely a prop. By this time, Joe had given up the piano. (Provided by the Riley family)

Joseph P. Riley Jr. receives his diploma from Citadel President Gen. Mark Clark, spring 1964. Riley had a distinguished career at the military college, serving as a member of the Summerall Guards drill platoon. (Provided by the Riley family)

Riley takes the oath of office for his second term as Charleston mayor from civil rights pioneer Septima Clark as his father holds the Bible, January 1980. Riley was re-elected without opposition, a luxury he would have again four years later. (Photo by Tom Spain)

Mayor-elect Riley addresses the crowd at the Gaillard Auditorium on hand for his victory party, Dec. 9, 1975. Riley stood on a chair and spoke only briefly, as he hadn't prepared a victory speech. He'd spent the day campaigning, not writing. (News and Courier archives)

Riley with his sons, Bratton (left) and Joe at their downtown home during his first term as mayor. Riley tried to keep his public duties separate from his private life, and spent as much time with his family as possible. (Provided by the Riley family)

Riley and Charlotte at the Spoleto Festival 1991, just before their 25th wedding anniversary. (Photo provided by the Riley family)

Riley keeps three framed collages of photos on the wall of the Isle of Palms beach house, most of them showing the family at play over the years. When not at City Hall, Riley spends a lot of his time outdoors. Joe III is on the left photo, Charlotte is in the top right corner picture and the center photo shows Riley with Bratton. (Photo by Wade Spees)

The things you do as mayor. Riley hams it up with "Mrs. Claus" and Abner the Charleston Mouse while planning the decoration of King Street Square for Christmas 1988. (Photo by Tom Spain)

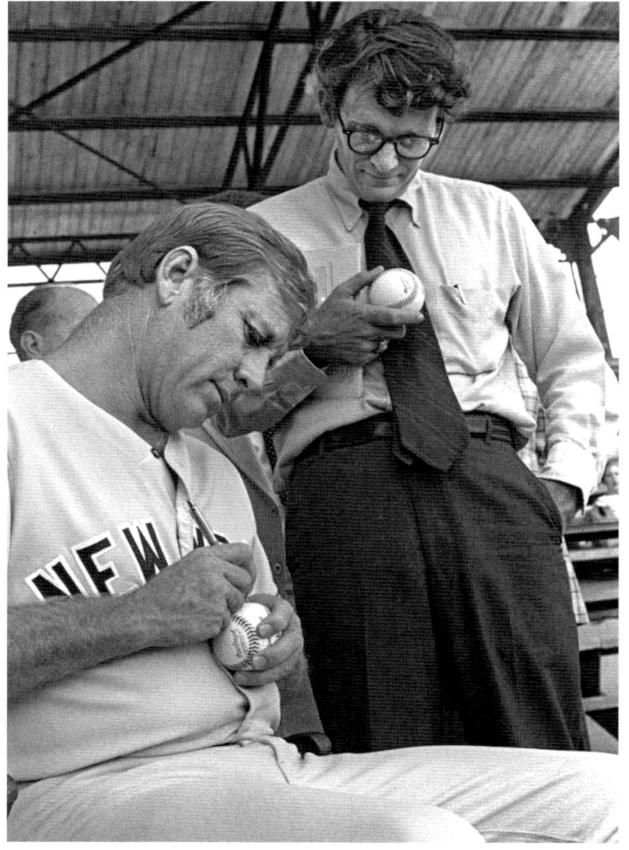

Riley, an avid baseball fan, took advantage of Mickey Mantle's appearance at College Park on July 20, 1978, to get a few balls autographed for his collection. (Photo by Brad Nettles)

The mayor throws out the first pitch on opening night at the stadium that bears his name, April 7, 2008. "I just try to get it to the catcher's glove without it hitting the ground," Riley said. (Photo by Wade Spees)

The iconic photograph of Riley being twirled by actor and River-Dogs co-owner Bill Murray, from opening night 2011. The image would inspire the figurine the team gave away on the night of Riley's final first pitch as mayor in July 2015. (Photo by Wade Spees)

The mayor surveys the damage to Hampton Park on Sept. 29, 1989, a week after Hurricane Hugo devastated Charleston. Riley mourned the loss of the park's great live oaks. His sons learned to walk in the park. He was close to tears during this tour. (Photo by Brad Nettles)

Riley appeared on The Oprah Winfrey Show when the television host brought her popular show to Charleston in the aftermath of Hugo, October 1989. Winfrey raved about Riley's efforts to restore the city. (Photo by Brad Nettles)

The "Get in Step with South Carolina!" march began on April 2, 2000, as Riley led hundreds on a protest march from Charleston to Columbia to force the state Legislature to take the Confederate flag off the Statehouse dome. Note Riley's bulkiness – because of death threats, he was forced to wear a bulletproof vest. (Photo by Bill Jordan)

The mayor in his City Hall office, Nov. 9, 1995, just after winning his sixth term. It doesn't look much different today, although it is a little neater now – and includes photos of his grandchildren. (Photo by Mic Smith)

Riley talks with his longtime friend, law partner and campaign manager Capers Barr outside of Mason Preparatory School during the 2011 mayor campaign; which would be his last. (Photo by Leroy Burnell)

Riley celebrates his 10th and final mayoral campaign victory at Jason's Deli in West Ashley, Nov. 8, 2011. The mayor is high-fiving longtime supporter Fritz Fielding while Capers Barr stands off to the right. (Photo by Wade Spees)

The mayor talks about completing Interstate 526 during a meeting of Charleston City Council at City Hall on Nov. 13, 2012. Note the famous Trumbull portrait of Washington behind him. (Photo by Wade Spees)

Riley listens to a reporter's question about an East Side drug bust during a press conference in City Council chambers, May 2, 2001. Police Chief Reuben Greenberg is on the left. (Photo by Wade Spees)

Riley's family poses on the deck of the Isle of Palms beach house. From left, Bratton, Bratton Jr., Riley, Joe Riley III, Mary Gail, and Charlotte. (Provided by the Riley family)

The mayor spends as much down time as possible fishing with family and friends. Here he displays a redfish he caught – and released – while angling with former law school classmate Thomas Boulware. (Provided by the Riley family)

Riley never missed a Charleston Christmas parade, and insisted on walking the route long after his family and staff insisted he ride in a car. This is from the Dec. 2, 2012, parade as the mayor makes his way along King Street. (Photo by Dave Munday)

Riley visited West Ashley resident Geraldine Rivers' home and talked to her, Kelly Hamlette and Cherlania Brown about school discipline. This was one of the mayor's "listening sessions" he did prior to launching his final campaign. (Photo by Robert Behre)

The mayor pays his respects to the nine Charleston firefighters who died during the 2007 Sofa Super Store fire just prior to the 2010 memorial service. Riley was on the scene the night of the fire, and persuaded City Council to buy the site for a park. (Photo by Wade Spees)

"Comforter-in-chief" Riley held Danielle Downing during a news conference as police asked the public for clues in the murder of Downing's brother, Jermel Tyler Brown, who was killed under an interstate overpass in July 2009. (Photo by Grace Beahm)

President Barack Obama presents Riley with the National Medal of Arts on Feb. 25, 2010, in the White House's East Room. Riley was an early supporter of Obama and has remained close to the president, who eventually delivered the eulogy at the Rev. Clementa Pinckney's funeral in Charleston. (AP Photo by Charles Dharapak)

Riley's leadership is largely credited for Charleston's reaction to the killing of nine Emanuel AME Church parishioners in June 2015. Here, the mayor attends a prayer vigil for the victims at Morris Brown AME Church a day after the slayings. From left, state Rep. Leon Stavrinakis, state Rep. Wendell Gilliard, Riley, Gov. Nikki Haley and U.S. Sen. Tim Scott. (Photo by Grace Beahm)

The mayor sits alone in a pew at Emanuel AME Church on July 2, 2015, just moments before a news conference to announce a college scholarship fund in the name of the Rev. Clementa Pinckney. (Photo by Lauren Prescott)

In the Arena

Only one man had ever won four mayoral elections in Charleston history, but almost everyone in the city expected Riley to soon join that short list. For nearly 12 years, he had barnstormed Charleston promoting one grand plan after the next, and he showed no signs of slowing down. He had baffled pundits by skipping the 1986 governor's race and, at 44, was still a young man. No one believed a politician as successful as Riley would simply walk away from public office.

By the spring of 1987, most people had decided the mayor wasn't going anywhere.

So it came as no surprise when, on April 14, Riley stood on the front steps of Charleston Place and told a crowd of 200 people that he would seek re-election for a fourth term. This time would be different. Riley had a challenger – his first since 1975 – and the Republican Party was campaigning against him with a litany of complaints: He was too liberal, had too much power and had served too long. These charges would become the campaign themes of the opposition, the criticism he would hear for the next six months, and the mayor addressed them in his opening statement.

"I had no desire to be mayor for life … or wear out my welcome with you," Riley said. "Our work isn't finished. If I were to step down now, I feel I would be leaving more unfinished business than I am prepared to leave."

He cited ongoing marquee projects including the waterfront park, the visitors center and the aquarium. He talked about the need for serious drainage improvements throughout Charleston, a Highway 61 expressway, a new bridge to James Island. These were all huge undertakings, and it was no coincidence that he launched his campaign in front of his greatest triumph. Riley considered the complex a symbol, a monument to the idea that lofty goals were within the city's reach.

Charleston had seen more change during Riley's tenure than at any point in its history, and he promised more. Of course, that was the problem for some people. Riley had dramatically increased tourism, which kept some downtown residents perpetually agitated. It did not matter that all this new business increased property values or had revived a once-moribund local economy. These critics dismissed Riley's efforts to strike a balance, to protect Charleston's oldest neighborhoods. In the past year the city had adopted rigid rules to rein in the horse carriage business, forcing tour buggies to take pre-selected routes so that no one street was clogged with horse traffic at a given time. Such gestures meant little to some downtown residents. They said none of those things would be an issue if not for Riley.

Riley's opponent, Roy DeHaven, played to those fears perfectly. On the same day the mayor announced his re-election bid, DeHaven called Riley and his associates a "pack of wild dogs" feeding off the federal government. He claimed Riley ignored the city's real needs – as well as a rosebush he had planted as part of a West Ashley beautification project. The bush died, the Republican lamented, and had to be replaced at taxpayers' expense.

After years on the back bench, the Charleston County GOP was feeling confident in 1987. There was only one Republican on City Council, but several others had announced their intentions to run against Democratic incumbents. The party decided against nominating any others, however, until they saw the Democrats' slate. The Charleston County Republicans had one goal, new Chairman Edward Holst told The News and Courier. "We want conservative government in the city of Charleston. We don't want puppets … (who) when the mayor pulls their string, their heads bob up and down."

Riley believed the vast majority of Charleston residents supported his agenda, that the Republican grousing represented only a small number of downtown residents. If City Council supported his plans most of the time, well, he attributed that to the logic of his reasoning – not arm twisting. And if people thought he focused too much on tourism, too bad. He would not alter his plans, not even in an election year. That was apparent when he appointed a committee to save the Old Slave Mart on Chalmers Street – yet another tourist attraction in a mostly residential neighborhood.

The Old Slave Mart was the oldest black history museum in the country. The building was the site of an actual marketplace where human beings were bought and sold for eight years beginning in 1856. Before that, slaves were often sold on public sidewalks – a practice some locals detested so much that the city eventually banned the practice. Since the Civil War, the building had housed everything from a black tenement to an auto repair shop. In 1938, Miriam Wilson turned it into a public museum filled with African and African-American arts and crafts, as well as relics of the slave trade. In the 1960s, Judith Wragg Chase and Louise Wragg Graves took over Wilson's work.

For years, the sisters had turned down offers from the city, the Charleston Museum, the College of Charleston and even the Smithsonian Institution to buy the building and their collection. But they were now both in their 80s and feared what might happen to the collection if they died before making arrangements. Although they had rebuffed the city's previous overtures, federal assistance and grants to the museum had dried up, and the sisters could no longer keep the doors open.

Chase said the Old Slave Mart would close once a going-out-of-business sale cleaned out the gift shop.

Riley cringed at the idea of a public auction, the collection scattered to the wind. He wanted to keep the Old Slave Mart Museum open; the mayor felt it was important to tell Charleston's whole story. Although the city had ample Civil War tourist sites and museums, the Old Slave Mart was the only Charleston facility that dealt exclusively with African-American history in sufficient depth. And Riley wanted more monuments to black history, not fewer.

The mayor's idea did not come at the most comfortable time in South Carolina. For months, the entire state had been debating whether the Confederate flag should fly atop the Statehouse dome. In late 1986, Jim Clyburn, at the time a state Human Affairs commissioner, questioned The Citadel's use of the flag and its band's performance of the fight song "Dixie" during football games.

Clyburn soon expanded his crusade to the Statehouse, where the flag – the rectangular Confederate Naval Jack – had flown since 1962. The banner had been hoisted originally to mark the 100th anniversary of the Civil War, lawmakers said, but was never taken down. Clyburn said the flag sent a bad message and he wanted it gone. That prompted death threats against Clyburn and his family. More proof that in South Carolina, old times were not forgotten.

The News and Courier was filled with letters to the editor for months, most of them supporting the flag and "Dixie." The comments were harsh and, although most letter writers claimed there were no racial overtones to their arguments, a few made blatantly racist statements. One person claimed blacks in public schools were holding the white kids back. It was an ugly reminder that civil rights were still a struggle in South Carolina. Riley quickly stepped in to defend Clyburn.

On April 4, 1987, the mayor published an op-ed in The News and Courier calling for the flag to be removed from the Statehouse. He tried to strike a conciliatory tone, noting "the pride that many have in the Confederate flag and 'Dixie' should be easily understood and honored. The negative feelings that many have about the same uses of the Confederate flag and 'Dixie' should be easily understood and honored as well. I believe that we can do both – and we must."

The flag is a reminder of those who fought and died gallantly, Riley wrote, but noted that it had been appropriated by people – including the Ku Klux Klan – to promote Jim Crow laws and oppose civil rights. The mayor said everyone should agree that using the flag in such a fashion is improper – something the Sons of Confederate Veterans also said. Riley argued the best way for the great-grandsons and great-granddaughters of those who fought in the Civil War to remember their ancestors was not to fly the flag on the Statehouse dome, but to give it a place of honor in museums and historical exhibits.

"My belief is that those who fought for the South in the Civil War and lost would much prefer their flag to be treated with this respect and honor rather than having it fly as a pennant on the third rung of any flagpole," Riley wrote.

Riley could not help but think he spoke with some authority on the subject. His great-grandfather Henry Oliver had been a decorated soldier for the South, so Riley truly was the descendant of a Confederate veteran. But unlike his ancestor, he had no interest in wallowing in the sweet misery of the Lost Cause. He suggested "Dixie" should be played only as a hymn, sung slowly as a nostalgic song of times past, not as an aggressive anthem. He said when "Dixie" is sung as a war cry, like at a football game, "many white people are standing and cheering, (but) our black friends are often sitting quietly, if not nervously, wishing the time would quickly pass. For they know that some of those who are cheering are doing so because deep down in their hearts, they wish that the racial progress we have achieved had never occurred."

The mayor tried to appeal to Southern manners. He asked flag supporters to put themselves in the shoes of their neighbors, to not do anything to make them uncomfortable, uneasy or sad. This was an important step to removing "yet another barrier to black and white Southerners achieving social and economic progress together." Riley had tried to strike a balance on Southern heritage, but many people did not see it that way. Soon, the letter writers attacked the mayor alongside Clyburn.

Lawmakers feared that Clyburn's and Riley's public relations campaign might get out of hand, and solicited a state attorney general's opinion on who had the right to take down the flag – and who didn't. The opinion, released in mid-June, said that neither the governor nor the state Budget and Control Board – the quasi-legislative and executive branch panel that actually ran much of the state – had the power to touch the flag. Only legislators could remove the Confederate Naval Jack from the dome, and they had no intentions of doing that.

Riley didn't worry about raising the ire of conservatives in an election year. He knew protesting the Confederate flag could hurt him politically, but he believed it was his job to preach equality and try to improve race relations. He had promised to do that when he first ran for office. Few people questioned the mayor's commitment to civil rights, but still he was criticized on occasion. Some African-Americans complained he did not hire enough minorities to work for the city, and that he did not do enough to nurture new black businesses. But those complaints were rare; most African-Americans gave the mayor their unconditional support. Even City Councilman Robert Ford had become a vocal supporter.

At the state Democratic Convention in May 1987, Ford noted that Riley presided over a racially mixed council and had appointed black citizens to positions of high authority in the city, not the least of which was a strong police chief. "Charleston doesn't have a black mayor," Ford said, "but we have Little Black Joe." The News and Courier editorialized that when a black public official could make such a joke without anyone getting offended or raising a fuss, it was a sign that Charleston had come a long way – and Riley deserved the most credit for that.

The mayor's devotion to racial harmony ran head first into the First Amendment less than a month later, when the Ku Klux Klan requested a permit to parade through the streets of Charleston. Riley did not want to see these buffoons marching through his city and considered denying the permit. But his attorneys argued the march constituted free speech and, without any good reason, the city couldn't turn down the group. The Klan would like nothing more than a lawsuit against the birthplace of the Confederacy to keep its name in the papers.

Riley agreed to issue the permit, but that didn't mean he couldn't have a little fun at the Klan's expense. First, he picked the date for them – Sunday, Aug. 2. It was one of the hottest weeks in the city, and the mayor liked the idea of the men in white sheets feeling the heat. Then he urged residents not to show up for the parade – not even to protest – because the Klan was staging the parade only for publicity.

The police and The News and Courier made the same plea, but it did little good. More than 2,000 people lined the parade route that Sunday. The Klan was scheduled to depart from Marion Square and march south on Meeting Street, west on Broad and back up King Street to their original starting point. Lowcountry police agencies sent about 300 officers to make sure there was no violence, and forced Klan members to go through metal detectors to prove they weren't carrying guns or knives.

The Grand Dragon was met in Marion Square by Police Chief Reuben Greenberg, who showed up to explain the rules of their parade permit. If the Klavern leader was surprised to see a black man leading Charleston's police force, he probably had enough sense to keep his thoughts to himself. Greenberg was not only a big man, he had a gun. The Klansmen agreed to the rules and set out on their way, some of them carrying signs that said "Wake up, white people" and "KKK here to stay." Of course, one of the Klansmen carried a Confederate flag.

What the Klan did not anticipate was the leader of the parade. Riley – who did not often let his dry sense of humor show publicly – suggested to Greenberg that the parade deserved "special" attention. So the chief decided to lead the procession personally, and on horseback. As the sweating, white-robed members of the Ku Klux Klan walked along Charleston streets, getting spit on and yelled at by black and white protesters, they were forced to look straight ahead at a Jewish black man – and a horse's ass.

Roy DeHaven used the KKK march to highlight the differences between himself and the mayor. He agreed the group was despicable, but said he would have forced the Klan to march in a circle at Brittlebank Park instead of letting them clog downtown streets. The message was clear: Riley contributes to peninsular traffic woes. DeHaven, a local real estate broker, had been campaigning since November 1986 and rarely let a week go by without finding a way to criticize Riley or the city.

Earlier in the year, City Council decided to raise the mayor's salary to $82,500, which would make it one of the highest-paying jobs of its kind in the nation. Council members argued that Riley had earned every penny of it, but a few pointed out they weren't raising Riley's pay, only the mayor's salary. Anyone who got elected would be entitled to the same amount. Riley went to his office during the debate – he didn't want to stay in the room so that opponents of the move could speak openly. But that wouldn't stop DeHaven, who told civic groups through the summer that $60,000 was enough. Council eventually settled on $73,800 for a new salary, although Ford – now one of Riley's strongest supporters – argued that this mayor was worth between $200,000 and $300,000 a year.

After years of criticizing Riley, the councilman had warmed to the mayor. At one council meeting, Ford spoke eloquently – and at great length – about a woman from his district hired to work at Charleston Place. The job allowed her to buy her own house, to live the American Dream – and it was all because of Mayor Riley's efforts to bring jobs and revitalization to the city, Ford said. This woman was the reason the city of Charleston, and the mayor, had worked so tirelessly to build the hotel and convention center.

Bill Regan thought the story wonderfully illustrated how much Charleston Place had done for the community, the woman the very personification of Riley's vision. After the meeting, Regan asked Ford if he had a way to contact the woman he'd mentioned. Ford looked confused by Regan's question, and then remembered his speech. "Oh that," Ford said. "I just made all that up." He was only trying to help.

Not that Riley needed any assistance – DeHaven was helping the mayor's campaign enough for everyone. In June, DeHaven suggested the city test Spoleto performers for AIDS. He said the president wanted select groups tested for the virus, and it would be prudent to check out all the artists filing into the city. At a news conference called for this sole purpose, DeHaven said City Council should "defend its citizens and visitors alike, and the testing will encourage both safe and high-risk people to be responsible while in Charleston."

When reporters asked him about DeHaven's suggestion, Riley was barely able to respond. "His comments are ridiculous. I don't think they merit any more comment than that."

DeHaven would not back down, expanding his net a few days later to suggest some city workers be tested as well. The county Republican Party's executive committee applauded his stance, even though DeHaven was forced to admit he had to refund a few campaign donations as a result of his position. Still, he continued his strategy of making outrageous comments in an effort to gain traction. At one point, he claimed the Democratic Party paid black people to vote.

Finally, one month before the election, DeHaven tried to revive a decade-old feud between Riley and the city Fire Department. He said firefighters were quietly complaining that the mayor forced them to sign a "loyalty oath" prior to voting. The "oath" was actually a letter the state Supreme Court ordered all public employees to sign acknowledging they weren't contract workers. A recent court ruling had found that an employee handbook could be legally interpreted as a contract of sorts – and contracts meant unions, so the court stopped any confusion before it could start. But DeHaven said the letter was a message to firefighters: Vote for Riley or lose their job.

DeHaven's campaign playbook could have been taken from the minutes of any downtown neighborhood association meeting. The people still upset over Charleston Place and the proliferation of tourism provided the candidate much of his ammunition. He parroted claims made by these groups, telling reporters that Riley had let city services decline while over-reaching with annexation and "building pyramids" to himself. He took sly swipes at allegedly liberal causes, criticizing the city for spending tax dollars on the Spoleto Festival. That gave Riley the opportunity to point out the city's $70,000 investment had amounted to a $60 million economic impact on the Lowcountry.

In the end, none of those tactics benefited DeHaven. On election night, Riley took 81 percent of the vote – winning all 38 city precincts in a landslide that suggested he'd never had more support. DeHaven was gracious in defeat, and said his campaign suffered because elected Republican officials failed to publicly support him. Of course, most elected Republican officials did not routinely go around making such outrageous statements. And most of them had no desire to take on Riley, because they realized the mayor wasn't going anywhere.

Weeks after the election, The News and Courier and The Evening Post asked readers to rank the most powerful people in the Lowcountry, and the mayor won overwhelmingly. The papers noted the irony of this, as the criticism of Riley in 1975 held that he was too mild-mannered and not powerful enough to lead the city. Riley joked to the papers that "I haven't heard that recently." In fact, most people felt exactly the opposite by the end of 1987.

Riley's victory revived the speculation that he would soon seek higher office. While discussing a move to make municipal elections nonpartisan, Herbert Fielding – by then a state senator – told The News and Courier that he was doing his best to launch a 1990 Joe Riley gubernatorial campaign. Most people already believed Riley was eventually headed for Columbia or Washington. None of them considered the idea that he might just stick around. No one had ever run for a fifth term as mayor.

Two weeks after his fourth inauguration, Riley met Strom Thurmond on Concord Street to break ground for the city's waterfront park. The 12-acre park had undergone significant redesign since the mayor first proposed the idea. Gone was the "festival marketplace" to link the park to the Market. The city also had decided against building a pier on the harbor that would run the length of the park. Instead, Riley wanted to restore the marsh along the shore. The mayor said the park would return the city's focus to the harbor, offer more water access for locals and tourists, and alleviate traffic for the neighborhoods South of Broad.

Elizabeth Gadsden Woodward – who along with her late husband, Charles, had put up half the money for the land – was on hand to watch the ceremony as Thurmond and Riley took gilded sledgehammers to drive the first pilings into the ground. Thurmond gave his piling a good smack and it sank into the ground mere inches. When Riley's hit his, however, the whole piling disappeared into the ground. Mugging for the cameras, Thurmond grabbed Riley's arm and said, "I knew he was a good mayor, I just didn't know he had such large muscles."

Of course, it was a trick. City workers had rigged the piling to drop into the earth the second the mayor struck it. But it was a nice metaphor for Riley's growing power. One poll had just ranked Riley among the 12 most-powerful mayors in the country.

That winter, Riley was having less success with another waterfront project – one that initially wasn't even his plan. Sen. Fritz Hollings had asked the mayor to consider a city partnership with their alma mater, The Citadel, to build a new basketball arena on the banks of the Ashley River. The military college was facing a $7 million price tag to renovate McAlister Field House. The gym was 50 years old, had terrible acoustics and no air conditioning. Maj. Gen. James Grimsley, president of the college, wanted to give McAlister a makeover, but several members of the Board of Visitors wanted a whole new facility. They feared Riley would not agree to a joint-operated arena, so they sent Hollings to lobby him.

As predicted, Riley was not interested at first. But he slowly warmed to the idea, perhaps because North Charleston Mayor John Bourne was planning to build his own coliseum. Riley knew an arena in North Charleston would draw people away from the city, and he didn't want the competition. Finally, he decided the waterfront land on Lockwood Drive would make an ideal setting, especially if the arena also included a convention center. The mayor agreed to work with The Citadel, and city staffers drew up plans for a $20 million arena. Riley began talking to members of the Legislature, hoping to get partial funding from the state's upcoming bond bill.

Riley worked for two months before the Board of Visitors abruptly changed course and decided to renovate McAlister Field House. Citadel officials said the city's plans would make the arena more suited to conventions than basketball and, at an estimated price of $29 million, the facility would cost far more than they wanted to spend. Suddenly, Riley was forced to sell the college on an idea its board had brought to him.

It was annoying, but some people thought it was just politics. North Charleston voters had agreed to float $20 million in bonds for a coliseum, and Grimsley wanted the renovation, so lawmakers persuaded the Board of Visitors to back off. Although it wasted months of time, Riley later said it was a good example of the simple truth of development: Sometimes the greatest blessings are unanswered prayers.

When the arena project fell through, it left a large swath of land on the Ashley River wide open for development.

The mayor's 1988 inaugural address had focused largely on efforts to revive the city's East Side, but an offhand remark about a potential new park garnered the most attention. Riley said the city was trying to buy the Angel Oak tree on Johns Island. The 1,400-year-old live oak – the largest tree of its kind in the Lowcountry – was believed by some people to be the oldest living thing east of the Rocky Mountains, and had become a minor tourist attraction. But the tree was not only privately owned, it also sat well outside Charleston's city limits.

The idea to acquire the tree had first come to Riley more than a year earlier. The owner, a local developer named S.E. "Speedy" Felkel, almost lost the tree in a tax dispute. The Internal Revenue Service said Felkel owed $4.3 million in back taxes and planned to seize nearly all of his property – including Angel Oak. Riley pleaded with the IRS to sell the tree to the city instead of putting it up for auction, but nothing ever came of it. Felkel settled with the feds an hour before the auction.

Riley had not forgotten the lost opportunity. He thought Angel Oak would make a great city park, and feared Felkel might eventually lose the tree or sell it – and an important piece of Lowcountry history would be gone forever. The city was having a formal appraisal of the land done, the mayor said, and would pay fair market value. Sounding very much like the Godfather, Riley said, "I feel sure our offer will be accepted." And if not, Riley was willing to invoke eminent domain and take it.

The area of Johns Island where the tree sat – near the intersection of Maybank Highway and Main Road – was not part of the city of Charleston, but state law at the time allowed a city to declare eminent domain outside its borders so long as the land taken was used as a park. Attorneys for the city helpfully pointed out the law to reporters, confident they were on firm legal ground.

Felkel was not interested in selling and called the mayor's efforts a hostile takeover. He said the tree was a family heirloom – he'd bought it 24 years earlier – and this was no different than Riley walking into his house and taking the family Bible or his "one-of-a-kind Rembrandt." Felkel knew exactly how to play the victim and paint Riley as the bad guy. And it worked.

Johns Islanders said the mayor had damaged his reputation by trying to take someone's private property. Dana Beach, conservation chairman for the Charleston branch of the Sierra Club, warned that the dirt road leading to the tree should not be paved if the city acquires it. Even Frank Gilbreth, in his Ashley Cooper column, could not support the mayor this time.

Gilbreth said taking Angel Oak was a terrible precedent that could eventually allow the city to seize historic downtown homes and declare them treasures too valuable to rest in private hands. The criticism was gentle, but Gilbreth's disapproval gave Riley pause. He always believed he would win any debate if he had Ashley Cooper on his side. And this time he didn't.

Within a week, Johns Island residents sent Riley a petition signed by 2,800 people opposed to his plan. State legislators announced efforts to change state law so the mayor couldn't take property outside his city limits. By spring, Riley and Felkel were called to testify before legislative committees. Felkel used his sudden fame to try to make some money. In April, he announced that he might turn the Morris Island lighthouse into a tourist attraction. He had bought the 19th-century tower in the 1960s for $25,000 and said he wanted to restore it and open it – if Riley didn't want to take that, too.

When one newspaper reporter asked Felkel why he was so busy acquiring Low-country landmarks, he said, "I just like old things."

By late spring, the entire fiasco had become a joke. The Legislature dropped its bill and the city backed off its eminent domain threats. During an annual American Cancer Society fundraiser, in which local celebrities were jailed until they raised money for the charity, Sheriff Al Cannon arrested Riley on a charge of "coveting thy neighbor's tree." The mayor pleaded guilty, although he declared his innocence on charges of trying to build one too many coliseums in town and illegal fishing for an aquarium.

The aquarium – or the S.C. Marine Science Museum, as he called it – remained at the top of Riley's priority list, but it was not faring well in Columbia. When Gov.

Carroll Campbell asked the Legislature to cut the aquarium money from its bond bill, Riley claimed it was regional politics. He said the governor wanted to funnel all available state funds to his hometown of Greenville. Perhaps, the mayor said, "it might be time to oppose the Greenville Arts Center."

Riley and Campbell sat down to talk less than a week later, and the conversation did not go well. The governor tried to make his argument sound non-political. He said it bothered him that Charleston wanted to fund fish over children, while Riley pointed out the aquarium would make money for the state and was an educational center that would benefit children. The mayor's powers of persuasion did not work on the partisan Campbell, but he had better luck with the Legislature. When lawmakers passed a bond bill in June, it included $9.5 million for the Marine Science Museum.

Riley spent the rest of the summer trying once again to lure James Islanders into the city and urging Charleston County not to move its offices to North Charleston. County Councilman Burnet Maybank said "Little Joe" couldn't accept the fact that Charleston would soon no longer be the largest city in the county. Riley argued the county had an obligation to maintain a presence in the historic district and it would be a mistake to fragment county government. The fight over the County Courthouse was still going on when U.S. Supreme Court Justice William Rehnquist arrived to dedicate the new Federal Courthouse Annex across the street.

But all that was inside baseball, as Riley called it, and he soon turned his attention back to the aquarium. In October 1988, Riley launched a campaign asking city voters to dedicate $9.5 million in bonds to what he now called the South Carolina Aquarium. Riley said that money – coupled with $9.5 million from the state and private donations – would be enough to build the $23.7 million facility.

Riley took his campaign to the Chamber of Commerce and the schools, and then made a public presentation at the Dock Street Theatre. The mayor said he was confident the city would recoup its investment within five years and, by then, the area would see a total economic impact of nearly a quarter-billion dollars. The aquarium would house 200 live exhibits, more than 5,000 aquatic animals and a 300,000-gallon ocean tank. And, he said, it would attract private businesses to the waterfront. City Council had decided to locate the aquarium on the Cooper River just north of the Dockside Condominiums.

On Nov. 8, voters were in a generous mood. Two-thirds of county residents agreed to chip in on Mayor Bourne's North Charleston Coliseum and Mayor Riley won 75 percent support for his aquarium bond referendum. "I feel the citizens of our city are enthusiastic about this wonderful opportunity and feel strongly that its educational, environmental and economic benefits will make it an extraordinary asset for our community," Riley said.

The mayor was amazed. He had been in office 13 years, and in that time had built a major hotel and conference center, acquired a waterfront park and started an international arts festival. Now, he would soon have an aquarium. Charleston was changing, becoming a more popular tourist destination each year. As a result, the city's economy was doing better than most of South Carolina – and the country.

As 1988 drew to a close, Riley was even more optimistic than usual. Almost everything was going his way, Charleston's way. The city was healthier than it had been in decades, perhaps centuries, and seemed poised on the edge of a renaissance.

For the moment, he could not see the storm clouds on the horizon.

September 21, 1989

A cluster of thunderstorms over Senegal, The Gambia and Guinea-Bissau moved off Africa's westernmost coast on Sept. 9, 1989. Almost immediately, the storms began a delicate meteorological choreography that forecasters call a tropical wave. The winds of the storms began to move in concert, picking up speed as they churned over the Atlantic Ocean 1,000 miles north of the equator.

Within a day, this low pressure system organized enough to officially become the 11th tropical depression of the year. The storm was 125 miles southeast of the Cape Verde Islands, a very dangerous place for a tropical system to form. Most years, there are usually only two Cape Verde storms – but they are almost invariably the largest, most powerful systems of the hurricane season. Storms born on the cape have to cover the most distance over warm, open water, giving them ample time to organize and grow – and gain strength.

For three days the depression traveled due east at 12 degrees north latitude. After the first, an eye began to take shape and it was classified a tropical storm. Late on Sept. 13, the system was 1,100 miles east of the Caribbean's Leeward Islands. A low pressure system to the south nudged the storm on a west-northwestern course, and by the next day it was just 400 miles east of Guadeloupe. Finally, it had reached hurricane status. It was given the name Hugo.

The winds closest to the storm's eye were moving at 150 miles per hour and gaining speed.

For a brief time, Hugo's wind speed topped 160 mph, enough to classify it a Category 5 hurricane. It had been downgraded to a Category 4 storm by the time it passed between Guadeloupe and Montserrat, and even without a direct hit, Hugo did enough damage to leave 10,000 homeless and five dead. Then, around 2 a.m. on

Sept. 18, the eye passed over the southwestern corner of St. Croix. Hugo's 140 mph winds damaged or destroyed 90 percent of the buildings on the island. Nearly all of St. Croix's vegetation was laid waste. Nine more people died.

From there the storm passed by St. Thomas, lashing it with hurricane-force winds before crossing over the Puerto Rican islands of Vieques and Culebra, where one yacht recorded its top gusts at 170 mph. Culebra took the brunt of the damage, but Hugo also spread its wrath across the northeastern corner of Puerto Rico near Fajardo. Vieques and Culebra lost 80 percent of their wooden buildings, leaving 30,000 people homeless and causing more than $1 billion in damage. Another nine people were killed by the storm.

Hugo's Puerto Rican landfall weakened the storm somewhat. Its winds slowed to 100 mph and the eye began to break apart. But as it settled in over the North Atlantic, Hugo began to reform, its winds regaining their speed, eventually reaching nearly 140 mph. It was moving northwest, its path preordained by an upper-level low over Bermuda and a low-pressure system in the Gulf of Mexico. Hugo was barreling across the Atlantic at 25 mph on Sept. 20 when the National Weather Service issued a hurricane watch for more than 400 miles of U.S. coastline between Fernandina Beach, Florida, and Cape Hatteras, North Carolina.

Charleston sat roughly in the middle of the watch area.

In September 1989, Riley was busy trying to persuade county voters to support a November bond referendum for his aquarium. County Council had agreed to put the question on the ballot, and the mayor wanted to assure everyone that the South Carolina Aquarium would pay its own way before the regular naysayers began their smear campaign. And, as usual, they would.

Riley had had a busy, but largely uneventful, year. He hosted the U.S. Conference of Mayors' summer convention in June, reached a deal with the state for the city to operate the Old Exchange Building and made substantial progress on his plan to build a new main branch of the county library on Calhoun Street. At the same time, Riley was championing a plan by private developers to rebuild the old Charleston Hotel – a grand, Greek revival building that stood on Meeting Street for more than 120 years before it was torn down in 1960.

The razing of the old Charleston Hotel was largely considered the greatest preservation disaster in the city's history. Riley was smitten with the idea of a reproduction of the building – even though the owners planned to use it for office space, and even though it called for the demolition of the Heart of Charleston Motel, home of a diner the mayor frequented regularly with his staff. The Board of Architectural Review was unimpressed by the design for this new Charleston Hotel, however, and when board members asked the developer to go back to the drawing board, the idea was scrapped.

Riley was having better luck with his own pet projects. The waterfront park was 60 percent complete, the city was about to add a pier and docks at Brittlebank Park and council had just bought a piece of land next door to the James Island Yacht Club for another park – sparing residents from a dry-stack marina the former owner had been planning there for years. Demetre Park, as the city called it, would prove immensely popular.

Adding green space to the city was one of Riley's oldest goals. Since first taking office he had wanted to dramatically increase the number of parks. The Lowcountry was a unique, beautiful ecosystem that he believed should be preserved as much as possible. He knew that, with the area's growing population, such areas would become even more important to Charleston's quality of life. He didn't realize it at the time, but much of his work would soon be undone.

Charleston followed Hugo's path through the Caribbean with the mild concern of any coastal town that hadn't faced a major storm in decades. The papers had published daily stories on the storm's destructive wake across the Atlantic since Sept. 12, when it was just a tropical storm. On Sept. 16 the National Weather Service in Columbia told Charleston reporters that the city appeared to be out of harm's way – "for now." It was more comfort than anyone needed at that moment.

In the late 1980s, weather forecasting was not nearly as sophisticated as it would become just a decade later. Cities had little advance warning of storms. There were no computer models spitting out projected tracks every few hours, no way to determine what might happen in the days ahead. Hugo was one of the first hurricanes to get so much attention from the media in advance of its arrival, but it was still muted compared to what would come by the turn of the century. As late as Sept. 18, the National Hurricane Center said an East Coast landfall was uncertain. It did not appear the time had come to panic.

Riley had never faced the prospect of a catastrophic storm. No major hurricane had hit South Carolina since Gracie in 1959, although the 1981 Tropical Storm Dennis had caused enough flooding problems in Charleston that the mayor was forced to request federal funds to help with the clean-up. He realized that if a minor system like Dennis could flood city streets, a major hurricane could be devastating and deadly. Riley, who called the storm a "HURRI-cane" in the Lowcountry manner of putting emphasis on the first syllable, knew little about storms – but he knew how to listen. When the weathermen talked about the high over Bermuda and the low over the Gulf guiding the storm, Riley had a sense that Hugo's path was fairly clear and predetermined, and Charleston's hurricane drought was over.

On Tuesday morning, Sept. 19, the mayor gathered his staff at City Hall to work out a storm plan. By then most locals were growing more concerned with Hugo's trajectory, and Riley's people were no exception. He told them there was no use bemoaning their bad luck – they should look at it as an opportunity. Government does a lot of unpleasant, regulatory things like sending out tax bills and issuing parking tickets. This was their chance, he said, to help people at a time when they need it the most.

"If we can do the best job any city has ever done preparing for a storm, then the benefit to the city and the county will be a long-term positive impact," Riley told them.

The mayor did not like negativity, had never understood politicians who focused on how bad things were. He preferred to maintain an air of optimism and hope in the face of just about any situation; that was simply his personality. But the storm tested his resolve. Riley told Charleston's top administrators that the city was at war and the enemy was just over the hill, waiting to strike. The message was they could not let their guard down for a second; they had to remain on high alert throughout. "If we let up for a minute, the enemy will come over the hill and kill us."

The mayor asked Barbara Vaughn, the city's ombudsman and public relations officer, to gather advice from other cities that had suffered direct hits from a hurricane. He suggested she try Gulf Coast towns that had suffered through Hurricane Camille 20 years earlier. Ask them, Riley said, what they learned that wasn't in the books, the manuals on storm preparation. What did the experts miss, what did these cities learn from their horrible experiences? It took Vaughn about an hour and a half to return with pages of advice and frightening warnings.

City officials in Galveston, Corpus Christi, and little towns around Mississippi told Vaughn to evacuate as many people as possible – that was the single most important thing to do. The most dangerous part of a hurricane is rising water. The surge that follows a hurricane comes out of nowhere – a wall of water that can envelop an entire town, trapping people, drowning them. Most of the Gulf Coast officials Vaughn spoke with made one final, terrifying point. They said that no one ever sees a storm surge on television because, when it comes, there is no one left to film it.

There was no simple way to get residents to evacuate. Some people never take a storm warning seriously; there are always knuckleheads and thrill-seekers who treat impending doom like a party. One mayor told Vaughn, "Cry wolf if you have to" to get people to leave. But, they cautioned, there is a political risk to that. If the storm doesn't hit, some people will be upset they were inconvenienced. But saving lives is far more important than politics. As the mayor later recalled, his counterparts said he must "thread the needle between fear and panic." Riley decided the best way to convincingly show people the severity of the situation was to let them see how seriously he took it.

Riley called a news conference at noon on Wednesday, Sept. 20 – hours before the National Weather Service issued a hurricane watch or Gov. Carroll Campbell declared a state of emergency. He chose to speak with reporters in front of City Hall, where workers were boarding up the windows of the nearly 200-year-old building. This was not coincidence. That sort of storm preparation was just the sort of action that attracted TV cameras, and Riley wanted everyone to see City Hall battening down the hatches.

Riley told reporters the city was simply being prudent. He warned people against throwing hurricane parties or standing on The Battery as the storm came in, because he didn't want to risk his police force to save people from poor behavior. He repeated what other mayors had told Vaughn almost verbatim. "This is not funny, and it is not a spectator sport." The smart thing to do, Riley urged residents, is to be ready for the worst.

"There is no downside to being overly prepared," Riley said. "The citizenry must not be lulled into a false sense of security. This is a dangerous killer hurricane and the combination of its winds and high tides could produce a storm and dangerous effects the like of which very few people in Charleston have ever seen."

Most people took the warning seriously. Residents rushed to the hardware stores for plywood and supplies as the city gave out free sandbags. This would help protect property, Riley said, but it would not offset all the danger. Although shelters were being opened around the city, Charleston County Council Chairwoman Linda Lombard asked people to consider leaving the peninsula if they could – even in advance of an evacuation order. Riley, who joined Lombard at regular news conferences, made the same plea and urged churches to contact their elderly members to make sure they could get to safety. "This is a time when the people in the community should reach out and care for each other."

Riley followed his own advice. His son, Joe, was already safe in Columbia, attending classes at the University of South Carolina, and would soon be joined by his grandparents. Big Joe had rented hotel rooms in Columbia and gathered up his usual rambling entourage of friends for the trip. The mayor sent Bratton with Charlotte to her mother's house in Camden, far enough from the coast that he felt they would be safe. He didn't want to have to worry about his family because he wasn't going anywhere. City Hall would serve as the command base and, if there was a storm, Riley would ride it out in the mayor's office.

Police Chief Reuben Greenberg met with the mayor before his Wednesday press conference to plan their strategy. Already, Greenberg had sent most of his officers home to get their families on the road – the city did not want its emergency personnel worrying about their loved ones while trying to rescue others during a storm. The chief explained that he would have police stationed at key points around the city if it looked like the storm was going to hit. Riley told Greenberg to make sure his force was at full strength because he would not tolerate any looting. It's bad enough when a city goes through the physical destruction of a hurricane, Riley said, but looting can destroy a city's character – and its honor. Greenberg took the message seriously.

That night Gov. Campbell urged the residents of all barrier islands to evacuate. Campbell said he wouldn't hesitate to issue an order forcing everyone out of all low-lying areas if the storm didn't veer off its current path, as forecasts predicted. At that point, the governor said, the situation "does not warrant panic, but prudence." Most public offices would be closed the next day, Thursday, Sept. 21, in case the National Hurricane Center's watch turned into a warning. But neither the news, nor the forecast, would improve overnight.

The hurricane warning was issued at 6 a.m. on Thursday, Sept. 21, even though the potential strike area had not been narrowed. Charleston was already getting 40 mph wind gusts and rain from the storm's outermost bands, but forecasters still said the storm could hit anywhere between Fernandina Beach and Cape Hatteras. The weather was bad enough that people had taken notice. Hours after the warning went out, Interstate 26 was clogged – the 100-mile trip to Columbia taking up to eight hours. Those who remained in the city cleaned out hardware stores and supermarkets, stocking up on supplies. They worked through heavy rain and increasingly harsh winds. The outer edges of Hugo were closing in. Even if it didn't hit Charleston, the city would likely see heavy damage.

Although storm shelters were open around the county, city workers realized that many public housing residents were still in danger. The Ansonborough Homes sat on low-lying ground just a block off the Cooper River. If there was any storm surge, they would no doubt be flooded. Riley asked the Red Cross and the county to set up a shelter downtown, but everyone he talked to said that wasn't safe – the entire peninsula could end up underwater. Riley knew he couldn't just send poor downtown residents to a shelter on Rivers Avenue in North Charleston – they wouldn't go. So he decided to turn the Gaillard Auditorium into a shelter. He sent workers knocking on doors, asking people to come and ride out the storm in the auditorium. That order likely saved at least a dozen lives.

At midday the roads leading out of Charleston were jammed as thousands of people fled inland, but the peninsula was largely deserted. An eerie silence had fallen on Broad Street by the time Riley and Vaughn set out for the county's emergency headquarters in North Charleston to meet with Lombard and other officials. Riley blew through the streets at a quick clip, passing swaying palm trees as he raced to the latest news briefing. The storm was about 200 miles away and he wanted to tell people to use the time they had left to get out of the city. Later, neighbors of Riley's sisters would say they had planned to stay until they saw the mayor on television. When Riley said they should leave, they took it seriously. Eventually, about 150,000 people evacuated along South Carolina's coast.

As darkness fell, state officials and forecasters still held out some small hope that Hugo would take a last-minute turn, get caught in the Gulf Stream currents and pass Charleston far offshore. Perhaps the city would get only a glancing blow. It was the last optimistic thought most people in South Carolina would have for a long time.

The mayor spent the evening visiting shelters, trying to reassure people they would be safe indoors. At Garrett High School, the CBS news program "48 Hours" interviewed him briefly, the reporter telling him that the storm did not appear to be turning – and it was only hours off the coast. Weather forecasts now predicted it would make landfall somewhere between Hilton Head and Myrtle Beach. In other words, Charleston was the bull's-eye.

Riley tried to keep up an optimistic front, but he knew there was little question anymore – the storm was coming. He quickly gathered up Howard Chapman, the city's transportation director, and Kerri Morgan, a News and Courier reporter, and left the school. Crammed into the cab of a heavy-duty city truck, they set off down Meeting Street toward City Hall – the wind occasionally picking the truck up and dropping it back on the road. If this was the edge of the storm, Riley thought, he did not want to see a direct hit. As he dodged fallen tree limbs, Riley's bag phone began to ring. It was Bob Sheets, director of the National Hurricane Center.

"Charleston is Ground Zero," Sheets said. "It's going to be a dead hit on Charleston Harbor."

It was exactly what Riley had feared, and it didn't help to hear Sheets recite the tracking data. The storm was picking up speed, moving toward the coast at nearly 30 miles per hour. Hugo's winds were 138 mph, its eye a monstrous 40 miles wide, and it was pushing a storm surge of between 12 and 17 feet. Landfall was expected to come just before high tide. Hurricane Hugo had the potential to be the Storm of the Century.

Morgan later said the mayor's eyes got wide as he listened to Sheets. But he remained calm, clung to his usual stoic manners even as he dodged debris on Meeting Street. He had barely slept the night before and was running on pure adrenaline. As he raced down the peninsula, Riley would later recall, he knew they were "cutting it a shade close." When he hung up with Sheets, Riley turned to Chapman and Morgan and simply said, "We have to get back to City Hall. We have a lot to do."

When they reached 80 Broad St., Riley gathered reporters to send out the only message he could offer: a prayer. "All we can do is pray now and hope that all the precautions we have taken will be sufficient." He was resigned to catastrophe; it was out of his hands. But, the mayor told reporters, as beautiful as Charleston's historic buildings were, they could be rebuilt and replaced. Human life could not.

Riley was back in his office when the power went out at City Hall. Water was pouring into the basement, shorting out circuits. City workers had gotten a generator for the building, but the mayor would not let them go outside to crank it up. From a peephole in the plywood covering his window, he could see slate shingles flying through the air – projectiles that could slice a person open. Riley would not risk anyone's life for a little power, and told his staff to light candles. Without the hum of electricity through the building, he could hear rainwater continuing to pour into the basement. It had begun.

Hurricane-force winds reached the city by 10 p.m., bending palm trees, stripping roofs of their shingles and toppling street signs. An old tree in Washington Park next to City Hall fell on a gas line, forcing firefighters out into the storm to stop the leak. A fire, they knew, would quickly spread across the city, fueled by the roaring wind. Riley sat with his staff in the mayor's office, listening to the chaos on a police scanner. Windows at the Medical University had been blown out by the gusts, and Hugo had claimed its first roofs of the night.

A hurricane is a nearly perfect, self-sustaining storm. It is powered by a low-pressure center, drawing energy from the evaporation of water on the ocean's surface. The moist air rises and forms rainclouds. The Earth's rotation forces the storm's winds into a counter-clockwise motion as they churn toward its center, its eye. The closer the wind to the storm's eye, the stronger it is. As Hugo approached Charleston Harbor, the winds circling its eyewall were about 135 mph, enough to classify it as a Category 4 hurricane on the Saffir-Simpson hurricane wind scale. By any measurable standard, it was a monster.

When the inner bands of wind reached Charleston, the damage began immediately. Utility poles bent under the pressure, electricity cables snapped loose and transformers exploded. The entire city was plunged into darkness, sparing residents the sight of the carnage. Trees that had stood for 100 years were ripped out of the ground, church steeples were toppled. Hugo found every building with structural weakness and knocked it down. The air pressure caused windows to explode, the shattered glass a crescendo to a violent symphony playing throughout Charleston.

Across the city, people who could barely stand in the wind were struggling to survive. Rescue workers fought to save East Side residents who had remained in their homes. On Sires Street, a man and several children were pinned inside a building when it collapsed. They would remain there throughout the night. The residents of a Perry Street house listened as their home creaked and groaned before finally falling down around them. Another man was trapped when his Moultrie Street house gave up and collapsed.

Hugo's destructive force was constant, almost in concert. The Meeting Street Piggly Wiggly, Second Presbyterian Church and the City Market lost their roofs at the same time a giant crane at the Ports Authority's Columbus Street Terminal crashed onto the docks. Nothing in the city was spared. The wind tore a chimney from the Aiken-Rhett House, broke the Palladian window at the Joseph Manigault House and ripped up 86 newly planted trees in Riley's waterfront park.

The storm was so large it engulfed the entire county simultaneously. On Johns Island, people using Haut Gap Middle School's gym as a shelter watched as one of the building's walls buckled. In West Ashley, the steeple at Blessed Sacrament fell and the press box at St. Andrew's High School's football stadium was blown away. Even the fiberglass Coburg cow, a local icon that stood on a spinning sign along Savannah Highway, had simply vanished. And the ocean was beginning to slice Sullivan's Island and the Isle of Palms to pieces.

Sullivan's Island Police Chief Jack Lilienthal had stayed behind to make sure everyone left the island. Satisfied that he was the last man on the island, he turned his patrol car toward Ben Sawyer Boulevard. The wind was rocking his car, threatening to knock it off the road, by the time he reached the Ben Sawyer Bridge. As he drove onto the superstructure, the chief could feel the bridge twisting beneath him. When his tires finally hit the Mount Pleasant pavement, Lilienthal looked in his rearview mirror just in time to see the swing bridge wrenched off its pedestal. The road he had been driving on seconds before was now lying in the Intracoastal Waterway.

Across the harbor, City Hall withstood the punishing winds better than most structures in Charleston – but the mayor feared that could change at any minute. Riley could feel the building rocking, hear its walls creaking under the pressure. Finally, he walked down to the first floor to look out a peephole in the plywood covering the front doors. He saw a huge patch of sheet metal rolling down Broad Street like a ball of tin foil, bouncing off the fence at St. Michael's Church before finally stopping. He thought to himself, "Oh, no, somebody lost their roof."

Riley returned to his office just in time to see the first water plop onto his desk. Then, more rain began pouring through the hallway trap door that led to the roof. It had been City Hall's roof that the mayor saw tumbling down the street, and now the building was flooding. Reporters and city staff ran to City Council chambers, where they tried to decide how best to protect the priceless art collection – which included Trumbull's Washington portrait. They debated taking down the paintings but decided they were safer on the walls, vertical.

Suddenly, Riley burst into the room and ordered everyone to move downstairs. The second and third floors were no longer safe, he said, and the basement floors were slick with rainwater leaking in through the sandbags. The only dry place in City Hall was the first floor, which sat just about 12 feet above street level. Barbara Vaughn would later remember that moment as the instant she first felt real fear. They were trapped.

The leading edge of the storm pummeled Charleston for nearly two hours. And then, all at once, there was nothing. When the eye passed overhead, the wind stopped as if someone had flipped a switch. It was like a dream. One minute, 135-mph wind was whipping through the streets, the next there wasn't even a breeze. The stars were visible overhead. As the storm moved onshore, the entire peninsula was sitting in the middle of its eye. It was an unsettling peace, and a temporary one.

Riley and some of his staff wandered into Broad Street as the eye passed overhead. It felt like they were in a glass dome inside the storm, something meteorologists called the stadium effect. They saw City Hall's roof lying on the sidewalk, and the street was littered with palm fronds, but Riley could see no catastrophic damage. So far, it appeared, Broad Street was holding up well. Doug Smits, the city's chief building officer, decided to test a pay phone on the corner. He punched "0" and amazingly enough got an operator on the line. Smits asked her to place a call to his family in Moncks Corner, and told her where he was calling from. The operator agreed to put the call through, but said she didn't believe he was standing on the corner of Meeting and Broad. No way, she said, could anyone survive this storm.

The false security of the eye lured hundreds of people into the streets, and Chief Greenberg sent a bus full of police officers rolling down King Street to patrol for looters. Already some people had decided to take advantage of the chaos, and Greenberg wanted to stop them before things got out of hand. The officers soon found people trying to force their way into downtown businesses, and went to work. Just after midnight City Hall staff heard Greenberg yelling over the radio, ordering police officers to use their night sticks on the looters.

"Don't arrest anybody," the chief said. "Beat 'em. We have no place to put them."

The storm would soon subdue any looters the police could not catch. Forecasters predicted the eye would pass over within 45 minutes, a small window of calm before the second half. Riley did not wander far from the shelter of City Hall – he'd promised Charlotte he wouldn't take any stupid chances. He knew his window of opportunity to survey damage was tight, and he couldn't see anything anyway. Without its street lights, Charleston had been thrown into an eerie, inky blackness.

Riley gathered the City Hall staff around the radio and called a crew of workers stationed at the Garden Theater. Then he delivered the second half of his pep talk. "OK, you've done it. You've done the best job any city has ever done in preparing for a storm," the mayor said. "Now, we're going to do the best job any city ever did in recovery." Riley knew it was time to prepare his people for the aftermath, even though he was not sure what the second half of the storm would bring.

He did not know the worst was yet to come.

As the eye moved inland, the back side of Hugo rolled ashore, showing Charleston the true power of a major hurricane. The storm's second act was more devastating and deadly than the first, its wind stronger. Roofs and church steeples surrendered immediately, and great live oaks in Hampton Park were torn out of the ground. A trio of buildings on Hayne Street crumbled under the force. Riley noted with as much interest as fear that the storm sounded very much like a train rolling through downtown. The noise was amazing, terrifying, and announced the arrival of the very worst the storm had to offer: the storm surge.

Hugo's timing could not have been worse. High tide was due just after midnight, which meant the storm's surge would arrive when the harbor water was cresting – and that threatened to raise the sea level in Charleston by as much as 17 feet. That wall of water slammed into The Battery and quickly spilled over it, flooding East Bay Street and bursting through the doors of the city's most recognizable mansions. Some of those homes would soon have six feet of water in their parlors. In those houses where the owners had stayed behind, they watched the seawater creeping up grand staircases toward them with no signs of slowing down. One downtown resident stood on his staircase, watching in horror as the surge brushed against his first-floor chandelier.

The Ansonborough Homes had nearly six feet of water in them at the height of the storm, nearly covering the ground-floor apartments and weakening the entire structure. On the west side of the peninsula, the water rushed onto Lockwood Drive, the surge driving sailboats from the City Marina into the street. Sullivan's Island and the Isle of Palms were almost completely overcome, with hundreds of houses washed away. On Goat Island, behind the Isle of Palms, the storm stacked dozens of boats like discarded children's toys. But the surge was at its absolute worst in McClellanville.

Thirty miles north of the peninsula, hundreds of people had taken shelter at the old Lincoln High School. McClellanville was in the path of the storm's northern edge, which brought with it the greatest storm surge. Inside Lincoln's cafeteria, McClellanville residents could just make out dark shapes on the windows and soon realized it was water creeping up the panes. Cars floated by and one man saw a coffin bobbing in the waves. Soon, the water breached the school, flooding the cafeteria. The people climbed onto the tables but quickly found themselves standing in the rising water. By 3 a.m., some were covered up to their chests, holding children high above their heads. If the surge did not recede soon, they knew they would die.

For those people and many others, it seemed the horror would never end. But in truth, the back side of Hugo began to move inland about two hours after it reached the coast. From there, it would tear a path across South Carolina and hit North Carolina at Charlotte, leaving death and destruction in its wake. In South Carolina alone, Hugo destroyed 3,300 homes and damaged another 18,000. The bill for the devastation would come to nearly $6 billion. And 35 people were killed.

Riley had no way of knowing the extent of the destruction across the city. Although he had phone service, and even spoke to the governor around 1 a.m., there was no one out in the storm to offer first-hand reports. A man from the Federal Emergency Management Agency was stationed at City Hall and, at one point, Riley asked if he had any advice. The man said, "Save all your receipts." What a bureaucrat, Riley thought. He was looking for some checklist, not red tape. It would not bode well for the clean-up. And it did nothing to help at that moment. City Hall was still creaking against the strain of the wind, and the mayor wondered just how bad his city was suffering.

Riley believed he and his staff had done everything possible and planned well. By the time the eye passed, the mayor was confident that – at least in Charleston – no one had died. But as the second half of the storm punished the city, he was no longer sure. And he could not send his police and rescue crews out to investigate without risking more casualties. Finally, convinced there was nothing more he could do, Riley found a bare spot on the floor in the city attorney's office, lay face-down on the hardwood, and slept through the storm's final hour.

Hugo passed just as it came, under the cover of darkness. By 5 a.m. only the trailing winds remained, and the surge had started to recede. Before daybreak, Riley – not quite fresh from his nap – gathered up his staff and ventured outside to survey the damage left in the hurricane's considerable wake.

Most of Charleston's historic buildings were spared. They had stood for centuries, weathering other catastrophes, but none quite like Hugo. Some of them were scarred, disheveled and many were missing their roofs. It would take months, if not years, to repair all the damage. Of the $6 billion in damage inflicted on South Carolina, a full third of it would be in Charleston County. But the city had survived.

It seemed most of Charleston was covered in an ugly brown film. South of Broad, Meeting Street was blanketed in a thick layer of pluff mud that had been at the bottom of the harbor the day before. Broad was coated in mud up to Legare Street, but the surge had not reached City Hall. Daylight was an hour or more away, and it was difficult to see, but Riley could make out shapes – tree limbs, ruined cars, broken power poles. The debris nearly covered the street.

The mayor took his city truck up to King Street, finding only one building that had suffered catastrophic damage. The second floor of a photography shop in the 200 block had been sheared off and dumped into the street. Every awning, every decorative flourish in the shopping district had been blown away, stripping the city bare. But as Riley made his way back to City Hall, he noticed one thing had ridden out the storm, as improbable as it was. Atop the Post Office that stood overlooking the Four Corners of Law, the American flag – in tatters – was still flying.

The mayor stopped to wonder how he could restore order to this chaos. People would be waking up soon, he thought, and they would find a scene that no one alive in Charleston had ever witnessed. The city looked like a wasteland. The damage was serious, no doubt, but Riley knew they had been lucky. He tried to put the storm in historical perspective. Charleston had been through wars, fires, earthquakes and hurricanes – but it had always recovered. And it would again.

As he surveyed his beautiful, ruined city on the morning of Sept. 22, 1989, Riley knew the hard part was just beginning. He had spent nearly 15 years rebuilding Charleston, and now he would have to do it again. When he reached the steps of City Hall, he took one last look down Broad Street, considered the job ahead and had a singular thought.

We've got a lot of work to do.

PART III

Charleston Rising

After the Storm

At daybreak, Riley took a silent tour of downtown in the city pickup truck he'd been driving around since the week began. The truck had improbably survived the storm, and the mayor took Howard Chapman along for a more extensive survey of the damage wrought by Hugo. It was a short trip. Many of the roads that had been empty the day before were now impassable, cluttered with roofs, trees, even boats – the refuse of a killer storm.

The harbor was calm, almost placid, but the surge had left its watermark on Charleston's finest homes – a reminder that an angry sea had invaded only hours earlier. The streets were littered with trash that a day earlier had been the ornamental décor of one of the country's most handsome cities. Now it was just garbage, scattered road hazards waiting to be hauled off to a landfill. The city was largely deserted, and the emptiness lent a surreal quality to the scene. Finally, on lower King Street, the mayor found a couple picking through the remnants of their home. Riley stopped the truck, got out and hugged them.

There wasn't much he could say.

It seemed every square inch of the city had been touched by the storm. Hugo had inflicted more damage on Charleston than the Union military or the fires that ravaged the peninsula during the Civil War. The only comparison was the Aug. 31, 1886, earthquake, which destroyed 2,000 buildings and killed 27 people. The earthquake inflicted $6 million in property damage at a time when the entire city's worth was only $24 million. Based on inflation, Hugo had made a similarly proportional impact. Within a month, city officials would calculate the bill for storm repairs at $1 billion.

City Hall was a madhouse by the time Riley returned. The phones were ringing constantly – some people offering sympathy, others help. The mayor briefed Greenberg, fire officials and rescue workers and ordered city crews to start clearing the roads. That was the first order of business – make the city accessible for the National Guard and the Red Cross, which he hoped would soon deliver supplies. Everyone in the city needed water and food.

There were 137,000 people without power across the county, so even those who hadn't lost their roofs were miserable. Without electricity, much of their food would soon spoil. The temperature was approaching 90 and they would endure it without air conditioning – not a death sentence, but one more element of discomfort. The storm had affected everyone in some way. Even those who hadn't lost their homes were overcome with the emotional stress of living through disaster.

Riley believed the key to recovery was restoring as much normalcy as quickly as possible. He needed the power turned on so the stores could open, and garbage pick-up had to resume as soon as the roads were clear. Until then, the mayor knew he had to find some way to lift people's spirits, give them hope, and assure them that Charleston would get through all this.

Riley had not checked on his own home, but he was distracted much of the day by thoughts of his family. He hadn't heard from Charlotte, and it worried him. When he tried to call, he could not get through. Had the storm hit the Midlands worse than he'd heard? At one point, to no one in particular, Riley said, "I wish my sweetie would call."

Riley's family was just as concerned about him. His son, Joe, had been told by someone in his fraternity that the radio reported the Charleston mayor was killed in the storm. Joe didn't believe it – he knew his father wouldn't put himself in harm's way – but the phones were out in Columbia and he had no way to check. When the electricity blinked on for a couple of hours, Joe turned on the television. Soon, CBS showed video footage of his father and Sen. Hollings touring those areas hit hardest by Hugo.

Riley spent much of the day talking to the media. He knew the national news could help put out the message that Charleston needed help, so he divided his time between coordinating relief efforts and standing in front of cameras. Because he had hosted the U.S. Conference of Mayors summer meeting three months earlier, most of his colleagues had visited the city and, naturally, fell in love with it. Before the day ended, dozens of mayors from around the country called offering help. When Riley told the St. Paul mayor about all the trees in the road, Minnesota put two workmen with chainsaws on the next plane to South Carolina.

The entire country rallied to help Charleston. President Bush declared the South Carolina coast a disaster area, eligible for federal clean-up money, and Gov. Campbell immediately requested funds from the Federal Emergency Management Agency and the Small Business Administration. Riley converted the Gaillard Auditorium into a distribution center, and soon the trucks started rolling into town. For days, many Charleston residents would pass their time standing in long lines that snaked down Calhoun Street.

Of course, some people took advantage of the tragedy. Storm opportunists from out of town showed up selling ice for $10 a bag and chainsaws for $600. Some crews were cruising city neighborhoods offering to clear yards of debris – for $2,000 each. Riley compared this price-gouging to looting, and swore that if he caught anyone doing it, he would throw them in jail. By the day's end, the mayor would set a 7 p.m. curfew for the city.

Other towns across the Lowcountry established similar curfews, both to curtail the looting and because it was too dangerous to drive at night. Without street lamps, it was nearly impossible to see the trees and debris in the road. That afternoon, the mayor got a call from Larry Tarleton, executive editor of The News and Courier. Tarleton asked Riley to give the paper's employees an exemption from the curfew – not only reporters gathering information for the community, but the delivery crews as well.

"We haven't missed an edition in nearly 200 years," Tarleton said.

Riley only had to think about it for a moment. He spread the word to his police officers and the National Guardsmen patrolling the city to let newspaper employees pass. Later, the mayor would say he realized it was important – not just for journalism but because the newspaper was delivering information people could not get otherwise, not so long as the power was out. And Riley realized that a newspaper on people's doorsteps was one more bit of normalcy in a town starving for it.

Late that night, more than 14 hours after he had begun the day, Riley finally went home to get some sleep. Gibbes Street was dark and he had to feel his way to his door. Inside the house, the mayor found the entire first floor coated in brown, drying pluff mud – the storm surge had not spared his home. He and Charlotte had rolled up the rugs and moved them upstairs before she left, which saved them, but the floors and walls were a mess.

The house had lost part of his roof, and Riley would later discover that his heating and air-conditioning units were ruined. He was not particularly upset. The mayor had spent the day listening to one heartbreaking story of loss after another, and knew that he was going through what everyone else in Charleston had to endure. As tired as he was, Riley went to work wiping up the mud as best he could before he was overcome with exhaustion.

In the first week after the storm, Riley held two news conferences each day, always at the same time. Sticking to a routine was part of restoring normalcy, even if he only reported where to get ice the next day. He tried to end each announcement on a positive note, sometimes nothing more than the news that some ladies from a Mississippi church were delivering food the next day. Later, Riley learned that people would sit in their cars and listen to the news conferences on their radios – the only way many folks had to hear a broadcast.

Charleston proved itself resilient in those days after Hugo, most people doing all they could to make the best of the situation. Riley noticed that, without air conditioning, more people spent time on their front porches. Neighbors began to talk regularly, and that soon grew into community cookouts. It was as if Charleston had reverted to an earlier, simpler time. People also found their faith rewarded, their spirits lifted, when insurance agents descended on the city to settle claims quickly – and often generously. Later, people would joke that modern Charleston was built by Joe Riley … and Hugo.

One of the biggest problems the mayor faced after the storm was restoring electricity to the city. Without it, the stores could not re-open, more perishables were lost and people could not get back to work. South Carolina Electric & Gas had announced it might take between 17 days and three weeks to restore power to the Lowcountry. That was unacceptable to the mayor. As soon as Riley heard that news, he called the chairman of SCE&G at midnight on Sunday. He explained that Charleston couldn't wait that long. Every day the city went without power it sank deeper into economic depression.

The chairman said he understood and would do what he could, but Riley wasn't sure he had gotten his point across. So he dialed another number. A sleeping Peatsy Hollings answered the phone.

"I'm sorry to wake you, Peatsy, but I need to talk to the senator," Riley said.

The mayor asked Hollings to call the SCE&G chairman personally to stress the importance of getting the power on. Riley figured he might not have the clout to spur an entire utility company into action – but Fritz did. The next day, power trucks from around the South converged on the streets of Charleston.

Riley leaned on Hollings heavily in the weeks after the storm. Although the senator had spent most of his career as a legislator, Riley knew he had an executive's intuition. His term as governor had been transformational for South Carolina – Hollings knew how to get things done. The senator was eager to help his hometown, and didn't mind twisting arms to do it.

Eventually, though, Hollings became frustrated – he could never find Riley, could never get him on the phone. The lines at City Hall were perpetually busy; in fact, every time the mayor went on TV he gave out the number for the help line, and the phone banks lit up like they were hosting a telethon. So one day, as Riley was meeting with his staff in the mayor's office, a BellSouth technician walked in unannounced carrying a telephone. He explained that the senator had ordered him to install the phone on the mayor's desk – and only Hollings had the number. Riley could not argue with Fritz Hollings any more than the phone company, and just had to sit there and watch the technician work.

Anytime this new Batphone rang, Riley's staff snapped to attention. They knew Hollings needed an update, wanted to know what he could do to help – and they would have to get him an answer immediately. One evening, Riley had his senior staff gathered in his office when the phone rang. The conversation stopped as Riley picked up the receiver. The mood in the room was tense, no one sure what Hollings might need. But the mayor only listened for a moment and then said, "Do you want Darryl, or his other brother Darryl?"

It was a wrong number, but the mayor's response left everyone in the room doubled over laughing. They had no idea that Riley watched television, much less Bob Newhart sitcoms.

The phone came in handy when Hollings wasn't in town, allowing Riley to coordinate everything out of City Hall. But the senator came home every chance he got. Together, Riley and Hollings took a helicopter ride around the Lowcountry to survey the damage, the mayor straining to look out the window as they passed over Sullivan's Island. He wanted to see if he could spot his father's boat, which had been left tied up to the docks.

Sullivan's and Isle of Palms, where the mayor's own beach house sat, had been damaged much worse than downtown. Many houses had been washed away – though not the mayor's – and others had been reduced to so many piles of lumber. But there, amid the debris, Riley saw Big Joe's boat still securely lashed to six pilings – but the dock was gone. The random nature of the storm was amazing, and unsettling.

With the Ben Sawyer Bridge lying half in the waterway, most island residents could not find out if their homes had survived – and this was making them irate. National Guardsmen were stationed on the islands to keep people off until Sept. 26, when a ferry was set up. A permanent solution was weeks away, as the state Department of Transportation tried to figure out how to put the Sullivan's Island bridge back on its pedestal. But then, nothing was moving very fast in Charleston.

For the first few days, Riley put on his usual optimistic face and praised federal officials for helping the city. But by Wednesday, Sept. 27, he began to suggest that FEMA was not moving quickly enough. The mayor told reporters he wasn't sure "the extent of the damage from Hugo is understood yet at the federal level." Hollings soon joined in, as usual taking his criticism to the next level. The senator said he was embarrassed by the response from Washington. "Instead of management, we have mismanagement or no management."

Riley and Hollings bypassed the bumbling FEMA bureaucracy as much as they could. When the mayor's sister, Jane, heard from a friend in North Carolina that the Marines wanted to help, Riley had Hollings dispatch troops to McClellanville.

Riley called the general in charge of Fort Campbell, Kentucky, when he heard the base had a stockpile of industrial-grade generators on hand. Berkeley County had lost power to its sewer system, cutting off the most basic of services for thousands of people. The general agreed to deploy his generators, but FEMA tried to stop it. Agency officials said they could not authorize the use of military generators because no one had yet completed an assessment-of-need form.

"They have no power," Riley told the bureaucrat. "They don't need an assessment, they need help."

Riley asked Hollings to have the general send the generators, and they were soon on the way.

It took only a week of such roadblocks before Riley and Hollings declared open war on the federal government. At one news conference, Riley suggested to the FEMA coordinator that "respectfully, sir, we need to rev up the engine." The agency was bogged down in "a bureaucratic slowness. It would be dishonest for me to say otherwise." As usual, Hollings was even more blunt. He called FEMA "a bunch of bureaucratic jackasses." Riley publicly agreed with the sentiment.

Barely a decade old, FEMA was already a nightmare of red tape and inefficiency – the very stereotype of a federal agency. All the claims stations, where people were supposed to apply for assistance, were set up in the suburbs beyond the reach of the poorest downtown residents – a point Hollings made in his "jackasses" speech. And then FEMA quickly proved Hollings and Riley right with its response. FEMA coordinator Paul Hall said all requests for assistance had to go through Gov. Carroll Campbell's office; the agency would not respond to anyone else.

Hall even introduced partisan politics into the debate, claiming no government agency could compete with private business. But FEMA's problems stemmed more from a lack of common sense than anything else. National Security Advisor Colin Powell told Riley and Hollings he would send personnel and food from Fort MacPherson, Georgia, but FEMA stopped it. The agency ruled their help was not needed in Charleston.

The FEMA politics continued when President Bush flew into the Lowcountry. A presidential trip to a disaster area was common, but Bush chose not to visit Charleston, site of the hurricane's landfall. Instead, he toured Summerville with Mayor

Berlin G. Myers, who called the president "a courageous man." Of course, Myers – a staunch Republican – had also praised FEMA. A week later, Vice President Dan Quayle also showed up, and he met only with GOP officials in North Charleston and Berkeley County. Quayle's single visit to the city hit hardest by the storm came when he checked into Charleston Place.

The White House's decision to snub Riley looked even more petty because the Charleston mayor was already getting national praise for his efforts. His large network of contacts in the National League of Cities and the U.S. Conference of Mayors had brought in as much help, if not more, than FEMA. When talk show host Oprah Winfrey taped her show at the King Street Palace on Oct. 5, her first words upon taking the stage were, "Where's the mayor?"

Winfrey said she had never heard such positive comments about a mayor, perhaps a better endorsement than Riley ever could have gotten from Bush.

Riley was led onto the stage and Winfrey hugged him. With an audience of 20 million watching, the mayor – wearing a "Charleston: We're Going Strong!" T-shirt – outlined the city's relief efforts and listed the things Charleston would need in the coming weeks. When the show aired, a new round of aid flooded into City Hall.

Eventually, so many relief workers showed up that Riley had to give them rooms at the Francis Marion Hotel. The hotel was once again going through bankruptcy, but the city made a deal with the bank to provide insurance. Suddenly the city had ample room for its out-of-town help. Marion Square became a parking lot for utility trucks and heavy machinery, most of them sporting out-of-state license plates. By the end of the month, Riley declared Charleston 65 percent "back to normal."

The mayor conceded, however, that final 35 percent would take far longer. In fact, it would take years. Three years after Hugo, St. Philip's steeple would still be encased in scaffolding. It would be nearly a decade before Market Hall reopened its doors. But the city was working overtime. In the six weeks following the storm, 72,000 truckloads of debris were taken to area landfills. Normally, the city collected only 17,000 in a year. Much of the overflow was hauled away by sanitation workers from neighboring states.

At one point, a woman told the mayor that she had seen a Charlotte garbage truck in her neighborhood, and it brought a tear to her eye. Riley told her yes, our friends are helping out.

Before the mayor even had the city's power turned back on, he was thinking about how to jump-start Charleston's economy. Riley knew the storm had threatened the entire community's livelihood, particularly the tourism industry. It was crucial to let people know the city was open for business, that it had not been destroyed – a perception that could harm Charleston's economy for years. While he was still coordinating the crews clearing streets, Riley called David Rawle to City Hall to help him craft a message.

The mayor wanted a succinct way to deliver two very different – almost contradictory – messages: tell the country that Charleston needed supplies, money and support; and at the same time let them know the city had not been destroyed. It seemed every anchorman who came to town stood in front of the three fallen warehouses on Hayne Street as they talked about the utter devastation Charleston had suffered. Riley did his best to put a positive spin on the stories. Every time he went on camera, he pointed at the Hayne Street rubble and boasted that those were just about the only buildings destroyed.

The slogan Rawle and Riley chose was "Charleston: We're Going Strong." It became the city's slogan, its bumper sticker. They had T-shirts made, which the mayor wore during all his television interviews. Soon, Riley began telling the national media that Charleston was open for business, bragging about the city's temperate fall weather or plugging the annual house tours. Some people criticized the strategy, and the mayor didn't want to sound like a huckster, but he knew the city's economy – and a lot of jobs – depended on tourism.

In his usual optimistic fashion, Riley promised that Charleston would be better than ever. In truth, the storm had demolished some eyesores no one had the heart to tear down, and exposed weaknesses in other buildings. Following Hugo, more of the peninsula was open for redevelopment than ever before. By the year's end, Riley would announce $56 million in new private investments around the City Market alone – including two office and retail complexes, as well as a new hotel on the site of the fallen Hayne Street warehouses.

But the city paid a dear price for the storm, too. Riley mourned the devastation to Hampton Park, which he had restored to its former glory over the past 12 years. Huge oaks had been ripped from the ground and scattered across the park. A week after Hugo, The News and Courier captured an image of Riley walking through the fallen trees showing as much sorrow as he would allow himself to display. This was where his sons had learned to walk. It was one part of the city he wished did not need to be rebuilt.

The storm had taken a toll on Riley. Most nights he got home after midnight and was gone again before 8 the next morning. Charlotte expected him to crash any day, and told reporters that he was running on pure adrenaline. He needed some time off, she said, but wouldn't take any. And even if he slipped away from City Hall for an afternoon, Riley was dealing with the problems Hugo had caused at his own home. He wanted to handle it himself, and even told his son, Joe, to stay in school when he offered to come and help.

When Big Joe heard this, he called his grandson in Columbia and said, "Get your ass down there and help him." Joe Riley III was caught between conflicting orders from his two namesakes – the two most powerful personalities in his family. Eventually, he followed Big Joe's advice, drove down to Charleston and spent a couple of days cleaning up the family garage.

There were some things, however, that Riley had to handle alone. His uncle, John Edwin Schachte Jr., died just a week after the storm. The mayor spent the evening with his devastated mother, but had to be back at City Hall the next morning. He took off long enough to serve as a pallbearer for his mother's brother. It was all the time he had to spare.

On Oct. 13, Riley finally took a break. He and Tom Bryant flew to San Francisco with their sons to see the opening games of the 1989 World Series. It was the fourth meeting between the A's and the Giants, but the first in 75 years – and the first since both teams had relocated to the Bay Area. Riley had planned the trip before the storm, and Bryant was surprised when the mayor called to say he was still going. He had debated canceling the trip, fearing it wasn't right to leave the city. But the cleanup was well underway and he needed a break. And nothing relaxed him like baseball.

They stayed in San Francisco, crossing the bay for the first two games in Oakland.

The A's won both on their way to the first four-game Series sweep in more than a decade. Riley caught up with the San Francisco mayor at one game, and enjoyed spending time with Joe and Bratton without the burden of city business hanging around his neck. The evening before they left, Riley, Bryant and the boys ate in San Francisco at Basta Pasta, an Italian restaurant. Shortly after they flew out the next morning – and hours before the scheduled first pitch in Game 3 of the Series – a powerful earthquake rocked the entire region, seriously damaging Candlestick Park and much of the city.

Just before the earthquake hit, two Salvation Army trucks had left San Francisco with relief supplies for Charleston. When he got home, Riley would return the favor. Based on the response the country had shown him, the mayor would never let another disaster pass without sending help and manpower from Charleston. He felt it was the least he could do.

Bryant felt bad – he'd taken Riley from a hurricane into an earthquake in little more than three weeks. But Riley just laughed about the dark cloud seemingly following him around. Later that week, he called Bryant and, in a conspiratorial voice, asked, "Think Basta Pasta is still there?" Riley could not help but feel relieved – he had made it through the worst month in modern Charleston history, and his city was bouncing back more quickly than even he had expected.

Riley's management of the recovery made him a statewide, even national, political figure. He had cemented his reputation as a calm yet decisive leader, a man unflappable in the face of tremendous odds. When Riley's childhood friend Pat Brennan visited over the holidays that year, he was amazed at the reception the mayor got just walking down King Street. They could hardly take a few steps before someone else stopped them, to thank Riley for saving Charleston.

"You would have thought he was the pope," Brennan recalled years later. "There were people coming up to him, taking his hand, crying, telling him that his leadership saved their lives."

Many people assumed Riley would ride that popularity into the governor's mansion. There was still time to launch a 1990 campaign, where he would face incumbent Gov. Carroll Campbell. Although Campbell was also praised for his leadership during the storm, he'd been accused of playing politics during the recovery – diverting more resources to his home base in the Upstate than the Lowcountry. Campbell often came across as a blatant partisan, and was not nearly as popular in 1990 as he would be in retrospect. And Riley's popularity at the moment was off the charts.

The Democratic Party was eager to co-opt Riley's growing fame, because times were slowly changing in South Carolina. Although Democrats still largely dominated the state, they were losing their grip. The party had held the governor's office continuously between 1876 and 1975, when Jim Edwards became the first Republican elected since Reconstruction. After Edwards, Democrat Dick Riley reclaimed the governorship for two terms, but then came Campbell. The Democrats held the majority in the Legislature, but their numbers were falling. The trend did not look good for the party. Still, they believed Campbell was vulnerable. That had more to do with the growing demand for Riley than Campbell's poll numbers.

In those months after the storm, the mayor was everywhere. The Association of Citadel Men named him Man of the Year and the University of South Carolina gave him an honorary degree when he delivered the commencement address that winter. The graduating class gave the mayor two standing ovations. And in January, both chambers of the Legislature would pass resolutions praising his work in the aftermath of the storm. Despite all those accolades, Riley never considered running for governor in 1990.

As much as Riley wanted the job, he simply had too much to do in Charleston. He wouldn't abandon the city for a statewide campaign. His friends told News and Courier columnist Barbara Williams that it was a cruel twist: Riley was in a perfect position to run for governor because of how well he had performed as mayor. But his devotion to the city kept him from following his greater political ambitions – at least for a while. The Democrats maintained their "draft Riley" campaign into the spring, even though the mayor repeatedly said he would not run.

Williams said that, at the very least, duty required Riley to seek an unprecedented fifth term as mayor.

By the end of 1989, that fifth term seemed like a foregone conclusion. Although the mayor predicted Hugo recovery efforts would mandate a city tax increase, voters still went along with his bond referendum to fund the aquarium. For the moment,

Riley could do no wrong. He proclaimed Spoleto would go on as planned, and the waterfront park would open on schedule – and no one questioned his ability to keep those promises.

Riley was determined to return Charleston to normal as quickly as possible, and he would not accept excuses or any delay. Every time people had to concede anything to the storm, it was a defeat that hurt the city's psyche. So when an Alabama company said it could not finish new light poles for College Park in time for the new season, Riley raised hell and called the president of the company. The order was put at the front of the line, and the stadium had its lights 48 hours before opening day. Hugo would not interfere with the start of baseball in the Holy City.

Riley intended for the city to be fully recovered by the end of 1990. But FEMA was not helping. The federal relief agency had offered Charleston $6.8 million less than Riley and his staff said they needed for repairs. In fact, FEMA officials disputed nearly every claim the city made. They said the $1.75 million needed to repair the City Marina was $500,000 too high, that Cypress Gardens needed only $1.5 million, and not the $2.5 million Riley requested. Finally, FEMA ignored Charleston's estimate that it would take $3.9 million to rehabilitate the Gaillard Auditorium, and offered $905,000.

The mayor said FEMA's offers were insulting and inept. The federal bureaucrats were overlooking many things that needed repair, and did not have nearly enough knowledge of engineering and construction to make such conclusions. Charleston County Administrator Ed Fava agreed with the mayor's allegations, saying that the government's repair estimates were ridiculous. The feud would continue for months.

On May 11, 1990, Waterfront Park opened to great fanfare. At the dedication ceremony, the Charleston Symphony played, the lights on the Pineapple Fountain were turned on for the first time and Riley talked about his 14-year "dream realized." The park had cost $14 million, although $1 million of that was repairing damage caused by Hugo. Crews had worked seven days a week to get the park open on time, another of the mayor's edicts that the storm not slow the city down.

The park was like nothing else in Charleston. Palm trees lined the water's edge, mingling with oaks and magnolia trees throughout its interior. Aside from the decorative Pineapple Fountain, there was a larger fountain at the foot of Vendue Range that invited children to get soaked. But perhaps the most attractive feature was the covered pier filled with oversized swings. Tourists and locals lined up nearly every day for a few minutes in those swings. In all, Waterfront Park was a much more inviting, and scenic, public space than even The Battery. Charleston attorney and historian Robert Rosen – an old friend of Riley – said the park might become the mayor's greatest achievement. But he said the name didn't suit it. Waterfront Park, Rosen said, should be called Riley Park.

But that name would soon be taken.

The mayor's standard operating procedure was to juggle several projects at once. No sooner than Charleston Place was finished, he was deep into planning the aquarium. And the same week he dedicated Waterfront Park, Riley approached The Citadel with plans to build a new baseball stadium. He suggested this new ballpark should sit on the college's property overlooking the Ashley River – the same land where the military school had considered building a new basketball arena. If The Citadel would donate the land, the city would offer the college a permanent lease for its baseball team in return. Riley envisioned a 6,500-seat stadium in the style of the new major league parks beginning to sprout up around the country.

Riley loved College Park, the stadium where his grandfather had introduced him to the game. It was, he told friends, "comfortable as an old shoe." But the South Atlantic League didn't feel the same, and league officials privately told the mayor they might move their team to North Charleston. Riley was horrified by the thought of losing another sporting venue. At first, city engineers tried to figure out how to build a new stadium at College Park, but the kind of park the city – and the league – wanted could not be shoehorned on that land. So Riley began to court his alma mater.

By summer, Riley was exhausted. The dispute with FEMA continued, Spoleto had taken up much of his time and he was on the hunt for money to build the new baseball stadium. Then a mild controversy erupted when he said city outlets couldn't sell tickets to the rap band 2 Live Crew's July concert at the King Street Palace. He knew the decision bordered on censorship, but Riley said it was a decision based on values.

"No one can tell me that the lyrics for "As Nasty As You Wanna Be' are not bad for children," the mayor said. "It's not a political issue, it's not a philosophical issue, and it's certainly not a racial issue."

Chief Greenberg defended the mayor's decision and, despite complaints of discrimination from Councilman Robert Ford, dispatched a large show of force to make sure nothing happened at the concert. Little came of the incident until near the show's end. The group was leading an expletive-laced rant against Riley when a hole in the Palace's roof opened up, dumping water on the rappers.

Riley took off from work for much of the summer. Between July and September, the mayor had three weeks of vacation with Charlotte in addition to several long weekends. He stayed in town most of that time, dividing his days between downtown and the beach house. He went shrimping and fishing, swam in the ocean, worked in the yard and played golf with Charlotte. The mayor called the summer "therapeutic." He would need that time off to finish the year.

By the fall, Riley had wrangled $12.8 million out of FEMA for repairs, but promised not to stop until he got the final $3.7 million he believed Charleston was due. He was also deep in negotiations for the aquarium's construction and lobbying City Council to support his baseball stadium. At the same time, he was gearing up for a campaign to implement a local option sales tax.

For years, Riley had argued that cities needed another revenue source to pay for new projects without constantly putting the costs on homeowners through property taxes. He finally won legislative approval to hold such a referendum countywide, and promised voters the sales tax would benefit them because visitors would pay much of the tab. By the fall of 1990, the city was approaching 4 million tourists annually, and those people spent a lot of money. Why not hit them up for an extra 1 percent? North Charleston Mayor John Bourne opposed the tax, and Riley spent much of the fall publicly feuding with him over it. Riley got the upper hand, barely. In November, the sales tax was approved by a razor-thin 53-vote margin. That was one less write-in vote than Riley got for governor, without even being on the ballot.

December was often a slow month for city business, but 1990 was an exception. On Tuesday, Dec. 4, Riley finally got the Angel Oak. The IRS had seized the tree from developer Speedy Felkel during another dispute over income taxes, but this time Felkel was unable to finagle a last-minute deal. Riley was ecstatic, and in the end even Felkel encouraged him to bid on the property. "If I'm not able to get it, I'd rather it go to them than anyone else," Felkel said. The city ended up paying $127,900 for the property, twice as much as Felkel had been offered a few years earlier. Riley promised to tear down the wall around the tree and open it up as a park for everyone.

That should have closed out 1990, but the mayor had one last piece of business. On Dec. 28, Jim Rozier, the new Berkeley County supervisor, was getting ready to be sworn into office when he got a call from Riley. At first, it was just pleasant chitchat – congratulations on winning the county's top political post and the like. Then the mayor hit him with the real reason for the call: City Council had called a special meeting and, within minutes, would annex Berkeley County's Daniel Island into Charleston.

"Which part?" Rozier asked.

Riley said everything except the spoil area at the very tip of the island. Rozier later said he felt like the mayor had broken into his home and absconded with the family silverware.

Daniel Island was an unspoiled gem in the Lowcountry – nearly 10 square miles of land, much of it waterfront, that was due to be developed in the coming years. The island, larger than the city's peninsula, sat between the Cooper and Wando rivers just upstream from Charleston Harbor. In the 18th century it had been home to one plantation, then two. By the early 20th century, it was mostly farmland when Harry Guggenheim bought it for $75,000. In 1971, the Guggenheim Foundation took over the land. A year later, plans for the Mark Clark Expressway were announced, and it looked as if the island would soon become a lot more convenient – and valuable. Plans for subdivisions were announced.

Berkeley County wanted to provide water, sewer and other services to the area, a deal that would help prop up the largely rural county's infrastructure. Now, Charleston was swooping in to take it all. Rozier felt betrayed, and told the mayor so. Riley said he understood – he expected a fight. But the deal was in motion. There was no turning back.

Riley had coveted the land for years. He called Guggenheim attorney Henry Smythe annually to make an offer and do his "due diligence." He lobbied the foundation, explained the island needed municipal services, that it should be part of the city. He had heard that the foundation wanted to build a gated community on the land akin to Hilton Head Island's Sea Pines Resort – and he did not think that would be good for the region. But no matter how much Riley talked, the Guggenheim Foundation remained indifferent.

The mayor likely would have continued with his soft-sell calls into the next decade, but Bill Regan overheard that North Charleston was making a move on the island. Riley and Regan knew North Charleston and Mount Pleasant wanted Daniel Island as much as the city. But if someone was going to take the Guggenheim land by force, Riley wanted it to be Charleston. It took Regan and Riley little more than a week to put together the deal. And at 4:59 p.m. on Dec. 27, they put the special-meeting notice on the front door of City Hall – although the mayor would later concede "it wasn't too noticeable."

On the evening of Dec. 28, 1990, City Council gave tentative approval to a plan to annex most of Daniel Island. Riley felt he'd pulled off one of the great midnight coups in Charleston history. This would allow the city to grow in another direction and block the efforts of other towns to encroach on Charleston's borders. Daniel Island would add significant property to the tax base and population to the city in the years to come.

But it also started a war, one that Riley knew could wipe out all the goodwill he had earned in the past year.

A Moveable Campaign

The Lowcountry was largely distracted by the unmistakable build-up to war in the Persian Gulf as 1991 began. Iraq President Saddam Hussein had invaded the tiny country of Kuwait, and the United States and a coalition of countries were threatening a retaliatory strike on the occupying Iraqi military. But in Moncks Corner, the Rotary Club was attacking Charleston for a similar foray into Berkeley County. The club awarded Joe Riley its "horse's ass" award for crossing their border and annexing Daniel Island.

The mayor was, the Rotarians said, no different than Hussein.

The city's surprise annexation did not go over well with many people. Mount Pleasant town officials protested the move, and North Charleston Mayor John Bourne called Charleston "greedy." In truth, they were upset they hadn't done it first. Since plans for the Mark Clark Expressway had been unveiled in 1972, Mount Pleasant and North Charleston had flirted with the idea of annexing Daniel Island – particularly after the Guggenheim Foundation announced it would build 6,000 upscale homes on the island.

Bourne denied allegations that his city had been plotting a similar move. Sure, he said, he had recently asked his city's sewer district what it would cost to provide service to the island, but he hadn't talked with landowners there in "months."

A week after its initial vote, Charleston City Council delayed final action on Daniel Island at the request of the Guggenheim Foundation. The group hadn't decided whether to challenge the annexation, and Riley wanted to give them more time if it helped avoid a court battle. The mayor was confident the city was on firm legal ground, and figured the Guggenheim lawyers would realize that sooner or later.

The city's method of annexation was unorthodox, to be sure. Under state law, an area could be annexed only through referendum – unless landowners representing 75 percent of the value of the land taken requested it. Bill Regan, who Riley later credited as the mastermind behind the legal strategy, realized the city could get the Guggenheim property without a vote if it annexed a large enough swath of land. As long as the foundation's holdings were worth no more than 25 percent of the total area, Guggenheim had no legal grounds to protest.

Riley and Regan approached Joe Griffith and Robert Knoth, who owned land to the north and east of the island. Their combined property was worth more than Guggenheim's farmland, so the mayor lobbied them. He sold the idea as "good citizenship" – annex into the city and help Charleston grow. They agreed, and Griffith subdivided his land among family members to create more "freeholders" – that is, people with a stake in the property.

Griffith also changed the designation of an island he owned from conservation to residential, increasing its assessed value (and leaving the county property assessor scratching his head). The city promised to reimburse him the difference in his property taxes until he sold the land. By every measure, both in value and the sheer number of land owners, Charleston met the 75 percent plateau.

The city had no problems legally, but Riley had to worry about public opinion. Even though he had raised the ire of some Berkeley County residents, most people treated the controversy as a joke. Frank Gilbreth, in his Ashley Cooper column, suggested turning Iraq over to Riley and praised his ability to take land away from rich Yankees. Even Fritz Hollings couldn't resist a few good-natured jabs. When WCIV opened its new building in Mount Pleasant, the senator noted that if Riley were there he'd probably try to annex the TV station.

Riley defended the annexation in his annual State of the City address, but was also trying to repair fractured relationships. He met with Mount Pleasant officials, promising the city would not annex north of their town limit, and had lunch with Berkeley County Supervisor Jim Rozier at the Colony House restaurant. Rozier asked Riley to pick up the tab – Berkeley County was boycotting Charleston, and he couldn't spend money there.

The Guggenheim Foundation sued Charleston to stop the annexation, but its attorneys realized the land would soon be part of a city – the only question was which one. The foundation asked for proposals from Charleston, North Charleston and Mount Pleasant before any court battle began. Riley's plan focused not on basic services, but on the parks and public spaces Charleston would build. He argued that Daniel Island had to be public, and its parks would define the island. The foundation lawyers were intrigued, but may have been swayed more by acquaintances at the National League of Cities, who praised Charleston and its reputation for smart growth. The Guggenheim Foundation soon dropped the lawsuit and accepted the annexation.

The foundation also had other concerns that persuaded them to join Charleston. The State Ports Authority wanted to build a new terminal on the island, and the Guggenheim board knew that would decrease the value of their land. The port had been renting a spoil area on the island to dump dredge material from the harbor, and rumor was the state might take surrounding land for expansion. The Guggenheim Foundation knew it couldn't beat the state of South Carolina, but Charleston and Riley might.

By March, the SPA announced that it might take as much as one-third of Daniel Island for a new terminal. Some SPA officials claimed that, without this new land, the port could have to shut down. Riley called the bluff and said it would be a waste of valuable property. Soon he had a study that said the island would be difficult for large ships to access. Then the city adopted zoning on the island that would bar industrial sites. The state filed a lawsuit challenging the zoning. The fight would continue for years.

Riley's fourth term as mayor was supposed to be his last.

He had planned to step down in 1991, reopen his law practice and perhaps start laying the groundwork for a 1994 gubernatorial campaign. He was ready to get off the political carousel for a while, but also felt a nagging sense of responsibility to the projects he had underway – the aquarium, the new baseball stadium, the development of Daniel Island. It was the same quandary he had found himself in before, one entirely of his own making. But there were other considerations, too. The mayor didn't feel he should leave office until all the damage inflicted by Hugo had been repaired.

The mayor opted for compromise. In April, Riley announced that he would seek an unprecedented fifth term, but warned voters that he might not finish it. He admitted an interest in the governor's office, perhaps the worst-kept secret in Charleston, and said he might run in 1994. Reporters questioned the wisdom of such full disclosure, but Riley felt it was the only honorable thing to do. If the voters decided four terms were enough, he would respect that.

"I assumed that by now it would be time to stop," the mayor said. "Actually, I never intended to serve as mayor this long. It seemed, however, there loomed opportunities for this community that I felt bound to seek, obstacles to overcome and goals to achieve. It seemed to me to be my duty."

The News and Courier's Barbara Williams opined that such a frank admission would be political suicide for most folks, but she suspected Riley could pull it off. Williams had followed him since his days in the Legislature, and knew better than to heed the tentative tone of Riley's announcement. Her next column carried a headline that read, "The race for governor is on – and count Riley in."

As it turned out, neither the mayor's political ambitions nor the Daniel Island controversy had any bearing on the 1991 election. Riley was the man who led the city through the Hurricane Hugo disaster, and that would not soon be forgotten. No one else even bothered to file for the mayor's race. The Republicans said they might put up a candidate in four years, but not this time. Joe Riley was basically given a fifth term as mayor by acclamation.

The summer passed quickly and, with no campaign to take up his time, Riley was able to focus on city business. In May, the visitor center and bus shed opened – nearly 15 years after the mayor had first proposed it. The new facility shifted tourism farther north on the peninsula than it had ever been, and opened Upper King Street to even more development. The revitalization of Charleston was quickly spreading. But the city's redevelopment would not come without some growing pains.

That summer, Riley was forced to deny accusations that the city's decision to close the Ansonborough Homes public housing project was an attempt to further gentrify the peninsula. Hugo had flooded the homes with more than five feet of water, and the city chose not to reopen them. The federal Department of Housing and Urban Development would not pay to rebuild public housing in the flood zone, and the city could not afford the expense – especially when housing officials were told any new development would have to be elevated.

At the same time, the city had begun a drainage project nearby at the corner of Calhoun and Concord streets. Workers planned to dig down a few feet and install drain pipes to alleviate flooding in the area. But once they broke ground, the public works crew encountered a horrible smell. At first, they simply covered up that spot and moved to a new one. They encountered the same smell at the second site, and finally decided they needed to figure out what was in the ground. They took Riley a sample of the soil and, after smelling it, he felt sick for three days.

The city eventually determined the soil had been contaminated by effluent from a coal-gasification plant that operated on Charlotte Street in the 19th century. The refuse from the plant was considered dangerous at 1,000 parts per million, and tests suggested the ground at Ansonborough Homes had about 40,000 ppm in it. The entire site would have to be cleaned up and capped. That ended any talk of reopening Ansonborough Homes.

Riley had promised earlier that he would not shut down the public housing project, which sat about a block from his proposed aquarium site. He knew he would catch grief over the reversal, and worried about whether he was doing the right thing. The mayor did not like the idea of displacing black residents, but the cost to rebuild was too great. The city would clean up the land, sell it and use the money to build scattered-site public housing in West Ashley and on Johns Island. It was the best they could do.

City Councilman Robert Ford and others claimed Riley had forced the Charleston Housing Authority to do his dirty work and get rid of the poor people. As Charleston grew, and real estate prices continued to rise, gentrification became a more prevalent concern. Already some complained that the East Side redevelopment threatened to make the area unaffordable for most of the people who had lived there for years. Now the city was shutting down public housing in the middle of the expanding tourism district.

Ford said the soil wasn't the problem, the land was simply too valuable to waste on poor people – a charge that would linger no matter how much the city denied it. But when the councilman called Riley a "dictator" during one meeting, the mayor told him to quit grandstanding.

"You got on it because you thought you could get some mileage out of it," Riley told Ford.

In July, Riley was drawn into yet another Spoleto controversy when festival founder Gian Carlo Menotti declared that he could no longer work with the management team. The maestro demanded the resignation of general manager Nigel Redden and a few other top executives. Menotti said either they had to leave or he would. The Spoleto board sided with Redden, but Riley defended Menotti – even when festival officials asked him to stay out of it.

The mayor knew Menotti was being difficult, but argued that he had created Spoleto and the city could not let him walk away. Eventually, Redden and Menotti's other targets quit, but two years later the composer was at it again. By the time Menotti threatened to quit in 1993, Riley was through defending him. He'd had enough of the drama. The mayor said the festival – which would still be called Spoleto – would go on without Gian Carlo.

"This time, he's made a big mistake," the mayor said.

The Spoleto back-and-forth dragged into September 1991, when Riley dedicated the new Angel Oak park and learned that Fire Chief Wilmot Guthke was retiring at the year's end. His search for a new chief was interrupted by the news that he was going to be awarded the National Trust for Historic Preservation's top honor for his work preserving historic Charleston. Suddenly, Riley was busy again – but not too busy for baseball. The Braves, which had become Riley's team, were in the middle of a playoff run.

Riley had made his usual trek to a couple of Atlanta games during the summer with Tom Bryant and Bratton – Joe had graduated from college and was working on a ranch in Idaho. By then, the mayor knew Ted Turner well enough that they usually got seats in the owner's box. But even at the game, Bryant noticed, Riley would sit with a bag phone, taking calls. He always had something else going on. Once, he handed the clunky phone to his friend. "Tom, daddy wants to talk to you," Riley said. "He's in the hospital."

Riley was back in Atlanta for the National League Championship Series between the Braves and the Pittsburgh Pirates, and then in Minneapolis for the Braves' first World Series appearance since moving to Atlanta. Even Joe flew in to meet his dad and brother, although he got there late. Idaho had been suffering bad fires, which cut down on available water, and Joe could only bathe in a creek. When he got to the hotel, everyone had already gone out for dinner. Riley left a note telling his son where to meet them, but added, "Take a shower first."

Although he won re-election without opposition, political reporters declared Riley a loser in the November elections because of changes on City Council. Independent candidate Maurice Washington had scored an upset victory and Democrat Ligure Ellington replaced the retiring Danny Richardson. Washington and Ellington indicated during the campaign they would not automatically vote with the mayor – even though Riley argued that no one on council did that. Still, The News and Courier said Riley had only five safe votes on the 12-member council.

Bratton held the Bible as Riley took his fifth oath of office in 1992. It was a sign of how long he had been mayor – during the 1975 inauguration his youngest son had been a toddler; now he towered over his father. During the ceremonies, Ford said he wanted to see the mayor do more to help minorities economically "for the next two or three years, depending on the outcome of the governor's race." Riley asked if that was an endorsement, and Ford said, "No."

Riley's fifth term started slowly. He renewed his push for a new ballpark, enlarged the size of the planned aquarium to 85,000 square feet and annexed more of James Island and the St. Andrew's Public Service District. But he spent much of the winter stumping for the presidential campaign of a young Arkansas governor.

Riley had sat on commissions with Bill Clinton – and his wife Hillary – in the 1980s, and liked them both. They were progressive and their politics largely matched his own. The Clintons relied on the mayor's influential stump speeches during the South Carolina Democratic primary, which the governor won in a landslide. Riley would eventually be the first speaker onstage at the Democratic National Convention in July. At Madison Square Garden, Riley used his spotlight to talk about the federal government's obligation to fund American cities adequately.

When he returned from New York, Riley went straight to his father's side. Big

Joe had spent much of the past year in and out of the hospital. As usual, the entire family had gathered at Big Joe's beach house in 1991 for the Fourth of July. But he wasn't feeling well; they thought he had a cold. When his condition worsened the next day, they feared it was pneumonia and took him to the hospital.

The doctors ran tests on Big Joe, the beginning of a long year of hospital visits. Since then, he had been admitted to Roper at least a half-dozen times. He always bounced back, and Riley thought it was just the rigors of old age. But later, Riley said he could look back and chart his father's decline from one July to the next.

The Riley kids were scattered by that time – Susanne was in Indiana, Mary in North Carolina and Jane still had children at home. Their mother couldn't handle it all on her own, so Riley took on the role of his father's medical advocate. He talked with the doctors, got to know the nurses, made all the decisions. He took his briefcase to the hospital, worked out of an office near his father's room. In the mornings Riley would get coffee, a sticky bun and the newspaper and take them in to Big Joe. They would sit for hours, talking about the news. If a nurse came in to check on the patient, Riley would turn his head or leave the room. He still couldn't stand needles.

Big Joe had been retired for a few years, but still could make news. Months earlier, his portrait had been unveiled at the State Ports Authority offices in commemoration of his eight years on the board and a lifetime as ambassador for the city. It was the last of many honors he would receive. Joe Riley Sr. had spent his whole life around politics, running campaigns, supporting his congressmen and governor friends, even doing constituent work for the pure joy of it – but he had never run for office. Big Joe had been content to work behind the scenes, lending his time to various charities and his church.

Public office, well, that had been for his son.

He was, without a doubt, proud of Riley. "He would say, 'Your mother and I are proud' – that's how he always said it," Riley would later recall. His only son had continued the family's tradition of public service in Charleston. And he had done more, and become more influential, than any of them. Big Joe had stayed out of the way, even though some people claimed he held great influence at City Hall.

"During campaigns, when people criticized me, he was ready to fight them," Riley recalled. "Daddy was a civic leader, so he was used to dealing with public officials.

But he never, ever, ever, ever asked for anything to help him, to get some piece of legislation that would benefit his business. He didn't like stingy people, people who would not donate to his causes, or do things for the community."

Riley did not much care what people said about familial influence, but his father did. For the most part, Big Joe watched from afar. He rarely rose to the bait to defend his son, no matter what anyone said. He was careful to make sure everyone knew Joe Riley Jr. was his own man. Big Joe understood the perceptions of politics.

Riley had not followed his father into the real estate business, but ultimately gave him the successor he'd always wanted. Five years earlier, Charlotte had started working at Joseph P. Riley Real Estate and, when he retired, she took over. Big Joe was happy. He had a large family, and long after he mostly quit talking politics, he still loved to ramble on about his four children, his 12 grandchildren.

In early August 1992, one of Charlotte's nieces died in Wisconsin. The family was heartbroken – the young woman had a child just before succumbing to cancer, which made her loss all the worse. Charlotte and Bratton left for the funeral, and Riley was scheduled to join them the next day. Before he went, however, he asked the doctor if it was safe to leave town. When he said, "It's up to you," Riley got worried and decided to stay.

Within a day, he got the call – his father was dying. Riley rushed to the hospital, and found Big Joe unconscious, but, "I think he knew I was there." Joseph P. Riley Sr. died on Aug. 8, 1992, a Saturday. He was 80.

Big Joe's funeral was held at the Cathedral of St. John the Baptist, a church steeped in Riley family history. Afterward the mayor escorted his mother, Helen, to the graveside at St. Lawrence Cemetery. Now he was the patriarch of the family, and in time most people would stop adding "Jr." to the end of his name. But it had never been a distinction that had bothered the mayor; in fact, Riley was proud of it.

"We didn't expect his death to happen, and the permanence of it was very hard," Riley later said. "He was a great man, a great father. He was a larger than life presence. I am thankful I had that year with him."

Weeks after he buried his father, Riley sent city workers to South Florida to help Miami and Homestead dig out of the debris left by Hurricane Andrew, a

Category 5 storm even more deadly than Hugo. The mayor had not forgotten the help Charleston had received three years earlier, and he believed in returning the favor – a sentiment Big Joe would have understood.

Riley could not help but publicly note, however, that FEMA moved much quicker these days, and suggested it might have something to do with Florida being a swing state, and this being an election year. But there was another election on the horizon that concerned him much more. James Island had announced plans to vote on incorporation that December, possibly creating a town that would stifle Charleston's growth.

Of course, that was precisely the idea. The incorporation's supporters freely admitted they were just trying to create a town-in-name-only to stop the city from annexing more of the island. Even though the proposed town of James Island would be the 17th largest municipality in the state, organizers said it would do practically nothing. The town would get its fire and garbage service from the island's public service district and would rely on the county sheriff's office to provide police protection.

Riley was not the only one outraged by the group's brazenness. County Council Chairman Keith Summey said if James Island incorporated, it would have to pay extra for police protection. Residents in each of the county's cities paid county property taxes, but the sheriff's office patrolled only unincorporated areas. Cities were supposed to have their own police departments. Otherwise, why become a town? It was a matter of double taxation, Summey said. But James Islanders didn't see it – their hatred of Riley blinded them to issues of equity. They argued if Mount Pleasant or Charleston didn't get their police protection from the county that was their fault. They didn't realize – or didn't care – that if the sheriff's office was forced to patrol cities as well as rural areas, everyone's county property tax bill would go up astronomically.

Even the Municipal Association of South Carolina – the lobbying arm of the state's cities – criticized the James Island ploy. The association said people shouldn't form a town unless the purpose was to provide residents a greater level of service; hating Joe Riley was not a good enough reason. But in December, the incorporation passed by about 30 votes. Before the end of the month, Charleston citizens would file a lawsuit challenging James Island's ability to put up a moat and call itself a town in name only.

In November 1992 the city reached an agreement to lease Citadel land on the Ashley River for a new baseball stadium, and signed HOK – the architects behind Baltimore's Camden Yards – to design it. It had not been an easy victory for Riley; some council members didn't want to spend the money. Luckily, regular Riley critic Councilman Larry Shirley was a huge baseball fan and saw the allure. The bigger problem came from council members who did not want to be in business with The Citadel, claiming racism and sexism was rampant at the military college.

Riley tried not to take the attacks on his alma mater personally, but by the winter of 1993 he could no longer avoid the debate. During a speech at the college, the mayor was booed by the Corps of Cadets when he initially declined to answer a question about whether The Citadel should admit women – which had become a national issue. Riley did not want to risk offending Citadel President Lt. Gen. Claudius Watts, who was sharing the stage with him. But finally he gave in to the Corps. "I guess you want me to discuss it."

"Having courage to stand by your convictions is one of the important things you learn at The Citadel," Riley said.

The mayor said he always favored equality, and that included admitting women to the school. But, he said, if he were governor he would not enforce his opinion on the college – the Board of Visitors could come to its own decision. The cadets and Citadel officials later praised Riley for having the courage to say that, because it ran contrary to most opinions on campus.

Riley had not only offered his personal opinion, he had issued a position statement. Because in February, he confirmed that he would run for the Democratic gubernatorial nomination in 1994. Gov. Carroll Campbell's second term was coming to an end, so it would be an open race – and Riley wanted to be first out of the gate. The mayor said a formal announcement would come much later, but basically he was already stumping for the job.

Over the next few months, Riley would stake out even more ground. As governor, he said he would take the Confederate flag off the Statehouse dome and put it on a new memorial to Southern soldiers. Then he promised that the only part of the state budget he would allow to grow would be education spending. Slowly, Riley was rolling out an entire platform, and his election seemed almost inevitable. State Republican Party Chairman Henry McMaster said Charleston Republicans had to find a way to derail Riley if they stood any chance of holding on to the governor's mansion.

But another disaster was looming, one that political reporters speculated would force Riley to abandon his campaign.

The mayor was in his office on a Friday afternoon in February 1993 when he got a call summoning him to Sen. Fritz Hollings' district office at the Custom House. He set out on a cold, windy, angry day, wondering exactly what he was walking into. Hollings sounded worried. When he arrived, the senator told him the Pentagon was about to issue a statement – nearly every Navy command post in Charleston could be closed within a year.

The Base Realignment and Closure Commission had been created in 1988 to increase Defense Department efficiency following the end of the Cold War. Two dozen bases around the country had been shuttered in the past five years, and the Pentagon was not through. BRAC had created a list of potential installations to mothball, and it included just about everything local: the Naval Shipyard, the Naval Base, the Submarine Training Facility, the Fleet and Mine Warfare Training Center, the supply center, the public works center and the hospital. Even the Naval Electronics Systems Engineering Center was a target.

The Lowcountry stood to lose about $1 billion in civilian and military payrolls, and 65,000 jobs, assuming the worst-case scenario. Riley knew this could be disastrous for the local economy, but later said there was an even more concrete fear. Thousands of local residents, many of them citizens of Charleston, might lose good, high-paying jobs.

North Charleston Mayor Bobby Kinard promised to fight for the base, but he was new to the job, did not have as many Washington connections and was often distracted by fights with his own city council. So Riley and Hollings stepped in and quickly put together a coalition of local officials to begin lobbying. They got to know commission members personally, divided them up and each had one over to their house for dinner. Riley spent much of the next two months in Washington, talking to members of the BRAC commission and testifying before defense committees. He even went on Good Morning America to defend the Charleston area's military heritage. He argued that 1989 defense cuts had already cost the area 20 ships and 18,000 jobs. The economic impact of further closings, Riley told the BRAC commission in May, is unacceptable.

But Riley and Hollings were lambasted when they suggested BRAC close the Naval Shipyard in Portsmouth instead – and clashed with President Clinton when he defended the Virginia base. Portsmouth Mayor Gloria Webb attacked Riley for his "unethical" behavior. Riley said Webb was a friend, and he understood why she was upset, but, "What we're doing is fighting for our economic life. And we've got a good case. In Norfolk this is jarring to them. They have assumed because they're so big, they could escape all this."

While the controversy simmered, local officials were also secretly working on a plan to salvage the Lowcountry economy if they lost. They hired a team to come up with a base realignment plan to bring other business onto the base. Riley knew they had to do something to combat the psychological damage. If people believed the local economy was going to fail, it could lead to a chain reaction where shopping centers, car lots and other businesses closed down. But they had to work in secret, Riley said, because if BRAC found out the city had an alternative plan, the bases were doomed.

They had hoped to avoid revealing their scheme, but it soon turned into Plan A. In late June, BRAC voted to close the Naval Base and Shipyard, costing the area more than 20,000 direct jobs and $620 million in payroll. The hospital and NAVALEX center had been spared for the time being. Hollings had told Riley that NAVALEX was more important than shipyard jobs. The senator wasn't sentimental; he knew those were old-school jobs, and technology was the future. Still, it was devastating. Sen. Strom Thurmond called it the greatest disaster to befall Charleston in his 90 years.

Riley was in the committee room when the announcement was made, and looked as if he hadn't slept for days. His aggressive lobbying would be controversial, and some BRAC members said he could be shrill in private, but the mayor was always the first to arrive for the hearings and the last to leave. They could question the decision to put up such an aggressive fight, but they could not question his commitment to the Lowcountry.

"I feel defeated," Riley told reporters. "They can say all the nice things they want to; the bottom line is, my community got eviscerated."

Soon after that, local mayors announced that the Navy base would be opened to private business, revealing the plan they'd had in the works for months. Riley said the base would make a perfect place for new industry to move in; the infrastructure was already there – rail, water, docks. "We're going to do what we did in this community after Hurricane Hugo."

Riley threw himself into the recruiting efforts so much The Post and Courier reported rumors that the mayor would soon call off his gubernatorial campaign to focus on rebuilding the local economy. The day of the announcement, reporters had asked how the base closure would affect his campaign, and he said it was the "farthest thing from my mind." But he would not quit, and said the rumors were false.

"I feel it is wishful thinking on the part of my opponents," Riley said. "Bottom line, it's not true."

In October 1993, early polling for the Democratic gubernatorial nomination showed Riley with a 21-point lead over Lt. Gov. Nick Theodore, his closest competitor. Theodore, a longtime Upstate politician, had been friends with Riley for years but the two men were worlds apart in style and personality. While Riley came across as chronically serious and earnest, even studious, Theodore was the archetype of the back-slapping, good ol' boy South Carolina politician. And like most veteran pols, Theodore knew how to play hardball.

While Riley was busy with Navy base business, Theodore was out schmoozing county party managers and racking up commitments. Theodore was building a machine. The mayor knew what was happening – a week did not go by without at least one supporter saying, "We're not seeing you out there." He knew he should have been out canvassing the small, rural counties of the South Carolina interior, but he was more concerned with Charleston's economy.

When he did begin to campaign, Riley was still talking about the economy. He started issuing 15-point plans to bring jobs and economic development to rural

South Carolina. The mayor felt that was the governor's primary job, and his interest in rural counties – many of them populated by minorities, few of them with enough jobs to go around – dated back to his time in the Legislature. Riley campaigned for governor exactly as he governed as mayor, by trying to do things. Trailing in the polls, Theodore chose to make Riley the issue.

Theodore's campaign reported that Laurie Thompson, Charleston's director of Housing and Economic Development, called a D.C. fundraising group during normal business hours – suggesting he was making campaign calls on the city's dime. Thompson told reporters he had used a credit calling card supplied by the campaign. Kerri Morgan – a reporter-turned-campaign spokeswoman – said it was funny to hear Theodore's camp complain about abuse of public office, since the lieutenant governor's press secretary was also his campaign spokesman.

But Theodore, desperate to close the polling gap, continued to attack. When the mayor released a plan to combat crime in South Carolina, Theodore claimed Charleston's crime rate had risen over the past 20 years and Riley had done nothing to stem the violence. Then he recruited veteran Riley critic Robert Ford, and the city councilman went around the state claiming the mayor had never done anything for black citizens in Charleston.

Riley was aghast. He believed his record on crime and racial issues was so strong that he would naturally attract a majority of the primary's black vote. But he was not out on the campaign trail touting his record, so Theodore defined him. A decade before "swift boat" became a household term, Theodore turned Riley's greatest strength into his greatest weakness. State lawmakers McKinley Washington, Lucille Whipper and Herbert Fielding came to Riley's defense, but it did little good.

By the time Theodore claimed Riley had raised Charleston taxes 37 times in 19 years, he had closed to within 7 points in most polls and collected $15 million in campaign contributions – twice as much as Riley. The lieutenant governor had seized the momentum, and the once inevitable Riley campaign and coronation no longer seemed such a sure thing. Riley friends feared the governor's office was slowly slipping away. Then, on May 2, campaign manager Michael Matthews resigned.

Matthews said he and the mayor disagreed on campaign strategy. With four Democrats in the primary, Matthews said he only wanted to make the runoff;

Riley insisted they try to win outright. Matthews' departure was not as serious as it seemed – Riley's inner circle actually ran things – but it started a minor exodus. Spokeswoman Kerri Morgan left the same month, and chief fundraiser Jim Cunningham followed. He complained it was difficult to get Riley to make the personal fundraising calls he needed to be competitive. Cunningham said Riley was "very serious about his job as mayor" – suggesting the mayor cared more about his current job than running for the next one.

Riley had said from the start he wouldn't let the governor's race interfere with his mayoral duties, but state party leaders thought he took that too far. They said part of the problem was that he was running a statewide campaign out of Charleston instead of Columbia. Bud Ferillo, a Democratic campaign consultant, said Riley didn't seem motivated; the people who wanted to support him couldn't find him. Don Fowler, a member of the Democratic National Committee, defended the mayor against such criticism. Fowler said it was facile to think every campaign had to operate identically, that Riley's lack of visibility was not an issue because the real stumping would not begin until the Legislature adjourned in June.

Riley knew he needed to be on the campaign trail. He was torn, but ultimately believed the Navy base redevelopment was "life and death for the community." It wasn't only the thought of an economic doomsday that distracted him, however. He was also working on the new baseball stadium, trying to secure a HUD grant for another redevelopment of the Francis Marion and negotiating with Saks Fifth Avenue to open a store on King Street.

Even Riley's friends were surprised at how little he allowed the campaign to distract from his day job. It wasn't as if the mayor was making a show for the public, it appeared he actually cared more about the day-to-day workings of the city than his campaign. To them, it seemed everything was an excuse to avoid the campaign.

Then, in late April, a tourist was killed in the historic district during an attempted armed robbery. It was the first fatal attack on a tourist in 25 years and, after his calls to the victim's family, Riley's attention turned to increasing police presence on the lower peninsula. Meanwhile, Theodore used the killing as proof of Charleston's spotty record on crime during Riley's tenure. The hits just kept coming.

Charleston certainly had issues that distracted the mayor from the campaign, but he was also struggling with a larger personal realization: Riley wasn't sure he wanted it bad enough. For a long time he had been inspired by Hollings, McNair, West and Dick Riley. After his first year in the Legislature, people had said to him, "You're going to be governor one day." He had thought about that while watching McNair and West give State of the State addresses, imagining how he would handle those issues.

He was first approached to run for governor 20 years earlier, in 1974, when Pug Ravenel was declared ineligible mid-campaign. Since then, he had been mentioned as a potential candidate almost every four years. After Hugo, the state Democratic Party hounded him relentlessly. But Riley had changed in his two decades as mayor. Now, instead of thinking about the governor's office, he fretted over his ongoing projects, what needed to be done in Charleston.

In all those years of waiting for his inevitable ascension to the governor's office, Riley had learned that being mayor was his first, best purpose. It was what he actually wanted to do.

That did not mean he would concede – he had never lost a campaign. By June, Riley was on the campaign trail, determined to make up for lost time and take the fight to Theodore.

A Greater Destiny

On June 2, 1994, a compromise to take the Confederate flag off the South Carolina Statehouse dome died when the General Assembly adjourned for the year. The Senate had offered to remove the flag and replace it with another banner elsewhere on the grounds, but House members facing re-election in November refused to negotiate for fear of complicating their fall campaigns.

The mood across the state was ugly. South Carolina had been bombarded with negative national publicity and faced a possible lawsuit over the flag from the NAACP. A week after the gavel fell, Sen. Darrell Jackson asked Gov. Carroll Campbell to order the Legislature into special session to salvage the Senate plan. Campbell said he would do that only if there was an agreement in advance – and lawmakers consented to work without pay.

Nick Theodore, the lieutenant governor and Democratic candidate for governor, quickly seized on Jackson's idea. He sent Campbell a letter, claiming the House hadn't had enough time to consider the Senate plan and pleading with the governor to consider Jackson's request. "I believe you agree that a resolution of this matter will be in the best interest of our great state."

Riley thought Theodore was grandstanding, making a play for the black vote – and a hypocritical one at that. He pointed out to reporters that Theodore was not even in the Senate chamber when the flag vote was taken.

The mayor said if he was elected governor, he would bypass the Legislature and take down the Confederate flag by executive order on his first day. "Effective leadership could have brought down that flag years ago and put an end to a divisive debate. We must bring down the flag as quickly as possible … so the state can then concentrate on the critical issues of reducing crime, improving education and providing more jobs for all our citizens."

The 1994 gubernatorial campaign had officially begun.

At a debate the following week, Theodore and Riley attacked each other so viciously the other candidates could hardly get in a word. Theodore renewed his claim that Riley had raised taxes in Charleston 37 times, and the mayor argued that taxes had gone down 30 percent as a result of his local option sales tax. Then Riley reminded the audience Theodore had been absent when the Confederate flag vote was taken in the Senate – just as he had been vacationing on a Greek island when South Carolina was decimated by Hurricane Hugo.

Since cranking up his campaign, Riley had gained on Theodore's fundraising lead and still held a 4-point advantage in most polls – which statistically meant they were tied. Although Theodore was well-versed in attack politics, two decades as a mayor promoting sometimes-controversial projects had honed Riley's street-brawler skills enough to make him a worthy foe. But his position as the erstwhile front-runner meant Riley not only had to fight the lieutenant governor, but the other Democratic candidates in the race. Soon, one of the other two, Attorney General Travis Medlock, dragged the mayor's family into the campaign.

At one rally, Medlock's wife ridiculed Charlotte Riley – mocking the mayor's announcement that, if he was elected, his wife would remain in Charleston to run the family real estate business. "Let me put everyone's mind at ease," Laura Medlock said. "Yes, when Travis Medlock is elected governor, Mrs. Medlock will move into the mansion with him." It was a cheap shot, but one that drew raucous applause from the Medlock-friendly audience.

Charlotte had never been fond of politics, did not want to be the candidate's wife, and had no desire to be the state's first lady. She would not stop her husband from running, but wanted as little as possible to do with it. Bratton had been put on "mom duty" to keep her away from the campaign as best he could. Charlotte couldn't stand to hear people attack her husband – and now they were attacking her. Riley would not respond to the jab for fear of dragging his wife further into the mudslinging.

Riley's sons were much more involved in the campaign. Joe had taken a staff job on the Senate Commerce Committee in Washington, and he and Michael Hollings – the senator's son – planned a D.C. fundraiser for Riley. Democrats told Joe it was crazy to try to raise money for a progressive politician in trendy, tony – and very conservative – Georgetown. But Joe had an ace; he'd called Pat Conroy and persuaded the author to make an appearance. Conroy's popularity was at an all-time high on the heels of a Hollywood adaptation of his novel, *The Prince of Tides*. And in Washington, nothing drew attention like celebrity. They raised $40,000 in a single night. Soon, Joe would fly to South Carolina to coordinate efforts in the rural, inland counties.

The primary was little more than a month away.

Theodore spent those final weeks on the attack. He claimed Riley had taken illegal campaign contributions from companies that did business with the city. A subsidiary of a local development firm, the Beach Company, had donated to Riley's war chest, as had the public relations firm of Rawle Murdy – owned in part by David Rawle. Riley said every contribution had been vetted against state ethics laws, and threatened to sue Theodore's campaign manager for slander. The mayor said the real issue was that Theodore took PAC money while he didn't. Between 1989 and 1992, Riley said, Theodore had personally accepted $7,000 in gifts and free trips from lobbyists while openly supporting legislation to ban such practices.

The negative campaigning didn't help either candidate, but appeared to hurt Riley more than Theodore. One week out, the lieutenant governor took a slight lead in the polls. Riley's camp had always known the public polls were skewed in his favor; their internal polling never showed them with a commanding lead. They assumed the initially strong numbers had much to do with the mayor sharing the surname of popular former Gov. Dick Riley. Still, with public polls giving Theodore the edge, he had the confidence to turn down Riley's challenge for six debates around the state. Theodore called it "an act of desperation." Then the Theodore campaign employed Robert Ford to tape a radio commercial claiming Riley opposed a Martin Luther King Jr. day for the city. Just the opposite was true, but the ad did the trick: Riley's support in the black community began to fade.

Riley believed his record was clear, and early polls suggested he was right. In June, he held a 32-point lead over Theodore among black voters. Of course, that is precisely why the Theodore camp attacked – and it worked. It seemed nothing was going right for Riley in those final days. At one campaign event in Charleston, a number of the mayor's supporters left the rally only to find city parking tickets on their cars.

The mayor's biggest hurdle, however, would not become apparent until just after the primary. A new state law restricted a person from voting in one party's primary and the other party's runoff during the same election cycle. Riley had strong support in Beaufort County, but there was a seven-way race for sheriff on the Republican ticket. Many people, unaware of the new law, opted to vote in the Republican primary to select a sheriff. Those voters would not be able to support Riley in a runoff.

It almost didn't matter. On election night, Theodore garnered 49.55 percent of the vote – not enough to win outright, but close. Medlock took 9 percent and Rock Hill businessman William Holler drew 4 percent. Riley came in second with 38 percent of the vote, and would face Theodore in a runoff two weeks later. From his campaign office in Columbia, Riley promised "the greatest comeback in South Carolina history." The mayor renewed his challenge for a series of debates, and said he'd come in second simply because the lieutenant governor was part of the state's formidable good ol' boy system.

"I'd say that extending a hand out to South Carolina's voters and calling them buddy apparently works in mysterious ways," Theodore responded. It was perhaps the most self-aware statement of the entire campaign, as Theodore had summed up his facile, but effective, campaigning style in a single sentence.

For the next two weeks, Riley campaigned tirelessly. He began each day by jogging through a different city and stopping to talk to voters. In one two-day period, he raised $275,000. He barnstormed the Pee Dee, courting black votes with former Atlanta Mayor Maynard Jackson, who vouched for Riley's civil rights record. His son, Joe, took over the Sumter County campaign office and came close to flipping the county, giving Riley as much of a lead as Theodore had during the primary.

At several campaign stops, Riley brought out fact sheets to take apart Theodore's "37 tax increases" claim. One of the alleged tax hikes was an increase in greens fees at the city's municipal golf course. Riley was on-point, focused and indefatigable. His friends said the mayor was moving like a man possessed. If he had campaigned that hard during the primary, they said, he could have won without a runoff.

On election night, there would be no concession, no victory speech. In the primary, Riley lost to Theodore by nearly 30,000 votes – now the mayor appeared to be just 2,000 votes behind. But no one would declare a winner. There were still uncounted ballots – and unanswered questions – the day after the runoff. A Williamsburg County election commissioner was forced to resign after he was caught tampering with ballots to help Theodore. The race was too close to call.

When the recount was finished, Riley lost by 1,609 votes – or, his friends lamented, one vote per precinct. The tide had turned, they said, and with another couple of days Riley might have won. The mayor had great support in the Lowcountry, but Theodore held a considerable edge in the Upstate and Midlands. Riley's progressive politics did not play as well inland as they did along the coast, even in a Democratic primary. The Beaufort County sheriff's race had cost the Riley campaign, and it didn't help that fellow Lowcountry son Arthur Ravenel had been on the Republican gubernatorial runoff ballot. Ravenel lost his race, too, falling to David Beasley. The difference was that Riley had never lost an election.

After the runoff, the governor's race devolved into a typical partisanship battle. Riley played the role of loyal Democrat, campaigning with Theodore when the lieutenant governor inevitably asked for his support. Others could not forgive the harsh primary so easily, however. The Post and Courier endorsed Beasley over Theodore, in part because of the shameless way he had distorted Riley's record on civil rights.

The Republicans won nearly everything in the Nov. 8 election – education superintendent, secretary of state, agriculture commissioner, lieutenant governor and, of course, governor. Beasley beat Theodore 50 percent to 48 percent – a margin of 23,000 votes. The GOP victory was in part a fierce backlash against the election of President Bill Clinton two years earlier, but also just the changing nature of South Carolina politics. It was the first time in the modern era Republicans had held the governor's and lieutenant governor's offices simultaneously, but it would not be the last. Soon, the GOP would dominate the entire state.

And no sooner than the election ended, some people began to plan a 1998 governor's campaign for Joe Riley.

Life went on.

The city of Charleston v. the town of James Island finally went to trial in July 1995, by which time the town had been operating for two years. The city's complaint was complicated, hinged on arcane state law, but Riley said the bottom line was that James Island had impeded Charleston's ability to grow – and was financed by tax money that rightfully belonged to other county residents and municipalities.

State law was clear: no town could form within five miles of another municipality without first asking to be annexed into the existing city – unless that new town had more than 15,000 residents. James Island claimed 18,000 residents, but city attorney Bill Regan pointed out the town reached that number only by patching together nine areas divided by waters that were already in the city. Basically, James Island ran through Charleston.

James Island attorneys argued that even if the town had broken every imaginable state law to incorporate, it should be allowed to continue operations because it provided services to residents. Those services, however, were limited to zoning decisions, issuing business licenses, planning a town hall – and receiving local option sales tax money. It was not exactly an argument that impressed Circuit Judge John C. Hayes III, or anyone outside the town limits. After all, two years earlier the town's founders had proudly declared James Island a town-in-name-only.

For Charleston this was simply a border dispute, but other municipalities around the county were deeply interested in seeing James Island dissolved. The issue was money. By becoming a municipality, James Island became eligible to receive a portion of the county's sales tax collections – dividing the pie into more pieces. This hurt cities that actually provided services – Charleston alone had lost nearly $300,000. Not only did James Island not provide any regular services, it planned to take sales tax money and divide it among residents. The town's entire operation was subsidized by the rest of the county. And with the rebate, town residents paid far less in taxes than anyone else – all while accomplishing their primary goal, which was to avoid annexation into Charleston.

James Island was flouting the very tenets of double taxation Riley had bemoaned for years, and did it at the expense of the county's largest economic generator – a tax base that ultimately benefited everyone. It galled the mayor. He had spent much of the past two years thinking regionally, working for the greater good outside his municipal borders. The mayor had been negotiating with county and North Charleston officials how best to use the Navy base. The idea was to open the base to private business, perhaps a shipyard, and persuade the State Ports Authority to expand its operations to the base rather than build a new facility on Daniel Island. The infrastructure the ports needed was already in place, Riley argued.

The mayor continued that work after both sides rested in the case of Charleston v. James Island.

In April 1995, Riley announced his sixth bid for mayor in a news conference at the old Citadel campus. The setting was intentional – the castle-like building on Marion Square, which in recent years had housed some county government and school district offices, would soon become a new hotel. It was yet more proof of how much the city had changed during his tenure. Riley promised to make Charleston the largest city in the state by 2000, and predicted King Street would be a vibrant, revitalized retail and restaurant corridor early in the 21st century.

The mayor would not get a free pass this election, not with the Republicans feeling more powerful than ever. Soon after his announcement, state Rep. Ron Fulmer said he would challenge Riley. Flanked by Carroll Campbell, Gov. David Beasley and Congressman Mark Sanford, Fulmer promised to slash the budget of every city department by 10 percent. He wanted to privatize the aquarium and city garbage service and promised to fix the city's drainage problems. Fulmer said he would serve only two terms – a not-so-subtle dig at Riley's 20 years in office.

Fulmer stuck to the new script of the Republican Party, and throughout the summer he attacked nearly everything Riley touched. He opposed the new baseball stadium, complained about the city's debt, recycled Theodore's claim of 37 tax increases. The mayor ignored most of the trash talk. Political reporters said the election would be a referendum on Riley. If that was the case, most Charleston residents appeared happy with the current management. In November, Riley won re-election with an overwhelming 75 percent of the vote.

By then, Judge Hayes had dismantled the town of James Island. He said the town's boundaries were not contiguous, that it had skirted state law to incorporate. He allowed the town to keep operating at a minimum level while it appealed, but it was clear Hayes believed the state Supreme Court would uphold his decision.

Riley took his sixth oath of office on Jan. 8, 1996, and many people assumed it would be his last as mayor. In two years he would run for governor again, and no one expected him to lose. But the mayor said nothing during the campaign about the possibility of not finishing his term, as he had in 1991 – a point most people missed. Robert Steed, a political science professor at The Citadel, told The Post and Courier after all that time as mayor, "it would be kind of natural to look for a different level, different challenges."

It was a fair assessment, but did not take into account the soul-searching Riley had done in the past year.

Riley ignored the speculation and the calls from the state party. He said nothing about higher office in his inaugural address, promising to devote the next four years to building the nation's best aquarium and minor league baseball stadium. The mayor said the city would try to enhance the lives of local children through better education and mentoring programs. "We must all believe passionately that we have not a single child to waste and that every child in our community is this village's collective responsibility."

Political reporters assumed this talk of education was the prelude to a statewide platform, but Riley was thinking about the school district's pending vote on the location of the new Academic Magnet High School. The mayor had lobbied school board members to use the site of the old Murray Vocational School, a neoclassical building on Chisolm Street. Riley wanted the school close to MUSC, the College of Charleston and The Citadel, but some people thought he just liked the idea of keeping the school, which was expected to be a success, on the peninsula. Meanwhile, North Charleston Mayor Keith Summey –the former County Council chairman – was offering the district two other sites.

Murray Vocational had housed some school district offices in recent years but needed extensive renovations, and Riley suggested the city might help. There were only two problems: City Council did not like the mayor making such an offer without its approval, and neither did some downtown residents. The Chisolm Street school building, after all, sat South of Broad.

City Council members accused Riley of treating them like potted plants, fueling the long-standing perception that council was expected to always do the mayor's bidding. Councilman Maurice Washington said City Council was a legislative body in title only, and several others claimed they knew nothing about the plan until they read it in the paper. A few threatened to hold up money for the renovation. The mayor told The Post and Courier he had talked to several council members before making the offer, but couldn't call a special meeting for everything that came up.

The Charlestowne Neighborhood Association eventually joined the protest, and the mayor accused the group of having a not-in-my-backyard philosophy. Living in a city, he said, meant that schools, shopping centers and residential areas must mingle and co-exist – a mantra he would repeat in the coming years. Council ultimately went along with his plan, but it took a 7-6 split with Riley casting the deciding vote. In the end, it didn't matter. The school board, blaming parking woes and the nearby Coast Guard station, gave Academic Magnet to North Charleston.

The school controversy had no lingering effects on council. In April 1996, City Council signed off on a $16.3 million deal to build a brick-and-concrete baseball stadium on the banks of the Ashley River – the place where Riley once envisioned a coliseum and convention center. The mayor said the stadium would be a gathering place, a clean, well-lighted destination where people could spend their evenings watching baseball. The Charleston RiverDogs, the city's most recent franchise, expected attendance to double once the stadium opened. Riley said it would be nothing less than "the best baseball park for a city our size."

"This community deserves excellent things, not mediocre things," the mayor said.

Riley planned to call the stadium Ashley River Park, a designation that needed only council approval. But in September, City Council voted to name the ballfield Joseph P. Riley Jr. Park. The idea came from Councilwoman Mary Ader, a Republican who had first taken office with Riley in 1975. She had been on opposite sides of the mayor many times, but she lobbied the rest of council to go along with her idea. It was simply the right thing to do, she said.

The debate suggested the rubber-stamp controversy of the previous spring was over. Even Riley's usual council opponents agreed with Ader. The mayor's abiding love of baseball, and his vision to build the stadium, made Riley Park the logical name. Councilman Larry Shirley, who often clashed with Riley, said it was the one instance when he believed in breaking his rule about naming things in honor of the living.

The mayor put up more of a fight than anyone feigning false modesty.

"I feel very strongly about this," Riley said. "I'm a servant of the people, and you don't name things after a servant." He said it would be enough to take his grandchildren to the stadium one day and bore them with the story about how, once upon a time, City Council had tried to name it in his honor. But council ignored his protests, and voted 11-1 in favor of naming the baseball stadium Joseph P. Riley Jr. Park. The mayor cast the lone dissenting vote.

The audience responded with a standing ovation and City Clerk Vanessa Turner Maybank read the name of the park – even as Riley interrupted her and said, "We'll work on that later." Quietly, he said, "The 'no's' have it. The chair rules the new name of the park is Ashley River Park." But no one would listen to Riley. There was no other name for a new baseball stadium in Charleston.

In September, Riley flew to Italy in hopes of reuniting Spoleto with the Festival of Two Worlds. Three years earlier, the collaboration between the two annual events had been severed when Gian Carlo Menotti quit Spoleto in a huff. Menotti forced artists to choose between the two festivals, and it had cost the city some talent – although certainly not all. Many performers had elected to remain associated with Charleston.

Nigel Redden had returned to Spoleto as general manager, and he and board chairman Homer Burrous asked Riley to join them for a meeting with Spoleto, Italy, Mayor Alessandro Lauretti at an opera festival. The mayor initially declined but reconsidered when he realized it might be a nice, albeit quick, trip for him and Charlotte. They would stay with Countess Alicia Paolozzi, who had homes in both cities – and originally suggested the joint venture to Menotti. Riley just hoped he could reason with Menotti.

The trip did not go as planned. Paolozzi was as warm and friendly as ever, but Riley didn't even see Menotti until the Spoleto mayor held a press conference – and then the composer barely spoke to him. Riley was disappointed, and more than a little annoyed by the drama. Charlotte later said Menotti acted as if he was playing out a tragedy from one of his own operas.

On Friday, just after he was presented with a gold Roman coin from Mayor Lauretti, Riley got a call that his office had routed through City Hall. That was no easy task, and he paused only a second to wonder what could be so important. But as soon as he heard his sister Jane say "Joe," he knew.

His mother had suffered a stroke. Riley and Charlotte said hurried goodbyes and rushed to the airport in Rome.

Helen Riley's health had been in decline for years, at least since Big Joe died. All her community work – the hours donated to the Association for the Blind, the Florence Crittenton Home, the Gibbes Museum and her alma mater, the College of Charleston – had slowed down in recent years, but she tried to stay involved. On Thursday, Helen had attended a meeting at her church. Her old friend Helen Debrux said she had been pleased to see her because "she doesn't always go." The stroke hit the next day.

Since his father's death, Riley had spent increasingly more time with his mother. He handled her finances, which weren't complicated, and got her help to keep up the Murray Boulevard house. He took Helen to all her doctor appointments, to lunch and to church. One story the mayor liked to tell was how, before she agreed to marry Joe Riley Sr., Helen named an amount that had to be in his bank account before the wedding. She wasn't greedy, or even money-oriented – she was just practical. Riley often said his father would not have been nearly as successful without her as a partner.

The mayor couldn't think of anything else as he and Charlotte raced back to the States, enduring long airplane rides, barely making connections. Finally, they got across the Atlantic and landed in New York. He called home only to find out he was too late. Helen Louise Schachte Riley died on Friday, Sept. 13, 1996. She was 81.

Riley felt guilty that he hadn't been by his mother's side, but she knew he was working on a cause close to her heart. Helen Riley's friends would later say she was so proud of everything her son did for Charleston – but especially Spoleto. All the flowers that adorned City Hall during the festival's opening were picked from her garden. It broke Riley's heart that he could do little more than eulogize her for the newspaper.

"She was the best mother in the world and her children's teacher, friend and guide," the mayor said. "We knew her complete energy went toward our best interests. She was also our father's true partner and a bright, intelligent person who graduated from the College of Charleston second in her class and did post-graduate work at Jefferson Teaching Hospital in Philadelphia, where she received a degree in medical technology. Mother loved Charleston very much and was so greatly interested in community affairs. Most of all, she was an inspiring, loving and caring person who will be greatly missed."

Although Riley was his father's son, he had inherited more of his personality from his mother. He shared her temperament, her quiet ways. She had raised him to love the Lowcountry, spending countless hours on the beach with him when he was a boy. Helen had supported his decision to forego the family business for law school, and remained his close confidante. He thought back to the old days when the family spent their summers at the beach. Big Joe couldn't stand silence, or being out of touch. He would call all his friends, leave messages, get tired of waiting and then go out on his boat – leaving Helen to take all the returned calls.

It made Riley smile to think about that, but sad to know he'd lost them both in a span of four years.

The city was negotiating to buy 90 acres of undeveloped land on James Island when the South Carolina Supreme Court took up the case of the island town's incorporation. Some City Council members suggested Riley wait for the outcome, but he wouldn't. The mayor said the city should preserve the pristine land overlooking the Stono River – home of earthen batteries left over from the Civil War – before someone turned it into a subdivision. Riley wasn't worried about the court.

On Nov. 18, the state Supreme Court dissolved the town of James Island. The justices were unanimous in their opinion that it had formed illegally by tying together nine separate patches of land separated by creeks and marshland already inside the corporate limits of Charleston and Folly Beach. "It defies the very concept of contiguity to suggest that one municipality may use an adjacent municipality's annexed territory to establish contiguity."

The town's supporters complained, said they did not want to be part of the city of Charleston because it had become too tourist-oriented. It was an unusual rationalization, since incorporation did not move them any farther from the tourist district. The Supreme Court ruling did little to change their lives – they would still get all their services from the county and public service district. Their desire to distance themselves from Charleston was a state of mind, and Riley had become the personification of what they did not like about the city.

One Saturday, Riley and Charlotte were driving across the James Island connector to buy something at a hardware store when the mayor spotted a bumper sticker. It said "Iraq hell, bomb Riley." He sped up to see who was in the car, but Charlotte told him to slow down. The mayor didn't care about the insult – he thought it was a scream.

The day after the Supreme Court ruling, the city of Charleston dropped off annexation petitions at James Island fire stations and its recreation center – and began mailing forms to every person who lived in unincorporated parts of the island. Within the first day, the city got more than 150 completed petitions, with more phone calls coming each day. The city wanted people to annex voluntarily, but needed requests only from owners of 75 percent of the property value in any area to take entire subdivisions. If James Island tried to form a town again, it would have far fewer households with which to broach that 15,000-resident threshold.

The town's organizers quickly asked the Supreme Court to reconsider the case, but it was too late.

By February 1997, South Carolina Democrats were getting antsy. Joe Riley was their chosen standard-bearer, their greatest hope of unseating an incumbent Republican governor in 1998. The party believed their nominee should be crisscrossing the state, laying the groundwork for the campaign, talking to the press, outlining issues. This proverbial candidate should make an announcement by spring at the latest. They did not want Riley to wait too long to engage, as he had in 1994.

No doubt, Riley had given the party some hope. For months he had been wading into state issues with increasing frequency. He derided the Legislature's ongoing lack of commitment to education funding, criticized the decision to open the Barnwell landfill to out-of-state nuclear waste and spent much of 1996 stumping for Democratic candidates around the state. Riley said he was only being a loyal party member, not trying to ingratiate himself to county political leaders. But he nevertheless was building up a lot of goodwill.

The Democrats did everything they could to entice Riley. The party persuaded other candidates to stay out of the race until the mayor made a decision. Basically, Riley was promised the nomination was his for the taking, a coronation-in-waiting. The timing was not bad. It wouldn't be an open race, but he would face a governor of questionable popularity. David Beasley had proven too reasonable and moderate for some Republicans, and enraged some right-wingers by joining the call to remove the Confederate flag from the Statehouse dome. Riley, in fact, had praised the governor's stance. But many people considered Beasley vulnerable, and the Democrats said they could lose only if they started too late. Riley agreed, said he was considering the party's offer.

"I don't have a self-appointed, precise deadline," he said, "but I've got to make a decision very soon."

When that decision came in March 1997, it was not the one most people expected. Riley said he would not be a candidate for governor in 1998, or any other year. He would never seek higher office of any kind. This choice, he said, had nothing to do with a loss of fire, desire or sense of duty. He had no fears about raising money or running against a sitting governor. It was only "a response to my family's wishes and my love and duty to them."

"The time is not now. The time was then … and I was unsuccessful," Riley told The Post and Courier's Schuyler Kropf.

It was not an easy decision. Riley was giving up the one office he had wanted since he was a young man. But he later said his only regret was that he would never have a chance to help the rural counties of the state. In the end, it came down to that sense of family his parents had instilled in him. Charlotte, Joe and Bratton had tolerated invasions of privacy and forgiven his absences for decades, and that was enough. "My family has willingly made sacrifices – generously, not begrudgingly," he said. This, he believed, was the least he could do for them.

Of course, Riley knew such an admission would only bring more attention to his family and, to spare them, he considered blaming his health. He had suffered a tough bout of pericarditis, a swelling of the membrane around the heart, shortly after the 1994 campaign. He thought about citing his numerous responsibilities in Charleston, and that wouldn't have been a lie. But he decided only the truth would satisfy the people who expected him to run again.

The mayor's friends had no doubt he was telling the truth – even though they did not like the decision. Bill Regan told the newspaper that many of Riley's friends were disappointed but unsurprised. Even Riley's critics took the news badly. Robert Ford, by then a state senator, said Riley could easily defeat Beasley. City Council members who were often at odds with Riley called it the state's loss, but admitted they were glad he was staying – they needed him. And Sen. Fritz Hollings, Riley's political mentor, called it devastating news for South Carolina.

"He's the best," Hollings said. "I don't know how you're going to get anyone with that track record and that charisma. The state is unlucky; the city of Charleston is very, very lucky."

Some Democrats suspected there was more to it, knowing that when a politician cites family reasons, they are often hiding something. A few speculated that Beasley's move to the center had unnerved Riley. More charitable party officials said the mayor was simply being realistic, that Charleston was his priority and he realized he couldn't devote enough time to the race. They had to come up with excuses, because none of them could imagine anyone walking away from an easy trip to the general election, if not the governor's mansion.

Finally, someone stepped forward to douse the conspiracy theories and corroborate Riley's story. At the end of the week, Elsa McDowell, who had become The Post and Courier's news columnist not long after the retirement of Frank Gilbreth, published an interview with the mayor's wife, Charlotte Riley.

For 20 years, Charlotte had studiously avoided the limelight, stayed away from ribbon-cuttings and city functions, and sometimes even stayed out of sight at inaugurations. She had no love for publicity or the public life – unlike most politicians, Riley never sent out the requisite campaign photos of the candidate with his family. But more than any of that, Charlotte could not stand to see her husband questioned.

She told McDowell that family was most definitely behind Riley's decision.

"I am the reason," Charlotte said.

In 1994, Charlotte had been mortified by the gubernatorial campaign. But she knew how much it meant to Riley, and so they had reached an understanding: if he was elected, she would stay in Charleston with friends and family while he worked out of Columbia. She thought it was an acceptable compromise, one she was comfortable with until the campaign began.

"That was before I had to watch someone I love read about the race every day and be torn apart," she said.

Riley struggled with his 1994 loss for a long time. It was his only defeat, and it came during his first shot at the job he'd always wanted. The mayor had considered a 1998 campaign, even though he realized during the last race that he didn't want to abandon Charleston. His consideration for Charlotte eventually resolved his internal struggle – some members of the family later said he couldn't bear to put her through another statewide campaign.

The Rileys had reached an accord: He would make no more forays into the dirty world of state politics, and she would live with his decision to be mayor so long as he wanted. In fact, Charlotte conceded, "You are doing what you are meant to do."

Joe and Bratton wanted their father to win the governor's office as badly as he did, but eventually agreed their mother was right. Joe later said he had no doubt a Joe Riley governorship would have been good for the state, but he feared what might happen to Charleston without his father at the helm. Hollings had been right, too: it may have been South Carolina's misfortune, but Charleston was very, very lucky.

Eventually, Riley came to see it in purely logical terms. If he had been elected governor, he might have served one, possibly two terms. And then what? He could have run for Congress, but most likely the Republican revolution would have quickly put an end to that. No, being mayor of Charleston gave him his best chance for the greatest amount of achievement. It was his destiny, and it was more than enough.

In retrospect, there is little doubt what would have happened. In 1998 a Democratic state representative named Jim Hodges – a man with almost no name recognition outside his small, rural district – trounced Beasley 53 percent to 45 percent. Hodges did this by focusing on education, as Riley would have. The only variable is that Hodges based his campaign almost exclusively on introducing a state lottery to fund college scholarships and other education programs. During Hodges' victory speech, many of Riley's friends thought, *That could have been Joe*. But when The Post and Courier asked Riley if he regretted his decision, he said no.

"I put my family first and that is my first responsibility."

More than a year after Riley said he would never seek a higher office, reporters were still looking for ways to give the mayor a promotion. Some speculated that U.S. Sen. Strom Thurmond – who was approaching his 96th birthday – might not finish his term. It would be up to the governor to appoint a replacement, and most prognosticators believed Hodges would appoint Riley.

The mayor dismissed the speculation, saying he was confident Thurmond would finish his term. Riley said if he continued his career in public service, it would only be as mayor of Charleston.

"I would say that's leaving the door pretty well shut," Riley said.

The New South

More than 6,400 people showed up for the RiverDogs home opener at Joseph P. Riley Jr. Park on April 7, 1997 – exceeding the new stadium's capacity, quite literally, right off the bat. The ballpark was a smaller version of the new Major League Baseball venues going up around the country, and by opening day it had inspired 1,200 people to buy season tickets. In their final season at College Park the RiverDogs sold only 100.

The stadium was built of brick and concrete and steel, reminiscent of old parks like Wrigley Field, but it was also decidedly high-tech – just one of three in the minor leagues with a video replay scoreboard. It was also the only stadium with such a majestic water view, making it a popular place not only for sports but people-watching. It was, as Riley had hoped, a true gathering place.

By the time the RiverDogs took the field, The Citadel's baseball team had already played a game in the stadium. Riley was on hand for both openers. Before throwing out the first pitch on this night, the mayor made a short speech about "the ballpark." He was still uncomfortable with City Council's decision to name the stadium after him and had insisted that at least a section of the park be named after Larry Doby, a Camden, South Carolina, native and the first black player in the American League.

Despite his protests, most people would simply call it "The Joe."

In his brief remarks, Riley dedicated the park to the baseball lovers of Charleston and hoped it would provide generations of fun and memories to warm the "infields of our hearts." He recalled his first professional baseball game a half-century earlier, when his grandfather Ned took him to opening night at College Park. He spoke of walking up the creaky steps of the grandstand behind the first base line as he held his grandfather's hand. Riley could not forget those details because it was the night he fell in love with the game.

"A generation later I began taking our sons to College Park," Riley said. "I would hold their hands as we walked up the same creaky steps. I introduced them to the game I loved and they watched me keep score as I taught them the nuances of this marvelous game. And now they teach me. These are memories I have for life. Tonight we open more than just a stadium for baseball. We dedicate a cathedral of memories."

Riley sat in the stands as the RiverDogs took a 5-0 lead in the first inning on the strength of two home runs – one of them a three-run shot. The team went on to beat the Cape Fear Crocs 6-3, a good omen for the new park. Although most of the excitement came in the first minutes, the crowd was into the game all night, screaming and shouting and cheering. It was, Riley would always remember, magical.

With the ballpark open, Riley turned his focus to the long-delayed aquarium project, which had been in the works nearly a decade before The Joe. The facility had suffered one setback after another since Ontario-based Ellis-Don company arrived in 1995. Preliminary work was delayed eight months after the construction firm claimed some of the pilings had shifted a few inches. Ellis-Don officials feared the building would not survive an earthquake and needed to make adjustments. The company wanted the city to pay its costs for the delay, but instead Riley filed a lawsuit. City consultants said the soil and foundation were fine, and the mayor suggested the company was trying to run up its bill.

"If, heaven forbid, there is a serious earthquake in Charleston, if there is one building still standing in the city, it will be the South Carolina Aquarium," Riley said.

Ellis-Don filed a countersuit, and the legal wrangling began. It was beginning to look as if the aquarium would not be finished in time for the anticipated 1999 grand opening.

The ongoing aquarium delays did not upset many downtown residents, who had renewed their complaints about tourists overtaking the peninsula. One group suggested closing all roads South of Broad to everything except local traffic. At the very least, the group said, tour buses should be banned from historic neighborhoods. Riley put together another tourism study committee – one that he would lead – to consider still more regulations.

Charleston was becoming more popular every year. Nearly 4 million tourists visited annually and, in the past two years, plans for 24 new hotels had been announced. Conde Nast readers ranked Charleston the fourth-best U.S. city for tourism. The city and the Convention and Visitors Bureau were doing their jobs well – too well for some locals. It didn't matter that the city had blocked new hotels from being built south of Calhoun Street, or that all those annoying tourists lowered property tax bills by $200 or more each year. There were simply too many people.

It also didn't matter to Riley critics that the rest of the world considered Charleston a model for urban design. The national Seaside Institute had honored Riley with its top award for 1997, praising him as "the man who cares the most about the quality of the design of the city, the quality of life in the city and the civic responsibilities of each citizen." The mayor had delivered Charleston from the 18th century to the 21st century; the judges said he should be in the White House.

The real problem for some people was change. Some were even mad the King Street Woolworth was closing after 95 years in the same location. The store's demise was a corporate decision, not the city's doing, but the message was clear: Change was simply bad. The Historic Ansonborough Neighborhood Association said the city's quality of life had declined and the mayor did little to prevent it. Riley told the group that Charleston was "dealing with the pace of success. Eternal vigilance is the price of a livable city."

Riley's tourism committee eventually recommended a plan to change bus routes, reduce bus traffic and limit the hours when commercial tours could operate – and City Council overwhelmingly adopted it. Despite the new rules, and the city's promise to ban gambling boats, many downtown residents complained that it was not enough. Some of them would have been more than happy to shutter the Convention and Visitors Bureau and leave the aquarium unfinished. Riley, who had heard such complaints for far too long, said these people did not understand the concept of urban living.

"It used to be you could find a parking place in front of that building on King Street because there wasn't any activity there. Now there are 1,200 public parking spaces within 200 yards of that building, which means you could get to that building more conveniently than you could get to any regional shopping mall in America."

Riley suggested some of these critics might be happier in the suburbs and, in April 1998, he gave them the option. The city unveiled development plans for Daniel Island, which included a commercial district nearly the size of downtown Charleston. Its neighborhoods would emulate pre-World War II towns with tree-lined streets, sidewalks and homes built close to the road. The island community held so much promise that the private Bishop England High School moved its campus from the peninsula to Daniel Island.

Downtown neighborhood groups warned that growth and tourism issues might be a factor in the 1999 mayoral election, a not so thinly veiled threat. Riley had not announced his re-election plans yet, but had proposed making municipal elections non-partisan. The mayor said partisan politics only created divides where none existed, that there was no Democratic or Republican way to pave streets. The city's fire department had just become only the 26th in the country to achieve the country's highest possible insurance rating, for instance, and that had nothing to do with any political party.

Critics said the mayor was attempting to neutralize the growing strength of the Republican Party, but in November 1998 more than 51 percent of voters approved the idea. The Republican Party quickly filed suit, and by spring 1999 the state Supreme Court threw out the results. The justices said the referendum was invalid because the city had not done enough to ensure privacy – such as failing to provide voting booths or folding ballots. Riley, undeterred, would soon try again.

On Jan. 12, 1999, Riley announced his campaign for a seventh term as mayor. He had sat down over New Year's weekend to list his goals for the coming year, the ongoing projects that needed his attention. There was the aquarium, of course, as well as his lobbying efforts for a new Cooper River bridge, the reopening of the Old Slave Mart Museum, an ordinance to curb late-night bar hours downtown and an expansion of the Charleston Museum – where he hoped to put the *H.L. Hunley*. The Confederate submarine had been discovered offshore in 1995 and there were plans to raise it within two years.

By the time he was finished, Riley had 120 items on his list. Clearly, it was more than he could do in the single year he had left in office. The mayor told reporters, "If the citizens would allow me, I would love the opportunity to try to continue to do them."

Two weeks later, City Councilman Maurice Washington hinted to reporters he might challenge the mayor. Washington was a Riley supporter in 1995 but had become one of his most ardent opponents on council. That did not make him unique. City Council was more divided than it had been in years. Council members fought over term limits, eventually dismissing the idea, and criticized each other for getting up to do interviews in the middle of a meeting. The times were changing quickly. In the 1997 election, Riley lost three council members who had been with him since 1975 and a fourth, Mary Ader, was forced to resign for health reasons in 1998.

Riley still worked with this new council fairly well, but the politics were becoming more contentious. In part, that was just the political climate. In the spring, the mayor imposed a three-minute rule on citizens who wanted to speak during council meetings. It was traditionally a chance for people to complain about traffic or drainage, but the public comment portion of the meeting had devolved into a regular gripe session. James Island resident Mary Clark showed up regularly to protest city annexations on her island. Another regular complained that council didn't do enough to stop drug dealers on the East Side. And one local activist had a running monologue about gentrification, in which he often made thinly veiled threats against Riley: "White people like Mayor Riley bring out the Denmark Vesey in me."

Washington was rarely a rabble-rouser but said he simply saw things differently from the mayor, and that's why he had decided to run. He conceded that winning would not be easy. "You beat Mayor Riley, you've earned the right to serve," he said. "That's the way it ought to be."

When the state Supreme Court ruled that the city could not hold a nonpartisan election in 1999, Washington chose to run as an independent. Riley filed to run as a Democrat – and Washington quickly called him a hypocrite. If the mayor supports nonpartisan elections, the councilman asked, why run on a ticket? Riley said running as an independent in a partisan election would be akin to rejecting his party, something he would not do. Political scientists told Post and Courier reporters that Washington's decision was a break for Riley, who might not fare well against a black candidate in a Democratic primary.

Race would be the dominant issue of the campaign. Washington accused the mayor of race-baiting when he mailed brochures touting his civil rights record to black households. At an October debate, Washington waved the brochure – which detailed Riley's position on the Confederate flag, the Martin Luther King Jr. holiday and affordable housing – and said, "This is an insult to me and should be an insult to every African-American."

Riley did not respond during the debate, and made no apology afterward. He called the brochure a positive piece of campaign literature that did not mention Washington. "A good question for the mayor of Charleston is what has been his record in civil rights for the African-American community. I was very proud of that, and I wanted to let voters know that."

Riley sent out the brochure in response to a mailer from Sen. Robert Ford – the former councilman – which claimed the mayor had never done anything for the black community. Washington denied any involvement and denounced Ford, but he was clearly relying on the black vote. His campaign was operating primarily in the city's predominantly African-American precincts, where a new poll showed Riley with 51 percent support compared to Washington's 24 percent. Even the mayor joked about it.

"I guess that poll took him aback today," the mayor said.

Riley felt he was on safe ground talking about race with Washington. Every other African-American on City Council had endorsed the mayor, and David Dinkins – the first black mayor of New York City – was coming to town for a Riley reception. Washington was a political chameleon, had run for office as a Democrat, a Republican and now an independent. Some in the black community viewed his shifting status as political opportunism and did not respond kindly.

On Nov. 2, 1999, Riley won his seventh term with 71 percent of the vote. He credited the win to the broad support he had across the community, but Washington had made a dent in the mayor's base: He won 12 of 85 precincts – something no one else had done against Riley in a mayoral election. The councilman also won 51 percent of the black vote, besting Riley by 102 votes. The mayor's campaign attributed that to Washington's laser focus on black wards. More than half of the 5,087 votes he got came from those precincts.

A few weeks after the election, Riley flew to Havana with the mayors of Baltimore and Knoxville, Tennessee, to talk about preservation. The Cuban government's capital had crumbled after decades of poverty and neglect – some people estimated that one of the city's historic buildings collapsed each day. The Baltimore and Knoxville mayors, fresh from a course at Riley's Mayors' Institute on City Design, toured the city to examine structures in desperate need of preservation. They also critiqued buildings constructed since the revolution that did not fit Havana's beauty. Baltimore Mayor Kurt Schmoke proclaimed the Russian embassy in Miramar the worst piece of architecture he'd ever seen.

"It violates every Joe Riley principle," he said.

Riley told the Cuban officials that preservation is one of government's responsibilities to its citizens. The public has a right to control anything it can see. He said Charleston's height limit on buildings was "the most important land-use decision our community has made." The mayor knew his audience, explaining that preservation is not elitism, an excuse to renovate mansions; it is a quest to save beauty, which nourishes everyone's spirit. Preservation, he argued, helped the poor more than the rich because the rich can travel to beautiful places.

"The poorer ones have no options to them other than their city," he explained.

The message Riley delivered to Havana officials was similar to a story he often told in preservation and urban design classes. Soon after Charleston opened Waterfront Park, the mayor jogged through it regularly. Every morning, he noticed the same man sitting on a bench, looking out over the harbor. His name was Clarence, a local who took odd jobs downtown, usually sweeping the sidewalk in front of businesses. Clarence was poor, and suffered from epilepsy. The mayor began to speak with him regularly, and one day asked why he was always in the park.

"It's so beautiful. I like to watch the sunrise and the ships coming in," Clarence replied.

The mayor said that is why he built Waterfront Park, why he fought to preserve land, to keep high-rises and gated communities off his city's most valued property. He always finished by telling audiences that they might be able to travel to Paris or Venice, but Clarence can't. And "we build our city for Clarence."

Pat Brennan, Riley's childhood friend, said he'd heard the mayor tell that story in large rooms more than once. "When he finishes, there's not a dry eye in the house."

Riley had defended that philosophy during the campaign, when Washington criticized the city for spending millions on a new baseball park, aquarium and the Charleston Maritime Center, which had just hosted the Around Alone single-handed sailboat race. At the time, the mayor noted that no one ever visits the Spanish Steps in Rome, or Central Park in New York, and asks how much they cost. "When we invest in public works," he said, "we should aspire to create something that is beautiful and lasting."

When he was sworn in for his seventh term in January 2000, however, Riley said his next four years would not be marked by any huge new project. He planned a $4 million renovation of Marion Square and an evaluation of the Gaillard and Memminger Elementary School auditoriums, but said his primary focus would be limiting the development of rural land outside of the city. He wanted to work with county officials to establish a greenbelt surrounding the Lowcountry's urban areas.

But there was one big-ticket project already in the mayor's long-range plans, a new attraction to rival the aquarium or Charleston Place. Riley wanted the city to become home to a national black history museum. More than 40 percent of the Africans brought to the country in bondage had landed in Charleston Harbor, and the city had a duty to tell that story.

"Charleston is a city that has always accepted the responsibility of preserving and presenting its history, but there is one aspect of Charleston's history that we have been quiet about presenting," the mayor said. "It is the history of African-Americans – their life and the role in our city and in the development of our country."

At that point, the museum was just a concept. But it was one the mayor would not forget.

History and race were still on Riley's mind in February when he and Columbia

Mayor Bob Coble began lobbying state lawmakers to take the Confederate flag off the Statehouse dome. Perhaps, they suggested, the flag could be moved to a monument on the grounds – an idea that had been considered six years earlier. The General Assembly had debated the flag issue for years but was at an impasse. People who believed it simply represented South Carolina's heritage were at odds with those who considered it an offensive reminder of the state's legacy of slavery. Most politicians had no desire to wade into the controversy.

Flag supporters accused opponents of stirring the pot, said there were no real racial problems in the state anymore. But in March, lawmakers did little to back up that claim when they once again refused to approve a Martin Luther King Jr. Day state holiday. Some of them said the state had too many holidays, a few said it would cost too much money and others said they would support a "Civil Rights Day" without honoring King specifically. Riley said Charleston lawmakers "should be ashamed of themselves" for making South Carolina look bad in the eyes of the nation.

Riley was appalled by the insensitivity of the Legislature. It seemed things in Columbia had not changed in the quarter-century since he first proposed a King Day holiday as a young lawmaker. He polled local business owners and found their concerns matched his own. The Confederate flag, coupled with the state's refusal to honor King, made South Carolina look backward and unattractive to outside industry. The mayor believed the General Assembly did not reflect the sentiments of the vast majority of South Carolinians, and he desperately wanted to prove it.

By late February, Riley had an idea. He would lead a march against the flag from Charleston to Columbia with hundreds – even thousands – of citizens in tow. If that did not sway lawmakers, perhaps a national shaming in the media would. It was a grand gesture, but he wondered if he wasn't crazy. Finally, he ran the idea past some friends and business leaders. They loved it.

The mayor announced his plan on March 15. The march would begin in early April, and it would be a five-day protest with more than a passing resemblance to Selma. Riley noted there were only 24 days left in the legislative session and people wanted the issue resolved before lawmakers adjourned for the year. "What we want is for America to know that it's not the people of South Carolina who don't want the flag to be lowered."

Any doubts Riley had about his scheme dissipated within days. Gov. Jim Hodges, Congressman Jim Clyburn, former Gov. John West, Bank of America CEO Hugh McColl Jr. and Darla Moore – the successful New York investor from Lake City – all pledged to join him on the march. Soon, calls from national newspapers and television stations started coming in to City Hall, expanding Riley's platform exponentially. He explained that he was raising money to defray the cost of shuttle buses, water, security and other services for the marchers. Before long, Riley realized he had tapped a nerve, he had started something. He just didn't know how many people might follow him on this trek.

On Sunday afternoon, April 2, more than 600 people gathered in Marion Square for the start of the march to Columbia. Many of the people were dressed as if they had come straight from church, and about a third were African-American. Riley was overjoyed to see a crowd that so closely mirrored the state's demographics – it made his point better than he ever could. The crowd painted a much more optimistic, and inclusive, portrait of South Carolina than its Legislature reflected.

After some brief opening remarks, Riley led the crowd out of Marion Square. A group of black housekeepers at the Francis Marion Hotel stood with their white managers waving and cheering as they moved out of the park. That scene would repeat itself along the sidewalks all afternoon as the marchers walked up Rivers Avenue through North Charleston and into Goose Creek. Only three protesters showed up that first day, one of them a young man walking alongside the parade, waving a Confederate flag. He asked some of the marchers if the flag had ever hurt them, and whether they thought he had the right to carry it.

"That flag is right where it's supposed to be," one woman told him. "It's in your hand walking down the street. Its place is not over the state Capitol."

The protests increased the following day as the gradually shrinking crowd marched up Highway 176. At several intersections, people parked to wave the flag and dare Riley's followers to take it down. After the third such display, David Rawle realized it was the same people moving from one crossroad to the next. Still, a State Law Enforcement Division detail watched the flag supporters closely. Riley had received at least one death threat, forcing him to wear a bulletproof vest and walk flanked by a security detail. By midday, blisters had formed on the mayor's feet and then burst, and the police took him to his motel in Harleyville for treatment.

Riley had returned to the front of the procession by late afternoon, just about the time the marchers passed a man with a Confederate flag sticker on his lawn mower. The man, a veteran of World War II and Korea, heckled the group as they passed. He said they were wasting time and gas.

"He fought for the American flag, and now he's showing us this confounded thing," one person in the procession said. "We've got our own civil war going on."

The march ended at Holly Hill on Monday night. When the group set out the next day, Riley led the way, talking on a cell phone most of the time. His gamble had paid off; he was inundated by calls from national media outlets. The entire country was watching this group of South Carolinians marching on the state capital, civil rights style, in a non-violent protest similar to the ones that had changed the country two generations earlier. Riley told one reporter, "We've told the story that the citizens of South Carolina, all walks of life, are working hard to bring the flag down. It is what I hoped for."

Security along the route increased dramatically when the march reached Calhoun County, where the death threat against Riley had originated. Someone sent the mayor an anonymous letter that promised "If you march your niggers through Calhoun County, I will put you in my gun sights." The hours the procession spent crossing that county were the most tense of the demonstration. But nothing happened, and by Wednesday night Riley and his followers reached the outskirts of Columbia. The next day they would walk into the city, onto the Statehouse grounds and join a rally already in progress.

The final miles attracted the largest crowd. The singer and Charleston native Darius Rucker joined the route, as did former Gov. David Beasley – whose efforts to bring down the flag two years earlier were to blame, in part, for his defeat. The mayor's wife and sister also drove up for the final stretch. Charlotte had stayed with Jane the entire week; Riley did not want her home alone when people were making threats.

The streets of Columbia were lined with supporters in those final miles, but when Riley reached the Statehouse he was greeted with protest signs. One of them claimed "Mayor Riley is ashamed of his own ancestors" and another read "Mayor Riley is picking cotton on a northern plantation." That particular sign did much to undermine the protesters' argument that their support of the flag had nothing to do with race.

Gov. Hodges met Riley outside the Statehouse and said, "You're tired and I'm tired of waiting to see the Confederate flag removed from the Statehouse dome." It may have been a scripted line, but it drew loud cheers from the weary walkers. A long line of speakers addressed the crowd before Riley took the podium and for the first time read from the threatening letter he'd received. It was a stark illustration of the contradictory message in the "heritage not hate" slogan.

During the rally, Senate President Pro Tempore John Drummond got the mayor's attention and whispered good news in his ear – he had gotten the two sides together. Drummond told Riley the Senate had agreed to vote on a Confederate flag compromise deal that would take it off the Statehouse dome. Riley had won.

One week later the state Senate voted 36-7 to remove the Confederate Naval Jack from the Statehouse dome, where it had flown for nearly 40 years. It would be replaced with a more historically accurate battle flag on the Soldiers' Monument overlooking the intersection of Main and Gervais streets. Sen. Robert Ford – who had been Riley's antagonist on City Council for so many years – had sponsored the bill and pushed it through with the help of Sen. Glenn McConnell.

The legislation not only removed the flag from the dome, it took Confederate flags out of the House and Senate chambers, as well as the Statehouse lobby. And, as importantly, the new law also created a statewide Martin Luther King Jr. Day holiday. The House quickly followed suit, and Gov. Hodges gladly signed the legislation into law.

If that had been all he accomplished, Riley would have had a good spring. But on May 19 the South Carolina Aquarium opened its doors, nearly 17 years after he first suggested it. The glass and concrete structure overlooking the harbor held hundreds of species of fish and wildlife from across South Carolina, with dual centerpieces of a re-created saltmarsh ecosystem and a two-story saltwater ocean tank. Schoolchildren from across the state dressed as goldfish and stingrays led the mayor and the governor into the $69 million facility.

"Joe, terrific job as always bringing your vision to reality for South Carolina," Hodges said. "This aquarium adds one more reason why people around the world will come to Charleston. This whole area will blossom and develop further."

Riley credited the grand opening to the voters who approved a bond issue and the donors who contributed millions more. He congratulated them all for facing down "the we-don't-need-another-fish-tank naysayers." The mayor recognized his family, all of whom "feel the slings and arrows that these complicated and therefore controversial projects cause." Finally, Riley thanked his parents, who were both alive when he began work on the aquarium.

By the spring of 2000, the seeds that Riley had planted in the 1970s and '80s had taken root and sprouted. Hugo had slowed things for a while, but the economic boom of the 1990s had made the city stronger than ever. Charleston had doubled its size in 25 years and its tourism industry was growing as quickly as its population. Anyone who had not seen the city in a quarter-century probably would not have recognized it. Before the year's end, Riley's primary focus would be growth management.

Because Charleston was becoming such an increasingly desirable place to live, the mayor said, the city had to tackle the problem of affordable housing before home prices were out of reach for most folks. The window was closing fast. This was the price of success.

Despite the delays, and the criticism that he had spent too much and built an attraction that was too modest in scope, the aquarium was initially a huge success. Within five months, more than 500,000 people would visit the alligators and sharks. But the economy, world events and a statewide boycott would soon conspire to slow that steady stream of visitors. Riley argued that all attractions saw a decrease in attendance their second year. And the aquarium's second year would fall in one of the most troubled periods in American history.

The Confederate flag was lowered off the Statehouse dome on July 1, 2000 – a day marked by more protests than Riley had seen at the end of his 120-mile march. The compromise, praised in the days after it passed, had really made no one happy. On the dome, the flag had been a speck on the horizon. At the Soldiers' Monument it was front and center at Main and Gervais, visible for blocks.

The NAACP made good on long-standing threats and declared a boycott of the state. McConnell and Ford argued that they had removed four flags in exchange for one on a monument, and the banner no longer occupied a position of sovereignty. But no one on either side liked the outcome. The NAACP attacked Ford, and the Sons of Confederate Veterans shunned McConnell.

Riley did not particularly like the compromise either. Earlier in the year he had asked the flag to be moved from the dome to the Soldiers' Monument, but he had envisioned a flag cast in bronze, not an actual banner flapping in the breeze. "Moving the flag from the top of the Capitol to the front of the Capitol is not unifying."

But lawmakers had compromised as much as they were willing to, at least for the foreseeable future.

Last Call

When Joe Riley was young, his father often lamented there was no place to get an ice cream cone on the Charleston peninsula. The city was quiet in those days, a time when real estate was cheaper than it had been in the years following the Great Depression. Tourism was a foreign concept, economic development a dream for other cities. For the most part, it was still that way when Riley took office.

But as the 21st century began, Charleston was suddenly a vibrant urban center, home to South Carolina's most eclectic and electric shopping district, an epicenter of tourism with theaters, parks and an aquarium spread across the peninsula. There was even a children's museum in the works. New businesses opened every week, and although some didn't make it, most did. All this success carried a cost. Home prices had escalated to the point they threatened to drive all but the wealthiest citizens from the peninsula. Although the city tried, it was a struggle to provide enough affordable housing for a diverse downtown population. It had all become so overwhelming that some City Council members proposed a moratorium on growth. That suggestion was promptly ignored, but clearly the city had to do something to maintain the quality of life in a city where suddenly everyone wanted to live.

The city seemed to impose new regulations on tourism every year, but still it was not enough for some downtown residents. They complained Charleston had simply become too loud. Locals, not tourists, were now a problem as well. The city's bar patrons often wandered into residential neighborhoods at all hours of the night, revelers roaming otherwise quiet streets. There was little doubt this led to increased crime, mostly vandalism and public intoxication. So in late 2000, at the mayor's urging, City Council passed a law that required all downtown bars to close by 2 a.m. Shortly after it took effect in early 2001, a coalition of bar owners sued.

The bar owners said the new ordinance would drive them into bankruptcy. Many of these bars catered to food and beverage industry workers who rarely got off work before midnight, and their business was the only thing keeping some of these bars afloat. The city had cut into their livelihood. The court refused their request for an injunction until the trial and, getting more desperate every week, the bar owners tried to negotiate with the city. They asked to stay open until 3 a.m., and when the city refused, pleaded for extended hours on the weekends. Riley and the council wouldn't budge.

But in July, a circuit judge ruled that the city could not force businesses to close at any hour – only the state could. By then several other Lowcountry towns had followed Charleston's lead and imposed their own late-night curfews. As a result, Charleston's bars stayed open later than those in surrounding communities, driving even more traffic to the peninsula. Riley found himself fighting for the rights of downtown residents while incurring the wrath of the businesses he had attracted to the Market and Upper King Street. It was a fight destined to go on for years, just another byproduct of success.

In the fall of 2001 and again in the spring of 2002, Riley weathered back-to-back stints in the hospital. In October, a biopsy revealed an early stage of prostate cancer. His doctors offered radiation and hormone therapy, but Riley opted for the quick fix – surgery. He had the operation in mid-November at Roper Hospital and was back at work by early December. To quash any rumors about his health, Riley invited reporters to talk to his doctors, who said the cancer had been completely removed and a recurrence was unlikely.

To prove he was still fit and spry, Riley made his annual walk in the city's Christmas parade – although staff tried to persuade him to ride in a car for once. He told Charlotte and his mother-in-law he would do just that, but at the last minute decided he could walk. When he saw his wife and her mother standing along the route, he got a stern look that told him he would hear about it later.

Four months later, Riley was back in the hospital, this time for a pinched nerve in his neck. The mayor had been in pain for nearly a year, a nagging ache in his arm and neck that wouldn't subside. He tried physical therapy, but finally agreed to have a herniated disk in his neck removed and the surrounding vertebrae fused. It was a routine surgery, but it left him sidelined for another three weeks. In six months, he missed six weeks of work, which bothered him as much as his health problems.

While Riley was convalescing in April 2002, a group of James Islanders were selling bumper stickers that read "Just Say No To Joe!" – the proceeds of which went toward the island's second attempt to form a town. The campaign was a success. A month later the island's incorporation was approved with overwhelming support, followed quickly by the city of Charleston's lawsuit. Riley's attorneys claimed the law that allowed James Island to incorporate was unconstitutional. Lawmakers friendly to the island had championed legislation making it legal for waterways and marshes to be "shared" by two municipalities. James Island was able to piece together disparate pockets of the island, jumping Charleston city limits, to form a town of more than 20,000 people – enough to get around other state laws that made it difficult for towns of less than 15,000 to incorporate.

Bill Regan argued that the Legislature had created "special legislation" to benefit only one area, which was illegal under state law. The town fought back, but made Riley the focal point of its argument. Mary Clark, the woman who had spent so much time at City Hall begging Charleston to stop annexing her island, was elected mayor of the town and promised, "They're going to be sorry." It was yet more work for the city's legal team. Soon, the city attorney's office would need reinforcements.

In June, a stray invoice for nearly $2,000 showed up among the city's outstanding bills. It was a routine appraisal for some property the city owned, but it seemed odd to Joleen Deames, assistant director of budget, finance and revenue collections. A quick check confirmed her initial suspicions – the company that submitted the bill, Appraisal Group of Charleston, did not exist. Deames looked through city records and soon found more invoices from the fictitious business, some dating back years. Next she sifted through a file of canceled checks and found several that had been cashed by the Appraisal Group of Charleston. When she examined the backs of those checks, she recognized the handwriting immediately.

The scrawl was clearly the penmanship of Danny Molony, the city's property coordinator. His father, Bobby Molony, was a good friend of the mayor's family.

Danny Molony had worked for the city more than a decade, managing 350 parcels worth more than $250 million. Although Molony reported to the city's chief financial officer, Steve Bedard, he had always enjoyed great freedom – and it appeared he had taken advantage of that autonomy. Bill Regan went to Molony's Meeting Street office the next day and told him he was under investigation and on administrative leave. Staff took his city phone, pager and keys to the building. Riley hoped it was a mistake, but the evidence was damning.

Molony was a popular guy around City Hall – nice, friendly, the first one to volunteer to help out with the Christmas party. He had a business background; he once ran his family's credit bureau. His brother, Michael, was a municipal court judge and his parents were community volunteers. It didn't make sense. But as Bedard's staff pored through city records they found more and more evidence that suggested Molony had been bilking the city for years.

Within a week, Bedard had evidence that Molony had embezzled more than $300,000 from the city dating back to 1995. He was fired the next day, and the city of Charleston formally pressed charges.

The mayor wanted to call Molony's father before the story got out, but he dreaded it. Bobby Molony had been a family friend longer than he could remember, longer than Joe and Bratton had been alive. Molony's birthday fell on his and Charlotte's anniversary, and they had made a tradition of exchanging gifts. When the mayor's sons were old enough to play golf, Bobby Molony was the one who took them. He was like a grandfather or uncle to the boys.

Riley was torn. He had little sympathy for criminals, and later said Danny Molony fit the bill of white-collar criminals perfectly: nice, eager-to-please, always there to help as a cover for their larcenous ways. The mayor wanted the city's money back, and he wanted Molony to go to jail. But he knew it would devastate the Molony family. Finally, he made the call and explained to Bobby Molony that his son would be charged with embezzlement.

"Is this a civil charge, Joe?" Molony asked.

"No, Bobby," the mayor said, "it's criminal."

On June 19, Molony was charged with embezzlement of public funds, a felony.

His bail was set at $300,000 – almost exactly the amount he had allegedly stolen.

It was the first case of public corruption to come out of City Hall in the 27 years Riley had been mayor. And since Molony's father was a Riley friend and supporter, the crime soon took on political overtones. City Councilman Robert George publicly speculated that Molony could not have acted alone and called for an external audit of city books. City investigators and police said all evidence suggested Molony had indeed worked alone, and Riley said George should not turn the crime into a political football. He said the city would implement new procedures to make sure no one could ever steal from the city again, but within a day the mayor agreed to hire an outside auditor. He realized anything less would leave lingering questions.

"Our citizens deserve to not have any doubts about whether or not we will fully answer every question raised about this," Riley said. "I want the citizens of Charleston to know that every possible thing is being done."

The results of the audit were forwarded to SLED and the FBI, the mayor said, so it wouldn't appear the city was policing itself – and because the FBI had a better white-collar-crimes unit than the state. Councilman Larry Shirley said it wasn't political to raise questions, but applauded the mayor for taking steps to "cast any doubt aside that there's a cover-up."

Still, the controversy would not go away so easily.

In September, Riley said he would run for an eighth term in 2003. The announcement was a surprise to nearly everyone – not the fact he would stand for re-election, but that he revealed his plans so early. Usually, the mayor held such announcements until the spring before the election. This time he made his intentions known 14 months out. The mayor told The Post and Courier he had too many projects underway to willingly walk away. Riley even referenced the two health scares that had sidelined him in the past year, noting he had fully recovered and, at 59, felt fine.

"I love the job that I have, and I want to keep it," Riley said. "I love working for the citizens of this beautiful city. I love working with them and for them and working to make this extraordinary city an even more wonderful and livable place."

Riley didn't promise an eighth term would be his last. But he hinted at it, even called it "likely." By 2007, the mayor said, he would be 65. Political scientists speculated Riley had made his intentions clear early because in 2003 the city would hold its first nonpartisan municipal elections, which no doubt would entice more people into the race. The mayor had fired a warning shot, they claimed. Riley disputed the analysis, said he never made a decision to run for office based on what anyone else did. But clearly he didn't mind scaring the competition.

Marc Knapp, a former City Council candidate, said he was considering a bid for the mayor's office and was glad to hear Riley would be on the ballot "because it'll keep everyone else out. Everyone else is afraid to run. I keep hearing from everyone that I don't have a chance, but it's time for a change."

Riley's challengers would have plenty of new campaign material from the courts by the time the 2003 election season began. In December 2002, the state Supreme Court reversed the Circuit Court and ruled that Charleston could order its bars to close at 2 a.m. The ruling set off a chain reaction, with Mount Pleasant, Charleston County and the town of Summerville soon passing similar curfews. Only Folly Beach chose not to enforce a mandated closing time. Two months later, a circuit judge declared the town of James Island defunct because, as city attorneys had argued, its gerrymandered municipal borders were legal only as a result of unconstitutional legislation.

That same month, federal prosecutors indicted Danny Molony and his son, Mark, on charges of embezzlement and money laundering. A six-month investigation revealed that Molony had not only disbursed funds to a fake company, he also made payments to a business owned by his son. In all, the Molonys had skimmed more than $400,000 from city coffers. Riley said the city would sue three local banks in an attempt to recover the stolen money. The banks were not involved in the conspiracy, the mayor said, but simply sloppy – they should not have allowed Molony to deposit checks without a signature. He had written only "for deposit only" on the backs of the city checks.

There had been other minor cases of embezzlement during Riley's tenure – once an employee was accused of stealing small amounts from the pro shop at the municipal golf course; another was allegedly skimming the till at the Angel Oak gift shop – but no one had ever taken money directly from city accounts. The controversy, and Riley's relationship with the Molony family, threatened to bleed into the campaign. It began when supporters of Jimmy Bailey said the former state representative would not allow tax dollars to be stolen.

The mayor's political foes claimed Molony had freedoms other city employees did not have – that he could write checks without authorization, that he had little supervision – and suggested this was because of his close ties to Riley. City Council members interjected themselves into the campaign, claiming Molony shouldn't have been hired in the first place because, in the 1980s, he had a substance-abuse problem. Councilwoman Anne Frances Bleecker, also a friend of the Molony family, argued that was no reason to not hire someone, but the insinuation was clear: Molony had gotten his job through his contacts at City Hall. But Riley said he did not hire Molony or direct any of his department heads to give him a job.

"His people skills were good," Riley told reporters. "Danny didn't need any advocates for him."

Riley said the city's finance department was not to blame for missing Molony's subterfuge, but still he had tightened up control of accounts. He planned to sue both Molonys to recoup the lost tax money and wished them both long prison sentences, even though he knew it would hurt the family. In fact, it would take the family longer to get over the scandal than it would take the mayor to get the city's money back.

If that weren't enough, Riley went into the campaign season with several people demanding that he fire Reuben Greenberg. The police chief had lost his temper in two highly publicized incidents that spring. On March 20, 2003, Greenberg confronted a group of Iraq war protesters in Marion Square like a man itching for a fight. He insulted their leader, saying, "So you're the crazy fat lady everyone's talking about."

The woman tried to shake his hand, but Greenberg refused. He said, "You're proof that fat people aren't only at McDonald's." The chief later told reporters he didn't appreciate the woman attacking "fine American boys" defending the country's interests in Iraq and that he supported his fellow Texan, President George W. Bush, "100 percent." Instead of apologizing, Greenberg made it worse. "I was wrong. She's not fat. She's obese. She's grossly obese. If she doesn't like that, she can do something about it, like the Atkins diet I was on."

A few weeks later, the chief attacked a local TV reporter attempting to interview him at the police station. There were some West Ashley residents trying to shut down an adult bookstore in their neighborhood, and Greenberg allowed them to take a police bus to Anderson for a court hearing. Some City Council members publicly complained this was not an appropriate use of taxpayer resources, and the reporter wanted the chief's response. Greenberg grew increasingly agitated during the interview and used foul language to describe council members before slamming his hand on a table and shouting, "Fuck 'em."

When the reporter followed Greenberg out of the room, the chief turned and poked him in the chest repeatedly, questioning his intelligence all the while. Councilman Bob George said the chief essentially assaulted the reporter, that he was "wound tight as a damn clock spring." Other council members were defensive, noting everyone was entitled to have a bad day. But there was a growing sentiment that it might be time for the chief to go.

Riley defended the chief as best he could. He called Greenberg "the finest police chief in America" and noted the city's crime rate dropped 38 percent in his first seven years on the job. The mayor's political opponents countered the argument by claiming the crime rate had been diluted because of the city's rising population. Even some Greenberg supporters on City Council conceded the chief could be frustrating.

"I could give him suggestions, but he won't listen," Councilman James Lewis said. "He gets defensive and thinks you're trying to tell him how to do his job. He doesn't listen to council members, and that upsets us sometimes."

Greenberg eventually apologized to the reporter, but not the protesters – or City Council. Riley did not reprimand the chief, but Greenberg told the media he had been punished by his wife. It seemed the chief could not open his mouth anymore without saying something inflammatory; even his apologies were controversial. He told The Post and Courier, "If I wanted to be nice and get everybody to like me, I would have joined the fire department."

Riley did not officially kick off his eighth mayoral campaign until June. He appeared at West Ashley Park on a hot Thursday morning in rolled-up shirtsleeves as loudspeakers blasted Jefferson Starship's "Nothing's Gonna Stop Us Now" across the suburban soccer fields. The mayor said in the next four years he would focus on making Charleston a more livable city and lure more high-tech jobs to the region. Four opponents had lined up against Riley – Bailey, Knapp, City Councilman Kwadjo Campbell and tour company owner Tom Doyle – and they were all eager to make the mayor the campaign's primary issue.

Bailey was the strongest challenger, the one whose jabs hit closest to home. He accused the mayor of failing to recoup $10 million Charleston Place owed the city, and said he would collect the money and use it to alleviate downtown traffic with a new bus service. He suggested Spoleto officials endorsed his candidacy. And he courted firefighters – a group the mayor had had his differences with over the years. Bailey said the city sent firefighters into fires wearing combustible gear and polyester uniforms, which could melt.

The campaign was largely a back-and-forth between the Riley and Bailey camps. Riley said Charleston Place had not repaid its loan because it had yet to turn a profit. Spoleto officials denied they supported Bailey. And Riley campaign manager Capers Barr noted that Bailey's $70,000 war chest included a $50,000 loan from the candidate – suggesting he didn't have as much support as it might appear. Fire Chief Rusty Thomas tried to put out the other fires. He conceded the department's polyester uniforms were not the choice of the National Fire Protection Association. But he claimed that, "As long as you have your protective gear on" the uniforms were not a problem.

The Charleston Firefighters Association, however, said "Jimmy is telling the truth" and endorsed Bailey.

Campbell said the mayor hadn't done enough for the black community, although he conceded Riley was no racist. Still, he accused the mayor of leading Charleston's gentrification efforts, and distributed one flier in black neighborhoods that claimed "a vote for Joe is a vote for your eviction." Riley's camp noted the mayor had created 5,000 affordable housing units in the city since taking office in 1975.

The 2003 mayoral race was perhaps the nastiest campaign in Riley's tenure. The candidates claimed the mayor devoted too much time, attention and resources to big-ticket projects like the baseball stadium and aquarium while letting city services languish. The mayor was forced to spend a lot of time reiterating that Charleston's basic services were top-notch. Doyle said he was put off by the tone of Riley's ads, noting that "There's almost a sense of 'What would we do without him?' It's almost a little schmaltzy."

Mostly, the candidates stuck to the same script – Riley had been in office too long, they would do things differently. Political scientists said the mayor was running a far more negative campaign than usual, and suggested it was because the campaign considered Bailey a formidable foe. Riley said he was running on his record, but spent an inordinate amount of time trading jabs with Bailey. Knapp said the race had devolved into the two men throwing stuff at each other like two kids in a sandbox. At one point Bailey said Riley had suggested he could be his successor – a claim the mayor denied.

The tone was so different from the mayor's past campaigns that The Post and Courier asked former Riley opponents to handicap the race. Most declared the mayor a safe bet for re-election, but Nancy Hawk said Riley was vulnerable because of the Molony controversy and the sheer length of his time in office. "I do think that a lot of people think it's time for a change," Hawk said. "This is the first year I said he could be beaten."

The months of negative campaigning had seemingly taken a toll. One poll taken just before the election said Riley had 47 percent of the vote locked up. The margin of error was 4 percentage points, which meant that the mayor either had enough to win outright, or faced his first runoff for the job.

On election day, however, Riley's campaign showed its superior organizational skills. Volunteers went door-to-door in every neighborhood, and Congressman Jim Clyburn recorded a phone message that went out to voters across Charleston. The mayor worked in West Ashley and on James Island, which were considered Bailey strongholds, and refused to cede any African-American communities to Campbell. As usual, Riley wanted to win every vote. A baseball fanatic, the mayor knew the importance of a good closer. One campaign worker joked that "the only place the mayor surrendered was the Bailey household."

Riley silenced all his critics that day. When it was over, the mayor won more votes than the four other candidates combined, taking 70 of 86 precincts to win outright with 57 percent of the vote. Bailey was a distant second with 32 percent and Campbell won 9 percent. Knapp and Doyle got 1 percent each. Although Bailey had cut into Riley's margins in West Ashley and on James Island, it wasn't enough to win most precincts. And the mayor took 61 percent of the vote in the city's predominantly black precincts.

The Post and Courier said that, in his toughest mayoral race ever, Riley had shown everyone "the depth of his support."

The Riley victory party was held at Jason's Deli in West Ashley, where the crowd chanted "Joe! Joe! Joe!" until the mayor took the stage. Riley's speech that night was a recitation of campaign themes – he talked about creating more green space in the city, solving traffic and drainage problems, and suggested he would dabble in education or anything else to improve Charleston's quality of life.

"In this urban nation, it is our responsibility to make our city the very best, to make it the safest, the soundest, the most beautiful and the most livable."

Within days, Riley vowed to crack down on drugs and continue the redevelopment of Upper King Street. By that time, his opponents were already talking about "next time." Campbell said he would run again, and his City Council colleague, Bob George, also admitted he had pondered a campaign as well. "I really don't see Joe Riley running again in four years, but ... anyone who would rule that out would do it at their own peril."

Riley was giving away nothing. Less than a week after the election, he told the newspaper this would likely be his final term – but he wouldn't commit to that.

"I wouldn't want to close any doors," Riley said.

In March 2004, a federal judge sentenced Danny Molony to 30 months in prison. His son, who had helped steal much of the $400,000 taken from the city, got 24 months. The judge ordered the two to make restitution of about $405,000, but so far the city had collected only about 10 percent of the money – $42,000. Most of that came from Molony's city retirement account. (By 2010, the city would recover all its money with interest – more than $450,000.) After Molony's hearing, Riley argued the sentence was not harsh enough. Under federal sentencing guidelines, the judge could have given Molony 37 months. Despite Molony's apology, the mayor said he should go to jail for as long as possible.

"It didn't mitigate the fact that he needed to be incarcerated," Riley said.

In June, the state Supreme Court refused to rehear the 2 a.m. bar closing case, effectively dismissing the bar owners' lawsuit. The next month, the justices upheld the Circuit Court ruling that the law which allowed James Island to incorporate was unconstitutional. Before the ink was dry on the ruling, James Island organizers vowed to try again. Soon, Riley was back at work trying to annex as much of the island as possible.

Riley devoted much of 2004 to building more affordable housing in the city. The national real estate boom had affected Charleston disproportionately, especially on the peninsula, as demand far outstripped supply. People who could no longer afford to live south of Calhoun Street were moving farther up the peninsula, driving up prices as they went – and forcing poorer people, many of them black, out of their homes. The mayor said the problem, in part, was caused by people from out-of-state buying up peninsular houses for second homes.

Downtown land prices even forced the city off the peninsula; much of the affordable housing Riley built was on Johns Island and in West Ashley, where money went a lot farther. Private developers had cornered the market on peninsular land, and were even investing in condominiums on the East Side. Councilman Kwadjo Campbell asked one developer to donate to his East Side initiative – a solicitation Riley said was improper.

The mayor had been feuding with Campbell since long before the 2003 mayoral race. Riley had accused Campbell of interfering with police investigations of drug dealers on the East Side, but nothing came of it. When the councilman asked a private developer to donate to his nonprofit, however, Riley filed a complaint with the state Ethics Commission. The fight continued into 2005, and Campbell did not help his case with a series of arrests. In quick succession, Campbell was charged with driving on a suspended license, driving a stolen car (which he said was not stolen) and possession of marijuana.

The weight of all those controversies was too much for the councilman. By the summer of 2005, Campbell was indicted on ethics charges and suspended from office by Gov. Mark Sanford. He pleaded not guilty but eventually was convicted on a few minor charges, paid a fine and served probation. Seven years later, in 2012, Campbell would receive a full pardon. But by then, his days of battling Riley were mostly over.

On July 16, 2005, the Arthur Ravenel Jr. Bridge opened to traffic between Charleston and Mount Pleasant, changing the city and its skyline forever. The cable-stayed bridge with twin diamond towers immediately became a symbol of the Lowcountry, its eight lanes a vast improvement over the narrow and rickety Grace and Pearman bridges. With a main span of nearly 1,550 feet over the Cooper River, the Ravenel became the third-largest cable-stayed bridge in the hemisphere.

The bridge had cost nearly $700 million, and was funded largely through the efforts of state lawmakers – notably its namesake – with considerable help from Fritz Hollings, who had recently retired from the U.S. Senate. It was the largest single infrastructure project in state history. The bridge was not a city project, but Riley took pride in it just the same – he had first pointed out the deficiencies in the Grace Bridge, which by the early 21st century had a safety rating of 4 out of 100. It had been more than a decade since the mayor first started lobbying for a new Cooper River bridge, and now he had it. But not long after the new bridge was opened, the mayor lost something else just about as important to him.

In the early hours of Aug. 7, 2005, a woman driving down Highway 61 in West Ashley spotted a truck weaving and swerving erratically ahead of her. The big Ford pickup, painted black and white with a light bar across its cab, ran off the shoulder, overcorrected and crossed the highway's center line. If a car had been coming from the other direction, there would have been a horrible crash. The woman called 911, worried that something was wrong with the truck's driver.

A few minutes later, the truck stopped dead in the middle of the road. The blue lights on its roof came to life, and Charleston Police Chief Reuben Greenberg stepped out of the cab.

Greenberg walked back to the woman's car and asked if she had called 911 on him. Before she could answer, he asked her why. The woman was scared, and told the chief that, but it only seemed to make him madder. He hit her car door with his fist and said, "Don't call the police." He then hit the door twice more before walking back to his truck and driving off.

A sheriff's deputy arrived a few minutes later, heard the woman's story and noted the knuckle prints on her car door. She decided to not press charges.

The next day, Riley called Greenberg's doctor. This was not the first report of strange behavior the mayor had gotten concerning his police chief. For months, people had reported seeing Greenberg's truck weaving around the city, sometimes driving so slowly that people dared to pass a police vehicle on a double-yellow line. Riley asked the doctor to call Greenberg in for a check-up, to make sure he was all right. "I need to know if he can do his job."

Then he called the chief and said, as a result of the incident (which had garnered a lot of media attention), perhaps he should take a couple of weeks off for his health.

Since his back-to-back blow-ups two years earlier, Greenberg had not become any less controversial. In early 2004 he enraged many African-American leaders with an off-hand remark about black-on-black crime. The prior year, 2003, there had been 57 murders in the region, 18 of them in Charleston – the city's highest total since 1969. Many of them involved black suspects and victims. In a Post and Courier story about the trend, Greenberg had said, "I refuse to take responsibility every time one black son of a bitch kills another."

The insensitive quote nearly cost the chief his job. City Council members criticized him publicly, and the NAACP demanded an apology. The mother of one shooting victim showed up at a council meeting in tears. Her son, she said, was an innocent college student planning a career in the military, and he did not deserve to be called a name. Riley again defended the chief as much as possible. He told the woman Greenberg was only talking about drug dealers killing other drug dealers.

"That's what Chief Greenberg was talking about. He was not talking about anything else," the mayor said. "I stand behind Chief Greenberg. I know his heart. I know what he meant."

The chief was finally forced to write a letter clarifying his remarks. When that didn't work, he apologized.

By the time Greenberg attacked the woman's car on Highway 61 in August 2005, Riley had been worried for months. The chief was fine in staff meetings, but his behavior outside City Hall had become erratic even by Greenberg's eccentric standards. Riley could overlook some poor driving, or the chief's occasional random mumbling, but he couldn't ignore an attack on an innocent motorist.

Riley did not want to fire Greenberg. He believed the chief was a transformative figure for the city – its first black police chief. He had been visible in the community, his popularity rivaling the mayor's in some areas, although he was certainly unpopular in other circles. But Greenberg had made a difference and, as a result, major cities such as Washington, D.C., and Chicago had tried to lure him away.

The chief was a colorful, sometimes controversial, character – Riley had realized that soon after hiring him. He was willing to let that slide in exchange for declining crime and the community relations value of having a black police chief. For years, the mayor had defended Greenberg repeatedly, and in January had named the new municipal building in his honor. But all that was over. Riley told the newspaper that attacking a motorist was "inexcusable."

A week later, Greenberg announced his retirement. Publicly, the chief cited "old age" and high blood pressure as the reason. Greenberg said he was happy to cap off his career in Charleston, where he would continue to live – although he and his wife would spend summers in North Carolina. Riley praised Greenberg for his service to the city. "Reuben Greenberg, just being himself, did more for racial progress than one can ever imagine or ever truly appreciate. He destroyed the myths of stereotyping."

Greenberg was all smiles at his press conference, but he was not nearly as happy in private. He had met with the mayor the day before, and it was a difficult talk. Later Riley said, "It was a hard thing telling Reuben it was time to go." He wanted to allow the chief to retire with dignity and on his own terms. But he had to go. Greenberg was disappointed and surprised, Riley said, but the mayor made it clear the decision was non-negotiable. It hurt Riley to lose Greenberg, but he had to put the city first – even ahead of his friend.

Within a month, the mayor had 40 applications from potential replacements. Before he closed his search Riley would have far more than the 100 resumes he got in 1982. Once again, he had his pick of chiefs. But that was no surprise.

Charleston was a much different place than it had been 23 years ago.

Into the Fire

On July 29, 2006, former mayor Palmer Gaillard spent the morning in West Ashley, a busy suburb that wasn't even part of Charleston when he first took office. Gaillard's landmark 1960s court victory paved the way for annexations across water, in turn launching the city's great expansion. West Ashley – site of the first Charles Town settlement – had been Mayor Gaillard's first target. Now it was where he got his hair cut.

By 2006, Gaillard spent most of his time tending his tomato garden and building cabinets in the garage of his downtown home. For his 85th birthday the previous year, his family had arranged for him to fly a vintage World War II fighter plane, much like the ones he had piloted in the war. He'd spent the day turning loops in the skies above the Lowcountry, gloriously retired from the grind of daily politics. He lived the dream life of an ex-mayor.

He had gone to West Ashley that morning – as usual – to get his hair cut, then stopped off at a McDonald's for coffee and breakfast. No doubt he ran into other retirees who recognized him as "Pah-mar," the former mayor. Shortly after 10:30, Gaillard left the restaurant, got in his Buick LeSabre and pulled out of the parking lot. He turned left onto Sam Rittenberg Boulevard, which required him to cross three regular lanes of traffic and two turning lanes. Gaillard probably did not see the huge Ford F-350 until just before it slammed into the driver's side door of his car.

The accident trapped Gaillard inside the car and emergency workers had to cut him out, eating away precious minutes. But it likely would not have made any difference. The former mayor died of internal injuries in the ambulance on the way to Medical University Hospital. Police ruled that Gaillard had pulled out in front of the truck; its driver was not ticketed.

Riley had remained fairly close to Gaillard, catching up at lunch now and then. He eulogized the former mayor by saying he planted the seeds of the modern city. His auditorium lured the Spoleto Festival to town, and his annexation strategies ensured the city's growth. Riley had expanded the city's borders far beyond anything his predecessor could have imagined, but he said that "Charleston today would be a shadow of what it is" without Gaillard.

With Gaillard's passing, Riley and Arthur Schirmer – the former councilman who served out the last four months of Gaillard's final term – were the only living Charleston mayors. Riley already had doubled Gaillard's time in office, but that year speculation was rampant as to whether he would seek a ninth term. Some expected him to pass the torch to David Agnew, one of his top aides. The mayor said he would make a decision soon to give others time to decide whether to run. But fate forced him to announce his intentions sooner than he intended.

Riley had spent the first half of the year on unfinished business. So far he had recouped $165,000 of the more than $400,000 Danny Molony embezzled from city coffers, and considered selling the former property manager's house to make up some of the rest. He spent weeks in Columbia, lobbying the State Infrastructure Bank – which had funded the largest part of the Ravenel Bridge – to contribute several hundred million dollars to finish the Interstate 526 bypass. The road ended at Highway 17 in West Ashley and Riley wanted to extend it onto Johns and James islands, eventually hooking into the connector leading to downtown. People had been trying to finish the road for decades with little success, but Riley was too determined – or stubborn – to give up.

The mayor, with the help of Councilwoman Kathleen Wilson, had spent the spring trying to entice more James Islanders to join the city before town organizers attempted a third incorporation. But by August the island had its referendum. It was a town once again. And as usual, the city found flaws in the way the island had gone about incorporating.

That same month, Riley introduced Greg Mullen as Charleston's new police chief. Mullen was deputy chief in Virginia Beach, where he had been on the force for more than two decades. Before that he spent years as a special agent with the Air

Force Office of Special Investigations. He was a strict, by-the-book lawman who believed in keeping people safe at any cost – Riley's kind of man. But the mayor upstaged the city's first new police chief in 24 years when he revealed that he would run for a ninth term.

The mayor had little choice: a reporter asked Mullen whether he had been given assurances that he would have a job beyond 2007. Riley said since the chief answers directly to the mayor, he felt it necessary to give Mullen some assurance of job security. So yes, he would run again. Riley said he had plenty left to do anyway.

Mullen would prove nearly as controversial as Greenberg, but for far different reasons. He was not a hothead, and rarely said anything inflammatory, but some people thought his zeal for public safety intruded into the lives of residents too much. He proposed installing a series of surveillance cameras around the city to help police do their job, as he'd done in Virginia Beach. And he cracked down on public alcohol consumption. This upset some downtown residents when he barred patrons of the semi-regular Art Walk from carrying their wine from one gallery to the next. Mullen said if guys couldn't stand on the corner uptown drinking beer, then society types couldn't walk downtown sidewalks with booze either.

Mullen was pleased to see his boss back him on all these decisions, contentious as they were. Despite his persona of being a social progressive, Riley was very conservative on crime issues. After the city's 17th homicide of the year, Riley once again asked state lawmakers to strengthen penalties for gun violence. He wanted repeat offenders subject to warrantless searches and longer sentences, particularly for people who commit crimes involving a gun.

"The laws are too weak, the sentences too short, and probation is a joke," Riley said. "We need more judges, more prosecutors, more public defenders, more probation officers."

Riley had asked for all of those things before, but his efforts never led to anything other than a new violent-crimes task force. The Legislature was too scared of Second Amendment advocates – and the National Rifle Association – to tighten gun laws, even against criminals. So the crime continued. In October, Mullen had to work another city homicide his first day on the job. When the Legislature convened in 2007, Riley unveiled an 18-point plan to fight crime with Mullen at his side. Again, his pleas fell on deaf ears.

And in February 2007, Gian Carlo Menotti died in a Monaco hospital at the age of 95. Riley had not spoken to the composer since they had passed a few words in Italy a decade earlier, although they had traded letters in the past year. Menotti had tried to persuade Riley to drop the Spoleto name from the city's arts festival. The mayor politely declined.

On Monday, June 18, Riley sat down to a casual dinner at home with Charlotte, eating off a tray while watching the Braves game on TV. The ballgame had just started when the phone rang. Riley got up to answer it; his fire chief, Rusty Thomas, was on the line.

"Mayor Riley, we've got a big fire at the Sofa Super Store on Savannah Highway," Thomas said. "It's a really big fire."

Riley thanked him for calling, hung up and sat back down in front of the game. It surprised him to hear from Thomas – the chief usually called only about the most serious fires, and the mayor wondered why he had this time. Maybe he called out of pride, Riley thought – they were doing a good job. But that didn't feel right, didn't sound like Thomas. Perhaps, he thought, this was a really bad fire. It worried him. He feared Thomas had actually called because he was scared. Riley put his food aside, got in his car and headed for Savannah Highway.

The Sofa Super Store sat on Savannah Highway about four miles south of the peninsula, beyond a half-dozen car dealerships and near the busy Wappoo Road intersection. When Riley arrived, the scene was pandemonium – firetrucks parked everywhere, black smoke filling the sky, emergency workers running through a maze of hoses. As he got out of his car, the first thing Riley heard was someone saying, "We can't find Captain Mulkey."

The Sofa Super Store was a boxy building, more than 42,000 square feet with plate glass windows in front and a flat roof. Most of the space was showroom, and inside the store couches were crammed up next to one another, leaving only narrow paths to walk through. When dispatch got the call at 7:08 p.m., the store was still open and at least several employees were inside. No one was sure whether any customers were in there.

The Charleston Fire Department had a station just a mile down the road, and its trucks were on the scene in less than three minutes. Every firefighter who responded knew the Sofa Super Store well, and some of them dreaded it – even called it a death trap. To professionals, all that furniture looked like nothing more than piles and piles of kindling – and the building had no sprinklers. They knew this because the fire department inspected buildings, worked out plans for how to fight fires in them. But they had no magic plan to combat a blaze in the Sofa Super Store. If it caught fire, they knew, it would be an inferno.

The first men on the scene spotted a fire behind the building, near the loading dock. The trash and debris were burning fast but when the firefighters walked into the showroom five minutes after the call, all they saw was light smoke swirling around the ceiling tiles. But then one of the men opened the door leading from the showroom to the loading dock, and the force of the fire ripped the door from his hand. Soon, the flames started creeping into the showroom.

Fire is little more than oxygen combined with any sort of fuel at ignition temperature. Wood combusts at 300 degrees Fahrenheit and cotton fabric ignites at around 482 degrees. The most protective clothing starts to burn at 572 degrees. The only thing a fire needs to spread is oxygen – and more fuel. Opening the door between the loading dock and a showroom filled with wood and fabric literally breathed life into a killer fire.

Thomas had heard the call while driving on the 526 bypass and got there within eight minutes. He was followed by several off-duty firefighters who just showed up to help – a common occurrence in most departments. The crews fighting the blaze needed as much manpower as possible; they were having trouble already. The water pressure wasn't great, and it didn't help that arriving vehicles kept driving over the hoses.

Within a few minutes, fire crews from the St. Andrews Public Service District arrived to help. They got there just in time to respond to another 911 call – a Sofa Super Store employee was trapped in the warehouse, surrounded by flames. He could not reach the door. The St. Andrews firefighters took that call, breaking through a wall to reach the man. They had him out in about three minutes.

By then, the fire inside the main showroom was getting worse, and the 16 firefighters inside were quickly running out of oxygen. But they would not retreat; they were looking for people – they had no idea if any customers or employees were trapped inside.

The smoke and fire quickly overtook them and they called for help on their radios. Around 7:32 Thomas heard a "Mayday" over the radio, and then another firefighter ominously said, "Car One (Thomas' call sign), please tell my wife … I love you." Another firefighter was praying over the radio, "In Jesus' name, amen." A few of the firefighters' distress signals had been activated, but no one answered when the command post tried to reach them by radio. Thomas called all his commanders and said, "Account for your men."

No sooner than the chief ordered a roll call, one of the missing firefighters appeared in the showroom window. He was trapped, disoriented, and it appeared he didn't know where the door was. Crews outside the building quickly broke the glass and grabbed him. But that allowed more oxygen – more fuel – into the showroom. The fire consumed the fresh air hungrily. Inside, it got hotter. And there were still more firefighters in there.

At 7:38, Thomas called for an evacuation – everyone was ordered out of the building. It was a lost cause. At least seven firefighters retreated and got clear of the blaze. But at 7:41, there was a flashover – an instantaneous ignition of every combustible material in the room. The entire showroom was engulfed in a huge ball of fire. It was a death sentence for anyone left inside.

Four minutes later, the Sofa Super Store's roof collapsed, sending a mushroom cloud of flame and black smoke into the evening sky.

Debris from the explosion and the fire rained down on the parking lot and Savannah Highway, forcing firefighters and the sizable crowd of spectators to scatter. That was it; there was no more fighting this fire. The best the department could do was to keep it from spreading. But there were still a lot of men missing. Engineer Art Wittner was aboard a truck pumping water into the building when the flashover happened. He jumped off the truck and ran toward the building. A chaplain saw Wittner and grabbed him in a bear hug.

"I've got to find my men," Wittner said.

The chaplain shook his head, "You're not going to find them, Art."

Wittner would be the only man from his station to survive the night.

Riley stood outside watching the blaze for a few minutes, then made his way to the emergency support trailer that had arrived. Fire captains, police officers and other emergency workers were inside, and soon Thomas burst through the door, took his jacket off and sat down. "Who are we missing?" the chief asked.

For two hours, firefighters fought the blaze – and trickling water pressure – before they had the Super Sofa Store fire under control. They were able to keep the fire from spreading to the gas station next door, but it was 10 p.m. before anyone was able to get into the showroom. When they did, crews quickly found the bodies of two firefighters sprawled among the charred remains of couches and armchairs.

By then, everyone knew there were more men inside, they just didn't know where – or how many. At 10:45 Riley told reporters that several firefighters were still missing.

When he first arrived and heard someone asking about Mulkey, Riley had assumed – or hoped – that he was simply behind the building, too busy to answer his radio. As darkness fell, however, he was no longer optimistic. As crews continued to sift through the showroom, Riley followed a chaplain to the Savannah Highway fire hall to brief the families gathered there. The mayor watched as the chaplain updated the wives and mothers, and saw the horror in their eyes. "They were in utter disbelief. It was unfathomable. It was so sad."

At 11 p.m., rescue crews found the bodies of two more firefighters, barely 30 feet from where they had recovered the first two. Fifteen minutes later, they found three more men in the south end of the building. By then the rain had started, exacerbating the smoke so much it was nearly impossible to see. Firefighters combed through the rubble into the night. Finally, at around 4 a.m., they found two more men in the northeast corner of the building. These were the last of the missing men.

Nine men had died in the Sofa Super Store fire. It was the worst loss of American firefighters since the World Trade Center collapsed on Sept. 11, 2001.

Riley drove back to City Hall in the early morning hours, his phone ringing every second. The New York Times, CNN, Larry King Live, as well as Sens. Lindsey Graham, John Kerry and Hillary Clinton all left messages. When former New

York Mayor Rudy Giuliani called to offer his sympathy, Riley nearly broke down. "These are heroic people who go into burning buildings, and they gave their lives. It's just so tragic."

Charleston had not lost a firefighter on the job since 1965, 42 years earlier. Now the city had lost nine in a single night. Riley told every reporter the same things: The Charleston Fire Department is among the best in the nation, the firefighters were heroes who died doing what they loved, and they would never be forgotten. Finally, the mayor said he did not know yet what caused the fire.

Two days after the fire, the county coroner's office said all nine of the firefighters died of severe burns and smoke inhalation. The men may have been trapped by the collapsing roof, but it did not kill them. It was hard to say whether they had lived that long anyway; their oxygen likely ran out minutes before the roof buckled under the intense heat.

The coroner also revealed the names of the fallen: Firefighter Brandon Thompson and Engineers Mark Kelsey and Michael French of Tower 5/Engine 10; Engineer Brad Baity, Firefighter Earl Drayton and Capt. Billy Hutchinson of Engine 19; Engine 16 Capt. Mike Benke and Firefighter Melven Champaign; and Engine 15 Capt. Louis Mulkey. Together, the men had more than 132 years of experience fighting fires. Riley declared a day of citywide mourning.

The questions started almost immediately, and they came not only from reporters but other firefighters: Why were there so many men in the building? What caused the fire? Why did it spread, and become so deadly, that quickly? Thomas and Riley said department procedures were followed properly, but a full investigation would follow. The mayor said the community deserved to know what happened.

The city largely shut down for more than a week while the men were buried. Firefighters from around the country came to mourn, and the sidewalk in front of the twisted, charred metal frame of the Sofa Super Store was covered in flowers, American flags, stuffed animals and photos of the men lost. Each funeral ended with processions more than a mile long, each firefighter accompanied to the grave by pumpers and ladder trucks from around the region. Mark Kelsey, the last of the nine, was buried in his Indiana hometown on June 26. The city paid for each service, per Riley's order.

By that time, investigators with the federal Bureau of Alcohol, Tobacco, Firearms and Explosives determined that the fire started at the loading dock behind the Sofa Super Store's main showroom. The loading dock had been filled with flammable objects – a desk, large rolls of wrapping plastic and furniture awaiting delivery. Initial reports said store employees often ducked outside to smoke on the dock, although they would not speculate as to whether an errant cigarette butt started the blaze. But one store employee told The Post and Courier's Glenn Smith that everyone knew that smoking on the loading dock was "a huge no-no."

The loading dock became a point of contention in the investigation. The city said the dock was illegal, that the Sofa Super Store had never gotten a permit to build it. But the bigger problem was the lack of a sprinkler system in the building. Because sprinklers were not required by law, many businesses opted not to install them – the cost was considered too high. The water company charged companies up to $50,000 for an extra line and nearly $2,000 a year in fees. Within a month of the fire, Riley asked the water company to drop those fees and asked the state to change the law and require sprinklers in all public buildings.

As the city revealed one problem after another at the Sofa Super Store, others began to blame the fire department itself for mishandling the blaze. Roger Yow, president of the Charleston Firefighters Association (a union that represented about half the city's firefighters), said the department's operating procedures were inadequate and needed to change. Yow said the city's safety guidelines did not meet national standards, the department often fought fires offensively when they should have adopted a more defensive stance. He criticized the department's command structure and said the city did not plan well enough for combatting blazes in buildings that were known fire hazards – like the Sofa Super Store.

Thomas told reporters it was easy to second-guess decisions, "But they weren't there, and I was."

The chief had been traumatized by the fire. He gave eulogies at each of the funerals, and his stories suggested he knew all the men well. Thomas had always said he hired everyone in the department, not a human resources worker. The fire department didn't even issue badge numbers because everybody knew each other by name. And Thomas had been around 31 years. His father had been the department's head mechanic, and Rusty was drawn to the life at an early age. He joined when he was just 18.

No one doubted Thomas' devotion to the department. Even as chief, he helped fight fires when he was on the scene, and he was always at the fires. About the only time he ever left Charleston was to pick up a new firetruck. Even those who did not care for his management style said he was a good man, but they questioned his tactics. He was, some people said, too aggressive in fighting fires, took too many risks. The city investigated the fire, and the mayor assembled a panel of experts to determine what went wrong, but it was the outside inquiries that would lead to the most trouble for the Charleston Fire Department – and for Thomas.

City Councilman William Dudley Gregorie, who earlier had announced his own mayoral bid, said he would address the fire department's policy flaws quickly if he was elected. Gregorie adopted the concerns of the firefighters' union and would repeat them throughout the campaign. Paraphrasing Albert Einstein, Gregorie said, "To keep doing things the same way, and expecting different results," is insanity. Riley accused the councilman of playing election-year politics.

"No one should be trying to make political hay out of this tragedy," he said. "If we discover any reason to change policies and procedures we will do that."

Riley did not formally announce his re-election campaign until Aug. 14, a day before the filing deadline. Besides Gregorie, the mayor would again face Marc Knapp, as well as police officer and East Side resident Omar Brown. Knapp and Brown campaigned on platforms of lower taxes and more emphasis on basic city services. Gregorie said much the same thing, but made public safety his strongest focus. The real issue for all of the candidates, however, was Riley.

The mayor's three opponents attacked him mercilessly throughout the fall. They questioned his commitment to civil rights, children's issues and affordable housing. They blamed his leadership for the Sofa Super Store fire – Knapp going so far as to say Riley was liable for the deaths of the nine firefighters. Gregorie said Rusty Thomas got his job only because of his daddy's connections, that he hadn't been the choice of retiring Chief Wilmot Guthke.

The campaign was so intense that Riley even joked about it in September, when his portrait was unveiled at City Hall. The painting, commissioned by various patrons of the arts, showed Riley standing in the St. Michael's Church tower, the city skyline behind him. It was a bright, colorful painting – much different from most other mayoral portraits in the building, almost all of which showed stern men in dark suits sitting behind their desks. Riley told the crowd it remained to be seen whether the painting depicted him in the early, middle – or final – year of his administration.

As it turned out, Riley had nothing to worry about. In November 2007, the mayor won a ninth term with 64 percent of the vote. Knapp got 5 percent and Brown took 2 percent. But Gregorie turned out to be far more formidable than just about anyone Riley had run against. Gregorie won 22 of 89 precincts, most of them in the northern peninsula area of his City Council district. His margins were not nearly as large in those districts as Riley had in his, particularly downtown, but no one had ever taken so many precincts against the mayor. That showing all but ensured Gregorie was not going anywhere.

In his victory speech, Riley talked about plans for an International African-American Museum and expanding regional planning. He mentioned the possibility of a light-rail commuter system for the Lowcountry and promised to lobby the state Legislature to create a pre-kindergarten program for 4-year-olds. And he said the city fire department would learn from the lessons of the Sofa Super Store fire.

Those lessons would begin within months.

Riley was still talking about the fire when he took his ninth oath of office on Jan. 14, 2008. More than six months later, the Sofa Super Store still dominated much of his time. In his inaugural address, the mayor said the city would make the Charleston Fire Department a national model. But it would not be easy.

The firefighters union wanted Thomas out – they largely blamed his mismanagement for the tragedy. They said breaking out the store's front window was a horrible mistake that fed the fire more oxygen and doomed the men inside. The union issued a long list of things it believed the department had done wrong: Some of the off-duty firefighters worked in street clothes; some firefighters had not worn their equipment properly that night, a few did not use their breathing apparatus when surrounded by smoke; the polyester uniforms were too flammable and unsafe; the booster hoses used to feed water to firefighters were too small to get adequate flow.

Thomas took the criticism hard, but vowed to stay. A report commissioned by the city blamed the fire on the store's multiple state and city code violations – it had an illegally constructed loading dock and did not store flammable materials properly. Riley said the store's owner was responsible for the accident. The store owner, in turn, said the mayor was simply a politician blaming him for his fire department's inadequacies. It did not help public perception when attorneys for the families of the nine firefighters said the city report looked suspiciously like their own lawsuit against Sofa Super Store.

Although SLED would eventually rule there was no evidence of criminal negligence, the public's perception was tarnished as national firefighter groups continued the criticism. There were too many firefighters in the building at one time, Thomas allowed his crews to hot dog fires in a way that was dangerous. City Council members and The Post and Courier's Glenn Smith continued to critique the incident. The pressure became almost unbearable.

Riley thought it was unfair that Thomas was taking all the blame. Rusty was a hard-working man who didn't mind pitching in and getting his hands dirty, and the mayor considered him one of the best workers he had ever seen. But he knew Thomas was a marked man, and would be hounded as long as he remained chief.

In the spring of 2008, the two talked about the best course of action several times. Finally, on May 14, Thomas said he would step down as chief at the end of June – near the one-year anniversary of the Sofa Super Store fire. Later, Riley said it was the only way to get past the tragedy. "We decided together it was best for him and the department."

Thomas' resignation would not end the criticism or the lawsuits, but it satisfied the firefighters for the time being. The city eventually bought the Sofa Super Store property; Riley considered building a new fire station there but ultimately decided a memorial park would be more fitting. The city would host a service there every year on the anniversary of the fire, and part of Highway 17 in West Ashley was renamed the Charleston Nine Memorial Highway. The mayor kept a plaque commemorating the firefighters behind his desk. By the end of 2008, he secured a federal grant to buy $678,000 worth of new equipment for the department.

Still, the mayor would fend off jabs at his fire department for years. Finally, more than three years after the fire, a study by the National Institute of Standards and Technology said that sprinklers would have contained the fire and saved lives, and concluded that breaking the front windows contributed to the fire's escalation and the deaths of the firefighters.

In early 2008, Riley surprised many people by endorsing a young Illinois senator for president. Barack Obama had spent some time in Charleston courting voters and the mayor, although most Democrats considered him a longshot with Hillary Clinton on the ballot. The mayor had known the Clintons since the 1980s, even stayed at the White House during President Clinton's term. Throughout the 1990s, Riley had enjoyed better access to the federal government than ever before. And that came in handy.

The federal courthouse needed a second annex by the mid-1990s, but the General Services Administration did not like the option offered by the city – a 19th century building that needed some renovation. The GSA was threatening to move out if it couldn't build a generic annex, which no one in Charleston wanted. Riley called the president and asked him to explain that some things just cost a little more in a historic district. Clinton promised to get it fixed, but nothing happened for months.

One day Riley's son, Joe, saw the president at an event in Atlanta. He introduced himself to Clinton and said, "You know my dad, Joe Riley – he's the mayor of Charleston." Clinton said of course, shook his hand and moved on down the line. When he was five or six feet away, Joe heard the president tell one of his aides, "Remind me to get Joe's courthouse fixed." A week later, the GSA accepted the city's plan.

Most people expected Riley to endorse Hillary Clinton in 2008, although some said privately that the mayor was deeply offended by the Monica Lewinsky affair. That wasn't Hillary's fault, of course, but friends believed it had cooled him to the Clintons. At the same time, Riley aide David Agnew had begun talking up Obama to the mayor. Then Charlotte mentioned how impressive she thought the young senator was. So Riley began to read articles about Obama, then his book *Dreams From My Father*. Eventually, he met with Obama and liked what he heard. He was a serious, intellectual man, Riley thought.

When Riley decided to endorse Obama, he called his cell phone – but the call went straight to voice mail. He left a message. Later, he learned that when Obama played his voice mail in campaign headquarters, a cheer went up in the room. If a white Democrat in South Carolina would endorse a black man for president, Obama's aides said, they might just have a chance.

When Obama was elected in 2008, he did not forget Riley. Within weeks, the mayor was in Chicago meeting with the president-elect's transition team to advise them on municipal-level issues. Riley was consulted more as the elder statesman of the U.S. Conference of Mayors than as the administrator of a midsize Southern city. While he was there, Riley put in a good word for Agnew – who put together the fundraiser on "the front porches of Charleston" that Obama referenced in his victory speech. By the time Obama moved into the White House, Agnew was named the administration's liaison to the country's mayors. Suddenly, Riley had the ear of White House senior staff.

Even before Barack Obama took office, Riley had lobbied for federal aid that would help cities combat the ongoing recession. But his efforts quickly ran afoul of Gov. Mark Sanford, who refused to let South Carolina accept any federal stimulus money. It went against Sanford's libertarian – and cheapskate – ways. Riley argued it was foolish, that not accepting the money did not mean it wouldn't be spent, just that it would go elsewhere. "Now is not the time for philosophical wanderings of the mind," the mayor said. But Sanford would not listen.

Nor would the Legislature listen as Riley lobbied once again for tougher crime laws. In January, the mayor – backed by Police Chief Greg Mullen and 9th Circuit Solicitor Scarlett Wilson – asked the General Assembly to ban convicted criminals from owning handguns or military-style rifles. The mayor also wanted the state to enact harsher penalties for the illegal use of military-style rifles, and create new offenses for anyone using a gun while possessing, selling or manufacturing drugs.

Lawmakers would not touch gun laws because of the National Rifle Association, which Riley soon learned the hard way. In September 2009, the NRA sent postcards to Charleston residents criticizing Riley for his membership in an organization called Mayors Against Illegal Guns. The postcards urged residents to "help him make the right choice between protecting your Second Amendment rights or continuing to be associated with those who actively oppose and undermine your firearm freedom."

Riley said he was against illegal guns, so anyone opposed to his position must be in favor of illegal guns. "I know what my constituents want me to do, to make it harder for criminals to get guns and close loopholes that make it easy for criminals to get guns," he said.

The NRA targeted Riley because the Mayors Against Illegal Guns had recently lobbied Congress for background checks on all gun-show sales and asked for cities to have more access to information that would help them trace firearms. Three years earlier, New York City had sued 15 gun stores for alleged illegal sales, including two from the Charleston area. The NRA said it opposed illegal guns sales, but it had a very narrow definition of what that meant.

By the fall of 2009, Riley had more pending problems closer to home. The town of James Island had won in Circuit Court, forcing the city to appeal its lawsuit to the state Supreme Court. It seemed the fight would never end. But the bigger issue was the arrival of the cruise ship trade, which initially seemed to be good news. Carnival Cruise Lines announced its ship, the *Fantasy*, would soon call Charleston home. The 2,056-passenger liner would depart from downtown weekly for trips to the Bahamas, luring thousands more visitors to the city each year.

State lawmakers declared the recession over in Charleston and Riley called it an important development for the local economy. Cruise ships accounted for only 1 percent of the city's visitor base, but the mayor said it was an important percent. He predicted cruise-ship passengers would take one look at the city and decide to vacation in Charleston in the future. The *Fantasy* would not only make money for the city, it was free advertising. Within a month, the port would suggest renovations for its decrepit passenger terminal.

The *Fantasy*'s first cruise from Charleston came quietly on May 8, 2010. It had been a relatively uneventful year. In February, the city began work on a statue of Denmark Vesey at Hampton Park, enraging some locals who did not want to be reminded of the free black man accused of plotting a slave revolt in 1822. Riley called him an important civil rights figure and said the monument added to the "substantially untold story of African-American history and life in this community" – something he planned to rectify with his African-American Museum.

Later that month, Riley received the National Medal of Arts for his work cultivating historic and cultural resources in Charleston – as well as for his role creating the Mayors' Institute on City Design. In the East Room of the White House, President Obama singled out "my great friend Joe Riley and the extraordinary work he's done in Charleston."

Back home, not everyone felt the same. Before the end of the year, preservationists and some downtown residents began a campaign against cruise ships – and Riley – that echoed the protests against Charleston Place three decades earlier. They accused the city of once again catering to tourists at the expense of residents' quality of life. What really upset them, however, was the city's support of the State Ports Authority plan to build a new passenger terminal.

The complaints were predictable: the cruise ships visiting Charleston were too large, there were too many of them, they were waterfront eyesores. The ships would pollute the harbor, their passengers would create traffic jams. If that had been all, Riley might not have gotten so angry. But some locals called in the Southern Environmental Law Center, which told City Council that cruise ships dumped "grey water" – semi-clean sewer water – just outside the harbor jetties. Riley dismissed the complaints as hyperbole. He did not realize it, but the mayor was in for another long fight with some very noisy downtown residents.

And he intended to make it his fight for some time to come. In December 2010, Riley announced plans to run for a 10th term. That day he was meeting with Pennsylvania Gov. Ed Rendell about a national infrastructure bank similar to the one South Carolina set up to fund the Ravenel Bridge. The two men knew each other from the U.S. Conference of Mayors, and Rendell was amused by the mayor's early re-election announcement.

"When I was mayor of Philadelphia, Joe was mayor of Charleston," Rendell told reporters. "When Ben Franklin was governor of Pennsylvania, Joe was mayor of Charleston."

Rendell's joke got a good response, but not everyone was laughing. Some City

Council members – who called the mayor "King Joe" behind his back – said Charleston didn't have a democracy, it had a monarchy.

And people were lining up to change that.

Top of the World

In October 2011, the readers of Conde Nast Traveler named Charleston the top tourist destination in America. The city had been in the magazine's top 10 consistently since 1993, and for the past three years had ranked No. 2 behind San Francisco – the reigning champion in 18 consecutive surveys. When Helen Hill, executive director of The Charleston Area Convention and Visitors Bureau, accepted the city's crown in New York City, she said, "It's like winning the Academy Award for tourism." Hill was right; they even had a celebrity there to hand her the award – Stephen Colbert, who grew up in Charleston.

The seeds Riley had sown decades earlier had borne fruit in a big way. The mayor thanked Conde Nast and its readers, sending along the message that "We look forward to the opportunity to show visitors what makes Charleston a great place to visit."

It was a prestigious honor, but the timing could have been better. The city elections were less than a month away, and some voters were not enchanted by the thoughts of even more tourists flocking to Charleston. Tourism – or rather, the overabundance of it – had become a contentious issue in the 2011 mayoral race. Some people did not credit Riley with revitalizing the city. They blamed him for luring all those people to town.

Preservationists and some downtown neighborhood associations had spent much of the year protesting the city's decision to allow an increase in cruise ship traffic. Residents who lived south of Calhoun complained about the traffic on days the Carnival *Fantasy* was in port. They argued there was little economic benefit to the city. A few of them said, quite frankly, those people were not the kind of visitors they wanted in Charleston. They even persuaded the National Trust for Historic

Preservation to consider adding the city to its "11 Most Endangered List."

After months of complaints, Riley was less than diplomatic with the critics. The port, he said, is a hub of activity and business – the maritime industry built the city, its architecture and culture. He accused the anti-cruise-ship crowd of attempting to make Charleston a gated community. "You want to 'preserve' a Charleston without waterborne commerce that never existed. We are not turning Charleston into a boutique."

It had been a tough year for the mayor. He spent much of his time trying to secure funds for a $154 million project that would alleviate flooding on the Crosstown Parkway. An arsonist had been burning old houses on the peninsula, and the police had no leads. His old friend and longtime city attorney Bill Regan had died. And no sooner than the state Supreme Court dismantled the town of James Island for a third time, there was already talk of a fourth attempt. Then, in October – during the hectic final weeks of his re-election campaign – the historic district went on the World Monument Fund watch list because of the cruise ships. Riley raised hell.

The mayor was so frustrated by the incessant harping over cruise ships he could hardly focus on his campaign. He had four challengers, but three of them had no real chance of getting out of single digits. Riley's main competition was Councilman William Dudley Gregorie, who in the 2007 mayoral election had won 29 percent of the vote, and 22 precincts. Experience had only made the councilman more formidable. Gregorie was deftly courting voters in Riley's own downtown districts by promising an administration more focused on residents than tourists. And he declared that, if elected, he would serve no more than two terms. It was just what the "Riley fatigue" crowd wanted to hear.

Two weeks before the election, an anonymous group called Citizens for a Better Charleston set up a website to smear the mayor. They accused Riley of raising taxes and "endangering the rich history of Charleston." The group said he had been in office too long – and they supported Gregorie. The councilman said he had nothing to do with the attacks, and didn't know who was behind them.

Riley's friend and campaign manager Capers Barr told reporters the group was an example of "mudslinging at its very worst." The mayor was hopping mad. He eventually found out where the group got its mail and scheduled a news conference in front of the building. With cameras rolling, he called the Citizens for a Better Charleston a bunch of "cowards." The group told media outlets – anonymously – they could not go public because they feared retribution from the mayor.

The group claimed they were part of a growing grass-roots majority, but there was little evidence of that on election day. All the people suffering Riley fatigue either didn't vote or didn't exist in sufficient numbers. On Nov. 8, Riley took 2 out of every 3 votes to win his 10th term. His 67 percent of the vote dwarfed Gregorie's 27 percent. The three other candidates combined for only 6 percent. Riley said the people had spoken, and they did not like the methods of a bunch of "scared fat cats."

But those people would not have to endure the reign of "King Joe" much longer. During the campaign, Riley had said his 10th term would be his last. "When this next term is over, I would be 72, and I think that will be the right time to have a job or activities that are at a different pace than what being mayor of Charleston requires. You cannot do this job or should not do this job at any kind of scaled-back level." This proclamation had little effect on the election. Some people asked him to reconsider, and others didn't believe him.

After the election, Riley reiterated his claim that he was done – whether anyone believed him or not. The mayor said he would not groom, nor endorse, a successor; it wasn't practical. The idea of a mayoral race without Riley in it was something that many politicians had dreamed of for years. Less than a week after the mayor swore he would never be on a ballot again, several City Council members announced that they were thinking about running in 2015. Even though most of them suspected the mayor really wasn't going anywhere.

On Jan. 9, 2012, Joe Riley III stood on the steps of City Hall and read the oath of office for his father to recite. Before he began, however, he asked if this was really the last time – a not-so-subtle dig at the people who did not believe the mayor would quit willingly. Riley laughed along with the crowd of 600 in the street, and said it was.

"So, for the last time," Joe began.

In his final inaugural address, Riley sounded more like a young idealist than a man who had held the same job for 36 years. He promised to fight the federal government until Charleston's harbor channel was dredged to a satisfactory depth, lobby the state to finish the 526 bypass and help fund the Crosstown drainage project. He proposed turning Charleston into a "silicon harbor" for biotech and science-based jobs. But the most inspiring moment of the speech came when the mayor talked about what it took to make a "Great City." He vowed that Charleston would not rest on its considerable laurels.

Riley used his address to send a message to the people protesting the cruise ships. In recent years, he often spoke of how the city had to be a living, breathing place – a place where people resided and worked and played in the same area. Now, he said, some people were trying to change the city into something it never had been.

"A new affluence has graced our city," the mayor said. "And with that, there may be on the part of a few the misunderstanding that they live in or have moved to a place that is like a gated community – affluent and exclusive. But that is not a great city."

The first year of Riley's final term was one of his most productive. In February 2012 he secured $88 million from the State Infrastructure Bank to fund his Crosstown drainage project. City Council approved his plan for a $142 million renovation of the Gaillard Auditorium, funded in part by a sizable – and anonymous – donation. The Gaillard work would not be finished until his final months in office; the Crosstown several years later.

Then James Islanders voted to incorporate a fourth time, but this time the mayor would not give them the satisfaction of a fight. The city's legal staff determined the town's incorporation was finally constitutionally defensible, so Charleston wouldn't spend the money to file suit. Riley sent a letter to the attorney who helped the town form, Trent Kernodle, that simply said, "Trent, I give up – Joe." But in fact, Riley had won. After all those years of fighting, James Island's town had only 12,000 residents and 2,600 acres of land worth $28.8 million. On James Island, the city had nearly twice as many residents and four times as much land worth four times as much.

In May, the baseball fan-in-chief was inducted into the South Atlantic League's Hall of Fame for his work building the stadium that bore his name. It was one of his favorite honors. But the mayor's biggest coup of the year came barely a week after his inauguration. In January, Riley was in Washington for the U.S. Conference of Mayors winter meeting, which – as usual – included a trip to the White House.

Riley wanted to use the visit to lobby for the only federal issue on his mind at the moment: the harbor. Companies around the world were developing larger container-ships each year, and they required more clearance to get into port. If Charleston's harbor could not accommodate these new ships, the city – and the state – would lose millions in business.

Harbor dredging was not historically a mayor's job. For decades, the state's congressional delegation handled dredging projects by including an Army Corps of Engineers earmark in the federal budget. But South Carolina Sen. Jim DeMint had recently derailed the entire budget process by going on a grandstanding crusade against earmarks. The fiscal conservative declared all earmarks "pork," and shamed his colleagues into banning the practice. The allegedly pro-business senator – who would soon quit the Senate for a lucrative job at the conservative Heritage Foundation – had almost succeeded in wrecking the state's largest industry.

By 2012, the only way to make certain a project was included in the federal budget was to get the White House to add it – a much trickier proposition than asking a congressman. Riley had requested a line item for Charleston Harbor in 2011, and the president and vice president promised to help, but things were not moving quickly enough for the mayor.

The meeting at the White House was really just a photo op for the nation's mayors, a chance for them to go home and say "I spoke to the president." Riley knew he would have no more than a few seconds and didn't want to sound like a broken record – the last time he had spoken to Obama it had been about the harbor. But Riley told himself he would be, as he later said, a "real nerd" if he didn't find a way to mention his concern. Finally, just after the camera flashed, the mayor thanked the president for his staff's work to make sure Charleston Harbor was in the budget.

Obama surprised Riley; he was well-versed on the issue. "George Will thinks it's a good idea," the president said. The conservative syndicated columnist had recently written a piece lamenting the bureaucratic red tape holding up the work on important ports – which was exactly Charleston's problem. The president had not only read the piece, he remembered it. He also recalled talking to Riley about it the year before. So President Obama turned to Valerie Jarrett, a senior advisor, and asked her to make sure Charleston Harbor was in the budget.

Weeks later, the photo of Riley with the president arrived in the City Hall mail. An Obama administration staffer had included a note with the photograph. It said, "Best use of 30 seconds in the history of the White House." In July, the Army Corps of Engineers said the Charleston Harbor dredging project had been moved up on the waiting list by four years. The next week, President Obama put it ahead of another year's worth of projects.

The mayor pulled off a similar coup in the fall, this time for the benefit of the 526 bypass. Charleston County Council was waffling because James and Johns island residents were lobbying against the road. It appeared council leaders did not have the votes to prevail so Riley offered to have the city take over. He argued that much of the road would be in the city anyway, and Charleston officials could partner with the state Department of Transportation as well as the county. Reluctant County Council members realized that turning the project over to Riley would be more politically damaging than taking the heat themselves, so they voted 5-4 in favor of completing 526. The mayor had forced their hand.

In December, a 20-year-old man walked into Sandy Hook Elementary School in Newtown, Connecticut, where he shot and killed six adults and 20 children before committing suicide. Aside from the 2007 massacre at Virginia Tech, it was the worst single-person mass killing in the country's history. The nation was shocked; the man had gunned down children. Riley was appalled and became one of the first to call for stricter gun controls in the wake of the tragedy. The mayor lobbied Congress to restore the ban on military-style weapons, asked state lawmakers to ban high-capacity magazines, strengthen background checks and close loopholes in laws that allowed people to avoid criminal background checks.

"Through purchases at gun shows, any individual can bypass the background check system and fill a house with weapons they are not legally allowed to purchase. This is ridiculous," Riley said.

The mayor continued his crusade in his State of the City address, and later in Washington and Columbia. Years of experience had taught him how to garner national attention, and he and other mayors harped on the issue for months. But Congress would not consider any tightening of gun laws, not even for 20 dead children. No one would stand up to the NRA.

Riley remained on the national stage for much of the year. In September 2013, he and other mayors visited the 16th Street Baptist Church in Birmingham, the place where a Ku Klux Klansman had bombed and killed four black girls 50 years earlier. It was a tragedy reminiscent of Sandy Hook, but with racial overtones. Riley spoke for all mayors inside the church, and afterward the leaders of the U.S. Conference of Mayors stood outside the church and asked the country to end racism and discrimination.

The conference had an ambitious plan to speak out against bias, reduce poverty and eliminate disparities in prison sentencing guidelines between whites, blacks and Hispanics. Riley told reporters he had real hope that the plan could make a difference. Most people were cynical, but the mayor's optimism seemingly had not waned through more than four decades of public life. But once again things would get worse before they got better.

In October 2013, Charleston was once again named the No. 1 tourist destination in America by Conde Nast. The readers of Traveler apparently did not deduct points for the ongoing lawsuit against the proposed new cruise ship terminal. The legal fight was a bigger pain for Riley than the hip replacement he had in November, keeping him out of work for a month. But by January 2014, the state Supreme Court tossed out the lawsuit.

Riley said the lawsuit was nothing more than an attempt to scare off the cruise ship industry, and in his State of the City address declared it a failure. He said the complaint was "almost laughable." He dedicated the rest of his penultimate address stumping for bond referendums that would build new schools and libraries across the county. He announced that the city would break ground on its African-American Museum within two years, and bragged that violent crime in the city had dropped 17 percent in 2013, and 70 percent over the past seven years. Realizing he had only one more of these addresses to deliver, it seemed Riley was getting sentimental, even poetic. "This is the state of your city – old in history but ever so young in spirit."

As 2014 began, Riley was preparing for his inevitable departure. Already he was getting calls from reporters and filmmakers eager to do retrospectives and long interviews about his tenure. He agreed to most, and often talked about the guiding philosophy he had adopted decades earlier: When considering any project, he asked himself whether it passed the 25-year test, the 50-year test. Will this still be considered a good idea then? He could already answer that first question about some of his earliest projects, but still felt he had more to do.

Most people believed the verdict was already in on Riley. One month before the mayor and Pat Conroy were inducted into The Citadel Athletic Hall of Fame, New York Times columnist Frank Bruni posed the question: Is Joe Riley the most beloved politician in America?

His final two years in office felt like a sprint. By Riley's estimate, he had 53 projects in various states of development – the cruise ship terminal, the Gaillard, the African-American Museum and the Crosstown drainage project among them. He was also talking with the State Ports Authority about developing Union Pier, a dream he'd had since his first term. The mayor knew most of these projects wouldn't be finished by the time he left office, but he wanted to see them well on their way. At some point in the year, he calculated how many days he had left – and recited the number to at least one person just about daily.

Riley was too busy to be distracted by one of the city's biggest controversies of the year. Once again downtown residents were complaining about rabble-rouser bar patrons pouring into the streets at 2 a.m., but this time the concerns were coming from farther up the peninsula. Upper King Street had replaced the Market as the city's most-popular late-night hangout, and now people who lived north of Calhoun Street were frustrated just as much as French Quarter residents had been years earlier.

At Riley's urging, City Council passed a one-year moratorium on late-night bars on Upper King that October, which proved to be a controversial move. The mayor defended council, said he did not want the area to become Bourbon Street – a stretch of the city dead during the day and then alive at night. It wasn't healthy. Bar patrons responded to the moratorium by papering the city with posters featuring Riley's face and the message "Go to Bed." Soon, people started calling the image "Sleepy Joe Riley." The mayor said little about it. He would not be distracted by anything, even a little mockery.

Despite Riley's incessant countdown, the finality of his pending retirement did not sink in until Nov. 7, 2014 – 470 days to go. The Citadel Class of '64 had gathered at the college for its 50th reunion and the school's homecoming game. That afternoon, Riley and his classmates were on the parade ground listening to the Corps' a Cappella group sing "The Lion Sleeps Tonight" – a song popular during their time on campus – when Citadel President Lt. Gen. John Rosa made the announcement. The military college had created an endowed chair in American Government and Public Policy named in Riley's honor. He would be the first person to hold the seat, immediately after he retired from City Hall.

Bo Moore, dean of the School of Humanities and Social Sciences, said the college wanted to record the oral history of Riley's life and career, and his tenure as mayor. Moore said that "People 200 years from now will be looking at documents from the Riley administration." The mayor would also teach classes and lecture. Rosa said there was no better role model, no better mentor, than Riley – a Citadel man with the ring to prove it.

Riley told his classmates, and a crowd of hundreds, that a Citadel history class – a course that taught him the injustices of the Jim Crow South – had shaped his entire career. "The three major blocks in the early foundation of my personal and professional life were my family, my church and my education and training at The Citadel."

With his post-mayoral plans set, Riley felt more pressure than ever before. The first half of 2015 was a blur – there was never enough time in any day, his schedule was chronically overbooked. Appointments were canceled and shuffled, interviews postponed or turned down. He presided over the opening of Gadsdenboro Park across the street from the aquarium, kept tabs on the ongoing Gaillard renovation, fought efforts to allow offshore drilling for oil. Many days, he traveled the state in his city-issued Prius, toting design drawings of the African-American Museum to show potential donors. The state, city and county would fund $50 million of the $75-million facility, and he intended to raise the final $25 million privately. Riley would continue that work after he left office, but he was going to raise every cent he could while he was still the mayor.

In January, Riley scored a private meeting with President Obama while he was in Washington for the U.S. Conference of Mayors winter meeting. He used his time in the Oval Office to make a pitch for the African-American Museum, in hopes that the president could do something to help with the project. Obama was impressed with the idea, and Riley walked out of the White House optimistic that he had made a convert out of the president.

Back in Charleston, the sense of finality was overpowering for Riley. It truly was the end of an era. So many people were gone: his parents, Bill Regan. Ted Stern had passed a couple of years back, Reuben Greenberg in September. Herbert Fielding would not survive the year, passing away at 92. And that April, Mary Moultrie died. The woman who'd led the hospital strike during his first year in the Legislature had become a good friend and worked for the city for years. Riley eulogized them all, in the newspaper and at their funerals.

At the same time, others were writing eulogies to his career. National Public Radio, The New York Times, documentary filmmakers, local TV stations – everyone wanted a few minutes with him. Riley sat patiently for most of these interviews, answering the same questions over and over. He had known there would be some attention, but it was more than he expected. One of the biggest, and most important, events was scheduled for June. The U.S. Conference of Mayors planned a bash to celebrate the legacy of their dean – "America's Mayor" – at the summer meeting in San Francisco.

Riley could not afford to take the time – he had just over 200 days left in office. He hated to travel on a weekend, and didn't like leaving Charlotte behind. He considered not going or making it a two-day trip, but finally conceded this conference was too important. The city was slated to receive a prestigious livability award, one he would accept with Chief Mullen.

The mayor also knew there would be a surprise party – he could barely walk through a conference meeting anymore without big-city mayors stopping to take selfies with him. Finally, Riley realized this would be his last U.S. Conference of Mayors meeting as a member, the last chance he would have to address his colleagues as mayor. So he made the time, and planned to stay in California for three nights.

He would never make it.

Mark 4: 16-20

Charleston was quiet that night, a midweek lull in its normally busy tourist season. The streets of downtown were nearly empty, the city's usual revelry muted and muffled. The Spoleto Festival had ended a week earlier, the College of Charleston was on summer break and firefighters were preparing for a ceremony to mark the eighth anniversary of the Sofa Super Store the following night.

An oppressive humidity had settled over the Lowcountry a week earlier, leaving locals lethargic and desperately seeking their air conditioning. Even after the sun began to sink into the western sky, there was no escape from the smothering heat. It was June 17, 2015, and the brutal Charleston summer had come early. The locals realized it might not go away for a long, long time.

About 7:30 p.m., people started trickling out of Mother Emanuel AME Church near the intersection of Calhoun and Meeting streets. The church's quarterly conference had just dismissed following an hour and a half of boilerplate business, the induction of new ministers and a message from the district's presiding elder. By church standards, it was a fairly routine meeting; still the Rev. Clementa Pinckney – pastor of Emanuel for five years – had rushed to town from Columbia to attend.

Pinckney, a veteran state senator, had spent much of the week at the Statehouse, where the Legislature had returned after a two-week break to muscle through a budget impasse. It was frustrating; the state budget should have been approved by June 4, the mandated closing date for the General Assembly. As usual, partisan bickering had slowed the process to a crawl and South Carolina was just 13 days away from a new fiscal year with no operating budget.

Sen. Pinckney had used the ongoing budget debate to champion a cause dear to his heart: He urged his colleagues to increase state benefits for foster children. His argument was much the same as his ongoing efforts to expand the state's Medicaid rolls – there is great need. But Democrats in South Carolina did not get much say in what the state needed, and Pinckney was largely ignored by his counterparts across the aisle. But he would not stop trying.

Mixing politics with the cloth was nothing new for Pinckney, a minister his entire adult life and a politician with nearly 20 years of experience. The AME Church had a long history steeped in politics dating back to its formation. Mother Emanuel was the first AME Church in the South, formed in 1816. It had been the church of Denmark Vesey, the free black man who in 1822 had plotted a slave revolt to free Charleston's considerable African-American population. Vesey had hanged for his crime; his church had been burned to the ground. But the congregation would rise from the ashes time and again – after fires and wars and earthquakes. The faith of its congregants was unshakable.

Like many black Southern churches, Emanuel had played an important role in the civil rights era. Once, Andrew Young had spoken there; another time, the Rev. Martin Luther King Jr. preached from Mother Emanuel's pulpit. Coretta Scott King addressed striking hospital workers there the evening before her famous 1969 march through Charleston. Pinckney cherished that history, knew it well, and he would not be lax in his duties, even if it meant a harrowing, 100-mile commute at rush hour. He arrived just in time for the meeting.

Pinckney needed to return to Columbia that night – the General Assembly machine would slowly crank up Thursday morning for a continuation of the budget debate. But the church's regular Bible study was scheduled to follow the business meeting and he wouldn't miss it, even if it meant driving back to Columbia with the weariness of the day settling into his bones on Interstate 26. It was simply what he did.

For a moment, it looked as if Bible study might be cancelled – the quarterly conference had gone long and some people were hungry. It had been a long day, and the heat was tiring. The Rev. Daniel Simmons, a retired minister, suggested they postpone Bible study – probably realizing "Clem," as Pinckney was called, needed to get on the road. Simmons, a Vietnam veteran, had worked at the Department of Corrections before he retired, and knew how state government could wear on a soul.

Myra Thompson, a retired teacher, pushed for the Bible study to go on as scheduled. Her ministry license had been renewed at the conference and she was ready to talk about the gospel. "Let's do a little of it," Thompson suggested. The Rev. DePayne Middleton Doctor felt the same. She had just been introduced into the ranks of AME ministers, following in her father's footsteps. It would not do to start her career by skipping Bible study.

Thompson, Simmons, Middleton Doctor and Pinckney led the way to the large meeting room on the church's ground floor, just below the famous sanctuary. Eight others joined them, sitting in folding chairs around tables covered in white tablecloths. The room was often used for meetings, church dinners and informal gatherings. It was the most comfortable room in the building, surrounded by smaller rooms and offices. Soon after the lesson began, Pinckney's wife and daughter – the only other people in the building – retreated to his office and shut the door. There were 12 people remaining for the lesson; the oldest was 87, the youngest just 5.

Their lesson that evening was from Mark chapter 4, verses 16 through 20: "Others, like seed sown on rocky places, hear the word and at once receive it with joy. But since they have no root, they last only a short time. When trouble or persecution comes because of the word, they quickly fall away. Still others, like seed sown among thorns, hear the word; but the worries of this life, the deceitfulness of wealth and the desires for other things come in and choke the word, making it unfruitful. Others, like seed sown on good soil, hear the word, accept it, and produce a crop –some thirty, some sixty, some a hundred times what was sown."

The 18th century British minister and author Matthew Henry considered the parable from Mark 4 to be imminently important instruction on the nature of faith. It casts the church as a great field in which God's word is dispensed. Some people who hear the word are affected for a short time, but the lessons do not take root because their hearts and minds aren't "duly disposed" to receive them – "like seed sown on rocky places." This fleeting faith, Henry wrote, is a very dangerous thing, for it can be perverted and perhaps even used to justify evil. "The devil is very busy about careless hearers," Henry wrote. "Many continue in a barren, false profession, and go down to hell."

Before their lesson ended, the men and women of Mother Emanuel would come face to face with Matthew Henry's dire warning personified.

At 8:15, the Emanuel congregants were about halfway through their discussion of Mark 4 when a black Hyundai Elantra pulled up and parked near the church's side door. The car was so generic it might have been anonymous save for the tag on the front bumper, which read "Confederate States of America." Through church surveillance cameras, the driver was later identified as a 21-year-old high school dropout named Dylann Roof.

Roof grew up in Eastover, a rural town of 800 halfway between Columbia and Sumter, near Congaree National Park. He was a child of divorce, and moved from one school to the next, eventually repeating 9th grade before finally dropping out in his sophomore year. His family feared he was antisocial – he had no driver's license, no job, although he did have some friends. But most days he stayed in his room in his family's two-story log cabin, playing video games and apparently taking drugs.

The Internet seemed to be Roof's primary connection to the outside world, and there he was attracted to the websites and chat rooms of white supremacists – men who blamed all the nation's problems on African-Americans and other minorities. Racism is a refuge for the uneducated and paranoid, an excuse some people use to explain their own shortcomings. A substance-abusing dropout with no job, Roof fit the profile all too well.

The media firestorm of the Trayvon Martin case in Florida first drew Roof's attention to the world of white supremacists. Roof believed Martin had deserved to be shot by George Zimmerman, a self-appointed neighborhood watch officer, for doing nothing more than walking to his father's home after dark. Roof was content to believe Zimmerman's tale of having been attacked by the teenager, and he was angered by the media's attention to the case. He believed newspapers and television stations made too much of the killing while ignoring stories about black people killing whites, an opinion he likely picked up from the Council of Conservative Citizens' website.

Roof wrote on his own Internet page that he was outraged about "hundreds of these black on white murders" that were tallied by the Conservative Citizens. This led him to an interest in South Africa's defunct apartheid government, as well as Rhodesia – the name of the African nation of Zimbabwe when it was under white rule. He would pose for photographs waving the Confederate battle flag, wearing the banners of South Africa and Rhodesia on his jacket. In February, he had created his own website, called "thelastrhodesian.com," and used it to rant about blacks, Hispanics and Jews, just like other white supremacists.

Roof began telling people he was a segregationist. He told racist jokes, even to the black teens he knew. He clearly had trouble comprehending what was appropriate. In February, the same month he registered "thelastrhodesian.com" domain, Roof was arrested after questioning an employee at a Columbia mall store about its behind-the-scenes operations. He asked how many people worked in the store, when they closed. A store employee called police. When Roof was detained he was carrying a bottle of Suboxone – a prescription drug used to treat addiction to other narcotics. The effects of the drug are chilling: Doctors say regular use of Suboxone can leave a person practically numb, uninterested in most things, and impair the way the body handles emotion and stress. Roof did not have a prescription for the drug.

In April, Roof was arrested again, this time for trespassing – but the paperwork for his charge was filed incorrectly. That allowed him to avoid any problems when, later that month, he bought a .45-caliber handgun and several magazines of ammunition with the money his father had given him for his birthday. Soon, Roof posted photographs of himself holding the gun on his website.

Roof's online rants escalated quickly, and he began to include references to Adolf Hitler. His posts included pictures of himself at various Civil War sites around the state, including several in Charleston. One photo showed him burning an American flag. Roof wrote that he could not stand the sight of the flag. "Modern American patriotism is an absolute joke. People pretending like they have something to be proud of while white people are being murdered daily in the streets."

Roof announced on his website that he had decided he must act. He had to do something about the problems he perceived. "Some people feel as though the South is beyond saving, that we have too many blacks here. To this I say look at history. The South had a higher ratio of blacks when we were holding them as slaves. Look at South Africa, and how such a small minority held the black (sic) in apartheid for years and years."

"We have no skinheads, no real KKK, no one doing anything but talking on the

Internet," Roof wrote. "Well someone has to have the bravery to take it to the real world, and I guess it has to be me."

Roof wrote that he chose to attack Charleston because "it is (sic) most historic city in my state, and at one time had the highest ratio of blacks to Whites in the country." But like most white supremacists, he was a coward at heart. He wrote on "thelastrhodesian.com" that "I am not in the position to, alone, go into the ghetto and fight."

Ultimately, he may have chosen Emanuel AME Church because it was an icon in the black community, had been the congregation of Vesey – who white supremacists vilify above most other blacks. These people complained that Vesey's planned slave revolt could have resulted in the deaths of hundreds of white people – never mind that whites were holding most black people in bondage at the time. It made perfect sense to Roof's deranged mind.

Dylann Roof was Joe Riley's worst nightmare. He was the antithesis of the racial harmony the mayor had fostered in his city for decades. He violated the very gun laws Riley had tried to strengthen for years. And he flew the Confederate flag the mayor had been trying to remove from Statehouse grounds since the 1980s. Now this disturbed young man was on a collision course with Charleston. It was a disaster in the making, one for which there was no warning.

At 8:17 p.m., the gunman found the side door at Emanuel AME unlocked. He opened it, stepped inside and saw a dozen people sitting around tables discussing the Bible. Their first sight of him had to raise questions. Despite the heat, he wore dark pants and a long-sleeve gray shirt. He seemed shy, but spoke up to ask for the pastor. Pinckney told him that he was the church's minister, and invited him to join in their study.

The man took a seat next to Pinckney and listened quietly as the discussion continued. It confused him. The congregation had not judged him, did not question his presence – they simply welcomed him into the group. Certainly these people bore little resemblance to anything he had read about on the Internet. Later, the man would tell investigators that he almost could not go through with his "mission" because the people of Mother Emanuel were so nice to him.

But, as Mark 4 suggests, Christianity – "like seed sown on rocky places" – sometimes does not take root. As Matthew Henry wrote, those without roots can quickly revert to their old ways and "continue in a barren, false profession, and go down to hell."

At 9 p.m., the lesson ended and the group began a closing prayer. At that moment, the Emanuel visitor stood up, pulled the .45 from a pouch he wore around his waist and announced that he had come to kill black people. He pointed the gun at Rev. Pinckney, still seated next to him, and shot him at point-blank range. Pinckney had no time to react. In an instant, he was gone.

Although age had slowed the 74-year-old Simmons, he still had a soldier's instincts and lunged to protect Pinckney. The gunman quickly aimed at Simmons and shot him multiple times. He dropped to the floor, mortally wounded but still alive.

After Pinckney and Simmons fell, the man turned his gun on the rest of the worshippers. First, he fired on Sharonda Coleman-Singleton, a track coach at Goose Creek High and a minister at Emanuel AME. Then he set his sights on Thompson, Singleton's best friend, emptying his clip and quickly reloading. The remaining congregants fell to the ground to avoid being shot, but they could not get away. One by one, they were killed in cold blood: Middleton Doctor; Ethel Lance, a grandmother and the church's custodian; then Cynthia Hurd, a librarian with the county for more than 30 years. Hurd often worked late and missed Bible study, but she had the night off and decided to stay after the church's quarterly conference.

As she watched her friends dying in front of her, Felicia Sanders' thoughts turned to her 5-year-old granddaughter sitting beside her. She could not let this monster kill her baby. Sanders dropped to the floor, pulling the girl down with her, whispering in her ear to play dead. Somehow the little girl was brave enough to muffle her screams and followed her grandmother's instructions. The gunman was in such a frenzy he did not notice them among the other bodies littering the church floor. Sanders and her granddaughter were lucky; most of the people on the floor were shot several times, just to make sure they were dead.

When the man stopped to reload once again, Sanders' son, Tywanza, tried to reason with him. Wanza, as his friends called him, was a poet, a man of words – and he tried to use them to stop the killer. "You don't have to do this," he said. "We are no harm to you." Sanders was desperate to save his mother and his aunt, Susie Jackson. He did not make any sudden moves. Sanders' mistake was trying to reason with an unreasonable man.

The gunman told Wanza Sanders he was there to do a job, and had to finish it. He snapped a new clip into the .45 and shot Sanders next, then turned the gun on his aunt. Jackson, the matriarch of her family, was 87.

With the Bible study group scattered on the floor, bleeding and dying, the killer turned toward the same door he had come in through. Then he saw Polly Sheppard on her knees, praying, and walked up to her. He asked her if she'd been shot, and she admitted that she hadn't.

"I am going to let you live so you can tell the story of what happened," he said.

Then he turned the gun on himself, told Sheppard he was going to kill himself, and pulled the trigger. The .45 made a clicking sound, either because the gun had jammed or it was once again out of bullets. So he opened the door, looked both ways, ran to his car and drove away. It was 9:15 p.m. An hour had passed since he walked into Mother Emanuel.

Sheppard quickly discovered that Felicia Sanders and her granddaughter were alive, and Pinckney's wife and daughter also had survived, hidden in his office. Everyone else in the building was dead, or quickly dying. Simmons was still breathing, and Wanza Sanders was struggling to get up. "Where is my Aunt Susie?" he said. "I've got to get to my Aunt Susie."

Those were his final words.

Riley got the call from Chief Mullen around 9:35 p.m. The news stunned the mayor so badly he could hardly move. Mullen said a lot of people had been shot inside Emanuel, but they did not yet know how many. The shooter had gotten away, but the police were casting a wide net. The peninsula was on lockdown. Friends and family of the victims had started to arrive, the chief said, and he was directing them to the Embassy Suites around the corner. Riley told the chief he was on the way.

Riley had been sitting at home in a golf shirt and Bermuda shorts, no more immune to the heat than anyone else. When he hung up the phone, he started out the door but suddenly stopped. He had to change clothes. He realized the church elders would be in their suits, and feared that if he showed up wearing anything less it would be disrespectful. He went to his closet and stood there for a moment, frozen by the shock, staring vacantly at his wardrobe.

As Riley sped through the streets of Charleston in his Prius, his thoughts turned to Pinckney. Mother Emanuel was his church, but at first he was not worried about his friend. Riley knew the Legislature was in session and imagined the senator was still in Columbia. It was the same thought most elected officials had at first. Most did not realize Pinckney had driven down for the quarterly meeting and, as they heard news of the shooting, frantically called and texted him to offer their support and condolences. By the time police found Rev. Pinckney's phone, his voicemail was full.

Word spread quickly through the Mother Emanuel community. Sheppard had grabbed Lance's cell phone and scrolled through the contacts until she found a number for Willi Glee, an elder in the church. Glee had been at the earlier meeting, but left after getting some photographs from Hurd for a church display. When he answered his phone, Sheppard said, "He killed everybody. They're all dead." In less than an hour, Glee had alerted everyone he could. Much of the Mother Emanuel family would flock to the church.

Law enforcement officials swarmed the peninsula – city police, county deputies, SLED and the FBI – and quickly barricaded several streets. They fanned out through neighborhoods around the church, carrying rifles and leading search dogs while a helicopter hovered overhead. Investigators were having a hard time figuring out exactly what had happened because a bomb threat complicated their examination of the crime scene.

By midnight there were 300 people gathered at the Embassy Suites when the Rev. Norvel Goff, presiding elder of the AME district that included Emanuel, arrived to lead the group in prayer. Already people were holding vigils in the streets, and some family members stood outside MUSC, waiting to hear word about their relatives. One of them, Jon Quil Lance, had heard that his grandmother, Ethel, was in the church. "I'm lost, I'm lost," he said. "Granny was the heart of the family." It would be hours before Lance learned his grandmother's fate.

Most of the victims, including Lance, passed away before rescue workers reached them. Only Simmons fought for a while. Doctors tried to save him for hours, but eventually he, too, succumbed to his wounds. His death brought the toll to nine people.

Riley and Mullen stayed on the scene most of the night. At 1 a.m., Mullen surprised reporters when he said there was little doubt in his mind this had been a hate crime; in fact, it was the worst in South Carolina history. Riley's words were no less harsh. His disgust and anger came through as he told the press that "An evil and hateful person took the lives of citizens who had come to worship and pray together ... a most unspeakable and heartbreaking tragedy."

Riley promised the person who had done the shooting would be caught, and quickly. Within hours, police had recovered surveillance footage from the church's cameras and sent out images of the suspect and his car. Shortly after those photos showed up on newspaper and television station websites, the police began to get tips. One of those calls came from a woman who said the person in the video footage was her brother, Dylann Roof.

At 11 a.m. that morning, a woman in Shelby, North Carolina, passed a car that she felt certain was the one she had seen on the news. She called the police to report it, and soon afterward Shelby police pulled the car over and arrested Roof without incident 250 miles from Charleston. It had been 14 hours since the shooting.

Roof proved talkative and cooperative with the police. He waived his extradition rights, allowing South Carolina officials to move him to the Charleston County jail. There, he seemingly admitted to the crime, told investigators that he hoped his actions would spark a race war. But he conceded he almost hadn't gone through with it. He seemed confused by how kindly he had been treated by the Mother Emanuel congregation. They had not looked at him and stereotyped; they had welcomed him with open arms. It was chilling, as if he was programmed to hate, and to kill, even when reality ran contrary to all that he thought he knew. The seeds had been sown in a rocky place.

The national media descended on the Charleston area for the second time in less than three months. In April, a North Charleston police officer had shot and killed a fleeing suspect – an incident captured on a young man's cell phone. For more than a week, the Lowcountry was the focus of the nation's attention, and some predicted

North Charleston would become another Ferguson, Missouri. There had been protests of the North Charleston police, but there were no riots, no violence – despite the best efforts of out-of-towners, who tried to stir the pot. North Charleston had weathered the storm; now it was Charleston's turn.

But Charleston was no more prone to violence than its sister city. Residents held vigils for the victims, there were unity rallies and the community came together to mourn. The sidewalk outside of Mother Emanuel became a shrine, so many people coming to drop off flowers and cards that traffic became a concern. Eventually, the police put up barricades to prevent cars from parking on the sidewalk. Riley wanted to do something to allow the community to grieve together, to begin the healing he knew was necessary. He wanted to "instill the love and unity" Charleston had shown in the aftermath of tragedy.

The mayor's office quickly secured the College of Charleston's basketball arena, which sat a couple of blocks away from the church on Meeting Street. The city would host an evening prayer vigil on Friday night, 48 hours after the shootings. By Thursday afternoon, the city was planning its program and lining up speakers for the event. Riley scanned the itinerary and made one change: he asked them to add "What a Friend We Have in Jesus" to the program. He always enjoyed hearing that song when he visited black churches, and knew everyone in the city would recognize that particular hymn.

More than 4,500 people attended the Friday night service. The crowd prayed, sang and listened to local leaders and friends eulogize the slain congregation. The crowd joined in on "We Shall Overcome" and the mayor's request, "What a Friend We Have in Jesus." In his remarks, Riley said the gunman's racist beliefs belonged in the "dustpan of failed civilizations," and that if he thought he could divide the Charleston community, he had failed miserably.

"We share one thing in common. … Our hearts are broken. We have an anguish like we have never had before," Riley said. "In our broken hearts, we realize we love each other more."

The city of Charleston proved its mayor right. In the days after the vigil, thousands of Lowcountry residents lined the Ravenel Bridge, holding hands in a remarkable display of unity. Black community leaders attacked outside groups that had come into town, urging residents to take up arms against the police. Some thought the city's African-American community too docile, that years of life in South Carolina had taken the fight out of them. Instead, they showed great strength, God's strength, in turning the other cheek. And the families of the Emanuel victims showed amazing compassion the next week, when they stood in a bond hearing and forgave Dylann Roof for his trespasses.

Around the country, people watched as Charleston came together in tragedy as no other city had done, not since New York following the Sept. 11 terrorist attacks. The birthplace of secession and civil war still had its racial issues, but Charleston showed the world how a community can survive and draw strength from one another in crisis. Many longtime city residents and local leaders said it was not hyperbolic to credit the city's grace under pressure to Mayor Joe Riley.

For 40 years, Riley had molded his city into a tolerant, progressive community, a place where all people were equal, where civil rights mattered, where concerns were heard. He had delivered a 300-year-old city to the 21st century, and he accomplished it with much less consternation and divisiveness than other cities – in the South or the North. The mayor had taken a dying city and turned it into a vibrant, diverse and growing community as well as the nation's most popular vacation destination. He had proven it was possible for a city to be both of those things. But above all that, in Riley's final months in office, Charleston had shown itself to be more than a shrine to history. It was the model of a modern American city.

In tragedy, Joe Riley's true legacy was unveiled for the world to see.

EPILOGUE

Amazing Grace

If that were all, it would be enough.

By almost any measure, Riley's tenure had been a success – 40 years that changed Charleston forever. But before he left office the mayor would see one more of his goals accomplished; a feat he had been attempting for nearly three decades. It finally happened as a result of the tragedy that marred his final year in office, a silver lining to the darkest cloud over his years of public service. It all started at the prayer vigil two days after the shooting at Mother Emanuel.

At the TD Arena that night, none of the speakers stirred the audience quite as much as the Rev. Nelson Rivers III. He was rousing, funny and emotional as he spoke about the pain of loss. He told the story of Riley calling him about plans for the march on Columbia in early 2000. "That's when I knew he would be mayor as long as he wanted to be mayor," Rivers said. "Any man who would walk to Columbia out of a single conviction for uniting South Carolina, that's my kind of mayor."

Now, Rivers said, a man had slain nine people out of hate while flying the Confederate flag. It was time, Rivers said, to finally remove that flag from Statehouse grounds.

His call brought the people out of their seats, and it was a racially diverse crowd. Charleston County Council Chairman Elliott Summey and his father, North Charleston Mayor Keith Summey, were among those most touched by Rivers' remarks. By the end of the night, they decided to take up Rivers' cause and talked about replicating Riley's march to Columbia 15 years earlier. With the Legislature still in session, they hoped to force action immediately. They had support from the business community, and knew Riley would go along. The Summeys were going to announce their march the next week, but it turned out that no one needed to walk anywhere.

The morning before the vigil, Gov. Nikki Haley had been interviewed on national television and asked about the flag. She cautiously demurred, promising there would be a time and place to talk about the issue. To her detractors, it seemed the governor was punting – which was understandable. The flag had long been a sensitive political issue in South Carolina. It had come up most recently during the 2014 gubernatorial election when Sen. Vincent Sheheen renewed calls to bring down the flag.

At the time, Haley's campaign said the governor respected the bipartisan compromise that moved the flag from the dome to the grounds in 2000. If people wanted to revisit that, she said, it was a conversation for after the campaign. But when Haley declined to talk about the flag on the NBC and CBS morning shows that Friday, she was not dodging. In truth, Haley was quickly developing strong feelings on the issue – but she would reveal them on her own timetable.

The night of the Emanuel shooting, Haley had been up until 4:30 a.m., then turned around and left for Charleston at 8 a.m. after explaining what had happened to her children. It affected her deeply. She spoke to her husband, who was in Texas on National Guard duty, about it before spending the day at Morris Brown AME and meeting with Riley and other local officials. When images of Roof holding the Confederate flag and a gun were published, Haley had seen enough.

Over the weekend, the governor met with her staff at the mansion, fielded calls from presidential candidates who wanted her to take a stand. She asked them to refrain from jumping into the debate, promising she had a plan. For the next two days, she met with Republican and Democratic officials, the state's community leaders and Riley. Haley told them all the same thing – she would ask the Legislature to take the flag down immediately, during its extended session. And if they tried to delay until January, she would call them back into a summer session.

Both Democrats and Republicans were surprised. They assumed Haley would try to thread the needle, call for some form of compromise. Anything else was a political risk – especially for a Republican in South Carolina. But she didn't want a deal. Politicians and pundits assumed the governor was getting pressure from the state's biggest industries – companies like Boeing, Volvo and BMW. A few of the state's industry leaders had called and urged her to act, but they did so privately and offered no political cover. If the governor was going to do it, she had to go out there alone – or with as many elected officials who would stand beside her.

On June 22, Haley asked Riley to come to the governor's office. She was leaning heavily on him and former Gov. David Beasley – the two men who had taken the strongest stands against the flag. At the same time she put together a list of other officials she wanted with her at a 4 p.m. press conference that afternoon. Through her staff, she passed along a message: If they did not show up she wouldn't hold it against them, campaign against them or call them out. She understood what she was walking into. And she knew, at the very least, she would have Riley, Beasley and Congressman Jim Clyburn with her.

During the press conference, Haley talked about taking her children to Mother Emanuel for Sunday services, letting them learn the lesson that true love triumphs over true hate. And though she acknowledged the flag represented history, heritage and ancestry for some, for others it was an oppressive symbol of hate. She said the flag was the symbol of the state's past, not its future. If South Carolinians wanted to fly the flag on their property, that was fine. But it would no longer fly on Statehouse grounds.

"Today, we are here in a moment of unity in our state, without ill will, to say it's time to move the flag from the Capitol grounds," Haley said.

In her brief remarks, Haley delivered a message that was almost exactly the same as Riley had preached since the 1980s. And most of the state's congressional delegation and legislative leaders stood with them. Afterward, Riley praised Haley for exhibiting "leadership at this moment of sadness and crisis in our state."

The only problem was the 2000 compromise that moved the flag from the dome to the Soldiers Monument required a two-thirds vote to be amended, and no one was sure they could get that many lawmakers to go along. But now, after decades of consternation, the train was on the track. Soon, even business leaders came out in support of removing the flag. The pressure was on.

President Barack Obama had not been to Charleston since 2008, when he was a longshot candidate with the support of the city's longtime mayor. He returned on June 26 to deliver the eulogy at the Rev. Clementa Pinckney's funeral, an event so large it was moved to TD Arena, site of the mayor's prayer vigil a week before. The funeral set an attendance record for the basketball arena, and hundreds were turned away at the door after waiting all morning to get into a funeral that would run nearly five hours.

Air Force One did not leave Washington until the service had begun, but the president arrived well before his climactic slot on the program. He took the stage, standing over Pinckney's coffin, not at the traditional lectern of the President of the United States, but a simple stand draped with the flag of the AME church. That day, Obama asked the nation to find its grace in a speech that harked back to the powerful oratory that had helped get him elected. For most of the 40 minutes he spoke, Obama sounded more like a preacher than a president – recounting the storied history of the African Methodist Episcopal Church, its integral role in the black community for centuries. The man who killed the nine Emanuel parishioners, Obama said, may not have known about the church's past, but he had continued a long history of bombs, arsons and shootings at churches meant to control and terrorize people who only wanted basic human rights. This murderer wanted to start a race war, the president said, but he was too blind to see that he was being used by God.

"The alleged killer could not imagine how the city of Charleston, under the good and wise leadership of Mayor Riley, how the state of South Carolina, how the United States of America would respond – not merely with revulsion at his evil act, but with big-hearted generosity and, more importantly, with thoughtful introspection and self-examination that is so rarely seen in public life."

President Obama turned his eulogy of Pinckney – a man he knew, but not well – into his grandest address on race. He said lowering the Confederate flag was an act of grace, that the country had to confront the racial issues and gun violence plaguing the nation. He asked for "good people on both sides of the debate" to come together, and warned against falling into old patterns of making symbolic gestures but then doing nothing. And then, shocking everyone, the president broke into an a Cappella rendition of "Amazing Grace."

He could have been describing the city of Charleston.

Riley and Charlotte watched the president's eulogy from the front row with Vice

President Joe Biden, his wife and Michelle Obama. Afterward, the first lady told him, "Mayor Riley, you have been a shining beacon in this tragic event."

On July 9, nearly two weeks after the Rev. Pinckney's funeral, Haley signed a bill into law that removed the Confederate battle flag from Statehouse grounds. It had been a contentious fight in the General Assembly, but a mercifully short one. The Senate, after some bluster by a few back-benchers, passed the legislation relatively quickly. The House had taken longer as grandstanding, conservative flag supporters attempted to kill the bill with dozens of amendments. Ultimately, the momentum was too great and, around 1 a.m., the legislation was approved with massive – and bipartisan – support. Both chambers had easily exceeded the needed two-thirds majority.

The governor invited the families of the Emanuel shooting victims to the ceremony, and she signed the legislation into law in the Statehouse's second floor lobby flanked by former governors Jim Hodges, Dick Riley and Beasley. State Rep. Gilda Cobb-Hunter, an influential and veteran lawmaker from Orangeburg, choked back tears. She never thought she would see the day. Riley, who had waited just as long for the moment, was not there to witness it.

Haley had invited the mayor to the signing, but he missed the call. He was on Pawleys Island, where his wife's family held their annual retreat. Every year, Charlotte's relatives rented a row of beach houses on the Grand Strand and about 70 members of the mayor's extended family spent a week together. Riley never missed the week; it was the least he could do to make up for his long hours away from the family. Since the shootings, the mayor had been working 14 hours every day and, frankly, he needed the break. On that Thursday morning Riley was standing knee-deep in a muddy creek, a fishing rod in his hands, when he realized he hadn't checked his voicemail. When he heard the message from the governor, the mayor realized there was no way to extract himself from the mud and drive across the state in time for the ceremony.

Riley struggled with the decision of whether to leave for Columbia on Friday morning to watch the flag lowered. Finally, his son Bratton told him that he would always regret it if he didn't, so Riley – still Lowcountry to the core – took an outdoor shower beneath the beach house, put on a coat and tie and set out for the capital.

Just after 10 a.m. a Highway Patrol honor guard lowered the flag from the pole with more than 10,000 people watching from the Statehouse grounds and Gervais Street. The crowd was so deep they even crowded blocks down Main Street. As the flag of Gen. Robert E. Lee's Army descended, the crowd along the closest barricade chanted "U-S-A! U-S-A!" Some people cried and a few grumbled that the flag hadn't done anything to anybody, apparently dismissing what some people had done while flying it. Denise Quarles, Myra Thompson's daughter, told The Post and Courier she was not among those who cried. She simply cheered.

"Today was a day of being happy," she said. "It won't bring my mom back, but it does provide comfort to me and my family."

Riley called it a joyous scene, one that "I will never forget for as long as I live." He'd always had faith the flag would come down, that its days were numbered. He believed the people of South Carolina would one day demand it. As usual, the mayor saw the world as a reflection of his image of it, and considered South Carolina far more progressive than its reputation. But he conceded that he had given up seeing the flag lowered while he was still in office.

That afternoon, Riley drove back to Pawleys Island and his family. It was after 4 p.m. when he arrived, the brutal Lowcountry sun arching to the west behind him by the time he pulled up to the beach house. There were few people around; most were out for the afternoon. The mayor slipped inside and put on his swim trunks to celebrate the day's end, just as he – and his father before him – did almost every summer evening following a hard day at the office. He wanted to jump into the baptismal waters of the Atlantic Ocean.

He walked along the path through the sand dunes covered in sea oats and soon emerged on the beach, where about 30 members of his family were sitting around and watching the children play in the water. When they saw Riley step onto the sand, every one of them stood and clapped – a standing ovation. The mayor smiled, hugged his grandchildren and waded into the surf.

There was one more thing.

On July 24, Riley drove to the ballpark named in his honor to throw out the first pitch. It would be his final first pitch at a RiverDogs game as mayor. General Manager Dave Echols met the mayor and Charlotte at the side gate to usher them inside for an entire program put together without Riley's knowledge. This was the gathering place he dreamed would bring the city together, a place where memories would be made, and he had been right.

Riley could not take more than a couple of steps without someone stopping him to thank him for everything. Tony the Peanut Man joked that the night's Joe Riley and Bill Murray figurine giveaway was something the mayor had requested – that he'd been jealous of the Tony the Peanut Man bobblehead. Riley just laughed. When another woman asked him to please stay, to remain the mayor, Riley just touched her arm and said, "I'm not going anywhere." Here, he truly had the home-field advantage.

As he walked onto the field, Peter Frampton's "Show Me the Way" blasting over the public address system, the outfield video screen kicked to life, showing people filmed in various spots around downtown Charleston, all of them saying, "Thanks, Joe." The mayor glanced up at the tribute as he walked down the first base line, on his way to a television interview, stopping every few feet to sign autographs for people in the stands.

It was also city employees' night at the ballpark, and Riley spent his few public words thanking them for their work, recognizing one man as the winner of the year's city award for public service. He told them, "This is your night," but it was unmistakably his.

The RiverDogs presented Riley with two framed jerseys – home and away – each bearing the No. 40 for his years in office. The Atlanta Braves sent a bat signed by their latest Hall of Famers: Bobby Cox, Tom Glavine and Greg Maddux. RiverDogs President Mike Veeck told the crowd it was Riley's doing that there was professional baseball in Charleston. The crowd had never cheered louder for any home run.

Riley stood near the pitcher's mound with Charlotte, his sons Joe and Bratton, and his grandson Bratton Jr., as the team played a compilation video of tributes from various state and local officials. His old friend Alex Sanders called Riley "the most important Charlestonian since George Washington visited." Gov. Haley, Columbia Mayor Steve Benjamin, U.S. District Judge Michael Duffy all thanked him for his service. Chief Justice Jean Toal recounted the first time she met Riley, as a 9-year-old boy in his daddy's real estate office.

As the words echoed through the park, the mayor looked close to tears. All those people, all those compliments, had moved Riley and made him more emotional than he usually showed publicly. Over and over, these people credited him with making Charleston a better place to live. That simple summer evening took on an air of epic grandeur.

Finally, Riley took the mound to throw out the ceremonial first pitch. He did not take off his sports coat, but that did not belie a lack of seriousness. The mayor was ready. The trick, he explained, was to throw it high – aim for the catcher's head – because if you aim too low, the elevation of the mound would send the pitch spiraling into the dirt. Decades of watching baseball, of talking to the game's stars, of throwing out first pitches, had taught him that.

First the wind-up, and then a strong overhand throw that arced high, dipping as it sailed to the plate. The pitch was right down the middle, closer to perfect than anyone had a right to expect from the 72-year-old mayor. The ball hit the catcher's glove with a solid smack. A strike.

The mayor threw his hands in the air as 6,000 people screamed and clapped. They applauded the pitch, they applauded the culmination of a life in public service, they applauded him. Joe Riley stood taking it all in for a moment and then waved to the crowd.

Pat Conroy had summed up the sentiment decades earlier in *The Prince of Tides*. He was a son of the Lowcountry and a well-loved man. And it was enough, Lord, it was enough.

NOTES

I first interviewed Joe Riley in November 1997, little more than a week after I started work at The Post and Courier. Someone asked me to bat out a quick story about the city disputing its mid-Census population count and, dutiful new employee that I was, I called the mayor for comment. It was a forgettable little dispatch, but I remember being impressed by how easily I got the famous Charleston mayor on the phone, and how helpful he was. Reporters don't often have such thoughts – we are trained to be wary of all politicians.

I ran into the mayor occasionally over the next few years, although I never covered Charleston City Hall as a beat reporter. But it wasn't until I became a metro columnist in 2007 that I began talking to Riley on a regular basis. The world is a columnist's oyster, and the job frees you to write about almost anything – and one of my favorite subjects was local government. On occasion, I have run afoul of the mayor. If he thought I was wrong about something, or my criticism off-base, he would not suffer in silence. I can remember getting phone calls and letters from him, but I really can't recall the subjects. One time it had something to do with the city's St. Patrick's Day celebration, I think.

In the past eight years of writing opinion, however, I've found that I agree with the mayor far more than any other public official I've ever known. From my point of view, his heart is always in the right place. I attended his 10th and final inauguration and wrote a glowing column about the power of his speech that day. I was amazed he could still be so energetic, so enthusiastic and so inspiring after 36 years on the job. But that's the mayor. He is thoughtful about everything he does, and I hope that's come through here.

When Post and Courier Executive Editor Mitch Pugh and Managing Editor

Rick Nelson first approached me about writing this book, I was reluctant. Friends of the mayor had suggested a biography before, but I worried that I didn't have enough time to dig into a 40-year career and do the story justice. I knew the high points – everyone in Charleston does – but in a town this steeped in history, you have to know more than that. Attention to detail, and relationships, matter. Luckily, the newspaper allowed me to devote nearly all my time to the book. I needed it. I have followed the public business of Charleston for nearly two decades, but until this past year, I knew only a fraction of this story. I felt less guilty about that when friends of mine, some of them native Charlestonians, read this manuscript and said, "I didn't know that."

This book is based on dozens of hours of interviews with Riley, his family, friends and various other people who have had dealings with the mayor during his nearly 50 years in public life. I relied upon letters and city documents as much as possible, but my primary resource was the archives of The News and Courier, The Evening Post and The Post and Courier.

From 1975 to 2015, Mayor Riley was quoted, mentioned or the subject of somewhere between 325 and 775 local newspaper stories per year. That comes out to about 20,000 articles I had to read – or at least scan – in the course of researching this book. Most of the facts, and many of the quotes, herein come from those archives. Everything else is noted here.

Prologue

17 *Joe Riley feared:* Interview with Riley, Nov. 7, 2014.

19 *If you march:* Riley did not publicly acknowledge the existence of this letter to anyone but law enforcement officials until after the march. He mentioned it in his speech on Statehouse grounds at the conclusion of the march on April 6, 2000.

19 *For most of:* Interview with David Rawle, April 8, 2015.

23 *The news was:* Frank Santangelo recounted his examination of Riley and his instructions to him in a winter 2015 interview. Riley still has the running shoes Santangelo cut up for him.

PART I The Land of Opportunity

April 30, 1969

27 *The troops had:* This account of the 1969 hospital strike was compiled from various issues of The News and Courier, The Post and Courier photo archives and interviews with Mary Moultrie and Rosetta Simmons that I did in February 2007 for a retrospective on the strike.

35 *The situation is:* This quote from Riley is taken from a May 1, 1969, News and Courier article, "Legislature Reaffirms State's Stand on Strike." It was the first I'd heard of Riley taking up for the protesters, and convinced me to begin the story during the hospital strike, which was a major event in Charleston history. It marked a change in the city's political climate that culminated with Riley's election as mayor in 1975.

36 *Sanders had struck:* Interview with Alex Sanders, spring 2015.

40 *Ralph David Abernathy*: It's worth noting that Abernathy's "Letter from The Charleston County Jail" ran as a paid advertisement in The News and Courier on May 2, 1969. Today the letter would most certainly be news and run for free. It was an interesting contrast of the times.

The Rileys of Charleston

42 *Patrick and Ann:* Much of the Riley and Schachte family history was related to me by Riley's sisters, Susanne Emge, Mary Riley Chambers and Jane Riley-Gambrell, beginning with interviews on March 26, 2015. A brochure on Joseph P. Riley Sr. in The Post and Courier archives (no date) provides some early family history as well.

44 *Andrew J. Riley:* "Mr. A.J. Riley Passes Away," The Evening Post, April 22, 1924, provides much of the biographical information about Riley's paternal grandfather.

44 *The Evening Post called:* "Henry Oliver Passes Away," The Evening Post, March 14, 1910. Riley and his family did not discover that Oliver managed the 1883 renovation of City Hall until 120 years after the fact, when the building was undergoing another renovation and the mayor saw some old paperwork with his great-grandfather's name on it.

46 *Riley knew John:* The Schachte family history was based on genealogical in-

formation provided by Susanne Emge.

48 *Except for summers:* The early Riley family history was related by the mayor in a March 20, 2015, interview and by his sisters on March 26. Riley later confirmed his sisters' tales but was adamant he didn't throw "The Happy Cowboy" sheet music down the storm drain. He insists he can still point out the exact drain where it disappeared.

50 *His teachers would:* March 2015 interview with Dorothy Gnann, Sister Mary William. Gnann talked fondly of the mayor for nearly an hour one afternoon and, at the end of the conversation, said, "Don't put me in this book if you're going to blame Joe for that sofa fire. That wasn't his fault."

51 *Joe and Pat:* Interview with Pat Brennan, March 28, 2015.

A Lowcountry Heart

53 *Helen Riley made:* Pat Brennan, ibid.

54 *Joe played football:* Interview with Bill Robinson, March 2015 and Riley in July 2015. Robinson, apparently a starter his entire career, has a much different characterization of Riley's playing time than the mayor. The mayor had newspaper articles to back up his contention that he started for the second half of his senior year.

55 *Once Joe was:* Stories of Riley's teenage misadventures were recounted by his sisters with no small measure of glee. To the mayor's credit, he denied nothing and even added detail to some stories, including the one where he broke his parents' bottle of Scotch. At one point, his sisters apologized for not coming up with anything worse to tell on their brother. "We know he sounds too good to be true," they joked.

58 *That year a:* Pat Conroy. *The Boo*. Charleston: Privately printed, 1970.

59 *OK, Bubba, you've:* Interview with Riley, Jan. 21, 2015.

60 *Joe's decision to:* Riley's sisters recounted the discussion between him and his parents on his decision to attend law school instead of joining the family business.

62 *I remember we:* Charlotte Riley: "Dancer-at-heart delights in city's cultural awakening," High Profile by Dottie Ashley, May 24, 1997, The Post and Courier. This profile is worth noting as it is one of the few times the publicity-shy Mrs. Riley has ever been interviewed so extensively.

63 *Capers Barr had:* Interview with Capers Barr, Feb. 27, 2015. Barr later provided

me with a transcript of the letter which is quoted herein. Charlotte Riley says she and Ellie Barr persuaded Riley to write the letter; he says they may have nudged him, but he was going to do it anyway.

A Change is Gonna Come

64 *His father opened:* Interview with Herbert Fielding on March 2, 2015. I spent an afternoon at Fielding Funeral Home with the civil rights legend and found him so interesting I wrote a column out of the interview as well. Sadly, it was one of his last; he passed away in August 2015.

66 *For his entire:* The story of Riley going to dinner with his family was one of his earliest memories of racial issues in Charleston. He related this story in November 2014.

70 *Riley was not:* Riley recounted his days in the Legislature in a Feb. 5, 2015, interview.

72 *The Riley-Sanders amendment:* The mayor said the order of the names on the amendment depended on who was telling the story, and he was right. In a separate interview, Sanders called it the "Sanders-Riley" amendment.

75 *Riley and Barr:* Interview with Capers Barr, Feb. 27, 2015.

76 *Courvoisie explained that:* Riley and Conroy both recounted this story from their own points of view in the spring of 2015. I had the good fortune to interview The Boo in 2001 and although we talked about the publication of the book, he didn't mention recruiting Riley to lawyer it.

78 *That fall, Riley:* The mayor recounted this story on a plane to Washington, D.C., on Jan. 21, 2015. He had never talked about diverting campaign money to Fielding and Clyburn before; however, Clyburn has told the story often.

The End of an Era

82 *Any time Fielding:* Interview with Fielding, March 2, 2015.

82 *Goodstein quickly discovered:* Interview with Arnold Goodstein, March 2015.

84 *The speaker was:* Interview with Thomas Bryant, April 1, 2015.

85 *If you shoot:* Interview with Goodstein, March 2015.

88 *Riley told the:* Riley interview, March 20, 2015.

90 *Had he been:* Ibid. Riley's friends say if he'd been appointed chairman of the House Judiciary Committee, his career might have taken an entirely different path. But Riley says he would not have remained in the Legislature much longer regardless because he didn't like being away from home, and Charlotte didn't like him gone. By the time their youngest son, Bratton, was born, both had decided Riley needed to be in Charleston full time.

91 *The Legislature appointed:* Riley interview, Feb. 5, 2015.

93 *Eventually Riley was:* Riley interview, winter 2015.

The Campaign

97 *Throughout the fall:* Interview with Capers Barr, Feb. 27, 2015. Barr said there was no false modesty in Riley's claims, and that he'd never seen anything like the courtship leading up to the 1975 mayoral election. "He was literally asked to run. A lot of people say that 'people have been asking me to run,' but in Joe's case it was true."

97 *I'd never imagined:* Riley interview, March 20, 2015.

98 *I just want:* Interview with Thomas Tisdale, April 8, 2015.

101 *Big Joe was:* Riley interview, March 20, 2015.

101 *Besides, Riley said:* Ibid and interview with David Rawle, April 8, 2015. Riley's promise to serve only one term is, in retrospect, a big joke among his friends. The mayor swears he meant it at the time, but events intervened.

102 *Between the jogging:* Interview with Barr.

103 *Riley set up:* Riley interview, March 20, 2015.

103 *In April President:* Some of the information on Mayor Gaillard's background and career comes from his autobiography, J. Palmer Gaillard, Jr., *Boards to Boardrooms: The Life and Memoirs of J. Palmer Gaillard, Jr.* (Charleston: Privately printed, 2004).

105 *I was not:* Riley interview, March 20, 2015.

106 *Rawle hired Albert:* The story of the infamous 1975 campaign ads came from Riley and David Rawle, who said Riley's integrity was inspiring but, in the heat of a campaign, also a pain.

108 *As the campaign:* Interview with Tisdale.

109 *But no one:* Riley's sisters recall watching the 1975 campaign with horror

as their brother was smeared nearly every day. Mary said it got so bad she couldn't watch TV news.

109 *He then drove:* Riley interviews, spring 2015. The mayor conceded he hadn't spent much time on a victory speech because he had no idea whether he'd win. But he did recall going by to see his sons and his aunts before meeting Charlotte and his parents at the Gaillard.

Part II "Lift Every Voice and Sing"

Two Worlds

113 *Although he must:* Riley interview, March 25, 2015.

114 *The new City:* Riley 1975 inaugural address, City Hall files.

115 *Long after the:* Tom Tisdale told me the story of Riley and friends going into City Hall late on inauguration night to smoke cigars and drink beer. When I asked the mayor about it, he said, "That's not all – we rearranged the furniture, too." That's when I realized the book would have no shortage of material; the mayor was extraordinarily forthright.

120 *In August 1976:* Riley interview, April 15, 2015.

125 *One day a:* Riley interview, March 25, 2015.

128 *Herbert Fielding even:* Riley interview, January 2015.

A Golden Haze

133 *Riley understood this:* Riley interview, April 20, 2015.

135 *In 1920, the:* Stephanie E. Yuhl, *A Golden Haze of Memory: The Making of Historic Charleston* (Chapel Hill: University of North Carolina Press, 2005), 24-26.

137 *Before he even:* Riley interview, April 20, 2015. The mayor recalled some of the attacks – including the man City Councilman Danny Richardson had to tackle – but he never forgot a woman sticking her tongue out at him. He thought it was funny because she was so mad, and that was the worst thing she could imagine doing to him.

140 *In March 1978:* Riley interview, April 20, 2015. The mayor's dispute with the Hibernians was one of those episodes he considered part of his leadership duties.

He did not tip off the newspaper, but didn't shy away when it found out.

143 *Still, Riley's mayoral:* Ibid. There are probably people out there who still think the mayor ducked out of their reception to get to his next event. But Riley explained that going early and leaving early was just his way of making more time for his family.

144 *Riley sometimes found:* Thomas Tisdale interview, April 8, 2015.

145 *This prompted Bill:* Riley interview, July 30, 2015. The mayor found it hilarious that the city was, however briefly, landlord to a strip club. He's right–it is.

A Walk in the Park

148 *Riley thought Murray's:* Riley interview, March 25, 2015.

148 *Privately, he even:* Thomas Tisdale interview, April 8, 2015.

149 *The foundation was:* Riley interview, March 25, 2015.

151 *The next week:* Riley interview, July 30, 2015. President Carter's call to the mayor was a source of great confusion among his friends – and the public. The News and Courier assumed the call came at his office, but Riley swears he got the call at his house on a Sunday evening. And he says his friends are mistaken, he did not swear while on the phone with the president.

153 *His friends later:* David Rawle interview, April 8, 2015.

154 *Joe, you are:* Riley interview, March 25, 2015.

155 *Bill, that's a:* Ibid.

158 *That summer, Police:* The story of Chief Conroy and company's sail to Florida was recounted by Tom Tisdale and Riley in separate interviews, April 2015.

160 *Riley couldn't believe:* The letter Riley wrote to Preservation Society President Norman Olsen Jr. ran in its entirety in The News and Courier. Riley did not leak the letter, however; Olsen gave it to Frank Gilbreth. Apparently, Olsen thought it would make the mayor look bad. It didn't.

The Chief

163 *The city looked:* Riley interview, April 20, 2015. This is one of the mayor's favorite stories, the tale of how he wooed the Washington Light Infantry to the wilds of the Upper Peninsula … at Meeting and George. More than three decades later, the militia resides in one of the toniest areas of the city north of Broad.

164 *On March 14:* Riley's trip to Taiwan is recounted using a series of articles the mayor wrote for The News and Courier in May 1981. His series was informative, funny and well-written. He did the same when he took a European trip for similar purposes. He considered it part of reporting to his employers, the citizens of Charleston.

170 *Privately, he asked:* Riley interview, March 20, 2015.

172 *His resume stood:* Ibid.

173 *Riley planned to:* The mayor did not seem particularly disturbed or surprised by the racist calls when he hired Chief Greenberg. But he was amused by longtime reporter Eddie Fennell's tenacity at getting the story. From a March 20, 2015 interview.

173 *Greenberg didn't know:* Reuben Greenberg and Arthur Gordon, *Let's Take Back Our Streets,* (Chicago: Contemporary Books, 1989).

174 *I gave him:* Riley interview, March 20, 1015.

High-wire Acts

179 *Every summer, Riley:* Interview with Bratton Riley, spring 2015.

180 *Similar thoughts crossed:* Riley interview, May 6, 2015.

184 *But Thurmond had:* Riley interview, April 20, 2015. The mayor may have disagreed philosophically with Strom Thurmond, but he was impressed by his professionalism. Although a Hollings partisan, Riley came to respect Thurmond – even if he did not always endorse him.

185 *Riley later conceded:* The mayor says he has a good relationship with Hartnett these days, and still doesn't understand why his childhood friend was so offended by his endorsement of a Hartnett opponent. To Riley, it was just business – nothing personal.

188 *The Spoleto bill:* The hysterical story about Delilah Wallenda's tightrope walk comes from an interview with David Rawle, April 8, 2015.

190 *In January 1985:* Riley letter to Jacquelin Robertson, Jan. 10, 1985, City Hall files.

In the Arena

198 *Riley agreed to:* Riley interview, March 20, 2015.

199 *After years of:* Bill Regan told this story to Post and Courier reporter Robert Behre years ago.

202 *That winter, Riley:* Interview with Riley, May 6, 2015. This is one of those things where the mayor says, "Thank heavens for unanswered prayers."

September 21, 1989

210 *On Tuesday morning:* Riley interview, June 5, 2015.

210 *The mayor asked:* Interview with Barbara Vaughn, May 28, 2015.

212 *Riley followed his:* Interviews with Riley, Joe Riley III and Bratton Riley, spring 2015.

217 *Riley could feel:* Riley interview, June 5, 2015.

218 *Riley gathered the:* Riley interview, July 24, 2015.

221 *The mayor took:* Riley interview, June 5, 2015.

Part III: Charleston Rising

After the storm

225 *His son, Joe:* Interview with Joe Riley III, spring 2015.

226 *We haven't missed:* Interview with Riley, June 5, 2015. My good friend Larry Tarleton, executive editor at The Post and Courier when I was hired, has also told me this story.

226 *Late that night:* Riley interview, June 5, 2015.

227 *That was unacceptable:* Ibid.

228 *Do you want:* I heard this story from several City Hall staffers, including Barbara Vaughn. It's a peek at Riley's dry sense of humor.

229 *But there, amid:* Riley interview, July 27, 2015.

230 *They have no:* Riley interview, June 5, 2015.

232 *The mayor wanted:* Riley interview, July 27, 2015.

233 *When Big Joe:* Interview with Joe Riley III, spring 2015.

233 *On Oct. 13:* Interview with Tom Bryant, April 1, 2015.

234 *When Riley's childhood:* Interview with Pat Brennan, March 28, 2015.

239 *Riley had coveted:* Riley interview, June 22, 2015.

A Moveable Campaign

242 *Riley and Regan:* Riley interview, July 27, 2015.

245 *The city eventually:* Riley interview, June 22, 2015.

246 *Tom, daddy wants:* Tom Bryant interview, April 1, 2015.

247 *Riley had sat:* Riley interview, Jan. 21, 2015.

247 *When he returned:* Riley recounted the year of his father's declining health in a June 22, 2015 interview. He spent the better part of a year looking after his father and said, "I was glad we had that time together."

251 *Luckily, regular Riley:* Riley interview, June 22, 2015.

251 *During a speech:* Riley said his hesitation to talk about women at The Citadel was one of geography. When he was asked the question, the mayor was sitting next to Citadel President Claudius Watts, who opposed co-ed matriculation, and didn't want to embarrass him by disagreeing in front of the Corps.

252 *The mayor was:* Riley interview, June 22, 2015.

256 E*ven Riley's friends:* Some of the mayor's acquaintances felt his heart wasn't in the 1994 governor's race, but his friends knew he just refused to put a campaign ahead of his job. Riley conceded in a June 22, 2015, interview that he had some mixed feelings – but that didn't mean he would concede the campaign. It seems his ambivalence came from the idea of leaving the mayor's office.

A Greater Destiny

259 *Bratton had been:* Interview with Bratton Riley, spring 2015.

260 *But Joe had:* Interview with Joe Riley III, spring 2015.

261 *A new state:* Ibid.

267 *The mayor put:* Riley was not putting on airs; he seriously tried to stop City Council from naming The Joe after him. But of all the things the mayor built in the city, most friends agree the baseball stadium was the one to name after Riley, because he loves the game so much.

268 *On Friday, just:* Interview with Jane Riley-Gambrell, spring 2015.

268 *Since his father's:* Interview with Riley, June 22, 2015.

270 *One Saturday, Riley:* The mayor still laughs about this bumper sticker, a story he told in conversation on May 6, 2015.

272 *Of course, Riley:* Riley interview, June 22, 2015.

273 *Finally, the Rileys:* Ibid.

The New South

276 *A generation later:* Riley speech at RiverDogs home opener, April 7, 1997, City Hall files.

281 *It's so beautiful:* Pat Brennan first told me about Riley's "Clarence" speech and Riley related the story to me on July 27, 2015.

283 *Finally, he ran:* Riley interview, Nov. 7, 2014.

286 *During the rally:* Ibid.

Last Call

289 *When Joe Riley:* Interview with Riley, spring 2015.

292 *Bill Regan went:* Danny Molony's embezzlement of city funds was one of the most personal betrayals of Riley's tenure. He still hasn't gotten over what it did to the Molony family, but that didn't stop him from pursuing city funds to the point of taking the man's share of the family beach house. He related the story in a July 1, 2015 interview.

299 *By 2010, the:* This information concerning the recovery of the money Molony embezzled comes from a memorandum from assistant corporation counsel Susan Herdina to the mayor on March 8, 2010. City Hall files.

302 *The next day:* Riley interview, March 20, 2015.

Into the Fire

307 *On Monday, June:* Riley interview, July 1, 2015. The rest of the account of the Sofa Super Store fire is based on the reportage of the entire Post and Courier staff, in particular the work of Pulitzer Prize-winner Glenn Smith.

315 *In the spring:* Riley talked about the circumstances of Fire Chief Rusty Thomas' departure in a July 1, 2015, interview.

316 *In early 2008:* Riley recounted his relationship with President Obama over several days in January 2015, while we attended the U.S. Conference of Mayors winter meeting in D.C. He provided more detail in July 2015.

Top of the World

323 *On Jan. 9:* Riley's final inauguration was the only one I attended, and I was impressed with his speech enough to write a column about it – although I had forgotten it until I was researching this chapter. For a man going into his 37th year in office, Riley drew a crowd, closing down Broad Street. Even Bill Murray attended.

324 *Riley sent a:* Interview with Trent Kernodle, July 2015.

325 *But Riley told:* Riley told me this story in 2012 and The Post and Courier ran my column about the mayor saving our harbor money on the front page. He recalled more details of the conversation in January 2015.

328 *Despite the mayor's:* Riley's speech at The Citadel was the first event I attended with an eye toward writing his biography. He talked some about his days at the military college, which prompted the questions that informed the chapters on his early life.

330 *Obama was impressed:* Riley interview, January 2015.

330 *The U.S. Conference:* I had planned to travel to San Francisco with Riley for more interview time. But two nights before our flight, I checked The Post and Courier website after I had quit writing for the night and learned of the shooting at Emanuel AME. I knew right away the trip was off. The mayor's secretary called the next morning and told me what I already knew. A year of following Riley left no doubt in my mind where the mayor's priorities lay.

Mark 4:16-20

331 *About 7:30 p.m.:* This account of the shootings at Mother Emanuel came from various sources that week, none better than the narrative of events by my colleagues, Pulitzer Prize-winning journalists Doug Pardue and Jennifer Berry Hawes. Additional material came from Timothy Phelps, "Dylann Roof tried to kill himself during attack, victim's son says," the Los Angeles Times, June 20, 2015.

338 *Riley got the:* The timeline of the mayor's actions that night came from sev-

eral conversations with Riley throughout June and July 2015. Although he worked himself to the point of exhaustion for a month after the shooting, he kept in touch with me by phone throughout that time.

342 *Many longtime city:* I ended this chapter by giving the mayor credit for the city's reaction to the tragedy at Mother Emanuel. After a year of digging through his history, I did not think it was an overstatement to say he created the atmosphere that fostered such an empathetic, non-violent response. Over the next three days, I had several local officials say the same thing to me, including Charleston City Council members Bill Moody and Marvin Wagner, and Charleston County Council Chairman Elliott Summey.

Epilogue

343 *His call brought:* Interview with Elliott Summey, July 2015.

344 *The morning before:* This account of Gov. Haley's behind-the-scenes efforts to take down the flag comes from conversations with several key players, including Riley. A special thanks to Rob Godfrey for clearing up a few points.

347 *Haley had invited:* Interview with Riley, July 10, 2015. The mayor recounted his actions and feelings on his car ride back to Pawleys Island after watching the flag come down.

348 *That afternoon, Riley:* On July 24, following ceremonies for the mayor at the RiverDogs game, Meredith Blackwell described the scene on the beach that afternoon. She thought it was the most moving thing she'd ever seen. I think it's one of the best scenes in the book.

348 *On July 24:* I shadowed the mayor at the ballgame that night, hoping it would provide an uplifting ending to counterbalance the tragedy that marred much of his final months in office. It worked out even better than I had hoped.

ACKNOWLEDGMENTS

This book could not have been written without the immeasurable assistance and cooperation of Joseph P. Riley Jr. The mayor made time for me nearly every week for the better part of a year – and anyone who tried to get an appointment during his final months in office knows what a trick that was. On occasion we talked at City Hall, but usually I interviewed him in his car and even on airplanes. I'm sure he relishes driving in blissful silence now more than ever. But he patiently answered every question, no matter how inane, and for that I owe him my greatest thanks.

Although this is an authorized biography, I had complete editorial freedom. The mayor never tried to avoid tough questions or ask that anything be omitted from this story. I think that says as much as anything about the character of Joe Riley.

Barbara Vaughn has been my friend and ally in this from the beginning. At a moment's notice, she could find the 1975 inaugural address, 30-year-old letters, reports and speeches – or just about anything else. If she didn't know the answer off the top of her head, which was rare, she had it within minutes. For that, I am eternally grateful. The entire staff at City Hall was most generous with their time, too, and I owe special thanks to Mary Ann Sullivan, Laurie Thompson, Cameron Pollard and, of course, Cathy Baker.

At The Post and Courier, Publisher P.J. Browning and Executive Editor Mitch Pugh were tremendously supportive of this project and encouraged me to follow Riley as much as I needed. They didn't mind when I missed the occasional column, even if it meant fewer angry letters to the editor. Thanks to Pierre Manigault and John Barnwell as well. Several of my colleagues provided great insight into Riley and Charleston history, including Robert Behre, David Slade, Glenn Smith, Schuyler

Kropf and Tony Bartelme – all of us old-timers. Wade Spees and Matthew Fortner helped collect and choose the wonderful photographs in this book, and I couldn't have asked for more professional guidance. I also appreciate the help of my friends Leroy Burnell, Brad Nettles, Paul Zoeller, Laura Bradshaw, Mark Mulholland, Pam Gill, Liz Foster, Grace Beahm and Becky Baulch.

The mayor's family was tremendously supportive and helped me better understand his life outside City Hall. Thanks to Charlotte Riley, Joe Riley III and Bratton Riley. The "sisters" – Susanne Emge, Mary Riley Chambers and Jane Riley-Gambrell – were delightful. They provided many of the photographs in this book and spent an afternoon regaling me with stories of their childhood. And Meredith Blackwell related a story she thought extremely important. She was right.

Many of Riley's friends offered detailed recollections, and this book is much richer thanks to Capers Barr, Bill Robinson, Thomas Bryant, Alex Sanders, Arnold Goodstein, David Rawle, Thomas Tisdale and Pat Brennan. I even had the chance to interview Riley's grammar school teacher, Dorothy Gnann (Sister Mary William) and was fortunate to spend an afternoon with the great Herbert Fielding before he passed.

The novelist Pat Conroy, my personal hero, not only supplied the wonderful foreword for this book, he read the entire manuscript – which was both thrilling and scary to me – and offered great insight and anecdotes. Echoes of his novels haunt these pages, and it was an honor to work with him. Thanks also to Margaret Evans.

Also thanks to my old P&C buddies Tom Spain and Bob Kinney, as well as Courtney Kingston, Kristen Milford and Gill Guerry at Evening Post Books. They nursed this project along during a busy and difficult year, which my family endured with great help and understanding. Thank you all.

And a final nod to my very good friend Rick Nelson, managing editor of The Post and Courier and the editor of this book. He believed from the beginning and I couldn't have done it without him. Thanks, man.

Brian Hicks
Charleston, South Carolina
September 24, 2015

INDEX

D

S

ABOUT THE AUTHOR

Brian Hicks is a metro columnist for The Post and Courier in Charleston, South Carolina, and the author or coauthor of seven previous books. He has written about Southern history and politics for more than 25 years.

Hicks' journalism has appeared in national and international publications since 1986. He has been featured on CBS Sunday Morning, National Public Radio, the Discovery Channel, National Geographic and in Smithsonian magazine. He has won more than 30 journalism awards, including the Society of Professional Journalists' Green Eyeshade Award for humorous commentary and the South Carolina Press Association's award for Journalist of the Year.

His previous books include *Sea of Darkness, City of Ruin, When the Dancing Stopped* and *Ghost Ship*. His *Toward the Setting Sun* and *Raising the Hunley* were selections of the Book-of-the-Month Club, as well as the History and Military Book Clubs.

A native of Tennessee, he lives in Charleston.